AF743986

PRAISE FOR *CENTERS OF POWER*

"Drs. Berke and Schneider have managed to show convincingly how basic concepts of psychoanalysis and Kabbalistic thinking overlap and deal—within different theoretical perspectives—with fundamental problems of the human psyche, in health and illness. While reviewing central aspects of both disciplines in close comparative analyses, they are able to provide the psychoanalyst with a clear and comprehensive understanding of the Kabbalah for the modern mind. By the same token, they convey a clear and profound summary of contemporary psychoanalytic understanding to the expert in the Kabbalah. By the same process, the educated layman may acquire an intelligent, thoughtful introduction to the relationship between psychotherapeutic thinking and the spiritual dimension of an important field of Jewish religion. It is an important, thought-provoking contribution to the very actual discussion of the encounter of religion and psychological science in the light of our present knowledge of the unconscious determinants of behavior."—**Otto F. Kernberg**, past president, International Psychoanalytical Association

"In writing about the Kabbalah and psychoanalysis, Joseph H. Berke and Stanley Schneider have written their own 'Book of Splendor.' What they have done is to integrate the mystical and ineffable spirituality of the Kabbalah along with all its numinous radiations with other disciplines, such as psychoanalysis, cosmology, mathematics, and physics. The result is a remarkable and highly credible work. Their summary of the principal aspects of the Kabbalah mystic is clearly explicated. Their review of the history of psychoanalysis is alone worth the price of the book. One of the remarkable things about this book is that the writing style is anything but mysterious, which is so unusual considering the content of this book. I recommend it not only to psychoanalysts, psychotherapists, and other mental health workers but for the lay public as well." —**James S. Grotstein**, M.D., author of *Who Is the Dreamer Who Dreams the Dream? A Study of Psychic Presences* and *A Beam of Intense Darkness: Wilfred Bion's Legacy to Psychoanalysis*

"This extraordinary book is an attempt to determine man's place in the world, spiritually and metapsychologically, by exploring two disciplines—psychoanalysis and Kabbalah. Joseph Berke and Stanley Schneider, two world-renowned psychoanalysts and authors, attempt to build a bridge between these disciplines that deal with the nature of man's existence and the various forces that affect his life. The erudite interlocution between the multilayered conceptualizations of psychoanalysis and the rich mystical thinking of Kabbalah, sprinkled with moving clinical vignettes from the world of therapy and with marvelous Hassidic tales and anecdotes, makes it an academic achievement as well as a fascinating journey into man's psychic and spiritual world. I highly recommend this book for its originality and scholarship, and for its readability and clarity of exposition."—**Ilany Kogan**, training analyst, Israel Psychoanalytic Society

"Schneider and Berke have succeeded in drawing together two disciplines in a manner so skillful that it makes one wonder why these powerful connections have not been made before. It is a tribute to their scholarship and humanity that they have achieved this. Anyone concerned with healing and self-knowledge will benefit from reading this book."—**Paul Williams**, joint editor-in-chief, *International Journal of Psychoanalysis*, 2001–2007

"In this fascinating work two leading figures in the world of psychotherapy take us on a journey of discovery, beyond some of the conventional paradigms of our time. Most of these paradigms concern borders—the border and imagined division between scientific rationalism and spiritual experience, between secular modernism and religious traditions, between Western culture and ancient Hebrew texts. *Centers of Power* deconstructs these borders and demonstrates parallels and interconnections at every step. Like an up-to-date form of Renaissance scholarship, on any page you might find a reference to the Zohar, to Freud or Jung, to Einstein, to the Talmud and a Chassidic story. The 'centers of the power' refer to the center point of a person, of a level of being, of a way of looking at the world, of a scientific system, of a level of mystical tradition, of a journey. According to Rabbi Shneur Zalman's Tanya, the central point of every level of being is Truth. All points of Truth join together reaching above to the Infinite and below to the lowest level of existence. The theory of the authors is that if you can locate the point of Truth in psychoanalysis, in contemporary culture, in yourself, and in life, then, since all levels of Truth interconnect, instead of division there is unity. It is a beautiful idea. How can it be achieved? How can we find the center point of Truth and genuine power in every system? The ancient teachings of Jewish mysticism, Kabbalah, and their expositions in Chassidism, particularly of the Chabad school, provide an answer. In *Centers of Power*, Kabbalistic and Chassidic models are used to explore therapy, culture, and life. These models and insights provide a new order or paradigm, in which there are opposites, yet they join; there is fragmentation, yet it leads ultimately to Tikkun, Repair. This book, true to its spiritual sources, is fueled by the ancient image of the correspondence between the microcosm and macrocosm. When the therapist helps the client achieve Tikkun, when the Chassid in contemplative prayer achieves inner Repair of his or her fragmented self, when the reader makes a new discovery about Being and Nothingness on the microcosmic level—then the macrocosm too is affected—the Tikkun is not only of an individual self but of the world. Enjoy the journey."—**Tali Loewenthal**, director Chabad Research Unit, London

"The relationship between the self and the soul, as well as higher influences on a physical and metaphysical plain, are of fundamental importance for achieving an understanding of ourselves and our place in the world. In this remarkable study Dr. Joseph H. Berke and Professor Stanley Schneider show how much Jewish mystical concepts, as reflected in Kabbalah and Hasidic thought, are deeply intertwined with psychoanalysis and contemporary culture. The book invites us to explore new, elevated, and more sophisticated levels of awareness of different dimensions of reality. Everyone, regardless of their religiosity, should make it a priority to read this book. In so doing they will greatly enrich the spiritual and psychological structure of their lives."—**Rabbi Nathan Lopes Cardozo**, founder and dean, the David Cardozo Academy, Jerusalem

"Joseph Berke and Stanley Schneider are highly skilled Torah observant therapists. *Centers of Power* illustrates the close connection between Kabbalah, the soul of Torah, and psychoanalysis, the study of the deeper dimensions of the psyche. Most importantly, the authors demonstrate how these disciplines help to heal the hurts and divisions that people suffer between their head and their heart, between their inner worlds and outer worlds, and to gain meaning in their lives. I heartily commend it."—**Rabbi Shmuel Lew**, London

"*Centers of Power* guides us in the profound interplay between psychoanalysis and Kabbalah, culling insights and sparks that flow between them. This book reminds us that psychoanalysis not only interlaces with neurology, but also with deep spiritual concerns and touches problems of personal concern to many of us today. It is a book of faith and a book of learning and contributes to our exploration of who and where we are."—**Michael Eigen**, editor, *The Psychoanalytic Review*

Centers of Power

Centers of Power

The Convergence of Psychoanalysis and Kabbalah

Joseph H. Berke and Stanley Schneider

JASON ARONSON
Lanham • Boulder • New York • Toronto • Plymouth, UK

Published in the United States of America
by Jason Aronson
An imprint of Rowman & Littlefield Publishers, Inc.

A wholly owned subsidiary of
The Rowman & Littlefield Publishing Group, Inc.
4501 Forbes Boulevard, Suite 200, Lanham, Maryland 20706
www.rowmanlittlefield.com

Estover Road
Plymouth PL6 7PY
United Kingdom

Copyright © 2008 by Jason Aronson

All rights reserved. No part of this publication may be reproduced, stored in a retrieval system, or transmitted in any form or by any means, electronic, mechanical, photocopying, recording, or otherwise, without the prior permission of the publisher.

British Library Cataloguing in Publication Information Available

Library of Congress Cataloging-in-Publication Data

Berke, Joseph H.
Centers of power : the convergence of psychoanalysis and kabbalah / Joseph H. Berke and Stanley Schneider.
p. cm.

Includes bibliographical references and index.
ISBN-13: 978-0-7657-0500-6 (cloth : alk. paper)

1. Psychoanalysis. 2. Cábala. I. Schneider, S. (Stanley) II. Title.

BF175.B453 2008
150.19'5—dc22 2007032830

Printed in the United States of America

∞™ The paper used in this publication meets the minimum requirements of American National Standard for Information Sciences—Permanence of Paper for Printed Library Materials, ANSI/NISO Z39.48-1992.

DEDICATION

. . . But with whoever is here, standing with us today before Hashem, our God, and with whoever is not here with us today.

—Deuteronomy 29:14

. . . Those who are here in this world, and those who are not, for they will be born, but aren't yet with us. . . . These are the souls that will be created . . . (and are represented by the souls that are present).

—Midrash Tanchumah, Yitro, chapter 11

We are laid asleep
In body, and become a living soul:
While with an eye made quiet by the power
Of harmony, and the deep power of joy,
We see into the life of things.

—William Wordsworth, "Composed a Few Miles
above Tintern Abbey," July 13, 1798

FOR . . .

Our relatives of generations past

Our relatives of the present

Our relatives of the future

Contents

Acknowledgments

Shree Berke

Nathan Lopes Cardozo

Michael Eigen

Gedaliah Fleer

David Friedman

Yitzhak Ginsburgh

Mendel Gordon

Shmuel Lew

Kate Loewenthal

Tali Loewenthal

Ephraim Rosenstein

Ann Schearer

Adele Schneider

Chana Schneider

Shabtai Teicher

The Littauer Foundation

The Jay and Hadasa Pomrenze Foundation

We are especially grateful to Art Pomponio, our editor at Jason Aronson, who commissioned this book on behalf of Jason Aronson and has been very helpful in seeing it through to publication.

Introduction

The point of studying Kabbalah is to help us understand our relationships, our goals and generally our purpose in life. Psychoanalysis casts this same function in a modern cloak and can enable us to love and to live. How all this can happen is an excellent reason for exploring the interplay of these two complementary disciplines.

The predecessors of modern psychoanalysis engendered intense speculation about the mind and its functions. They encompass the lives of Sigmund Freud and Carl Jung, whose ideas and practices dominate the development of psychoanalysis in the twentieth century. Others—Alfred Adler, Eugene Bleuler, Pierre Janet, to name but a few of Freud and Jung's important contemporaries—also made major contributions to the study of normal and abnormal psychic phenomena, intrapsychic structures, interpersonal relationships, transpersonal (spiritual) realms and the dynamic interplay of all of these elements.

These clinicians, in turn, were rooted in the work of nineteenth-century figures such as the French neurologist Jean-Martin Charcot, known as the 'Napoleon of Neurosis.' Moreover, the psychiatrist Richard von Krafft-Ebing, the philosopher Arthur Schopenhauer and a host of lesser known leaders of the liberal intelligentsia of the Spiritualist movement, both in America and Europe, all contributed to the burgeoning analysis of the 'psyche,' the 'self' and the 'soul.'

Perhaps their most significant predecessors in the eighteenth century were Franz Anton Mesmer, after whom 'mesmerism' or hypnosis is named, and his disciple the Marquis de Puységur. The discoveries they made led directly to the work of Freud and Jung. But unlike Freud's meticulous interest in scientific methodology, and apparent lack of religious or spiritual concerns, Jung tried to interweave his own thinking with a collective linking to the insights and healing methods of 'ancient' or 'primitive' cultures. In particular, he was attracted to traditional practices of the shaman that are ever present in many parts of the world, yet remain mostly invisible because of the predominance of Western 'allopathic' medicine.

It may be surprising to note that many techniques used by psychoanalysts (after Freud) and analytical psychologists (after Jung), as well as their divergent methods of psychodynamic psychotherapy, are similar to, if not directly related to, the work of the shaman that still exists in many tribal or indigenous cultures. The shaman may or may not be identical with a tribal medicine man or witch doctor. Because he may incorporate magical practices in his work, these individuals have often been dismissed as ignorant and superstitious. However, shamen are skilled healers who utilize a keen sensitivity to the mental and emotional state of their clients. They analyze dreams, interpret internal conflicts, relieve guilt, promote healing regressions, overcome negativity and generally act as a positive projective focus, among an extensive array of functions. As the great scholar Mircea Eliade puts it, shamen are seers, they are specialists in the human soul (in modern terms read 'self') and the communal spirit (read *geist*). They are at home in the highest realms (spiritual universes) and the lowest ones (netherworld of the unconscious).[1]

Even before the appearance of modern psychological theories and techniques, shamanistic healing can be considered to be the predecessor of psychoanalysis and related treatments. Notably, the shaman, like the psychoanalyst, utilizes psychological techniques as well as his own personality to influence and overcome mental disorders. Later we shall discuss how shamanistic healing has continued to play an important role in psychologically and spiritually oriented treatments through the teachings of the great eighteenth-century Jewish mystic Israel Baal Shem Tov and the role of the Rebbe in Hasidic circles.[2]

From the standpoint of modern mainstream practices, one of the most important milestones was the discovery of animal magnetism by the eighteenth-century French doctor Franz Anton Mesmer and its refinement by his disciple the Marquis de Puységur. Mesmer believed that magnetic fluids or currents could pass between himself and his patients to effect a cure of otherwise intractable mental as well as physical conditions. By all accounts, Mesmer possessed an extraordinary degree of personal magnetism, that is, charm and authority, which he used to 'tune in' to his patients and provoke 'a healing crisis' during a period of 'magnetic sleep' or trance. Puységur realized that this trance had nothing to do with a physical fluid or energy, as his teacher asserted. Rather the active agent in the cure was the iron will of 'the magnetizer,' the therapist. Puységur concluded[3]:

> I believe in the existence within myself of a power.
> From this belief derives my will to assert it.
> The entire doctrine of Animal Magnetism is contained in the two words: *Believe* and *want*.

Subsequently, the theoretical focus changed from physical to psychological forces, while the curative process, which first became known as 'magnetic sleep,' evolved as 'artificial somnambulism,' 'mesmerism' and finally 'hypnotism.'

Meanwhile, 'spiritualism,' the belief that spiritual forces, particularly spirits of the deceased, could communicate with the living, took hold in America and later in Europe. These phenomena were said to manifest themselves with the help of a medium, a sensitive intermediary, who deployed trances, 'artificial somnambulism' and other procedures like automatic writing, to conjure spirits and effect contact. Both mesmerists and spiritualists influenced each other in expanding the study of the 'special forces,' those 'unconscious forces,' that generate aberrant states of mind and being.

By the turn of the century psychiatry had increasingly turned away from a static theory of mind toward a dynamic view of mental functioning. By dynamic we mean interactive, a constant flow of psychic forces both within the mind and between individuals, like a swirling, interacting world within worlds. This dynamism was fed by many sources, including new paradigms in physics, physiology and philosophy.[4]

Freud and his colleagues struggled with this increasing effort to comprehend the human personality in terms of a whirling dynamo of interests, conflicts, forces and interactions, much of which lies outside of conscious awareness. In France this effort crystallized in the person of Pierre Janet, a philosopher who studied medicine in order to pursue psychopathological research and eventually followed Charcot at the Salpêtriere. Janet stressed the importance of rapport in a therapeutic exchange and elucidated many dysfunctional psychological mechanisms, such as subconscious fixed ideas. In fact, Janet coined the term 'subconscious' (superseded in psychoanalytic theory by the term 'unconscious'). Janet's flow of ideas was like a seminal stream that enriched several major schools of thought. His theory of 'subconscious fixed ideas' was taken up by Carl Jung as 'a complex,' while Janet's well-developed psychology of religion complemented Jung, as well as other thinkers such as Henri Bergson and William James.

Janet furnished 'the loss of the sense of real' to Eugene Bleuler's conceptualization of schizophrenia and the sentiment *d'incomplétude* to Alfred Adler's views on inferiority. Janet's contributions to psychoanalytic psychology have been a matter of controversy, yet the emerging body of psychoanalytic theory was clearly aided by Janet's work on hysteria, psychological tension ('cathexis' and 'decathexis') and 'somnambulistic influence' (transference relationships).

Of these various schools of thought, the two most relevant to our book are those of Freud (psychoanalysis) and Jung (analytical psychology). Jung maintained a close association with Freud over a four-year period from 1909, after he finished his apprenticeship at the Burghölzli Clinic in Zurich. Indeed, at one point Freud began to look upon him as his heir apparent. Yet their differences in background (Swiss Christian versus Viennese Jewish), temperament (religious versus nonreligious) and outlook (transcendental versus scientific) mitigated against their continued collaboration. Jung also strongly disagreed with Freud's theory of psychosexual development and the universality of the Oedipus complex.

Jung left the psychoanalytic movement in 1913 and spent several years in relative professional isolation and self-reflection before his own theory of psychological types (introversion versus extroversion) was published in 1921. This was followed by his elucidation of universal primordial images, which he called the archetypes. These included the *shadow* (negative side of the self), the *anima* and *animus* (feminine and masculine components of the psyche), the *wise old man* (the Great Father) and the *magna mater* (the *old wise woman*, the Great Mother). Together they make up the *collective unconscious*, which Jung postulated is not a collection of psychic elements of which we are unaware or unconscious of, rather a powerfully active sustaining force that exists in every person and is part of a universal source.

In his later writings Jung explored paranormal phenomena, spiritism, alchemy, Eastern religious experience and mysticism. He believed that man is naturally religious, a view not far removed from that of the Baal Shem Tov. He coined the term *numinosum*, which has to do with the opening of the self to transcendent God-filled experience, and he claimed that there existed a religious instinct as powerful and fundamental as the sexual or aggressive forces described by Freud under the rubric of *Eros* and *Thanatos*.[5]

Jung's concerns with demonic possession and after-death experiences seem far removed from Freud's systematic, detailed analyses of instinctual development, from oral to anal to phallic impulses and attendant phantasies. Yet both men shared a fascination with the deepest recesses of psychic experience as well as the universal manifestation of these experiences in the form of symbols and metaphors, myth and ritual. They were also very willing to utilize this knowledge in pulling their patients back from the brink of madness.

Freud's ideas went through a process of continual revision, elaboration and reelaboration until the end of his life in 1939. A brief summary of his work shows that psychoanalytic theory went through three major evolutions: the theory of dammed-up-libido, the theory of mental conflict and the theory of object relations.[6] Some of these elaborations were carried out by Freud himself, aided by his immediate colleagues, while the latter was developed in part by Freud, but in particular by Melanie Klein and later psychoanalysts.

The theory of dammed-up libido was akin to classical physics. Psychic energies, initially identified with sexual energies (libido), built up and needed to be discharged. Otherwise stored-up energies (inhibitions) constricted mental activity and resulted in illness.

The theory of mental conflict became the classical theory of Freudian psychoanalysis and remains of central importance to the present day. The conflicts described existed on several different levels: between inner reality and outer reality, between parts of the self (inner reality itself) and ultimately between people (interpersonal relations). At first Freud stressed the conflict between unconscious impulses and the demands of reality. Then he focused on the conflict between parts of the self. He called this the structural theory because it had to do with the structure of the self, in particular the self as divided into the id, the ego and the superego. Finally, he said that the most fundamental conflict was between *Eros* and *Thanatos*, the life and death instincts, between innate life seekingness and innate destructiveness. As the British psychoanalyst John Steiner points out, when destructive forces become installed as permanent features of the personality, then severe disability and invalidity inevitably follow.[7] Frequently this process erupts as a state of continuous negativity that is initially located within the self, and secondarily between the self and others. This results from the projection of negative impulses onto external people or things. Such projective mechanisms enabled Freud to discover the transference relationship by which people relate to each other as figures from their past experience (object transference) or as aspects of themselves (narcissistic transference). The negativity explains why transference relationships are so often charged with hostility.

Each of these analytic theories incorporated major aspects of ones that preceded it. Thus early ideas about sexual repression (hysteria) evolved from the clash between instinctual forces (*Eros* and *Thanatos*). This conflict, in turn, was elaborated upon by Melanie Klein into a theory of infant development whereby the control of destructive forces within the self (envy, chaos) was the primary factor in determining emotional and psychological maturation. In the first few months of life this takes place by splitting the self into different parts. Along with this splitting, she described the splitting of the object (focus of the baby's attention) into good and bad images and/or relationships (good breast and bad breast, warm, nurturing mothering and cold, rejecting mothering). The infant's psychic structure is built up by a continual process of introjection (taking in) and identifying with these images and relationships, or by projecting and getting rid of them (psychic evacuation).

What we call personality is an amalgam of veneers by which we engage others or retreat from them. These provide a myriad of excuses for repairing and not repairing what we want to protect. Psychoanalysis, and related disciplines of psychoanalytic psychotherapy, is an interpersonal intervention that utilizes the study of projective and introjective processes (transference and countertransference transactions) to help people to reconstitute themselves when their lives begin to decompensate (become mentally or characterologically symptomatic). It also helps people whom Freud himself did not believe could be treated.

It is not without a certain degree of irony that Kleinian analysis has been beneficial not only for individuals suffering from psychotic disorders (which Freud termed 'narcissistic neuroses'), but also for helping to repair the rift, at least to some degree, between psychoanalysis and analytic psychology, between Freud and Jung. Kleinian psychology now comprises a major stream of Jungian thought and practice.

In this study we hope to provide a similar service, by reuniting psychoanalysis with one of its principle sources, Kabbalah, the Jewish mystical tradition. The parallels to psychoanalysis and to understanding the deepest levels of the personality that we find in Kabbalah are striking. Mysticism itself is an attempt to transcend ordinary understanding in order to try and 'know' on an experiential and cognitive level the 'inner reality' of the Divine Majesty—God. The mystic endeavor is to attain this state of union without getting lost in the Divine abyss, without sinking.[8] It derives from the Greek *mystikós*, meaning to reveal to initiates the mysteries of their existence. From a further perspective, Kabbalah reveals the essential nature of being. It touches the most profound dimensions of the self and of the soul.

Through an understanding of Kabbalistic principles, as with psychoanalytic ideas, 'man' can supercede time and timelessness as well as space and spacelessness and can bridge the gaps between this lower, material world and the upper, spiritual domains. In this way he can also begin to have more control over his own destiny.

In the earliest days of studying Kabbalah, two types of mystical lore developed, the 'work of the chariot' (*ma'aseh merkavah*) and the 'work of creation' (*ma'aseh bereishit*). The practitioners of the former are called 'those who descend to the esoteric level of the chariot.' The mystical experience is given as the metaphor 'entering the Garden/Paradise.'[9] This is based on the first chapter in the Book of Ezekiel, where the Prophet Ezekiel witnessed a vision of a fiery chariot ascending to the heavens and also described the Divine Majesty on the throne of glory.

The 'work of creation' is the study of mystical cosmology and cosmogony (the origins and nature of the universe). This is a systematic discipline relegated to the initiated and not to be studied in public because of the danger of Gnostic and heretical misunderstanding of the difficult and sensitive subject matter. The rabbis summed this up: "One is not allowed to investigate that which is above and that which is below, that which is before (temporally in the future) and that which is behind (at the earliest beginning), but only that which is from creation onwards."[10] It is essentially an exposition of the first chapter of Genesis.

Two books, in very esoteric form, summarized the study of mystical Kabbalistic literature until its 'exiting from the closet' in the twelth and thirteenth centuries. The Book of Creation (*Sefer Yetzirah*) is ascribed by traditional Kabbalists to have its origins with Abraham. However, modern scholarship states that it was composed somewhere between the third and the sixth centuries. There are thirty-two secret paths to wisdom in the book which refer to the twenty-two letters of the Hebrew alphabet and the ten primordial numbers called *sefirot.* (The numerical value of these letters or group of items is thirty-two, which in Hebrew equals *lev* or heart.) The book deals with the fundamental powers of the elements of creation and also contains elements of *merkavah* (chariot) mysticism with allusions to the animals (*chayot*) mentioned in the Book of Ezekiel.

The second book is called the Bahir or *Sefer Ha-Bahir* (Book of Illumination). Traditionally this work has been linked with Rabbi Nechuniah ben Ha-Kaneh of the first century, but modern scholarship places it in the twelth century in Southern France. In the Bahir early Gnostic ideas found their way into the mainstream of Jewish mystical thought. It also provides the first reference in Kabbalistic literature to transmigration of souls. The book is particularly concerned with letter mysticism, stressing the shape and sounds of the letters and vowels. In additon, there is an allusion to the *sefirot* as a metaphor of man as a 'spiritual tree.'

But the most important work of the Kabbalah is the *Zohar* (Book of Radiance or Book of Splendor). It emerged mysteriously in Castile, Spain, toward the end of the thirteenth century, like a 'Roman candle.' Composed mostly in a lyrical Aramaic, once the *lingua franca* of the Middle East, it is a mosaic of biblical commentary, medieval homily, spiritual fantasy and mystical exposition. In fact, the *Zohar* is often described as the Bible of Kabbalah.

The *Zohar* is divided into several sections. The largest section, the *Zohar* proper, consists of a dialogue on parts of the Torah delivered in the form of discussions of a group of second-century rabbis and scholars in Palestine, led by the noted mystic Rabbi Shimon bar Yochai. Most of the interchanges deal with inner or esoteric meanings of the Biblical text. Traditionally, Kabbalists attribute authorship to Shimon bar Yochai and his contemporaries. But it is generally agreed that the bulk of the *Zohar* was compiled or written by Moses de Leon of Guadalajara, Spain.[11]

In the *Zohar* the material world is the visible reality of unseen reality. Only masters of the hidden wisdom can perceive total reality. The *Zohar* explores the nature of the cosmos and the relationship between a transcendent God and a finite world. One of the major themes of the *Zohar* has to do with how the Godhead, the *Ein Sof* (the Infinite), becomes manifest in creation. The central doctrine of the *Zohar* is how, when and where human actions (religious life, performance of good deeds, mystical meditation, sins and improper thoughts) can evoke or disturb the highest spiritual forces. The author of the *Zohar* is interested in the theosophical mysteries that convey the inner meaning, not the literal meaning, of historical and everyday events. In all this, man has a cosmic influence. Both the 'lower' material and 'upper spiritual' worlds have a symmetrical correspondence. Consequently, deeds, prayers and actions all have a significant input and can help determine one's fate.[12]

With the expulsion of the Jews from Spain in 1492, the study of Kabbalah and Jewish mysticism had reached a certain plateau. While there was still a lot of practical and theoretical activity, a certain 'glue' was lacking that could point Kabbalah toward a more unified, systematic approach. The Kabbalists of Southern France and Spain were mostly people who were interested in spreading their ideas only to their local circle of adherents.

But more importantly, the Spanish expulsion created a spiritual, social and economic catastrophe. Kabbalah began to focus on "death, repentance, and rebirth (which) were the three great events in human life."[13] Now that humanity was threatened by real outside, external forces, Kabbalism attracted many more adherents. There was a strong desire to break the 'curse' of the Exile by repenting. The textual source for this was the *Zohar*'s promise that redemption would come if the heads of the (Jewish) community or only one (Jewish) community would repent sincerely.[14] Looking for a better life led to an emphasis on studying about the soul. The concept of metempsychosis (*gilgul*) (transmigration of souls) attracted many interested followers who found an explanation for death, a difficult life and the opportunity (both in the positive as well as the negative) to return for another chance at rectification (*tikkun*) (reparation).[15]

In writing this book we are not unaware that we are addressing a secular as well as a religiously oriented audience and that many potential readers shun even the mention of God, Divinity, spirituality, mysticism and religion. Moreover we live in a secular age when leading intellectuals are militantly antireligious and anti-God. Thus, various concepts in Kabbalah that, in some circles and at other times, would be easy to grasp are now even easier to dismiss. Therefore we have tried to provide a framework where ideas about God could be related to theories of the cosmos and a consideration of spiritual reality contrasts with new paradigms in modern physics. Nothing is unimaginable.

Kabbalistic conceptions of multiple spiritual worlds are as difficult or easy to fathom as current discussions of ten- and twenty-six-dimensional space and multiple universes.

Moreover we must not forget that many readers may find current psychoanalytic theories about 'inner reality,' 'psychic energies,' 'inner objects' and 'intersubjectivity' no less phantasmagoric. Freud may have longed for psychoanalysis to become mainstream, but given the vast predominance of biological and behavioral theories and treatments, this is far from the case. Most people simply are alarmed to know what goes on in and between themselves and others.

For all the above reasons we have structured our discussions to allow for the interweaving of Kabbalistic and psychoanalytic ideas over and over and over, from different angles, and in diverse contexts. Like similar flavors coming at distinct points of a meal, we intend and hope that they will eventually flow as a harmonious whole that will be intellectually and emotionally satisfying. Our aim is no less than to demonstrate, as described both in psychoanalysis and Kabbalah, that by redeeming one person, one can rectify the universe.

Let us add one further point. Our text is not gender specific. We use the term 'man' to refer to men and women and 'mankind' to refer to mankind and womankind. To do otherwise makes for a very choppy dialogue. Perhaps it is even more important to note that it is hard to find one term that denotes the fact that we all come from the same source.

NOTES

1. Mircea Eliade, *Shamanism* (Princeton, NJ: Princeton University Press, 1964).
2. Rabbi Yisrael (Israel) ben Eliezer, 1698–1760. He is generally known as the Baal Shem Tov (Master of the Good Name) or the Baal Shem (Master of the [Divine] Name) or simply by the acronym the Besht. The Baal Shem is the acknowledged founder of Hasidic Judaism and was an inspired and inspiring healer, teacher, and mystic. He lived and worked in an area that is now part of the Ukraine.
3. Armand-Marie-Jacques de Chastenet, Marquis de Puységur (1751–1825). This quote is from Henri Ellenberger, *Discovery of the Unconscious: The History and Evolution of Dynamic Psychiatry* (New York: Basic Books, 1970) 70–74.
4. Ellenberger, *Discovery of the Unconscious*, 289.
5. Andrew Samuels, *A Critical Dictionary of Jungian Analysis* (London: Routledge & Kegan Paul, 1986).
6. John Steiner, "The Aim of Psychoanalysis in Theory and in Practice" *International Journal of Psycho-Analysis* 77 (1996):1073–83.
7. Steiner, "The Aim of Psychoanalysis," 1074–75

8. Moshe Idel, "Prophetic Kabbalah and the Land of Israel. In *Vision and Conflict in the Holy Land*, edited by R. I. Cohen. (New York: St. Martin's Press, 1985).

9. Cf. T. B. Haggigah 14b.

10. Genesis Rabbah 1:10

11. Moses de Leon, 1250–1305. For extended discussions of the origins of the *Zohar,* see Encyclopedia Judaica, Vol. 16 (Keter Publishing, Jerusalem), 1194–215; also the internet encyclopedia Wikipedia at en.wikipedia.org/wiki/Zohar, 1–7.

12. The only complete English translation was edited by Harry Sperling and Maurice Simon in a six-volume work published by the Soncino Press, 1931–34. The language used in this work is convoluted, difficult, and often out of date. A major new contemporary translation is currently being prepared by Daniel Matt and published by the Stanford University Press (Pritzker Edition). As of 2006, three volumes of a projected twelve volumes have been published.

13. Gershom Scholem, *Major Trends in Jewish Mysticism* (1941; New York: Schocken Books, 1995), 249.

14. *Midrash Ha-Neelam* in *Zohar Chadash*, 23d.

15. Gershom Scholem, *On the Mystical Shape of the Godhead* (New York: Schocken, 1991), 197–250.

Chapter One

Reality, Worlds and Universes

From his earliest stages of development to the end of his life, 'man' is never alone. He is always part of an interactive process: emotionally, cognitively and physiologically. This interactive interplay can be termed 'influence.' Sometimes the 'influence' may be dyadic (mutual) or triadic (three parties) or more. Sometimes it may be active or passive. Looking at the concept of 'influence,' one can ask many questions: How much are we influenced by forces beyond the commonplace? Are there outside powers that influence thoughts and actions? Are there outside factors that affect our behavior?

Both Kabbalah, the Jewish mystical tradition, and psychoanalysis have developed philosophical and theoretical structures to explain the nature of existence as well as the varied forces that affect our lives. We intend to explore both disciplines to see how, when and where they interact with each other in order to determine 'man's' place in the world spiritually and metapsychologically.

Kabbalah is a God-based revelation that supposes a Creator, an Infinite Being that cannot be contained, fully defined or ever completely understood. This is not the same as a religion or religious-based outlook. Many secularists have understood that a Higher Being created our world and the universe that contains it. Often they come from religious family upbringings but cannot reconcile religious doctrine or dogma with scientific validation. Einstein and Freud are two examples of many.[1]

Initially it appears that when Freud began to develop his theoretical formulations of psychoanalysis, he unwittingly postulated a kind of "secularized Jewish mysticism."[2] However, in order to advance his new 'science,' Freud tried to keep it as far as possible from being tainted as a 'Jewish science.' Since almost all of Freud's colleagues, students, followers, admirers and even detractors were Jewish, a non-Jewish person, Carl Jung, was recruited in order to add a non-Jewish and secular perspective.[3] But the ploy did not and could not work, for Jung was the son of a Swiss Reformed Evangelical minister and was a firm believer in both religious and spiritual influences.[4]

According to Kabbalah, creation is not and could not be a secular event. The whole creation process was initiated by an All-Encompassing and Infinite Source, the Godhead. In the beginning there was no room for anything else except the Godhead. This meant that there is an overwhelming power that takes up all the available time and space, which seemingly left 'man' without the ability to maneuver or control his life. This raises the question of free will vs. determinism, issues that we will discuss in detail in forthcoming chapters. But then how can 'man' come into existence?

The answer that Kabbalah postulates is that God the Creator chose to withdraw or contract Himself so as to leave a primordial space within which creation and its aftermath could occur. The awesome energy of existence, akin to fiery furnaces at the center of the sun, was restricted in order to allow man physical and emotional 'space,' that is, to come into being, so that free will could exist too, and so that 'he' would not be overshadowed by an all-controlling Creator. The ensuing contraction, called *tzimzum* in the language of Kabbalah, created a series of worlds that provided a 'vacated space,' and set into play a hierarchical order of separation between God and man.

Tzimzum includes more than just contraction, or a stepping back and withdrawal from a field of infinite light, so that 'man,' and by implication 'consciousness,' can exist and develop. *Tzimzum* also means, as we have just hinted, 'to conceal.' "For the doctrine of *tzimzum* refers to a refraction and concealment of the radiating emanation from the Godhead, in a number of stages and in a progressive development of degrees, until finite and physical substances become possible."[5] The light that is concealed leaves an energy residue or remnant in the 'vacated space' called the *reshimu*. And the light of the Godhead is not dimmed; it is present in the upper spiritual worlds and minutely filters its way down in controlled doses to the lower material worlds, by means of a thin, finely focused light called the *kav* ('the line of light').[6] This is how the light of God connects to mankind. Although God has contracted and concealed His energy, the energies remain forever. Kabbalists assert that it is 'man's' primary task to try to get as close as possible to this Source in order to suckle and obtain emotional nourishment and growth.

What we have been discussing also relates to recent developments in cosmology. Physics has struggled since the 1950s with trying to understand how the world began. Was it a conglomeration of gaseous substances that produced a chemical and electrical reaction? Was there a 'Big Bang' that ultimately took mass and energy and erupted into a cataclysmic cacophony of elements—both large and minute—in order to remain with a remnant of energy and light?[7] These questions about the macrocosm bring us to the forefront of Kabbalistic formulations.

If cosmology tackles the macrocosm, quantum mechanics is a very successful theory that is concerned with the nature of the microcosm. Moreover, it provides a bridge between a Kabbalistic perspective and a psychoanalytic understanding of influence. This branch of physics developed in the early part of the twentieth century and purports to explain the behavior of atoms, molecules and nuclei. It developed in a world influenced by Einstein's special theory of relativity, and revolutionized our understanding of elementary forces. Interestingly, in some ways, quantum theory is the opposite of Einstein's theory. While Einstein wrote about a smooth integration of the cosmos—time and space—quantum theory was concerned with miniature worlds, where subatomic particles are held together by disparate subelements devoid of any content. As the quantum physicist Michio Kaku noted: "Thus, the two theories are hostile opposites."[8]

Important for our understanding of these phenomena is the fact that quantum mechanics provides probabilistic results because the physical universe (the cosmos, the macroworlds and microworlds) is probabilistic rather than deterministic. This fits in with the Heisenberg Uncertainty Principle of 1927:

> . . . there is no way of accurately pinpointing the exact position of a sub-atomic particle unless you are willing to be quite uncertain about the particle's momentum. . . . Also, there is no way to pinpoint the particle's exact momentum unless you are willing to be quite uncertain about its position. To measure both accurately at the same time is impossible.[9]

We should not conclude that quantum mechanics has moved into a world devoid of a Creator. In 1935, Einstein, Podolsky and Rosen noted a paradox (referred to in the literature as the EPR Paradox): "There really is some underlying clockwork that keeps the universe running, and that only gives the *appearance* of uncertainty and unpredictability at the quantum level. . . ."[10] Just as Kabbalah has within it the known and the unknown, and the certainty and uncertainty, there is a Godhead Creator, Master Watchmaker who is controlling the world(s) stage. "This quantum uncertainty ensures that the microworld is a turbulent and jittery realm."[11] The EPR Paradox follows well the Kabbalistic possibility of the simultaneous existence of several worlds and multiple worlds. What happens in New York has effects on what happens in Australia. Since there are multiple worlds and universes, there is always the possibility of influence from one world or area of the world, upon another world or area. These suppositions uncannily resemble the Kabbalistic dictum: "As above, so below."[12]

Are there parallels in psychoanalytic thought? What are the forces that influence our lives from within the mind or psychical apparatus, as Freud put it? Psychoanalysis describes different levels of consciousness: one more inner, the unconscious, and one more outer, the conscious. According to the founder of psychoanalysis, Freud, one could live in two spheres, levels or worlds, simultaneously.[13] On the conscious level, we live our lives in thought and action that we are aware of. This is called the manifest content. Then there is another level, the unconscious level or latent content. The unconscious level, likened metaphorically by Freud to that part of the iceberg that is beneath the surface of the water, has major influence in both thought and action over the conscious level, the above-the-water part of the iceberg. We are constantly influenced by the latent content, by the unconscious. It is the job of psychoanalysis to make the unconscious conscious so that we can have a more willful understanding and control over our lives. From another perspective, this allows us to be less bound by inner drives, what the Kabbalists term our animal self, and to be more able to exercise our inner essence, or what Kabbalists call our Godly soul.

Over the past 30 years, theoreticians such as the Chilean psychoanalyst Ignacio Matte-Blanco[14] have tried to link the emotional dimension of consciousness with a more formal physical description of classification. Matte-Blanco called this 'symmetrical logic.' Similarly, the American neurologist Antonio Damasio took consciousness a step further when he wrote about both the body and emotion as important partners in the 'making' of consciousness.[15] Feeling anxious, for example, is both an emotional as well as physical expression.

Recently there has been a proliferation of books on the close relationship between physicality and psychoanalysis. This brings us back to Freud's original "Project for a Scientific Psychology," where early on (1895!) Freud tried to tie in the body and psychology.[16] Since this "Project" was rediscovered in 1950, theoreticians have tried to put together Freud's original thinking in the guise of modern theory—until recently, but to no avail. Similarly, neuropsychologists with training in psychoanalysis have tried to tie in the physical and emotional.[17] Eventually we will show how these views link with Kabbalistic connections between spiritual and physical domains.

The convergence between the Kabbalistic concept of many worlds and the psychoanalytic concept of conscious and unconscious is striking. In both systems we have influences coming from hidden or secret worlds. In Kabbalah, it's the influence from spiritual realms upon man in his outer world. In psychoanalysis, it's the influence of the unconscious, the inner world, upon the conscious or outer world. In both systems, there is mutual influence from the microcosm to the macrocosm, as well as from outer to inner. We have already touched upon the influence of the spiritual on the material ("As above, so below"). Kabbalah also describes the reverse flow, from 'man' to God, by a variety of means, especially by the power of prayer. In order to understand these streams better, we need to explore both disciplines in greater detail.

Kabbalists posit the existence of a cosmos that contains four basic worlds ranging from the realm of God to the realm of man. Each of these worlds is a stage in the process of creation. They allow for different attributes of the creative power of God to achieve expression. These realms are arranged in order of the revelation from God to man, and since man is not capable of experiencing the direct energy or light of the Divine, there is the necessity of having filters (in psychoanalysis, we call these 'censors') so that there is distance between man and God.

It's important to note that some scholars use the terms 'world' and 'universe' interchangeably. We think it useful to differentiate these terms. Worlds are spiritual domains, while universes encompass spiritual domains and their interrelationship.

One of the oldest Kabbalistic texts is the *Sefer HaBahir* (*The Book of Bahir—The Book of Illumination*). Mystical tradition attributes it to Nechunya ben ha-Kanah of the first century C.E., and it is sometimes known by his name. It surfaced in Provence, France, at the end of the twelfth century, just as the study of Kabbalah was reemerging in public. Gershom Scholem, who was one of the first scholars to bring Kabbalah into popular awareness in the twentieth century, considers it to be "the first book that adopts the specific approach and the symbolic structure characteristic of Kabbalistic teaching . . . (it) is of the utmost importance as the only extant source for the state of Kabbalah as it was when it came to the notice of a wider public, and for the early stages of its development prior to its dissemination beyond limited circles."[18]

The *Sefer HaBahir*, in its brief 12,000 words of text, discusses the ten *sefirot* (Divine attributes of God) in the context of the creation of the world, utilizing the concepts of light and power. For our purposes, it makes the important connection[19] between the lower, material world and the upper, spiritual world, each represented by and embodied in ten *sefirot*.

The *sefirot* refer to "metaphysical principles or to stages in the creation of the world."[20] These are revelations of the essence of reality. They are the attributes of the Godhead as represented by qualities that are to be found in 'man.' An academic specializing in literature has referred to the *sefirot* as "complex figurations for God, tropes or turns of language that *substitute* for God."[21] The etymological source for *sefirot* is probably *sappir* ('sapphire, brilliance')—a reference to God's overwhelming radiance. It is also related to the Hebrew word *saper*, 'to express or communicate.' These linguistic etymologies convey the Kabbalistic idea that the *sefirot* communicate, filter and transmit Divine intentions and energies to the physical world.

We find in the *Sefer HaBahir* that the Hebrew word for 'world,' *olam*, is derived from the same root as *alam* ('concealed').[22] From here we can learn that the higher world, the one closest to God, is concealed from man. God is known as the King of the 'Universe,' and, in a play on words, can also mean the King of 'concealment.'[23] Since we are dealing with higher and hidden or secretive worlds or universes, we are describing movements from more concealed to more revealed domains. We can also describe this metaphorically as movement from a higher level (the Divine) to a lower level (man).

The highest level (or, the most inner or secretive), the top level that is immediately above the four worlds, is that of *Adam Kadmon* (Primordial Man). In this world or universe we have the first reference of the Divine light flowing from the *Ein Sof*, the One without end or limit. Since the Creator is infinite, He is not definable, and nothing but He can exist. The analogy is to being in the center of the sun where nothing material can exist, only pure energy. We, as humans, cannot fathom what the *Ein Sof*, or infinity, or pure energy, is all about. The process of creation and the philosophical understanding of man's existence are beyond our capacity to comprehend. Hence, we call *Adam Kadmon* 'nothingness,' *ayin*. This is to highlight and dramatize that we are not capable of understanding God Himself. "The word *nothingness*, of course, connotes negativity and nonbeing, but what the mystic means by Divine nothingness is that God is greater than any *thing* one can imagine, *no thing*."[24] *Adam Kadmon* serves as the mediator between the Infinite and infinite acts of creation.

The *Zohar* (*The Book of Splendor*), which is the most important Kabbalistic work of mystical teaching, defines the 'without end,' the *Ein Sof*, in the following manner:

> The cleaving of those offering-up sacrifices reaches until the *Ein Sof* . . . for all the will of the wills are contained within the *Ein Sof*.[25]

> He grasps all, yet no one can grasp Him. . . . No one but He can fill all the worlds.[26]

While theoretically a Creator exists in an absolute sense, Kabbalistic writings assert that every aspect of the creation process came into existence only because it was willed. Since God possesses *unlimited* will, all aspects of His creation are part of *limited* will. Only when there is movement from potential to actual is the will revealed. Since God wishes to reveal His will gradually, in stages, this gives man the opportunity to try to correct an imperfect world, thereby generating his own choices—as we shall discuss in a forthcoming chapter when we review the never-ending debate between 'free will' and 'determinism.'[27]

In order to understand the transformation of Kabbalistic ideas and theory into a more 'modern' cloak—and eventually, as we would argue, into psychoanalysis—we need to look at the development of Hasidism, which is the active expression of the Jewish mystical tradition. This mystical revival movement began in Southern Poland and the Ukraine in the eighteenth century. The Hasidic movement[28] was 'begun' formally by Israel ben Eliezer, known as the Baal Shem Tov (Master of the Good Name), and continued by his disciple, Dov Ber, known as the Maggid (preacher) of Mezhirich. Eventually the movement spread out to three main areas:

a. Ukraine, where Levi Isaac of Berdichev and Nachman of Bratslav were the main figures.
b. Lithuania, where Aaron of Karlin and Schneur Zalman of Liadi were the main figures.
c. Poland-Galicia, where Elimelech of Lizensk was the main figure.

Hasidism was a unique offshoot of the Kabbalistic ideas which then had reemerged from concealment in the late twelfth century in France and Spain. One might say that Hasidism is Kabbalah 'in practice.' Moshe Hayim Luzzato and Schneur Zalman of Liadi were two of the most important figures in the transition from a Kabbalistic to a Hasidic mode. The former wrote about his influence by a celestial spirit or teacher whom he called his *maggid*, and who brought him spiritual revelations. This was very similar to Joseph Karo, the late-fifteenth-century codifier of the Code of Jewish Law and a Kabbalist, who also had a *maggid* who talked to him and provided him with direct spiritual and mystical revelations at night. The latter, Schneur Zalman of Liadi, was the founder of the CHaBaD, or Lubavitch, dynasty. He was an astute Kabbalistic scholar who developed a theological and philosophical system of Hasidic thinking and belief that was first promulgated in his *magnum opus*, the *Tanya*. The book is divided into two parts: "The Book of the Benonim" ("Book of the Intermediates") and "The Portal of Unity and Belief."[29]

The *Tanya* states, "All the upper and lower worlds came into being out of nothingness."[30] Below the world of *Adam Kadmon* are the four worlds, or universes:

a. the world of *Atzilut* (emanation), containing the main attributes of God.
b. the world of *Beriyah* (creation), denoting the beginning of materiality.

c. the world of *Yetzirah* (formation), including a variety of spiritual entities that connect materiality and spirituality.
d. the world of *Asiyah* (making), including physical materiality.

Striking parallels to Kabbalistic constructs can be found in the psychoanalytic system. Just as the Kabbalistic system has the concept of inner, more secretive worlds that are not easily accessible, so too do we find in the psychoanalytic system inner worlds, known as recesses of the mind, that are not easily accessible. The Kleinian scholar Bob Hinshelwood makes the following interesting point: "The notion of the unconscious is one of the few concepts that have remained relatively unchanged in the course of the development of all the schools of psychoanalysis."[31] In effect, while the field of psychoanalysis has undergone many revisions, changes, additions and deletions, the basic notion of a secret, nefarious world having influence over a conscious, reality-based world has remained constant.

The nefarious, 'evil-lurking' unconscious is responsible for many of the underlying negativity that governs one's psyche. One example is given by Sigmund Freud:

> . . . such people cannot endure any praise or appreciation . . . they react inversely to the progress of the treatment. Every partial solution that ought to result, and in other people does result, in an improvement or a temporary suspension of symptoms produces in them for the time being an exacerbation of their illness; they get worse during the treatment instead of getting better. They exhibit what is known as a 'negative therapeutic reaction.'[32]

Another is given by a follower of Melanie Klein, Herbert Rosenfeld: "(Klein) conceived of the death instinct as a primary anxiety in the infant related to the fear of death, while Freud generally denied that a primary fear of death was in existence."[33] There is always a dark, mysterious nether world that draws us downward.

Sigmund Freud needed to account for the 'pull' emanating from inside the person's soul. In fact, as we shall see in the next chapter, Freud was quite specific when he used the words *psyche* or *seele* to denote 'soul' rather than 'mind.' He obviously was referring to an emotional part of the person that could account for a certain mysterious drawing power. Freud posited the existence of two major psychical systems: the unconscious and the conscious.[34] He conceived of the preconscious as a subpart of the system conscious. The preconscious can become fully conscious by focusing attention on it (attention cathexis) or by emotional engagement (emotional investment).[35] In the unconscious realm, Freud felt that there were strong instinctual feelings and thoughts that were repressed because of their threatening potential to the conscious, everyday psychic system. While these feelings and thoughts were not readily accessible to conscious thought and feeling, they had a potential major impact through their secretive, inner workings. They were able to affect and effect conscious feeling, thought and action. This became known as the topographic theory.[36]

The ultimate goal of psychoanalytic principles of treatment is to be able to render the unconscious conscious. Then we may become aware of the secret world of the unconscious and be on friendly terms with it. This will enable us to get a handle on our inner world. We can see a parallel here to the Kabbalistic upper (spiritual) worlds, which also influence the workings of the lower (material) worlds. Psychoanalysis also tries to reach the inner dimension of the unconscious, because of its profound effect upon the outer conscious world.

Significantly, we can trace the influence of worlds described by Kabbalah from the unconscious (or totally outside formal awareness) world of emanation, to the preconscious or semiconscious worlds of creation and formation, to the conscious (or at least potentially conscious) world of actualization.

Atzilut (emanation) is the world closest to the Godhead. Therefore the term *atzilut*, which derives from the word *etzel,* means 'nearby.' This beginning of the four worlds marks the separation between the 'world of unification' (the domain of the Godhead, from where emanation begins) and the 'world of separation' (the beginning of the four worlds). The essence of this world marks the emergence from potentialty into actuality—from the concealed power of the Creator to the actualization and effectuation of change in the lower worlds.[37] The *Sefer Yetzirah* (*Book of Creation*) refers to them as the "Ten *Sefirot* of Nothingness."[38] They are undifferentiated in this world and do not operate independently in this world.

The world of *Beriyah* (creation) is the beginning of a separate realm outside the domain of the Divine. In this world we have the beginning of separation from the Godhead. Aryeh Kaplan, who has expounded on Kabbalah in many books, notes that the term *beriyah* derives from the Hebrew root 'to create' and from the Aramaic 'to be outside.'[39] Therefore, metaphorically, this is the world of the Throne and the Chariot, images that convey the vehicle that is the transitional link to God.[40] They are the medium through which the *Ein Sof*, the Infinite, has come down toward man.

The third world is the world of form or formation, *Yetzirah*. This includes spiritual entities called angels—another step removed from God. It also denotes spiritual forces that are closest to our physical domain. Angels are mediators between our physical world of action and higher spiritual realms. Adin Steinsaltz, the Talmudist and philosopher, notes that there are countless number of angels, each one possessing a unique character and personality. "An angel is by definition the constant, unchanging manifestation of a single emotion or feeling . . . the task of angels is mediation, to maintain two-way communications. . . . They serve as emissaries of God. . . ."[41]

Such ideas parallel the concept of 'transitional object' coined by the psychoanalyst Donald Winnicott.[42] He demonstrates that there exists a mother-infant world and the world where the infant is more independent and separate.

The last world is *Asiyah* (actualization). This is man's world of action or actualization. Here the physicality interacts with the spirituality of the above worlds. It is at this level that man can reach awareness that his body can serve as a container capable of receiving spiritual energies. In order to allow such spirituality to be accessible, 'man' has to tone down the physicality of his being and allow himself to 'float' in a 'sea of nothingness.'

These domains describe the differing spiritual dimensions of existence. Freud, however, had great difficulty accepting the fact that there were such transcendental levels.[43] This was one of the reasons that Freud and Jung separated. When Jung was 'anointed' as 'crown prince' of the psychoanalytic movement in 1909, it was precisely at the time (1909–1911) that he was dabbling in mythology, the occult and astrology. Freud wrote about his correspondence with a friend who disagreed with Freud's treating religion as an illusion.[44] His friend called the religious feelings that he had "a sensation of 'eternity,' a feeling as of something limitless, unbounded . . . 'oceanic' . . . the 'oneness with the universe' . . .," or, as we have just mentioned, 'a sea of nothingness.'

Freud had to "admit once more that it is very difficult for me to work with these almost intangible qualities."[45] As a scientist, he had trouble dealing with abstract feelings and emotions. In contrast, Carl Jung tried to interject some mystical and occult thinking into a revised theory of understanding unconscious phenomena. Jung's early works contained within their titles the words 'so-called occult,' 'spiritualistic medium,' 'symbols of rebirth,' 'the collective unconscious' and 'the soul and death,' to list just a few. Jung was willing to extend his observations to the parapsychological world, which allowed him access to the realms of the hidden, unconscious worlds. Jung's concept of the unconscious, influencing world, consisted not only of our inner emotional life and our relationships with other humans (a pre–object relations theory), but also "animal and plant, and even that of inorganic matter and the cosmos itself."[46]

Freud somewhat modified his thinking in 1923 with the elaboration of the psychic system, not according to levels of depth of consciousness (as in 1900) but rather according to slices of the psyche along a longitudinal axis. This was the beginning of the tripartite theory of the id, ego and superego. While

Freud's interest in promulgating this theory was to focus on the conflict between instinctual drives and the outside, real world, he still felt the need to stress that there was an inside, internal world that was constantly influencing and pressuring the outside, external world. The thesis was the same: pressures from inside influence reality that is outside. What Freud had not developed was the potential for influence from the outside on the inside world. At the moment we seem to have a one-sided theory of influence.

Melanie Klein developed Freud's ideas through play therapy and the psychoanalysis of young children. Over the years she expanded her thinking to include the emotional world of the adult and the 'child inside.' Klein broke from Freud's restrictive view that overly emphasized the mechanistic stimulus-response theoretical framework. Freud's drive theory posited a one-person framework. On the contrary, Klein and her followers (collectively known as the British school of psychoanalysis) formulated the concept of a dyadic relationship between internalized images or representations of parents and their functions (called 'objects,' and when split into bits and pieces called 'part objects'). She saw the influence that these 'inside objects and part objects' had on the mind, emotionality and physicality. Klein further recognized an entire range of introjective and projective processes, including projective identification and introjective identification, as the means by which multiple worlds of 'internal objects' were created. In this she carried forward the views of her teachers, Karl Abraham and Sandor Ferenczi, two of the founding fathers of psychoanalysis. It is intriguing to consider the conscious and unconscious influences of their backgrounds. Both Abraham and Ferenczi were Jewish, as was Klein. The Ferenczi family name was originally Fraenkel. Ferenczi's father, Baruch Fraenkel (who changed the name after moving from Poland to Hungary), was a bookseller and purveyor of mystical texts.[47]

Klein and her followers emphasized internal interrelations within a two-person framework. Initially, Klein did not ignore external relations. However, she did not believe that these were the province of psychoanalysis. Others, particularly in the United States, focused on an active interactive relationship emanating from both parents and children. In the paradigm of infant-mother they saw the possibility of both sides influencing one another. Heinz Hartmann tried to develop an ego psychological way of viewing behavior. However, he didn't go far enough in leaving Freud's stuckness with the scientific instinctual discharge theory. While the psychiatrist and psychoanalyst Margaret Mahler, who worked with very disturbed symbiotically attached children, tried to carry this further with her theory of separation-individuation, she still had the infant responding to the behavior and feelings of the mother.

In the late 1970s and early 1980s, other psychoanalysts advanced Mahler's theory and expanded it to include the importance of the influence of the infant on the mother—not just the mother on the infant.[48] Here we have a perfect parallel of dual influence from above to below and from below to above (as in prayer), or from inner to outer and outer to inner. This dual influence theory in psychoanalysis comes closest to paralleling the dual-influence theory of Kabbalah. So the dictum "As above, so below" became "As above, so below" *and* "As below, so above."

Subsequently, the Scottish psychoanalyst Ronald Fairbairn took the bold leap of rejecting Freud's instinct theory and instead replaced it with the concept of object relationships. As Fairbairn stated, "Libido is not primarily pleasure-seeking but object-seeking."[49] One will always strive for a relationship to a satisfying object. Other British psychoanalysts complemented the work of Klein and Fairbairn and strove to perfect the understanding of the interactive, dyadic process between the patient and his desired objects.[50] The move was to perfect the understanding of the interactive, dyadic process between the patient and his desired objects. Today, the study of intersubjectivity seems to be another medium for trying to understand interactive processes, as it focuses ". . . on the interplay between the differently organized subjective worlds of the observer and the observed."[51] The analytic work that takes place is within the realm of ". . . *subjective reality*—that of the patient, that of the analyst, and the psychological field created by the interplay between the two."[52] The American psychoanalyst Thomas Ogden called the creation of the analyst and analysand a blend or merger—"the analytic third."[53]

Fairbairn and his followers, known as object relations theorists, stressed that man was born with an inherent desire for social interaction. This placed a major emphasis on the will and desire of the patient, as well as the will and desire of the object of choice. This interactive, dyadic relationship intensified the concept of will to be able to be paralleled by both sides of the equation. Man's free will is found in both sides of the object relations continuum.

The Kabbalistic view of God enabling man the 'space' for free will is paralleled in the object relations view, whereby man has the ability to interact with the other because of an innate desire to 'join' the other. This in Otto Rank's terms is that "the experience must affirm the individual's will."[54] Whereas the *Zohar* writes of the 'will of wills' on the part of God and the will as found in man, in object relations theory we see that the desire for social interaction is a deeply imbedded desire or will for emotional growth and change.

NOTES

1. Richard Panek, *The Invisible Century: Einstein, Freud and the Search for Hidden Universes* (New York: Viking, 2004), 86.

2. David Bakan, *Sigmund Freud and the Jewish Mystical Tradition* (New York: Schocken, 1965), 25.

3. Yosef Hayim Yerushalmi, *Freud's Moses: Judaism Terminable and Interminable* (New Haven, Conn.: Yale University Press, 1991), 42.

4. Buddhism is another example of how mystical principles and ideas can be pursued apart from the belief in a deity or Godhead.

5. Jacob Immanuel Schochet, *Mystical Concepts in Chassidism* (New York: Kehot, 1988), 49.

6. See Shalom Ulman, *Maftaychot HaChochmah* (The Keys to Wisdom) [in Hebrew]. (Jerusalem, HaMesorah, 1996), 122; Shaul Boyman, *Miftachei Chochmat HaEmet* (Entrance to the Wisdom of Truth) [in Hebrew] (1936, Warsaw; republished in Jerusalem: no publisher, 1987), 26–32. Boyman published this book at age 23. He perished with his family in the Holocaust.

7. Daniel C. Matt, *God and the Big Bang: Discovering Harmony between Science and Spirituality* (Woodstock, Vt.: Jewish Lights, 1996).

8. Michio Kaku, *Hyperspace* (New York: Anchor, 1995), 113.

9. J. P. McEvoy and Oscar Zarate, *Introducing Quantum Theory* (Cambridge: Icon Books, 1999), 156.

10. John Gribbin, *In Search of Schrödinger's Cat: Quantum Physics and Reality* (London: Black Swan, 1991), 182.

11. Brian Greene, *The Fabric of the Cosmos* (New York: Vintage, 2004), 330.

12. This is quoted in the *Zohar* 3:247b as: "No drop comes down from above without having two drops come from below." This is also found in the Talmud, Ta'anit 25b.

13. Sigmund Freud, "The Interpretation of Dreams," vols. 4–5 of *Standard Edition of the Complete Psychological Works of Sigmund Freud*, ed. James Strachey (1900; London: Hogarth Press, 1981).

14. Ignacio Matte-Blanco, *Thinking, Feeling and Being* (London: Routledge, 1988), 19–23. Matte-Blanco discusses the way man conceives mental life, both conscious and unconscious processes, by emphasizing the inner world of thoughts and feelings.

15. "I propose that we become conscious when the organism's representation devices exhibit a specific kind of wordless knowledge—the knowledge that the organism's own state has been changed by an object—and when such knowledge occurs along with the salient representation of an object." Antonio Damasio, *The Feeling of What Happens* (New York: Harcourt Brace, 1999), 25.

16. This was Freud's attempt to synthesize natural science and psychology in a theoretical framework that could explain all of emotion. It was written in a two- to three-week period, was left unfinished, was never referred to, and was seemingly forgotten. As the story goes, Freud "did his best to destroy it." Freud, 1895/1950, "Project for a Scientific Psychology," in *Standard Edition,* ed. James Strachey, vol. 1, 290.

17. Mark Solms and Oliver Turnbull have written about the linkage between neuroscience and subjective mental states, like consciousness. What is exciting is the identification of neurological correlates for psychoanalytic concepts and ideas. Mark Solms and Oliver Turnbull, *The Brain and the Inner World* (London: Karnac, 2002).

18. Gershom Scholem, *Kabbalah* (Jerusalem: Keter, 1974), 312, 314–15.

19. As Scholem writes: "Everything in the lower world, particularly everything that has sanctity, contains a reference to something in the world of the divine attributes." Scholem, *Kabbalah,* 314.

20. Scholem, *Kabbalah,* 23.

21. Harold Bloom, *Kabbalah and Criticism* (New York: Continuum, 1993), 25.

22. Bahir 1:10. Aryeh Kaplan, *The Bahir* (Newburyport, Mass.: Samuel Weiser, 1979), 5.

23. Bahir 2:10. Kaplan, *Bahir,* 96. See also Aryeh Kaplan, *Innerspace* (Jerusalem: Vagshal/Moznaim, 1990a), 21.

24. Daniel Matt, "*Ayin*: The Concept of Nothingness in Jewish Mysticism," in *Essential Papers on Kabbalah,* ed. L. Fine (New York: New York University Press, 1995), 67.

25. *Zohar*, 2:239a.

26. *Zohar*, 3:225a.

27. Yechiel Bar-Lev, *Song of the Soul* (Petach Tikvah, Israel: Sefer ve Sefel, 1994), part 1.

28. The major 'players' in this new movement included Israel ben Eliezer (1700–1760), Dov Ber of Mezhirich (died 1772), Levi Isaac of Berdichev (1740–1809), Nachman of Bratslav (1772–1810), Aaron of Karlin (died 1772), Schneur Zalman of Liadi (1747–1813), Elimelech of Lizensk (1717–1787), and Moshe Hayim Luzzato (1707–1747). Luzato maintained that he was a 'true' Hasid, and that other Hasidim were not true Hasidim. However, he is viewed by many as a Kabbalist and not a Hasid. See Moshe Idel, *Kabbalah: New Perspectives* (New Haven: Yale University Press, 1988), 295 fn. 90.

29. In Aramaic, *tanya* means 'it has been taught.' The author, Schneur Zalman of Liadi, spent 20 years writing, revising and elaborating the text, and it is known as the 'Written Torah' of ChaBaD. The *Tanya* addresses those who express love and reverence for God through study and contemplation.

30. *Tanya*, chapter 20. See also: Moshe Hayim Luzzatto, known as the RaMHaL, a prominent eighteenth-century Italian Kabbalist and philosopher. See M. H. Luzzatto, *Sefer Ha-Kllalim* [in Hebrew], ed. C. Friedlander (B'nai Brak: Gittler, 1989), "Kllalei Maamar Ha-Chochmah," 12, p. 314.

31. R. D. Hinshelwood, *A Dictionary of Kleinian Thought* (London: Free Association Books, 1991), 467.

32. Freud, 1923, "The Ego and the Id," in *Standard Edition,* ed. James Strachey, vol. 19, 49.

33. Herbert Rosenfeld, "Destructive Narcissism and the Death Instinct," in *Impasse and Interpretation* (London: Tavistock, 1987), 127.

34. Freud, 1900, "The Interpretation of Dreams," especially chapter 7.

35. 'Attention cathexis' is the English translation of the German *besetzung,* 'investment.' This term meant the amount of emotional energy attached to any object representation or mental structure.

36. From the Greek, 'mapping of the mind.'

37. Scholem, *Kabbalah*, 96–105.

38. *Sefer Yetzirah*, 1:2–9.

39. Kaplan, *Innerspace,* 25, quoting the classic *Pardes Rimonim* (16:1) (Orchard of Pomegranates) of Moses Cordovero.

40. Cf. Isaiah 6:1 and Ezekiel 1:26.

41. Adin Steinsaltz, *The Strife of the Spirit* (Northvale, N.J.: Aronson, 1988), 45. See also Adin Steinsaltz, *The Thirteen Petaled Rose* (New York: Basic Books, 1980), 8–17.

42. Donald W. Winnicott, "Transitional Objects and Transitional Phenomena," in *Through Paediatrics to Psycho-Analysis* (1953; London: Hogarth Press, 1975).

43. Joseph H. Berke and Stanley Schneider, "The Self and the Soul," *Mental Health, Religion and Culture* 9 (2006): 333–54.

44. Freud, 1927, "The Future of an Illusion," and 1929, "Civilization and Its Discontents." See also Stanley Schneider and Joseph H. Berke, "The Oceanic Feeling, Mysticism and Kabbalah: Freud's Historical Roots," *Psychoanalytic Review,* in press.

45. Freud, 1929, "Civilization and Its Discontents," 64, 72. The friend was Romain Rolland, the Nobel laureate in Literature in 1915.

46. Frieda Fordham, *An Introduction to Jung's Psychology* (1953; Harmondsworth, Middlesex, England: Penguin, 1991), 63.

47. Tom Keve, *Triad: The Physicists, the Analysts, the Kabbalists* (London: Rosenberger & Krausz, 2000), ii.

48. Daniel Stern, Robert Emde and Stanley Greenspan.

49. W. R. D. Fairbairn, "Object Relations and Dynamic Structure," *Psychoanalytic Studies of the Personality* (1946; London: Routledge & Kegan Paul, 1986), 137.

50. Harry Guntrip, Donald Winnicott and Michael Balint.

51. George E. Atwood and Robert D. Stolorow, *Structures of Subjectivity: Explorations in Scientific Phenomenology* (Hillsdale, N.J.: Analytic Press, 1984), 42.

52. Robert D. Stolorow, Bernard Brandschaft and George E. Atwood, *Psychoanalytic Treatment: An Intersubjective Approach* (Hillsdale, N.J.: Analytic Press, 1987), 4.

53. Thomas Ogden, "The Analytic Third: Working with Intersubjective Clinical Facts," *International Journal of Psycho-Analysis* 75 (1994): 3–19.

54. Esther Menaker, *Otto Rank: A Rediscovered Legacy* (New York: Columbia University Press, 1982), 103.

Chapter Two

The Self and the Soul

The self and the soul are key protagonists of both the psychoanalytic and Kabbalistic worlds. But they are amorphous concepts, perhaps the self more so than the soul. What is the 'self'? What is the 'soul'?

The 'self' is a paradox. It is a specific entity, but also an exercise in ambiguity. Although it pertains to psychological realms, the term encompasses a plethora of meanings ranging from the interpersonal to the transpersonal. Most narrowly, the many definitions include identity and identifications, awareness and self-awareness, as well as a host of mental functions that Freud referred to as "the mental apparatus."[1] More generally, the self refers to a person confirmed in his *subjectivity*, someone who is the agent of his own thoughts, feelings, memories and actions. At the same time, the self is also a person confirmed in his own *objectivity*, the object of his activity and focus of his conscious experience.

Heinz Kohut, the psychoanalyst whom many consider to be the progenitor of self-psychology, contends that the self is essentially "not knowable in its essence."[2] Before reaching this conclusion he reviewed various attempts to refine the term ranging from personality structure to psychological center. Subsequently he described the constituents of the self: ambitions, ideals, talents and skills. A secure self is a cohesive whole. The converse lacks cohesion and remains a fragmented, chaotic mess. Ultimately Kohut did not assign a specific, that is, inflexible definition to 'the self.' While he may not have believed that 'the self' is ineffable, he did think that the term may be best left undefined.

Jungian or analytical psychology appears to provide a broader conception. It sees the self as "the unifying principle within the human psyche." Thus for Carl Jung, the self is both the center and the container of individual consciousness.[3] Ultimately 'the self' can be seen as a holographic representation of the universe. This view is not too dissimilar from the Kabbalistic idea of 'the soul,' which, as we shall soon discuss, ranges from the 'animal' to the spiritual, according to five hierarchical categories of soulfulness. These begin with a human essence embodied in physical form and conclude with a state of absolute unity with the Infinite.

Joseph Berke recalls the day he realized that he existed. It was a scintillating summer's morning in Newark, New Jersey. He was fourteen or maybe fifteen years old, and was ambling down Osborne Terrace, the street where he lived. He noticed the sky—it was bright blue—and the clouds, proud bundles of white, seemed to be dawdling in the sky. He stopped and looked, very intently, as if transfixed. Suddenly he realized that he existed, and that there was an 'I' who was also a 'me.' For the first time in his life he had a profound sense of himself, as a being, as a doer, as a separate and independent entity. Berke felt alive and was delighted to be an 'I,' and not an extension of his mother's life. Years later, he learned that this is what psychologist Abraham Maslow and others have called a 'peak experience.'[4]

That day he discovered his 'self.' But what is this 'self'? Well, in the first place, it had to do with a sense of his own identity. He existed in the world; in his beingness, his uniqueness and his aloneness; in time (over many generations); and in space (with family and friends). This was the beginning of his awareness of himself as a separate player in the complicated business of human relationships. Such awareness coincides with the view of philosopher Dan Dennett that 'the self' is "the Center of Narrative Gravity" around which all our memories and life-stories revolve.[5]

This description carries two major implications. One is that when a person has a clear sense of his own identity, he feels confirmed in his own *subjectivity*. He understands that he is the agent of his own thoughts, feelings and experiences, which began with and end with himself. In other words, this individual becomes the vessel that contains the light of his own being.

Second, when he feels confirmed in his *objectivity*, he becomes aware of himself as an object, the object of his own praxis, of his own mental and physical activities. The psychologist William James defined consciousness as "the awareness of being aware."[6] Here 'awareness' is the activity and 'being aware' is the focus, or the object of the activity. Similarly, to be the object of one's own activity can best be conceived as being the focus of one's own consciousness. We commonly express this experience by hyphenated words: self-awareness (as happened on that summer's day: Berke became aware of himself as an object of his own awareness); self-consciousness (a somewhat embarrassing awareness that someone else is aware of oneself);

self-esteem; self-image; self-love; self-preservation; self-punishment; self-reproach; and so on.

So it all seems very simple. The self has to do with an enclosed subjectivity (I becoming an 'I'), and an enclosed objectivity (I becoming a 'me'). And it refers to identity, one's sense or personal awareness of extending over myriad relationships. But the concept also has to do with ontology. Ontology refers to one's being in the world. This often gets lost when thinking of 'I-ness' or 'me-ness.'

Ontology raises fundamental problems of existence: How can I become an 'I,' and how can I become a 'me'? Or another way to pose this question is: What gives life meaning, and, more specifically, what gives meaning to my life?

Such questions relate to Stanley Schneider's near-death experience, which took place after a car accident in 1978. His feeling of hovering, entering and exiting his body during an operation clearly delineate the cloudy world of conscious, unconscious and psychic awareness. It is very difficult to pinpoint in which world he existed. The self and soul were one entity that merged and divided from moment to moment through that traumatic experience, all of which demonstrates the overlap between the domains of the self and the soul.

This brings one closer to the realms of Kabbalah and to the issues that the Kabbalists have addressed over two millennia. But first let us consider how psychoanalytic thought has touched bits and pieces of these concerns in some very interesting ways.

For a considerable time, analysts didn't talk about the self. Freud himself did not use the term. Instead they talked about an 'I' related to identity, more specifically the ego. 'Self' became synonymous with the 'I,' and generated considerable confusion. Was the self an 'I,' an 'ego,' an inflated identity as in narcissistic aggrandizement, the mind or what?

In fact, Freud used the term 'ego' to refer to the thinking apparatus of the mind. According to his structural model, he distinguished between the ego, the id and the superego.[7] Consequently, the ego became the part of the mind that has to do with thinking and with grasping or understanding inner and outer reality. So after a while, the central self became synonymous with mind, and also with parts of the mind, especially in translation. But Freud's terminology also has to be approached with some circumspection. As Bruno Bettelheim has pointed out, Freud's translators skewed his words towards the medical or scientific in order to gain acceptance for him, especially in the United States.[8] 'The ego' is a rather cold, technical rendering of *das Ich,* with its many layers of emotional undertones. Similar problems arise conveying the meaning of *das Es* and *das Uber-Ich* (usually translated as the 'id' and the 'superego'). Neither of these words equals 'the self,' although when discussing superego function, such as in depression, Charles Rycroft notes that hyphenated words such as self-punishment, self-reproach, self-accusation and self-blame have been commonly used to indicate the object or target of masochistic abuse.[9]

In the 1930s ego psychology became the dominant school of psychoanalysis in the United States. Its major proponents included Heinz Hartmann, Ernst Kris, R. M. Loewenstein, David Rapaport and Erik Erikson. Again the concept of 'self' was bypassed in favor of the concept of the ego and its development. So instead of trying to see persons as a whole, how they existed in and for themselves and in and for others, these practitioners narrowed their attention to a part of the mind, which they pursued with a rational, mechanistic rigor. Moreover their thinking was highly influenced by models of social adaptation.[10]

In many respects ego psychology thwarted a deeper understanding of the psyche. However, it did emphasize the importance of context in determining the unfolding of the ego or, in a larger sense, the self. As psychologist Richard Bentall points out, when constructing a self, the child internalizes historically and culturally determined values.[11] The implication is that one's concept of self varies from time to time and place to place. Thus in the contemporary United States we can and do refer to an 'individualistic self,' while in countries like Japan where a person cannot conceive of himself outside of a large social group, the emphasis is on a 'collectivistic self.'

The counterpart to American ego psychology is object relations theory, developed in England by Melanie Klein and her followers. The term 'self' became a much more dynamic term than 'ego,' and was utilized to describe the relational aspects of Klein's theories. This includes all the processes of separating good from bad, inner from outer, introjection from projection. Yes, Klein often used 'the self' synonymously with 'the ego,' but this was a much broader ego to do with functions, defense mechanisms and ways of coping with anxiety.

As Hinshelwood points out in his *Dictionary of Kleinian Thought*, if 'the ego' stands for a part of the mind that can be objectively described (that is, from the outside), then 'the self' refers to a person as subject, as the initiator and container of his own experiences, phantasies and complicated inner interactions.[12]

In a similar vein, Heinz Kohut developed a concept of self relations that went beyond the bounds of 'self' as the focus of itself (as in self-awareness) and 'self' as the focus of an outside observer, but a self that was the instigator of relationships. This is a relating self, an entity that engaged with others, both inwardly and outwardly.

Thus over several decades, the term gradually enlarged its meaning. From first denoting a static mental structure, it began to encompass the idea of a dynamic interrelating personality, a signified and signifier. This is certainly the case when considering the role of the self in the work of the existentialist psychoanalyst Rollo May and in the work of the progenitor of analytical psychology, Carl Jung.

May focused on ontology, the self as a center of being-in-the world. According to May, 'the self' shares four basic ontological characteristics, that is, qualities of being.[13] First, it is a center of personal existence (quite different from being egotistical or self-centered). Second, man (by which we mean humankind: mankind and womankind) continually strives to affirm this center. Third, he utilizes this center to engage other people. And fourth, the self is a center of consciousness. For man this refers to self-awareness, of himself as subject, and of others as object.

We would add a fifth criteria of beingness. Man seeks to preserve his center, even to the extent of hiding it from himself. This has a lot to do with the creation of a false self system, which we will detail later on.

Interestingly, in the 1960s a Peruvian-born American anthropologist, Carlos Castaneda, helped to solidify the idea of a personal 'center,' as well as the concepts of 'centralness' and 'centeredness,' through his best-selling books about Don Juan, a Mexican *brujo* or warlock and shaman.[14] In order to protect oneself from death, disease and injury and to assure personal safety, a person always has to find his place of power. Don Juan taught that somewhere, in every room, there was such a place. But to find one's place was to be absolutely centered in one's being. Therefore power became equated with finding one's personal center of balance, and affirming the epicenter of the self. Comparatively, Schneur Zalman, the first Lubavitcher Rebbe, writing in his epic work, *Tanya*, teaches that the central point of every level of being is the place of Truth, and that every person should try to attain this place.[15]

The *Zohar* also discusses the importance of polarization and centering.[16] If one is 'off' in any way, it emphasizes the need to tilt that person to a more 'right' or 'left' position. The modern term for this is 'off' or 'on' center. Such directionality has a basic meaning as in describing an overly physical or emotional person, someone who is too warm or too cold, or for that matter, too active or too passive. Hence the significance of finding the just-right center of balance.

This central 'selfness' provides the starting point for personal relationships. Without such a point, relationships are impossible. Otherwise people engage in partial relationships or pseudo-relationships or non-relational relationships. At worst, relationships become extremely threatening because the central non-point of one's existence is continuously in danger of being engulfed or overwhelmed by the reality of others' beingness. At best, one's 'self' is an entity in continuous relations with other 'selves' as part of a people-related, or as Kleinian psychoanalysts state, an object-related universe.

The result of possessing a stable personal center is not only that one can engage in such a universe, but that one can expand this universe through a state of self consciousness. Here, we and others like Rollo May do not mean 'self-consciousness,' which is an embarrassing looking at one's self as if from without. On the contrary, self consciousness has to do with a state of expanded consciousness, where one's core self becomes the creator of symbols and abstractions. Thus people and things—trees, leaves, stars, grains of sand and even oneself—all gain a plethora of new meanings. This connects with the findings of the 'logo-therapist' Victor Frankl, himself a direct descendent of the Talmudic scholar RaSHI and the Kabbalist Rabbi Judah Loew of Prague, who taught that the nature of existence has to do with gaining meaning through existence.[17]

Analytical or Jungian psychologists refer to the center of the self as "the original state of organismic integration," the place within oneself where one's personal being, one's innate self and one's archetypal potential meet. At different points in a spectrum of 'being,' Jung distinguishes between 'the self,' 'the soul' and 'the spirit.' But in practice he often uses these terms synonymously.[18]

At one end of this spectrum, Jung expands the concept of self to include both conscious and unconscious consciousness or experience. This is in contrast to 'the ego' that Jung, as Freud, reserved for the conscious mind. Jung also saw the self as a mediator of opposites within a human's central personality. This implies that there is 'a good self' and 'a bad self' and 'a coordinating self,' a part of one's being that orchestrates relations between the two polarities.

The 'shadow side of the self' is an entity often equated with the part of the personality that a person wants to conceal. From a Jungian standpoint, it is simply an acknowledgment that the Self is all encompassing.[19] Therefore it must also include the negative. These negative qualities represent the inferior, worthless, dangerous, primitive aspects of one's nature, something dark that needs to be kept in the dark, hidden like an internalized 'evil other.' This 'shadow side' is remarkably like the Kabbalistic concept of the *sitra achra,* meaning 'the other side.' This is the force for evil that exists within every person. Why evil? Because evil is disconnected from Divine Purpose, and is, therefore, unrestrained in passions and appetites. The 'shadow' is also the repository for 'Thanatos,' which is what Melanie Klein called the 'death instinct.' This is the terrifying impetus to death and dissolution against which the self is constantly struggling.

The 'soul' is one's primary, undifferentiated potential. It is the central, invigorating core of one's existence. In Kabbalistic thought, this is identical with the 'I' (*Ani*), which means a sense of undifferentiated beingness—in contrast to the 'self,' which is a differentiated or actualized essence. In Jungian psychology, with 'the psyche,' the soul is a nonmaterial, archetypal essence that can connect one's experience with all experience, one's being with all beingness, whether animate or inanimate. In other words, it is the part of the spectrum that integrates inner reality with larger realities, the particular with the universal, personal consciousness with cosmic consciousness.

Jung applied the word 'spirit' to the nonmaterial, ineffable component of being. But 'spirit' differs from 'soul,' because a soul may be incarnate or non-incarnated, but one's spirit is incorporeal, ethereal and detached from the body. It is much more like the Kabbalistic entity of the *tselem,* an astral body or astral projection, like an apparition or shade. A spirit cannot be specified or encompassed by definition or description. It is formless, imageless, spaceless and endless. Moreover, it can exist independently from a person. The Kabbalah scholar Gershom Scholem tried to explain this phenomenon:

> What is the nature of this element which . . . is referred to in the *Zohar* and other writings as man's *tselem*? Is this a Kabbalistic version of the doctrine of the 'self' as the deepest spiritual essence within man, or is it a version of the idea of an astral body or 'psychic body' within man, which constitutes a third, independent entity mediating between body and soul?[20]

For Jung, belief in the spirit world does not necessarily include belief in the soul.[21] But 'spirit' may be personified in visionaries or prophets. In many respects the Jungians see 'spirit' as the essential or basic unifying principle of the universe.

Herein lies the seeming difference between Jungian and Freudian theory. Analytical psychology yields a holistic conception of man, from the intrapsychic to the transcendental, while psychoanalysis is inherently deterministic and reductionistic, with little room for the self, the soul or the spiritual. It may come as a surprise that this scenario is quite misleading and, as we have previously explained, follows from the mistranslation of Freud's work.

Bettelheim has shown that 'psychoanalysis' essentially means soul-study or soul-investigation.[22] In German the emphasis is on the first word, *psyche*—soul, not mind. But in English the emphasis is on the second word, *analysis*, with all its scientific, systematic associations. Freud was a superb wordsmith, a master of literary German. It is often said that if he had not developed psychoanalysis, he could have become a great poet and dramatist like Goethe. He used words very precisely. As Nobel laureate Hermann Hesse stated: "[Freud's work] convinces both through its very high human and very high literary qualities . . . [his language] . . . is beautifully concise and exact in its definitions."[23] If Freud had chosen to refer to the intellect or mind, he would have used the precise German word *geistig,* meaning mental. On the contrary, he wrote *psyche* or *seele,* both of which mean 'soul.' But they tend to be misconveyed in English as 'mind.'

Thus, in 1905, Freud wrote in his paper, "Psychical Treatment" ("Treatment of the Soul"), as translated from the German by Bettleheim:

> 'Psyche' is a Greek word and its translation is 'soul.' Psychical treatment hence means 'treatment of the soul.' One could thus think that what is meant is: treatment of the morbid phenomena in the life of the soul. But this is not the meaning of this term. Psychical treatment wishes to signify, rather, treatment originating in the soul, treatment—of psychic or bodily disorders—by measures which influence above all and immediately the soul of man.[24]

Compare the above statement as translated by Bettelheim with the way it appears in the English *Standard Edition*, where the title is given as "Psychical (or Mental) Treatment." The following is the passage as translated by Strachey:

> 'Psyche,' is a Greek word which may be translated 'mind.' Thus, 'psychical treatment' means 'mental treatment.' The term might accordingly be supposed to signify 'treatment of the pathological phenomena of mental life.' This, however, is *not* its meaning. 'Psychical treatment' denotes, rather, treatment taking its start in the mind, treatment (whether of mental or physical disorders) by measures which operate in the first instance and immediately upon the human mind.[25]

Why are these excerpts important? Because to explore the self and the soul, and the interplay between them, it is necessary to preserve the richness of human experience, its emotional resonances, its inexactness and ambiguity. Bettelheim suggests, and we would agree, that a psychoanalysis was not meant to be a dry intellectual exercise. Rather it was more akin to the writing of a great novel, the unfolding of a person's 'hi-story,' and recovering of his narrative gravity.

So when Freud deployed *das Ich,* he was trying to convey far more than a part of the mind. He meant the 'I,' the whole of a person's subjectivity, and the 'Me,' the whole of a person's objectivity, the totality of his personality, his entire 'self.' And when Freud deployed *das psyche* and *die seele* he meant far more than mind. He was trying to convey the full import of a person's holy, timeless essence, that which was most spiritual and worthy in him. As Bettelheim stressed, "Freud often spoke of the soul—of its nature and structure, its development, its attributes, how it reveals itself in all we do and dream."[26]

He asserted that psychoanalysis is 'a spiritual journey of self-discovery,' or as we now understand, 'soul-discovery.'

How did Freud's intentions become distorted? Bettelheim concluded that the distortions had to do with the wish of English translators to make Freud's work more acceptable by making it more scientific. Consequently Freud's technique appeared to become more and more abstract, more and more impersonal. Instead of being concerned with man, it became concerned with mind. Then soul-study evolved into psychoanalysis, i.e. mind-analysis, from the corrupted translation of the word 'psyche.'

However, we think this is only partly true. The answer also lies in the complicated and contradictory personalities of Freud and his followers. They needed and wanted to prove themselves as scientists and doctors, and to establish a new practice and paradigm of healing. And to do so, they had to operate in a world that was extremely hostile to their Jewish identities and backgrounds. Thus we can speak of a revealed and concealed Freud, states that are comparable to the concepts of *niglah* (revealed/open/transparent) and *nistar* (secretive/hidden) in Kabbalistic teaching. The overt Freud reveled in the mind, its structure and typology, its repressions and cathexes. Concomitantly, the covert Freud delighted in the study of the soul, very much related to his Kabbalistic and Hasidic roots, going back at least three generations.[27]

Two of Freud's famous patients were the fifth Lubavitcher Rebbe (the RaShaB) and the poet H. D. (Hilda Doolittle). In the first case Freud (or his colleagues) went to extraordinary lengths to conceal the treatment, even to the extent of losing his appointment books for years at a time. But we know that the meetings went well from the diaries of the RaShaB's son (who became the sixth Lubavitcher Rebbe) and who attended at least some of the sessions with his father.[28] H. D., on the other hand, spoke openly of her treatment with Freud and was widely quoted about her experience. She exclaimed, "He is the midwife to the soul."[29]

We now intend to explore what is the Kabbalistic concept of the soul, and by extension, the self, which touched Freud and his colleagues, both overtly and covertly, consciously and unconsciously.

In the Jewish mystical tradition the soul is a person's holy, timeless essence. We refer to an entity that is both elevated, that is, exists in spiritual realms, and is part of our primordial source and the endless everything. Therefore the soul is transcendental in nature and orientation. It yearns for knowledge of the most creative and sublime aspects of existence. Not only does it surpass the self, but the soul necessarily seeks to obliterate it in order to achieve union with the infinite, which in Kabbalah is called the *Ein Sof*. And by so doing the soul acts to repair or rectify the chaotic threads of the universe.[30]

The *Zohar* asserts there are many paths to wisdom:

> One way is to contemplate the mystery of His Master. Another is to know one's self. Who am I? How was I created? Where do I come from? Where am I going? How is the body fixed to function? How must I give an account of myself before the Ruler of All? A third way is to know the secret of souls. What is this soul within me? Where does it come from? Why did it come into this body made of a stinking drop? A fourth way is to know and contemplate the world one is in. What is its purpose? And then to seek to know the supernal mysteries of the higher worlds and to know one's Master.[31]

Who is the Master to whom the *Zohar* refers? He is the primordial source, the Godhead. So knowledge of one's self and contemplation of one's soul go hand in hand. Both lead to an extraordinary capacity to 'see' and comprehend the microcosm and the macrocosm, the most interior realities and the most cosmic truths. Why is this the case? Simply because man, also woman, is made in God's image. By image we do not mean a picture of God, for no such picture could possibly exist. Rather we refer to the basic characteristics or creative powers of God, which in Kabbalah are called *sefirot*.

Collectively the *sefirot* are depicted as spheres organized in the shape of a man, or, in popular Kabbalah, as a tree.[32] Each sphere is a bundle of illumination as well as the vessel that contains this illumination or energy, like a torus that contains an energized plasma. Laibl Wolf clarifies the human metaphor of the *sefirot*.[33] Three *sefirot* surround the head. These are *Keter* (representing the Divine will), *Chochmah* (wisdom) and *Binah* (understanding). Internally, the head contains *Da'at* (knowledge); the neck, *Malkhut* (the *Shekhinah*, the feminine presence of the Godhead); the arms, *Chesed* (kindness) and *Gevurah* (severity); the torso, *Tiferet* (splendor); the thighs, *Netzach* (thrust) and *Hod* (trust); and finally, the genitalia, *Yesod* (phallus).[34]

In other schema the *sefirot* are organized differently, such as a geometric figure with ten points linked by twenty-two lines.[35] All of these images, whether of men or of trees or of geometric figures, are themselves members of four worlds of ascending and interconnecting spirituality.

As we previously discussed, when the universe was initially formed, the *sefirot* did not have the ability to relate to each other. They could take in energies, but not give them out. At a certain point the lower *sefirot*, also known as the *midot* or the emotional qualities of God, shattered. In consequence, the fragments or sparks of these vessels embedded themselves in anything and everything, including all souls, past, present and future. This shattering of the vessels created chaos (*tohu*).[36] According to Kabbalah, the whole point of our existence is to retrieve these sparks (from wherever they had became embedded), raise them to their proper spiritual level, and bring about a complete repair (*tikkun*) of all four spiritual worlds, arranged heirarchically from *Asiyah* (Actualization), through *Yetzirah* (Formation) to *Beriyah* (Creation) and *Atzilut* (Emanation).

Of particular significance to this discussion, the Safed school of Kabbalists developed the idea that knowledge of the roots of one's own soul was essential to achieve a personal *tikkun,* or from another angle, soul-actualization. They believed it was the task of every person to achieve the rectification of his life by discovering the sparks rooted in himself through a process of introspective extraction (*birur*), comparable perhaps during psychoanalysis to the long and difficult process of uncovering one's repressed thoughts and feelings.

In the eighteenth and nineteenth centuries Kabbalists would try to sift the sparks that pertained to their souls by 'going into exile,' literally wandering from village to village for months at a time.[37] The Kabbalist Moses Zacuto alluded to the importance of this process:

> . . . every man should investigate thoroughly in order to know the roots of his soul, so as to be able to perfect it and restore it to its origin which is the essence of one's being.[38]

However, there is a big difference between what contemporary psychoanalysis or popular psychology might understand as self-investigation and self-discovery, and what the Jewish mystics intended. For them, uncovering the roots of one's soul through the process of *birur* (introspective extraction) and achieving a personal rectification was like finding the missing bits and filling in the cracks in one's existence. It did not have to do with success, accomplishment, happiness or pride. Quite the contrary, they strove to obliterate the ego and overcome all attempts at self-enhancement. What these mystics wanted was to explore and determine the nature of their own unique spiritual life-task. In their terms this meant realizing their 'Godly soul' and transforming themselves into a conduit for God's values and God's will.

Sanford Drob explains that a person who seeks guidance from a Kabbalistic master or Hasidic Rebbe does not require psychological construction or reconstruction (as in psychotherapy or psychoanalysis).[39] He is much more concerned with finding a way to serve God and his follow man, according to his personality and circumstances. If he succeeds in this task, then he will gain personal satisfaction and fulfillment. This is 'good,' even more so when it originates in 'evil.' In this regard Drob continues:

> When the evil impulse is redirected, the divine sparks within the soul are liberated and return to their source in God. The individual whose energy is placed in the service of Torah and *mitzvot* does not act so much as an animal whose energy has been redirected and put to good use, but rather as a being created in

> God's image whose Godly soul can now act unencumbered by the forces of material desire.[40]

Quoting the *Zohar*, Drob adds:

> The perfection of all things is attained when good and evil are first of all commingled, and then become all good, for there is no good so perfect as that which issues out of evil.[41]

In Kabbalah and Hasidism, the difference between good and evil has to do with degrees of spirituality.[42] This is akin to the conflict between the sacred and the profane. 'Good' is that which connects one to infinite reality, or godliness. 'Bad' is anything that detracts from or conceals godliness. These distinctions can be seen in the structure of the soul.

The soul is the vitalizing or life force that transforms the inanimate into the animate, clay into flesh. According to the Hasidic philosopher Simon Jacobson, the soul is divine energy, 'the flame of God,' a little piece of the infinite that lies within.[43] It is a part of a person that exists beyond matter, beyond the body, beyond the senses. It is our essential identity, or *raison d'être,* the manifestation of the divine intent and vision in creating a particular human being. We once heard from Simon Jacobson the amusing analogy that the soul is to the body what the astronaut is to a space suit. If one takes the astronaut out of the space suit, then the suit is useless and quickly collapses. The same can be said about removing meaning from one's life.

According to the Jewish sages, there are four stages of revelation. These can be encapsulated by the Hebrew acronym 'PaRDeS.' This has been roughly translated as 'orchard,' and refers to increasing orders of complexity and concealment. The letter 'P' stands for *pshat,* which signifies the obvious, conscious meaning of things. 'R' is for *remez,* a hint of something deeper, as in a slip of the tongue. 'D' is for *drash*, deeper still, as in an allegory or dream. But 'S' conveys *sod,* the deepest, hidden, unconscious, concealed dimensions of reality. *Sod* is the domain of the soul.

In general the Kabbalah differentiates between two kinds of souls, the 'Animal Soul' (*Nefesh B'haimit*) and the 'Godly Soul' (*Nefesh Elokit*).[44] Both are spiritual entities, and as we mentioned before, represent undifferentiated potential. But the Animal Soul, also known as the 'Natural Soul' (*Nefesh Tiv'it*), tends to be corrupted and cut off from the Godhead by being surrounded by layers or shells of personal drives, volitions, cravings and vices, even though it is not synonymous with them. These shells or barriers are known in Kabbalah as *klipot* and are closely connected in psychoanalysis with what D. W. Winnicott termed 'the false self.' After elaborating upon the 'Animal Soul' (*Nefesh B'haimit*), we shall return to this comparison in greater detail.

It is important to keep in mind that the 'Animal Soul,' the *Nefesh B'haimit*, is not the same as the Freudian 'id.' While it is concerned with physical pleasures, including procreation, it also encompasses selfish, self-centered preoccupations. It is not necessarily concerned with what things are good for, but how they can be used to boost pride, ego and ascendancy over others. For this reason the 'Animal Soul' is often referred to in the Hasidic literature as the 'Animal Self'—in other words, something dark and coarse, like a grub or worm.

Yet, however distant it is from its source, the 'Animal Soul' is a spiritual, not a material, entity. It remains a starting point for spiritual transformation and transcendence, as in the creation of the *Benoni* or 'intermediate man,' a person who is able to overcome the weakness and wickedness in himself and become close to God.[45] The energies of the 'Animal Soul' are part and parcel of the life of man, both for good and for bad. But because the spiritual qualities of the 'Animal Soul' tend to be obscured by egotistic or narcissistic interests or *klipot*, the 'Animal Soul' is likely to be identified with evil and wickedness.

In fact, the negative qualities of the 'Animal Soul' are called, the *'sitrah achra'* or 'the other side,' and are closely identified with the *yetzer ha-ra* or 'evil inclination/impulse.' Of course, the *yetzer ha-ra* has its counterpart in the *yetzer ha-tov,* the 'good inclination/impulse.'[46]

In Kabbalah and Hasidut, the *yetzer ha-ra* or bad impulse is something, physical or spiritual, that comes between man and God. This includes any violation of the Ten Commandments, whose infractions against man's fellow men may be encapsulated as envy and greed, lust and jealousy. These 'sins' emanate from the world of *tohu* or chaos. In psychoanalysis this chaotic state of being can be subsumed, in Kleinian terminology, under the paranoid-schizoid position.

The purpose of *tikkun* is to retrieve the embers of the infinite that are embedded in every body, every self and every soul. One has to raise them to their proper spiritual levels in order to bring about a complete transformation of worlds, both personal and cosmic. Aryeh Kaplan describes this process of rectification as moving from *tohu* to *bohu,* where *bohu* means the rectified state of the vessel (mind, self, soul, *sefirot)*—literally, the 'it is in it,' referring both to the container and the contained.[47] Again in Kleinian terminology, this process is equivalent to the movement from the paranoid-schizoid position to the depressive position, and then to a state of inner integration (*refuah shleimah*: complete healing).[48]

But what if this movement does not take place? What if the 'Animal Soul' (*Nefesh B'haimit*) remains mired in the *sitra achra*, the side of evil? The distinguished Hasidic scholar, Adin Steinsaltz, describes four kinds of evil that emanate from the 'Animal Soul' (*Nefesh B'haimit*), according to the elements of fire, water, air and earth.[49]

Fire encompasses pride and anger. The former concerns narcissistic aggrandizement, or, in less technical terms, a swollen head, a puffed-up self, anything that falsely asserts one's preeminence over others. Conversely, people may make themselves excessively small in order to achieve the same effect.[50]

Anger and rage are the emotional consequences of frustrated pride, of anything that challenges the self-centered view that "I am Pharaoh, I created myself, I am God" and "You are nothing." Indeed, we all remember the reaction of the stepmother in the fairy tale of Snow White when she looks into the mirror and finds that she is not the fairest of them all.[51]

Water involves lust, hedonistic pleasure, desire for the sake of desire, sex for its own sake. It is close to the Freudian idea of the 'id,' a total solipsistic sensuality. But as everything contains its opposite quality, water is also an essential element in giving life (fertility) and maintaining life (suppleness).

Air conveys malicious gossip, boasting, boosting oneself with an expansive nothingness. Air actions are hot and insubstantial. But they take place in order to convince others that the 'airhead' is bigger and better than they are.

Finally, *earth* is sloth and melancholy, any action or mood that pulls or weighs one down. Or, it can act on others to bring them down, too. Sloth is malicious turgidness. Similarly, melancholy, like depression, is a heavy world-weariness that paralyzes the will and buries one's *joie de vivre* under tons of bile.

Each of these elemental responses—prideful preeminence, hedonistic pleasures, idle boasting and turgid melancholy—are examples of the *klipot*, husks or shells that make almost impassable barriers between the mundane and ultra-mundane dimensions of existence, between the profane and the sacred. According to Kabbalah, there are four such *klipot*, as alluded to in the first chapter of the book of Ezekiel: 'a storm wind,' 'a great cloud,' 'a flaring fire,' and 'a luminescence.'[52] The first three are totally impenetrable. Like hard nuts that cannot be cracked—there is no way to get through to the fruit at the core, or even to know that the fruit is there. Or, from another point of view, their concealment of truth, spirituality, the divine radiance or knowledge of the Godhead, is absolute. An egocentric darkness prevails in order to protect the individual from being touched by the divine energies that surge within him.

But the fourth *klipah*, the *klipat nogah,* is different. It derives from the level of luminescence and is often called the translucent or even transparent shell. This means that a person who can access the *klipat nogah* does not necessarily remain bound to his selfish preoccupations or encase himself in material impulses. Something of the goodness in him, an awareness of others' needs and a 'higher purpose' in life, remains accessible. And not only is he open to such 'goodness,' but he can choose to release or extract it from himself, and sanctify his existence. *Nogah* also denotes the power of interpretation, to see things from different perspectives and to connect different perspectives—just as psychoanalysts in the power of interpretation can connect the past with the present and future.

All four *klipot* are forms of soul armoring. But if the initial *klipot* try to maintain an iron-clad armor in order to hide a self-serving narcissism, then the *klipat nogah* is more like chain mail, which allows light free passage from without to within and vice versa. Moreover, it allows for the intermingling of good and evil, rather than the rigid splitting into black and white. Then we can see the emergence of complexity and ambiguity, which is a further expression of the luminescence that characterizes the *klipat nogah.*

In Biblical Hebrew the word for luminescence is *hashmal.* In addition to conveying illumination, it denotes intense energies, like a carrier of the Divine will. In modern Hebrew the same word means electricity. Significantly Aryeh Kaplan translates *hashmal* as "the speaking silence."[53] Here Kaplan is describing an illumination that 'speaks' from the darkest depths of the soul, the silence at the core of our being. We can speculate that Kaplan's translation links the *klipat nogah* with an aspect of Freud's structural theory of the mind, that is, the preconscious. Both provide hints of deeper recesses of meaning, in Freud's view, of the mind, and in Kaplan's, of the soul. And both are normally inaccessible except by an intense act of will. Even so, with both Freud and Kaplan there remain areas that cannot be consciously activated: with Freud, the unconscious, and with Kaplan, the Godhead (Cosmic Consciousness).

The *klipot* are the spiritual analogues of Freud's 'resistances,' Wilhelm Reich's 'character armor' and D. W. Winnicott's 'false self.'[54] These are organized forms of concealment by which an individual seeks to protect himself from overwhelming libidinal impulses. These impulses tend to be experienced as very threatening, invasive demands coming from within (oral, anal, genital excitement) or without (an over-stimulating, tantalizing parent). What is the threat? In the first place it may be a fear of fragmenting, a breaking of the mind-body container, because the bodily energies are felt to be too intense. Later on, it is a fear of exposure and humiliation, of being shown up as less good than a parent or sibling. In the latter instance a fragile self cannot cope with the anger and rage that such close comparisons conjure up.

All this leads a person to construct a secret life, based on avoidance and deceit in order to protect a 'true' or 'core' personality which would, if it could, be receptive to others. Sometimes the individual is aware that he or she is putting on 'a false face,' 'a false front,' or simply 'airs.' More often than not, this person is not aware that his or her 'false front' is a constructed personality based on multiple layers of denial and concealment. Inevitably he believes that this 'false self' is the 'true self' and vigorously resists any clarifications to the contrary. There are exceptions. Mary Barnes was a forty-five-year old nurse who felt that her whole life was a living lie and that the only way she could become real was to revert to babyhood and grow up again. Joseph Berke helped her to accomplish the task of rediscovering both her self and her soul.[55] As Mary realized, her life had became a total barrier to satisfying emotional or social relationships. She worked long hours and spent much energy trying to please others. Winnicott calls this kind of falseness 'the compliant self.' As he points out, ". . . compliance on the part of the infant is the earliest stage of the false self."[56] It is characterized by a lack of spontaneity and the need to fit in with and imitate others.

Winnicott suggests that a more extreme form of concealment lies with individuals who spend most of their lives both expressing and fighting a variety of physical and emotional symptoms that are well illustrated by obsessive compulsive rituals or addictions to plastic surgery.[57]

Most extreme are adults (or children) who immerse themselves in one aspect of their personalities to the exclusion of all else, such as thinkers who are 'all brain' or sportsmen who are 'all body,' and who get very anxious in the face of emotional and social relationships. At the same time these individuals may try to hide the brittleness of their lives by developing a 'caretaker self' to hide all true feelings or by splitting themselves into different personalities. This leads to multiple internal voids by the projection of threatening feelings (need, dependency, intimacy) inwardly into various sub-selves, or outwardly into others. Consequently 'caretaker people' tend to become intensely envious toward others whom they believe contain everything real and worthwhile, while they contain nothing good or nourishing.

As we have been discussing, the psychoanalytic idea of the 'false self or selves' is closely related to the Kabbalistic concept of the *klipah* or *klipot* (in the plural). The former erects formidable walls or armoring around one's basic or true personality. The latter consists of equally impenetrable shells or barriers against one's basic essence or soul. At first the reasons for these constructions appear to diverge. Winnicott points out that the 'false self' develops in order to protect a fragile container from intense id impulses, whereas the *klipot* hide severe egocentricity, which opposes holiness *(kedushah)* and self-abnegation. But in practice both the 'false self' and the *klipot* are provoked by the narcissistic fury that the subject is not the source of everything. In this regard, a prayer that is recited by observant Jews after every meal (served with bread) is quite relevant. It thanks God for everything He has given us. Otherwise we would 'be dependent upon the gifts of mortal men' and would suffer 'shame and disgrace.'[58]

According to Lurianic Kabbalah, in every person there is a more direct expression of, and yearning for, spirituality. This is the Godly Soul (*Nefesh Elokit*) which seeks to obliterate the self in order to bring about a complete unification with the Godhead. The *Nefesh Elokit* is transcendental in nature and aim, and is concerned with everything creative, sublime and holy.

Man's Godly Soul is that aspect of himself that lies beyond his biological or narcissistic needs. As spiritually oriented psychoanalysts such as Eric Fromm, Victor Frankl and Nina Coltart, as well as Hasidic masters such as the late Lubavitcher Rebbe, Menachem Mendel Schneerson would declare, the Godly Soul is a clarion call from one's inner being, from one's 'speaking silences,' which impart to every person his deepest sense of meaning and fulfillment. In contrast, Freud appeared to extract meaning from life by systematizing irrationality. As Sanford Drob points out, Freud intended to create 'a value free, purely secular psychology,' and often referred to psychoanalysis as "a secular priesthood."[59]

The *Nefesh Elokit* has a complex structure and can act as an hologram, where a part equals the whole. It is generally agreed that the *Nefesh Elokit* is divided into five levels: the *Nefesh*, or physical dimension of spirituality; *Ruach,* corresponding to emotionality and symbolized by the heart; *Neshamah*, corresponding to the intellect and symbolized by the brain; *Chayah,* also known as 'the living soul,' conveying volition or divine will; and *Yechidah,* signifying unification, the unity of all five levels with the Godhead. Within these, of course, there are even greater complexities, levels within level within levels.

It is important to mention, however, that the term *Nefesh* both refers to the general concept of soul, and to the specific first level of the soul. Which is which depends on the context in which *Nefesh* is used, or the general concept.

The *Nefesh* is the lowest level of the soul. It has to do with the relationship a person has with spirituality, with the 'infinite,' with God, by means of his physicality and through his activities. *Nefesh* is related to the world of *Asiyah*, embodied action, and is the vitalizing element of personal existence. Significantly, it is said that *Nefesh* does not survive physical death (unlike the other four dimensions of the soul which Kabbalists aver do survive death).[60]

All the first four levels of the soul describe ascending (more complicated, closer) forms of relationship with God. Commentators also point out that these dimensions of the soul denote ascending levels of consciousness, from the ordinary to the transcendental, from *pshat* to *sod*.[61]

The second level of the soul is *Ruach*. It literally means 'breath,' 'wind' or 'spirit.' It also denotes the relationship a man or woman has with God through emotional inhalation and exhalation, the passage of love and fear (awe) in and through the body, in and between others, as well as in and with the cosmos. Perhaps that is why Hasidic masters such as the Baal Shem Tov, Rabbi Nachman of Breslov or the Lubavitcher Rebbes, were possessed with *Ruach HaKodesh*, the power of divine inspiration, a transformative spirituality in conjunction with a power of thought that can redirect reality. The *Ruach* is a part of the spiritual world of *Yetzirah* or formation, which has to do with potential being actualized.

Ruach lies between *Nefesh* physicality and the transcendental states of consciousness conveyed by the *Neshamah* soul. As such, it is concerned with symbolization and integration—of the heart with the mind, of feelings with thoughts. We can say that to move from the *Nefesh* to the *Ruach* level of the soul is to change one's orientation from personal survival to communal belonging. Significantly, this movement parallels the emotional development of the infant from what Klein called the paranoid-schizoid position to the depressive position.

The *Neshamah* is the third level of the soul and exemplifies the relationship that a person has with the Godhead by means of the intellect. By intellect we do not just mean the capacity for logical, rational thought. On the contrary, the *Neshamah* soul brings together sudden flashes of perception (*Chochmah*) in conjunction with the body of one's experience. In so doing it yields a profound understanding of the interconnectiveness of things (*Binah*). The further interrelating of perception and understanding with the entirety of one's being yields knowing-from-the-inside (*Da'at*).[62] This is a non-dissociated, holistic knowledge, as compared to a detached, 'heady' knowing-from-the-outside. All this is part of the spiritual world of *Beriyah*, which means creation, the ability to bring new worlds and relationships into being.

The *Neshamah* denotes a transcendental consciousness that 'sees' far and wide, as it is able to rise above private preoccupations and the attendant blockages and divisions that becloud most individuals' psychological and spiritual concerns. The *Neshamah* is the power of integration and reparation. It acts spiritually as a healer acts materially. Its primary focus is to retune the energies of the world, to remove disharmonies and negativity, whether in this world or the next, whether in conventional time and space, or through 'non-local,' supra-temporal connections.

We have just described the movement from *Nefesh* to *Ruach* and then to *Neshamah* consciousness. Likewise we have discussed the three levels of souls that these spiritual entities represent. On the psychological plane the counterpart of this shift from lower to higher consciousness is the emergence from persecutory anxiety and chaotic thinking. Next there is the development of depressive anxiety and more cohesive thought processes. Ultimately we can see a post-depressive, integrated state where all the fragments of one's inner and outer worlds have been repaired and re-paired. Like *Neshamah* soulfulness, this is a state of awareness that very few people are able to achieve in their lifetime.

Kabbalists perceive these levels of heightened awareness in terms of light or radiance, called the 'inner light' (*Ohr HaPnimi*). The *Ohr HaPnimi* refers to degrees of soulfulness that a person can imbibe and internalize. But to the mind of the mystic the soul is a part of the mind of God. So how can one take in a radiance so infinite and ineffable? The answer lies in the 'garments' (*levushim*) that the soul wears and through which it is able to manifest itself. We shall address this issue shortly. What is important to note is that the radiance at the spiritual center of the *Nefesh*, *Ruach* and *Neshamah* souls lies internal to the person concerned. In comparison, the radiance of *Chayah* and *Yechidah*, the fourth and fifth levels of soul, lies external to the person concerned. *Chayah* and *Yechidah* exist as an 'encompassing light' (*Ohr HaMakif*) and are said to exert their influence from outside, by surrounding or enveloping the individual. This may be because *Chayah* and *Yechidah* are so much 'higher,' that is, closer to the Godhead. Otherwise the intensity of their infinite radiance would be uncontainable.

Chayah, 'the living soul,' is super-rational, transcendent will. It is an *Ohr Makif* that imbues the 'inner lights' (*Ohrot HaPnimim*) with power and direction. It corresponds to the world of infinite emanation (*Atzilut*), the ceaseless flow of divine energies that give an actualized potentiality to all things.

Through the work of the *Chayah* soul, it is possible for a person to complete the spiritual work of self-redemption. What does all this mean? We can view this from both a Jungian and Freudian understanding. From a Jungian perspective it is the "realization of the shadow," "the kindling of a light in the darkness of being." In contrast, Freudians tend to refer to redemption as overcoming the web of repressions.[63] In both spiritual and material terms we are talking about an ongoing process of overcoming conscious and unconscious chaos (*tohu*).

Other Kabbalists have referred to unconscious chaos (*tohu*) as "the thoughtless light."[64] For them, redemption is the work of transforming 'the thoughtless light,' unconscious *tohu*, into consciousness, an outcome with which Freud would heartily concur. Essentially this involves restoring the evil impulses of the *sitra achra* (the other side) to cosmic goodness and godliness. As Adin Steinsaltz points out, this is the influence of the *Chayah* soul, to bring about a state of complete integration of man with himself, and man with the source of his being.

> When the world of *Tikkun* realizes its task and the Vessel is finished, it will be able to contain the power of the World of *Tohu*. Then a third situation will have been created, higher than either *Tohu* or *Tikkun*, a world in which the infinite power of primordial *Tohu* will be within (controlled by) the perfection of the world of *Tikkun*. This world is beyond the known and prescribed and

> substantial. A world in which men are no longer creatures of rigid and finite design but can begin to act as combinations of both the infinite and finite in a single being.[65]

Such a combination of the infinite and finite in one person introduces us to the fifth and most spiritually advanced level of soul, *Yechidah*. *Yechidah* means unification, singularity and oneness. It describes a single, indivisible, transcendent entity. The *Yechidah* soul is a *makif*, a limitless light that surrounds *Nefesh*, *Ruach*, *Neshamah* and *Chayah*, and imbues them with exceptional energies.

In fact it is impossible to describe the *Yechidah* soul, for it is closest to the infinite source of everything. To describe it is to enclose it with words, and that would be akin to enclosing infinity, an impossible contradiction. As soon as one tries to enclose infinity with the intellect, it stops being infinite. Nonetheless, Kabbalists have tried over many centuries to penetrate the meaning of *Yechidah*.

Rabbi Dov Ber, the second Rebbe of Lubavitch (the Mittler Rebbe) approached *Yechidah* experientially, from the extreme bliss or ecstasy *Yechidah* can arouse when the soul is totally and completely connected to God.

> This is the category of essential binding and attachment . . . of 'surrounding and filling' . . . the category of *Yechidah* within him . . . of the binding of his 'essence,' known as 'cleaving,' where the soul cleaves and is drawn automatically as a result of the divine 'essence' in the soul herself. . . . It is this that is called actual divine ecstasy.[66]

As we see, the essence of *Yechidah* is attachment and connectiveness. It describes a simple oneness which, in turn, is derived from two Hebrew words, *echad* and *yachid*. *Echad* means 'God is One.' But within his oneness there is also a state of differentiation: four lower souls, four worlds, four different directions for the presence of God. Therefore the level of *echad* is known as 'God immanent'; *yachid,* however, means that there is only oneness and nothing else.

There also exists an 'Upper *Yechidah* Soul' which is related to *yachid*, like the inner core of the sun, pure, indivisible energy. The 'Upper *Yechidah* Soul' is associated with infinite power and intelligence, but far beyond mortal consciousness, which is why it is known as 'God transcendent.' It is a point where the soul relinquishes its individual existence and, in the idiom of the mystic, becomes part of the divine essence, a state of total, perfected, interconnectiveness of myriad levels of *Nefesh*, *Ruach*, *Neshamah* and *Chayah* with the cosmos.

Nonetheless, the question remains, how can one apprehend the soul? How is it possible for material man to perceive an invisible and ineffable spiritual entity? As we have already alluded, the solution to this problem involves the 'garments' (*levushim*) which Hasidut concludes covers the soul.[67] These garments include thought, speech and action. Thought makes conscious the unconscious. Speech enwraps consciousness in words. And both speech and actions concretize experience and communicate one's inner world to others. Together they represent different aspects of a person's personality. But personality is part of the 'self.' So what Hasidut calls the 'garments of the soul' clearly signifies 'the self.'

Now we can see how the self and the soul are so closely connected. The soul vitalizes the self. It carries the inner essence of a person into the material world. Meanwhile the self provides a skin for the soul, and actualizes soul potential. The self reflects "the Divine Spark within us."[68]

Perhaps Heinz Kohut provided the most moving connection between 'self' and 'soul,' and by extension, between psychoanalysis and Kabbalah, in his book *The Restoration of the Self*. In the epilogue, he ponders the capacity of art and artists to depict the central dilemma of our age, how man can manage "to cure his crumbling self." Kohut confides that nowhere has he found a more accurate account of the yearning to restore a shattered self than in Eugene O'Neill's play *The Great God Brown*.

Toward the end, the central character, Brown, contemplates his wrecked life and tattered soul. Kohut concludes, through the words of Brown: "Man is born broken. He lives by mending. The grace of God is glue."[69]

NOTES

1. The term 'mental apparatus' makes its first appearance in 1900, in "The Interpretation of Dreams," and expands its meaning, being referred to as 'agencies' or 'systems.' See Sigmund Freud, "The Interpretation of Dreams," vols. 4–5 of *Standard Edition of the Complete Psychological Works of Sigmund Freud*, ed. James Strachey (1900; London: Hogarth Press, 1981), vol. 4, p. 49; vol. 5, p. 537.
2. Heinz Kohut, *The Restoration of the Self* (New York: International Universities Press, 1977), 311.
3. Andrew Samuels, *A Critical Dictionary of Jungian Analysis* (London: Rout ledge & Kegan Paul, 1986), 135.
4. Abraham H. Maslow, *Religions, Values and Peak-Experiences* (New York: Viking Press/Penguin, 1970).
5. Daniel C. Dennett, *Consciousness Explained* (Boston: Little Brown, 1991), 431.
6. William James, *The Principles of Psychology* (New York: Holt, 1890).
7. Freud, 1923, "The Ego and the Id," in *Standard Edition*, ed. James Strachey, vol. 19.
8. Bruno Bettelheim, *Freud and Man's Soul* (London: Chatto & Windus/Hogarth Press, 1983), 40.

9. Charles Rycroft, *A Critical Dictionary of Psychoanalysis* (Harmondsworth, Middlesex, England: Penguin, 1972), 149–50. Charles Rycroft was a significant figure in the modern history of psychoanalysis. A consistent critic against the rigidity of psychoanalytic formulations, he resigned from the British Psychoanalytical Society in 1965, after defending a colleague against hostile attacks for a 'heretical,' anti-establishment paper.

10. Heinz Hartmann, *Ego Psychology and the Problem of Adaptation* (New York: Imago, 1958).

11. Richard Bentall, *Madness Explained: Psychosis and Human Nature* (London: Allen Lane, 2003).

12. Robert D. Hinshelwood, *A Dictionary of Kleinian Thought* (London: Free Association Books, 1991), 284–86.

13. Rollo May, Ernest Angel and Henri Ellenberger, eds., *Existence: A New Dimension in Psychiatry and Psychology* (New York: Basic Books, 1958). This is the first book written on existential psychology and it set the stage for the development of the humanistic psychology movement (Carl Rogers and Abraham Maslow).

14. Carlos Castenada, *The Teachings of Don Juan: A Yaqui Way of Knowledge* (New York: Pocket Books, 1968).

15. Schneur Zalman of Liadi, *Likutei Amarim: Tanya* [bilingual ed.], trans. N. Mindel (1797; Brooklyn, N.Y.: Kehot, 1984), 57.

16. *Zohar*, 1:16b, 2:176a. See also Daniel Matt's translation, *The Zohar*, Pritzker Edition (Stanford, Calif.: Stanford University Press, 2004), vol 1, 125. See also Stanley Schneider and Joseph Berke, "Discovering Oneself: Kabbalah and Psychoanalysis," *Midstream* 51 (November–December 2005): 24.

17. Victor Frankl, *Man's Search for Meaning* (New York: Washington Square Press/Pocket Books, 1984).

18. Andrew Samuels, *A Critical Dictionary of Jungian Analysis* (London: Routledge & Kegan Paul, 1986), 136–37.

19. Jungians capitalize the term Self to indicate that it is all-encompassing, that it includes negative as well as positive qualities. When once asked what 'the shadow' was, Jung replied testily, "simply the whole unconscious!" Ann Shearer, personal communication, December 2004.

20. Gershom Scholem, "The Concept of the Astral Body," in *On the Mystical Shape of the Godhead* (New York: Schocken, 1991), 252. Cf. Aryeh Kaplan, *Innerspace* (Jerusalem: Vagshal/Moznaim, 1990a), 94–95.

21. Samuels, *Critical Dictionary*, 140–41.

22. Bettelheim, *Freud and Man's Soul,* 11–12.

23. Quoted by Bettelheim, *Freud and Man's Soul*, 8.

24. Bettelheim, *Freud and Man's Soul*, 73–74. This is based on Freud's (1905b) paper "Psychical (or Mental) Treatment," in *Standard Edition*, ed. James Strachey, vol. 7.

25. Freud, 1905b, "Psychical (or Mental) Treatment," 283.

26. Bettelheim, *Freud and Man's Soul*, 4.

27. Marianne Krull, *Freud and His Father* (New York: Norton, 1986), 90.

28. Stanley Schneider and Joseph Berke, "Sigmund Freud and the Lubavitcher Rebbe," *Psychoanalytic Review* 87 (2000): 1, 39–59.

29. Bettelheim, *Freud and Man's Soul*, 36.

30. Joseph Berke and Stanley Schneider, "Repairing Worlds: An Exploration of the Psychoanalytical and Kabbalistic Concepts of Reparation and Tikkun," *Psychoanalytic Review* 90 (2003): 723–49.

31. Based on Song of Songs 18, quoted by Sanford Drob, *Symbols of the Kabbalah: Philosophical and Psychological Perspectives* (Northvale, N.J.: Aronson, 2000a), 373.

32. The *Pardes Rimonim* (Pomegranate Orchard) of Rabbi Moshe Cordovero (gate 23, part 16, namely, *etz*) makes the connection between the Tree of Life being 'man' ("For man is the tree of the field"—Deuteronomy 20:19) and the Tree of Life. The connection is contained in the joining of the Tree of *Atzilut* that draws its sustenance from Chochmah (*Zohar* Shemini, 40a). Gershom Scholem also refers to the schema of the *sefirot* as a tree. See Gershom Scholem, *Kabbalah* (Jerusalem: Keter, 1975), 106.

33. Laibl Wolf, *Practical Kabbalah* (New York: Three Rivers Press, 1999), 1965.

34. Usually, in the human metaphor, the *sefirah* of *Malkhut* is depicted as below the *sefirah* of *Yesod*. See supernal 'Man' in Aryeh Kaplan's *Sefer Yetzirah* (The Book of Creation) (Newburyport, Mass.: Samuel Weiser, 1990b), 151.

35. See figures 2 to 5 in Kaplan's *Sefer Yetzirah*, 26, 28–30.

36. Kaplan, *Innerspace*, 82.

37. Naftali Loewenthal, personal communication, December 2004.

38. Quoted in Shalom Buzaglo, *Mikdash Melech* (The Temple of the King) [in Hebrew] (1750; Jerusalem: Machon Bnai Yissachar, 1995), vol. 1, p. 176. Moses Zacuto (1620–1697) was born in Amsterdam to a Portuguese Marrano family and wrote several commentaries on the *Zohar*. Buzaglo was a Moroccan rabbi from the eighteenth century. Buzaglo's commentary often quotes from Zacuto's commentary.

39. Cf. Freud, 1937b, "Constructions in Analysis," in *Standard Edition,* ed. James Strachey, vol. 23, especially p. 259.

40. Drob, *Symbols of Kabbalah*, 381.

41. Drob, *Symbols of Kabbalah*, 381, quotes only part of the *Zohar*. The full quotation from the *Zohar* (2:184a) states: "The true light comes out of the darkness. For when this side (the darkness) is subdued, God's majesty is able to shine forth. And God's manifestations are, therefore, arising from the darkness. And there is no good, except that which emanates from evil."

42. Hasidism is essentially the active expression of the Jewish mystical tradition as expounded by the Baal Shem Tov (1698–1760). See Naftali Loewenthal, *Communicating the Infinite: The Emergence of the Habad School* (Chicago: University of Chicago Press, 1990).

43. Simon Jacobson, *Toward a Meaningful Life: The Wisdom of the Rebbe* (London: Piatkus, 1995), 4. This is an extension of Proverbs 20:27: "The flame of God is the soul of man."

44. See Menachem Mendel Schneerson, *On the Essence of Chassidus*, trans. Y. Greenberg and S. S. Handelman (New York: Kehot, 1998). In this book, the late

Lubavitcher Rebbe, Menachem Mendel Schneerson, discussed another soul, the *Nefesh HaSichlit,* the Intellectual Soul. He said this is a tool by which the Godly Soul can communicate with the consciousness of a person. Moreover, it is the means by which the upper spiritual realms can communicate with the lower earthy realms, and the Godly Soul can communicate with the Animal Soul. But he also said that that there is a *Nefesh HaSichlit*, an Intellectual Soul of the Animal Soul. We think it is less confusing to keep to the traditional picture of an 'Animal Soul,' *Nefesh B'haimit*, and a 'Godly Soul,' *Nefesh Elokit*, whereby each has an intellectual component that allows them to communicate with each other as well as denote spiritual and material realities.

45. The *Benoni* has been described by Rabbi Schneur Zalman of Liadi in the *Tanya* as a person whose moral character is intermediate or halfway between a *tzaddik* (a person with no evil inclinations) and a *rasha* (a person mired in egotistic desires). His deeds/merits are equally balanced between good and evil. In Hasidic thought, an intermediate man never sins in thought, word or deed, even though the evil inclination (*yetzer ha-rah*) still exists in his nature.

46. Joseph Berke, *The Tyranny of Malice: Exploring the Dark Side of Character and Culture* (New York: Simon & Schuster, 1988).

47. Kaplan, *Innerspace*, 82.

48. Berke and Schneider, "Repairing Worlds."

49. Adin Steinsaltz, *Opening the Tanya* (New York: Jossey-Bass, 2003), 61–63. Many different cultures and philosophical systems have emphasized these four elements. For example, in his book *Ocean of Wisdom: Guidelines for Living* (Santa Fe, N.M.: Clear Light Publishers,1989), 44–45, the Dalai Lama writes: "Many Eastern philosophies, and in particular Buddhism, speak of four elements: earth, water, fire, and air. . . . These four elements are better understood in terms of solidity (earth), liquids (water), heat (fire) and energy (air)." Here the Dalai Lama is trying to describe the process of the creation of the physical universe, in contrast to Steinsaltz's description of the creation of the emotional universe.

50. This is well conveyed by the Yiddish expression: "*Mach sich nit azoi klein—du bist nit azoi grois!*" ["Don't make yourself so small—you're not that big!"] Berke, *Tyranny of Malice*, 125.

51. Berke, *Tyranny of Malice*, 75–76.

52. Kaplan, *Innerspace*, 147.

53. Kaplan, *Innerspace*, 147.

54. Josef Breuer and Sigmund Freud, "Studies on Hysteria," in *Standard Edition*, ed. James Strachey, vol. 2; Wilhelm Reich, *Character Analysis*, 3rd ed. (New York: Farrar, Straus & Giroux, 1980). Reich (1897–1957), a psychoanalyst (until he broke with establishment psychoanalysis in 1934), developed the concept of character armor. Reich defined this as the sum total of typical character attitudes, which an individual develops as a blocking against emotional excitations, resulting in body rigidity, lack of emotional contact—'deadness.' Donald W. Winnicott, "Ego Distortion in Terms of True and False Self," in *The Maturational Process and the Facilitating Environment* (1960b; London: Hogarth Press, 1972). Winnicott's (1896–1971) training as a pediatrician and

psychoanalyst enabled him to describe early environmental failure, the good-enough mother, and the omnipotence of the infant, in terms of a true and a false self.

55. Mary Barnes and Joseph Berke, *Mary Barnes: Two Accounts of a Journey through Madness*, 3rd ed. (New York: The Other Press, 2002).

56. Winnicott, "Ego Distortion," 145.

57. H. Donahue, "My 5-Year Addiction to the Knife," *London Times*, September 1, 2004, 4–5.

58. *Siddur Tehillat Hashem*, trans. Rabbi N. Mangel (New York: Merkos L'Inyonei Chinuch, 1978), 91.

59. Sanford Drob, *Kabbalistic Metaphors* (Northvale, N.J.: Aronson, 2000b), 278.

60. Hasidism maintains that the *Nefesh* does survive physical death, at the gravesite of the person concerned.

61. Leonora Leet, *The Kabbalah of the Soul: The Transformative Psychology and Practices of Jewish Mysticism* (Rochester, Vt.: Inner Traditions, 2003).

62. Together these three configurations of the intellect—*Chochmah*, *Binah* and *Da'at*—comprise the upper, intellectual triangle of *sefirotic* 'man' or the *sefirotic* 'tree' and are known by the acronym ChaBaD.

63. C. G. Jung, *Memories, Dreams, Reflections* (New York: Pantheon, 1963), 358. Freud, 1939, "Moses and Monotheism," in *Standard Edition*, ed. James Strachey, vol. 23, 86.

64. Leet, *Kabbalah of the Soul*, 276–77.

65. Adin Steinsaltz, *In the Beginning: Discourses on Hassidic Thought*, ed. and trans. Y. Hanegbi (Northvale, N.J.: Aronson, 1995), 10–11.

66. Dov Ber of Lubavitch, *On Ecstasy*, ed. and trans L. Jacobs (Chappaqua, N.Y.: Rossel Books, 1963), 64, 66, 67.

67. Schneur Zalman of Liadi, *Tanya*, 14.

68. Quoted by Niel Micklem in "I Am Not Myself: A Paradox," in *Jung's Concept of the Self: Its Relevance Today.* Papers from the Public Conference, Jungian Postgraduate Committee, British Association of Psychotherapists, no. 3, p. 4.

69. Kohut, *Restoration of the Self*, 287.

Chapter Three

Will, Free Will, Determinism and Motivation

A philosophical and theological debate has been around for thousands of years, preoccupying Greek philosophers as well as Talmudic scholars, reaching its apex during the medieval period. If God is all knowing, all seeing, all present, then how can man have free will? However, if we take the other side of the argument, and man does possess free will and is morally responsible, then we have a religious and philosophical problem in light of the belief in Divine omniscience, predestination and Divine Providence.

The Talmud[1] summarizes the problem quite succinctly: "All is in the hands of Heaven except for the fear of Heaven." This seems to leave man without any possibility of controlling his own fate. If a Higher Authority (this could be a belief in God, morals, the law of the land, etc., not necessarily a Deity) is in charge and determines or controls man's thoughts and actions, where is the opportunity for man to take responsibility for his life? In effect, man can take the position that since he has no control over his thoughts or actions, then he can technically disclaim any responsibility for good and evil, life and death. Yet, is that so? In essence, what we need to look at is: where is the fine line separating a higher control from man's input?

If we leave, for a moment, the conceptualization of the determinism argument in theological terms (i.e., the place of an Almighty, All-Encompassing Power), then we can view determinism as a philosophical, if not psychological, ideology which holds that every event is the result of antecedent causes. There are no 'miracles' or totally random occurrences. All conscious choice is based on unconscious antecedents. So on the surface it would seem that determinism contradicts the concept of conscious choice or free will. Yet several philosophers (Thomas Hobbes, David Hume and William James, to name just a few) and many psychoanalysts have tried to reconcile the two viewpoints.

Let us expand this discussion with a brief consideration of Eastern philosophical concepts. There, determinism is best expressed in the Buddhist doctrines of independent and dependent origination. 'Independent origination' is a principle of causal dependence:

> . . . all conditioned things and events in the universe come into being only as a result of the interaction of various causes and conditions. This is significant because it precludes two possibilities. One is the possibility that things can arise from nowhere, with no causes and conditions, and second is that things can arise on account of a transcendent designer or creator. Both these possibilities are negated.[2]

Buddhism clearly defines determinism as a causal relationship, yet it is not dependent on a creator in the equation of life. The principle of 'dependent origination' is a theory of parts and whole:

> . . . the very idea of 'whole' and 'wholeness' depends upon the existence of parts. Such dependence clearly exists in the physical world. . . . So when we consider the universe in these terms, not only do we see each conditioned thing as dependently originated, we also understand that the entire phenomenal world arises according to the principle of dependent origination.[3]

Nonetheless, while dependence or determinism, according to this thesis, removes the possibility of a creator, it does take into account the idea of causality.

Determinism in Western philosophies is most clearly associated with Isaac Newton and Albert Einstein. Newton, of course, was the seventeenth-century scientist who discovered the influence of gravity. To both Newton and Einstein "the notion of free will, that we are masters of our destiny, was an illusion."[4] In physics, if we were able to calculate the position and motion of all particles and sub-particles in the universe, then we would have infinite precision for any given time—past, present or future. This was Newton's vision:

> . . . the universe was a gigantic clock, wound at the beginning of time and ticking ever since because it obeyed Newton's three laws of motion. . . .[5]

This view was supported by the French mathematician Pierre Simon de Laplace, who was a scientific advisor to Napoleon Bonaparte. He insisted that using Newton's laws, one could predict the future with absolute certainty. When Laplace gave Napoleon a copy of his masterwork, *Celestial Mechanics*, the emperor exclaimed, "Sir, you have written this huge work on the heavens without once mentioning God." Laplace replied, "Sire, I felt no need of that hypothesis."[6]

Similarly Einstein declared: "I am a determinist, compelled to act as if free will existed. . . . Everything is determined . . . by forces over which we have no control . . . for the insect as well as for the star. Human beings, vegetables, or cosmic dust, we all dance to a mysterious tune, intoned in the distance by an invisible player."[7]

Newtonian mechanics, however, has been totally overturned by the Heisenberg Uncertainty Principle, which clearly concludes that we cannot know both the location and velocity of a particle with infinite precision.[8] The Uncertainty Principle is itself the cornerstone of quantum mechanics, the predominant and most successful model of physical reality that currently exists. This theory introduces chance into the universe and avers that the best we can hope for in determining the outcome of events is an approximate calculation of their happening. Obviously, determinism cannot be congruent with the Heisenberg Uncertainty Principle.

According to Jewish philosophical teachings, the opposing view of determinism was originally advanced by the Essenes, who attributed everything to predestination and the will of God. The Essenes were a Jewish religious sect that flourished in the land of Israel during the last two centuries B.C.E. up until the Roman conquest and destruction of the Second Temple in Jerusalem in 70 C.E.[9] Today we can see that Christian doctrines and theosophy are very similar to the Essenes' beliefs. There are even suggestions that John the Baptist was either an Essene or close to them.[10]

Determinism takes the view that whatever happens is determined in advance either by Divine knowledge and judgment or by causal necessity. In this regard, the Sadducees and the Pharisees, two Judean sects that flourished during the last two centuries of the Second Temple period, had oppositional ideas about social and religious tenets and ceremonial practices. The Sadducees, following Epicurus, denied the existence of Divine Providence in the affairs of man, and denied the doctrines of resurrection and the immortality of the soul. With the destruction of the Second Temple in 70 C.E., the Sadducees lost their social and ideological center and they disappeared as a sect. The Pharisees, also known as the 'separatists,' were followers of both the Written Law (the Torah or Pentateuch) and the Oral Rabbinic interpretations (the Talmud and Midrashim). They believed in the immortality of the soul, the resurrection of the body, Divine Providence and freedom of will. This meant that they took the dual position of recognizing the sovereignty of God and the freedom of man to choose.

Several medieval Jewish philosophers attempted to wrestle with the paradoxical free will–determinism issue. Yehudah Ha-Levi, in his theological novel *The Kuzari*, attempted to handle the paradox of free will.[11] Specifically, he asked how is it possible for man to have freedom and free choice if he is bounded by a Creator and there is causal necessity? The metaphor he used was that of a picture frame, where the frame represents the boundary that cannot be crossed. That boundary is Divine sovereignty or causal dependence. Yet, man is free to draw anything he wants in the picture, as long as he stays within the frame. This corresponds to the Rabbinic statement:

> God created six organs for man, three over which man has no control and three over which he has control. The three not in his control are the nose, eye and ear. . . . The three under man's control are the mouth, hand and feet.[12]

The meaning is that perceptual input is not under man's control, but verbal pronouncements, actions and movements are. Interestingly, Alexis de Tocqueville, an aristocratic Frenchman who came to the United States in 1831 and wrote on American institutions, morals and society, made the following observation, a very similar comment to Yehudah Ha-Levi's metaphor of the picture frame:

> Providence did not make mankind entirely free or completely enslaved. Providence has, in truth, drawn a predestined circle around each man beyond which he cannot pass; but within those vast limits man is strong and free, and so are peoples.[13]

Likewise, Maimonides strongly rejected the notion of determinism in any manner. He was one of the greatest Jewish philosophers, a codifier of Jewish Law and a physician with many published medical treatises.[14] Maimonides, also referred to by his acronym, RaMBaM, strove to re-work his philosophical system with Aristotelian philosophical principles and was cognizant of Arab Muslim philosophy. His well-constructed philosophical system had a major influence on Thomas Aquinas. In a strongly worded chapter in his 14-volume work, Maimonides stated that man had the freedom to choose whether to do good or evil. He referred to those who held deterministic beliefs as 'the fools of the world.' The RaMBaM believed that God does not force man to do anything.[15]

In the Kabbalistic framework the concept of God's will or desire is known as *ratzon*. *Ratzon* is the correlate to free will and determinism. There are two types of *ratzon*: the first is known as 'simple will' and is the Infinite power that encompasses all that 'was, is and will be,' also known as the *Ein Sof*, the Infinite.[16] An implication of the 'simple will' is that it can never be tampered with or altered.

The second form of will or desire, *ratzon*, is more limited and is mediated through the ten *sefirot*. As we have previously described, the *sefirot* are emanations or derivatives from the *Ein Sof*. They are a more limited type of will that give mankind the power to control and modify his thoughts, feelings and actions. This is a 'secondary' type of will that is within man's domain; it provides an element of choice or free will. This is because the *sefirot* progress from the Godhead through the world of emanation (*Atzilut*) to the increasing material worlds of creation (*Beriyah*), formation (*Yetzirah*) and finally, the world of human activity (*Asiyah*). Each of these worlds contains ten *sefirot*, in descending order, such that the lowest *Sefira* of one world (*Malkhut*) energizes the highest *Sefira* of the world below. As shown on the Etz Chaim, this is always *Keter,* itself depicted as a crown. It is the head or highest *Sefira* for that world and symbolizes the will inherent in it. These *sefirot* comprise a hierarchical array that allows the infinite energies of the *Ein Sof* to interact with the limited will of man. Or, to put it another way, they enable the Divine to establish a reciprocal channel of intentionality to do with man's everyday thoughts and activities ("As above, so below").

In clearer, terms, the first type of *ratzon* refers to God's desires, which are infinite and boundless. In this regard Moses Cordovero, one of the greatest of the sixteenth-century Safed Kabbalists, wrote: "Since He, His will and wisdom and understanding are one, and they are true qualities of His essence. . . ."[17] On the other hand, the second type of *ratzon* refers to what God has willed and which 'man' can effect.[18] One can refer to the former *ratzon* as the 'higher will' and the latter *ratzon* as the 'lower will.'

This 'lower will' is materialistic and not necessarily theistic. In many respects it was elaborated by one of the early psychoanalysts, Otto Rank, one of Freud's 'favorite sons.' In terms of his clinical practice, Rank placed the onus of responsibility upon the patient, for he observed that within an individual there resided a causality—not coming from outside influences or sources. He clarified:

> Only in the individual act of will do we have the unique phenomenon of spontaneity, the establishing of a new primary cause.[19]

What does this mean? We shall consider Rank's arguments in greater detail shortly. But to put them in the context of a lower, albeit human will that exists in an imperfect world, we need to return to the Kabbalistic framework that we have been discussing, and, in particular, ideas about the creation of the universe.

Undoubtedly, the Almighty, being all-encompassing, without limit or bounds, could have easily created the world to be a perfect entity. If that had been the case and a perfect world was created, then what could be man's purpose in life, as there would be nothing for man to contribute to the perfection of this world? Therefore, a less-than-perfect world was created so that man, with his ability and capacity for free will, would be able to perform good deeds and try to change and perfect the world. The lower, or limited, *ratzon* was used by God in order for man to have input by means of the *sefirot*. In this way, His self-restraint allows man a hand in altering the state of the universe.

On the other hand, the higher will (*ratzon*) does not have to be articulated in action. Just the fact that there is *ratzon* is sufficient for the object to be formed and created. As the RaShaB, Rabbi Shalom DovBer Schneersohn of Lubavitch, wrote: ". . . the creation of matter stems from God's utterances and speech, while the creation of form stems from His desire and will. . . ."[20] By saying that He 'willed something' we are saying that it has been physically made. When *ratzon* desires to do something, the object comes into existence immediately with the *ratzon*. Similarly, the eminent Kabbalist Shlomo Elyashiv wrote: "When it arises in God's *ratzon* to have something exist and attach form to it, it then exists without any differentiation between the desire to cause and the existent resultant."[21]

In the Hasidic way of thinking, the Divine Will is referred to as *Ratzon HaElyon*, the Supernal Will. The first leader of the CHaBaD (Lubavitch) dynasty, the Alter Rebbe, Rabbi Shneur Zalman of Liadi, in his major work on Hasidic thought, the *Tanya*, shows that our material world, the last in the series of emanations through the *sefirot,* is the ultimate objective of the Creation of the World. The observance of the commandments enables us to unite with God's will. Since, as a whole, the commandments represent God's will, then each commandment is a part of His will.

> Just as the organs of the human body are completely united with one's soul and are surrendered to it, so too is the life-force animating the performance and fulfillment of the commandments completely surrendered to the Divine Will which is clothed therein, and this life-force becomes, in relation to the Divine Will, like a body to a soul.[22]

Kabbalah asserts that when God constricts (via *tzimzum*) His freedom of choice (i.e., *ratzon*), a space is established in which man can operate. It is essential to note that even though all events (past, present and future) may be known to Him, this fact in no way limits or restricts man's exercise of his free will. On the contrary, the Almighty, being complete, good and all-inclusive, lacks nothing, and desires to share His goodness. The Kabbalists call this sharing of Divine attributes 'imparting.' This desire to impart is the positive energy that sustains man with the continuous gift of life. God's desire to impart parallels man's desire to receive; this is the (lower) will of man.

But the 'higher will' and the 'lower will' do not necessarily flow evenly or continuously. There are restrictions to the application or even existence of both the Divine and human will, which occur when the Infinite cannot be contained by the primordial vessels (the *sefirot*). Then the light of creation spills over and breaks the containment that these vessels provided. This event is known as *Shvirat HaKelim* ('the Breaking of the Vessels'). The shattered bits and pieces, the 'shards,' fall over and into everything. The ensuing chaos is a catastrophe, because the shards or fragments restrict the freedom of will and are responsible for the existence of evil. They replace purity of being with impurity of thought (as we shall explore in the next chapter). However, as we shall see, this 'catastrophe' also gives life meaning and purpose. Man gains the ability to strive for perfection in order to rectify (*tikkun*) the impurities and evil in the world.

At this point we can begin to ask the question, how does all this compare with a psychoanalytic understanding of the concepts of determinism and free will? How does psychoanalysis view the role of the therapist in working with a patient?

Early in his career, Freud wrote that the therapist needs to be careful not to impose his ideas upon the impressionable person's psyche:

> . . . it is suggestion which is the objectionable thing: the suppression of a free personality by the physician, who also retains a directing power over the sleeping brain in its artificial sleep.[23]

With all the care Freud took to ensure that the patient would be allowed freedom from suppression on the part of the therapist, he nonetheless had difficulty shaking his scientific deterministic approach. Twelve years later Freud wrote:

> Many people . . . contest the assumption of complete psychical determinism by appealing to a special feeling of conviction that there is a free will. This feeling of conviction exists; and it does not give way before a belief in determinism.[24]

And still later, Freud referred to ". . . the illusion of Free Will."[25] Freud was not yet able to allow himself to accept the fact that maybe one could actually have free will. The drives and instincts found in the unconscious would always, in Freud's view, have an impact on the psychical thoughts and actions of the individual.

Almost from the beginning of his career, Otto Rank had difficulty with Freud's absolute view of determinism. He suggested a theory of free will that could function side-by-side with Freud's principle of causality. Around 1924, Rank, together with Sandor Ferenczi, began to pursue more active techniques that focused on the here-and-now, on real relationships and the conscious mind and will, rather than on past history, transferences and the unconscious.

> I have pursued to its ultimate consequences the principle of causality which Freud applied to psychic events in a naïve 'physical' way, and had been led inexorably to a point where I simply had to derive mental phenomena from a 'causality of willing' in order to understand them.[26]

Rank was a forerunner of ego psychology, object relations and interpersonal theory, existential psychology and what Carl Rogers later came to call client-centered psychotherapy. The importance of Rank's contribution cannot be understated. Rank was one of the early pioneers in the psychoanalytic tradition who tried to break out of the restrictive mode of a purely biological foundation upon which Freud had built the early beginnings of psychology. Rank did not deny the biological underpinnings (he referred to this as 'the creature in man'), but he placed a major emphasis on the human elements of consciousness, such as self-awareness, and how this becomes expressed in the exercise of the will:

> The causality principle means a denial of the will principle since it makes the thinking, feeling, and acting of the individual dependent upon forces outside of himself and thus frees him from responsibility and guilt.[27]

Esther Menaker studied under Jesse Taft, an analysand of Rank, and also trained under Anna Freud. She sums up rather nicely how Rank's theory contributed to our understanding of motivation and the unconscious:

> It is the inability to affirm his own will, as well as to affirm the obligatory aspects of life and to take responsibility upon himself for functioning within the limitations of this framework, that characterize the neurotic character. It therefore becomes the task of therapy to help the individual to free himself from the fear and guilt which have inhibited such affirmation, that is, to liberate his individual will.[28]

Yet, she added, Rank's theoretical framework on the concept of the will is not without its complications.

> In insisting on the biological reality of the birth trauma and the need to assimilate and overcome it as the single driving force behind all our personal and cultural achievements, Rank extended his view of the causality of motivation beyond reasonable proportions: oversimplifying and overgeneralizing it at the same time.[29]

Is motivation an objective or subjective phenomenon? If we accept determinism and causality as obvious facts, where does that leave a person's motivation or will? The humanistic psychologist Abraham Maslow noted that there is a hierarchy of needs:

> The original criterion of motivation and the one that is still used by all human beings except behavioral psychologists is the subjective one. I am motivated when I feel desire or want or yearning or wish or lack. . . . So far as motivational status is concerned, healthy people have sufficiently gratified their basic needs for safety, belongingness, love, respect and self-esteem so that they are motivated primarily by trends to self-actualization (defined as ongoing actualization of potentials, capacities and talents, as fulfillment of mission, or call, fate, destiny or vocation), as a fuller knowledge of, and acceptance of, the person's own intrinsic nature, as an unceasing trend toward unity, integration or synergy within the person.[30]

Still we are left with the troubling question regarding the interrelationship between determinism, causality, will and motivation. What is under one's control and/or subject to deterministic causes? The psychologist Fred Pine attempts to 'blend' the extremes into a more coherent, flowing whole. He posits that ". . . there is present from birth a built-in, prewired motivational tendency, but these undergo developmental transformation; and it is the developmentally evolved motives that are worked with in the clinical situation."[31] This statement might bring the various possibilities into a sort of mutual co-existence.

Over the last several years, the theoretical frameworks of neurology and psychoanalysis have sought a common ground. Psychodynamic concepts are now being explained in neurological terms and a new scientific framework for understanding subjective experience is developing. Francis Crick[32] was one of the first scientists who put his finger on the 'problem':

> . . . you, your joys and your sorrows, your memories and your ambitions, your sense of personal identity, and free will are, in fact, no more than the behavior of a vast assembly of nerve cells and their associated molecules.[33]

Others have advanced parallel ideas in psychoanalysis and neuropsychology, even going several steps beyond Crick's assertions. To wit:

> At the level of organization of the basic-emotion command systems . . . at this primitive level of organization . . . the self is still essentially a passive mechanism. Although it triggers motor programs, it lacks *choice*. It is dominated by what Freud called the 'repetition compulsion.' In short, this primitive self is devoid of *free will*. From the neuroscientific point of view . . . the essence of 'free will' appears to be the capacity for *inhibition*—the capacity to choose *not* to do something.[34]

In contrast, the Texas psychiatrist Peter Polatin has focused on understanding the flow of will and motivation. He delineated how the will unfolds developmentally, in three stages: "The *counter-will* arises to oppose parental restrictions. The *competitive* will comes when the child aspires to do and possess things done and possessed by others. The *positive* will arrives when the individual has evolved his own standards."[35]

Polatin fit his developmental view into an interpretation of Rank, and showed that there seems to be an emphasis on the will developmentally occurring in all individuals according to a predetermined master plan. However, we know from our clinical work with children and adolescents that the will does not always follow a normal pattern of development; sometimes we find children and adolescents trying too hard. Their will is operating in a skewed and distorted pattern and they push, demand and exaggerate their emotions and behavior in order to elicit a response from others—generally adults. This can be directly expressed (verbally or by actions) or indirectly expressed or emoted (via projective and introjective processes).

In his relating to disturbances in cognition, Swiss psychiatrist Eugene Bleuler, who is famous for his studies of schizophrenia, noted that ambivalence was part and parcel of a psychotic disturbance of affect. Affect is the driving emotional force seeking expression, and ambivalence is the blocked correlate to emotional expression. Some may term blockage in the affective realm as a precipitate to serious emotional problems. Others may utilize the term 'paralysis' or 'stuckness' to describe the inability of the person to motivate himself to move forward for growth—in other words, a loss of will power. Significantly, Bleuler did not believe in a clear differentiation between sanity and madness.[36]

A psychoanalytic correlate for this is Freud's concept of the 'quota of affect.'[37] Affect may be increased, decreased, displaced or discharged. What is important is that the affect is not available for use. This can be seen in our patients as the blunted affect that Bleuler was referring to, or as the paralysis that we see in people who became terribly frightened to 'take risks.' This sometimes presents as a traumatic expression.

Interestingly, today we view consciousness as a complicated combination of neuroscience, artificial intelligence and psychological processes. If we only viewed consciousness as having a scientific basis, ". . . what would happen to our sense of moral agency and free will?"[38] This understanding, together with Rank's proposal to move away from the deterministic, reductionistic, mechanistic and causal way of viewing emotions and behavior, directs us toward a different and multifaceted way of understanding.

A similar way of thinking was the basis for the evolvement of object relations theory, as we previously have begun to discuss. In the United States, following the publication of Freud's tripartite structural model in 1923, early analysts viewed the ego as being in a central position as a mediator between the internal instinctual drives (the id) and the outside world.[39] Anna Freud[40] elevated the ego to a 'special' place, with emphasis on seeing the ego as a central agency in regulating emotion via the use of defense mechanisms. Anna Freud, however, at this time still viewed the instinctual drive theory as the primary energy system and raised interest in the status of the ego as a *system*.

In the 1940s and 1950s, psychiatrist Harry Stack Sullivan, also a pioneer in the treatment of schizophrenia, criticized ego psychology for being too static a theory of mind, and, by extension, of volition. He argued that social factors were also a determining factor and demonstrated that the patient's social, cultural and family context was influential in both normal development as well as psychopathology. While Freud's theory was one of drive reduction (via discharge), ego psychology added the dimension of the autonomous functioning of the ego. This meant that there was an area of psychological development outside the fixed realm of the instincts. The ego was conceived as having its own psychic energy that propels it, and this is a separate entity from the conflictual drive/instinctual energy of the id.

Sullivan and others added to this realization by developing an interpersonal theory that asserted the importance of social relationships.[41] Thus he moved far beyond the position of Heinz Hartmann, who was still very much committed to combining a drive (in our terms, deterministic) theory with an ego theory that he called an adaptational theory,[42] where the ego can be at odds with itself. Hartmann postulated a theory of ego strengths, focusing on the patient's internal push to health rather than Anna Freud's more negative view of defenses based upon ego weaknesses. Nonetheless, even though Hartmann made major moves toward an object relations theory, he still was not able to totally let go of the deterministic view.

In contrast, the object relations school, as we have begun to discuss, emphasized the importance of intra-psychic (the mental representations inside one's mind) and inter-personal (the 'real' people outside oneself) relationships. It itself was an outgrowth of British developments in psychoanalysis, which viewed the state and character of objects as the essential part of a psychological theory of development. This is opposed to the purely Freudian school of instincts and causality and the proposed modification of the ego psychologists, who still focused on instinctual impulses as part of their theory.

Melanie Klein was a leader in focusing attention on the world of internal object representations, introjections and projections. In effect, entire worlds exist and dramatically unfold within each person. Part objects are bits and pieces of images and urges, emotions and thoughts. Their interplay gives rise to extremely complicated constructs or 'internal worlds,' which may be based almost completely on fantasy (mental representations of instincts) or on actuality, or, as is usually the case, on a combination of both. Klein saw that everything in the 'real,' external world reverberates within this internal world. Or, as the Kabbalists put it, "As above, so below." Concomitantly, one's thoughts, feelings and actions are largely determined by how the internal world connects to the outer world. For example: if I interview for a job, how the interviewer is perceived in my inner world (whom he reminds me of, how I think he's relating to me, etc.) will determine how I see him in the 'real,' outside world. Through her understanding of the fantasy life of the infant and small child, she was able to merge both concepts of instinct as well as object. Yet, over the years, Klein's followers had increasing difficulties in maintaining the absolute links between instinctual and object relations.[43]

As we pointed out in the first chapter, Fairbairn rejected Freud's instinct theory. Instead he replaced it with his concept of object relationships, which focused on the observation "that libidos are not primarily pleasure-seeking but object-seeking."[44] He insisted that one will always strive for a relationship to a satisfying object. The explosive growth of the use of mobile phones or of the internet illustrates this process very well. The object relations theorists stressed that man was born with an inherent desire for social interaction. This placed a major emphasis on the will and desire of the patient, as well as the will and desire of the person (part or whole, transferential or actual) of choice. This interactive, dual relationship expands the concept of will to include both sides of the equation. Man's free will is found in and on both sides of a relational continuum. Thus, to parallel Kabbalistic thought, we might conclude "As inside, so outside," in addition to "As outside, so inside."

The counterpart of the mystical view that God enables man to have the 'space' for free will is the psychoanalytic view that man has the ability to interact interpersonally because of an innate desire to 'join' with another. In Otto Rank's terms, this exemplifies the 'affirmation of the will,' an intense desire for interpersonal exchange. This also involves both a quasi-deterministic quality—the innate desire on the part of the infant or adult to make emotional contact with the other (object seeking person)—as well as a here-and-now desire to be engaged in pleasurable object-related activities. Therefore, we can see an indeterminate confirmation of the reality of reciprocal relationships and reciprocal wills.

However, the question still remains, does free will or independent choice exist? Is it real or an illusion? The classical analysts tended to be deterministic. They contended that peoples' activities and life choices could be accounted for by their early experiences and basic impulses. Contemporary analysts are more eclectic. They understand that character and personality have many inputs, including a probabilistic array of intra-psychic and inter-personal relationships that take place within a hierarchy of secular frameworks: biological, social, legal, moral, political and so forth.

Their Kabbalistic colleagues might agree to a comparable differentiation depending on the operation of the Godly framework. The closer certain events or activities are to the Divine, the more they reflect the *Ratzon Elyon*, the 'Higher Will,' which cannot be tampered with or altered. But the farther that human activities and life choices are from the Godhead, the more they reflect a secondary type of *ratzon*, the 'Lower Will,' which takes into account the influence of the Divine, but which is not predetermined. Here 'man' has freedom of action and freedom of choice. The basic distinction is that the former occurs *on or as part of* the Godly framework, while the latter occurs *within* this framework.

Thus, it seems that free will depends on the frame in which it functions. Fracture the frame, and chaos will follow. One reason for this can be found in one of the Hebrew words for sin, *aveyrah.* In Hebrew 'sin' does not just mean bad or evil. That is a moral judgment and consequence of the influence of an *aveyrah* that transgresses, or goes beyond the bounds (of the frame). To sin is to commit a transgression, to fly too high (Icarus), to ape the Creator (Dr. Frankenstein) or to become a law unto oneself (Adolf Hitler, Chairman Mao, Gamal Abdel Nassar, etc.).

From another angle, a similar outcome occurs when a person possessed of the 'Lower Will' tries to go beyond his capacities and takes on the mantle of the 'Higher Will' or Godly Self. Politically this is commonly connected with nationalism, the secular religion of our age. Thus Hitler identified his Being with the *Urvolk,* the mystical primary horde of the German nation, Mao with the Proletariat, and Nassar with the Arab masses.[45]

Judaism itself can provide many examples of rabbis, scholars, even Kabbalists, who identified their individual, lower will with the higher, Divine will—with catastrophic results. Perhaps the most noted example is the seventeenth-century Torah prodigy, Shabbatai Zevi. As a young man he became extremely proficient in the oral law (the Talmud) and esoteric literature (Kabbalah). He gained many followers at a time of great despondency, when Jews were under attack by the Cossacks and were yearning for a leader who would take them out of their misery. Zevi enticed many people with magical practices and 'illuminations,' when he would deliberately break all religious conventions. He referred to himself as 'The Messiah,' a title confirmed by a number of his prominent disciples, also Kabbalists.

In 1666 Zevi identified with the 'Higher Will' by proclaiming himself 'the anointed' and preparing to march on Turkey to establish a new kingdom of the Jews. Ten of thousands of Jews from all over Europe and the

Mediterranean basin prepared to march with him. There could have been a bloodbath, as the Turkish sultan had him arrested and readied his execution. In the end, Zevi converted to Islam and was given a big pension. But his apostasy precipitated a pervasive demoralization in the Jewish world, as well as a fear of the mystical literature that continues until this very day.

These examples, whether of politicians or Kabbalists, illustrate the perversions of Will, all of which can destroy goodness, which itself can be defined as a connection with the Infinite. In consequence, such perversions unleash the forces of evil—pain, death and destruction—into the world.[46]

NOTES

1. A body of teaching comprising civil, religious, sociological and philosophical discussions. The time frame for writing and redaction was somewhere between the early third century and the sixth century C.E. This quotation comes from the tractate of Berachot, page 33b.
2. Dalai Lama, *The Four Noble Truths* (London: Thornsons, 1997), 12–13.
3. Dalai Lama, *Four Noble Truths*, 13.
4. Michio Kaku, *Parallel Worlds* (London: Allen Lane/Penguin, 2005), 154.
5. Michio Kaku, *Hyperspace* (New York: Anchor, 1995), 115.
6. K. C. Cole, *The Universe in a Teacup* (New York: Harcourt Brace), 68. Quoted in Kaku, *Parallel Worlds*, 154.
7. Denis Brian, *Einstein: A Life* (New York: Wiley, 1996), 185. Quoted in Kaku, *Parallel Worlds*, 154–155.
8. Werner Karl Heisenberg (1901–1976) was a German theoretical and nuclear physicist who won the Nobel Prize in 1932 for his Uncertainty Principle.
9. There has been much controversy regarding the etymology of the name Essene. There are those who feel that there is a cognate similarity to the word: *hasidim* ('pious ones') or to the Syriac *hasin* ('pious one'). Another theory relates it to the 'secret chamber of secrets' during Temple times—*hasha'in* ('secret or silent ones').
10. David Flusser, *Jewish Sources in Early Christianity* [in Hebrew] (Tel Aviv: Ministry of Defense, 1980).
11. Yehudah Ha-Levi (1075–1141) was a Spanish poet, philosopher and physician. His masterpiece, *The Kuzari*, was written sometime between 1130 and 1140, in Judeo-Arabic—Arabic language dialects written in Hebrew script. The full Arabic title is *The Book of Kuzari: An Argument for the Faith of Israel*.
12. Midrash Tanchumah, portion of Toldot, chapter 21. Midrashim are Jewish commentaries on the Hebrew scriptures compiled between 400 and 1300 C.E., and are based on exegesis, metaphors and legends.
13. From Tocqueville's *Democracy in America*, 1835. Quoted in neuropsychiatrist Peter Whybrow's book *American Mania: When More Is Not Enough* (New York: Norton, 2005), frontispiece.
14. Moses Maimonides (1135–1204).

15. Hilchot Teshuvah, chapter 5. Saadia Gaon (882–942) was an important source for this idea. Saadia Gaon was influenced by Aristotelianism and Moslem *Kalam* philosophy. See his *Book of Beliefs and Opinions*, ed. Samuel Rosenblatt (New Haven, Conn.: Yale University Press, 1948), Treatise 4, 3:152. A contrary view is that of the Spanish philosopher Chasdei Crescas (1340–1410), who critiqued the Aristotelian rationalist tradition in Jewish thought, as represented in Maimonides' writings. Crescas tried to draw a clear line with regard to determinism and free will. Julius Guttmann, the contemporary Jewish philosopher, noted that "[Crescas] . . . agrees with indeterminism insofar as he accepts its basic tenet concerning the possibility of events . . . on the other hand, determinism is correct if we center our attention, not upon the essence of single individuals, but upon the causes which work upon them." Julius Guttmann, *Philosophies of Judaism* (London: Routledge & Kegan Paul, n.d.), 238.

16. Moses Cordovero, *Shiur Koma* [in Hebrew] (Jerusalem: Yeshiva Kol Yehudah, n.d.).

17. Moses Cordovero, *Or Ne'erav*, 6:3. I. Robinson, *Moses Cordovero's Introduction to Kabbalah: An Annotated Translation of His* Or Ne'erav (New York: Yeshiva University Press, 1994). See the major Kabbalistic text, the *Zohar*, III:129a and 288b, where the simple *ratzon* of God is referred to as ' the will of all wills.'

18. Moses Cordovero, *Pardes Rimonim*, 4:4, 42a–44a. Moses Cordovero, *Pardes Rimonim* (Orchard of Pomegranates) [in Hebrew] (Jerusalem: Yerid Hasefarim, 2000).

19. Otto Rank, *Will Therapy and Truth and Reality* (1945; New York: Knopf, 1950), 44. In order for the individual to feel understanding and comfortableness, "the experience must affirm the individual's will." Esther Menaker, *Otto Rank: A Rediscovered Legacy* (New York: Columbia University Press, 1982), 103.

20. S. D. B. Schneersohn, *Kuntres Etz HaChayim: The Tree of Life* [in English] (1905; New York: Sichos, 1998), 8.

21. *Leshem Shvo v'Achlamah*, sha'ar A, chapter 8. The author, Shlomo Elyashiv (1841–1925), was also known by the name 'Baal HaLeshem.' S. Elyashiv, *Leshem Shvo v'Achlamah* [in Hebrew] (Pietrekov: Zederboim Press, 1909).

22. Schneur Zalman of Liadi, *Likutei Amarim: Tanya*. Bilingual edition, trans. N. Mindel (1797; Brooklyn, N.Y.: Kehot, 1984), chap. 23.

23. Sigmund Freud, "Review of August Forel's Hypnotism," in *Standard Edition of the Complete Psychological Works of Sigmund Freud*, ed. James Strachey (1889; London: Hogarth Press, 1981), vol. 1, 94.

24. Freud, 1901, "The Psychopathology of Everyday Life," in *Standard Edition*, ed. James Strachey, vol. 1, 253.

25. Freud, 1919b, "The Uncanny," in *Standard Edition*, ed. James Strachey, vol. 17, 236.

26. Otto Rank, *Psychology and the Soul* (1950; New York: Perpetua, 1961), 171.

27. Rank, *Psychology and the Soul*, 171.

28. Menaker, *Otto Rank*, 48.

29. Menaker, *Otto Rank*, 74.

30. Abraham Maslow, *Toward a Psychology of Being* (New York: Van Nostrand Reinhold, 1968), 22, 25.

31. Fred Pine, *Drive, Ego, Object and Self* (New York: Basic Books, 1990), 96.

32. Francis Crick in 1962 shared the Nobel Prize for Physiology of Medicine with James Watson and Maurice Wilkins. They shared the prize for discovery of the structure of the DNA molecule and a beginning understanding of the genetic code.

33. Francis Crick, *The Astonishing Hypothesis: The Scientific Search for the Soul* (New York: Simon & Schuster, 1994), 3.

34. Mark Solms and Oliver Turnbull, *The Brain and the Inner World* (London: Tarnac, 2002), 280–81.

35. Peter Polatin, *A Guide to Treatment in Psychiatry* (Philadelphia: Lippincott, 1966), 86.

36. Franz Alexander and Sheldon Selesnick, *The History of Psychiatry* (New York: Harper & Row, 1966), 211–16, 235–37.

37. Freud, 1894, "The Neuro-Psychoses of Defence," in *Standard Edition*, ed. James Strachey, vol. 3, 60.

38. Daniel Dennett, *Consciousness Explained* (Boston: Little Brown, 1991), 24.

39. Tripartite: id, ego and superego.

40. Anna Freud, *The Ego and the Mechanisms of Defense* (1937; New York: International Universities Press, 1971).

41. Harry Stack Sullivan, *The Interpersonal Theory of Psychiatry* (New York: Norton, 1953).

42. Heinz Hartmann, *Ego Psychology and the Problem of Adaptation* (New York: Imago, 1958).

43. This group met intermittently during the war years to try to advance the ideas relating to objects and instincts. This was an outgrowth of what came to be known as the Controversial Discussions, theoretical discussions that were deliberately not supposed to arrive at a scientific 'truth.' The Controversial Discussions brought together the warring factions of Freudians and Kleinians and even led to the beginnings of a new group: the Middle Group of Independents. See Robert Hinshelwood, *A Dictionary of Kleinian Thought* (London: Free Associaton Books, 1991), 253–55.

44. W. R. D. Fairbairn, *Psychoanalytic Studies of the Personality* (1952; London: Routledge & Kegan Paul, 1986), 137. This paper was originally presented in 1946.

45. Joseph Berke, *The Tyranny of Malice: Exploring the Dark Side of Character and Culture* (New York: Simon & Schuster, 1988), 319–20 (Hitler), 318–19 (Nassar).

46. Gershom Scholem, *Sabbatai Sevi: The Mystical Messiah* (London: Routledge & Kegan Paul, 1973).

Chapter Four

The Way of the Great Dragon: Good and Evil, Life and Death

According to the *Zohar*, the 'Great Dragon' has to do with the energies locked up in the darkest recesses of the self. It is related to the left, sinister, shadow side of man, and by extension, to the left column of the *sefirot* diagram, to judgment and severity. When untempered by kindness, the forces involved can be extremely dangerous, hence the image of something monstrous and life-threatening. Significantly, Kabbalah itself has been described as the 'Way of the Great Dragon,' meaning the unfolding of conscious awareness of the 'dark matter' in order to unblock and reclaim the light hidden therein.[1] In other words, we refer to the process of 'de-repression.'[2] But what is this area of conflict and negativity that can comprise such a large and mysterious part of our personality?

Psychoanalysis recounts that there is an ongoing battle between 'Eros' and 'Thanatos,' the life and death impulses in every person. From this perspective, evil is the triumph of destructiveness over constructiveness, death wishes over life wishes, hate over love.[3]

Initially Freud believed that the malicious attacks on people or things were secondary to what he called Eros, the life force. Later he concluded that destructive forces were equal in importance and power to life-enhancing ones. This idea is close to the old Persian (Manichaeism) world-view, whereby the spirit of evil (*Ahriman*) and the spirit of good (*Ormazd*) fight for predominance on equal terms.[4]

Freud's conclusion was strongly supported by his follower, Melanie Klein, who argued that envy is the earliest direct manifestation or externalization of the death instinct. Indeed Freud had discussed a hatred that opposed love, that is "older than love." Yet, on the other hand, he argued that love and hate arise from different sources. Freud connected envy with displeasure, and with fragmentation and chaos, while he identified love with pleasure, and with integration and structure.

Freud's formulations echoed an earlier account by the philosopher Immanuel Kant. Writing in *The Metaphysics of Morals* in 1797, Kant had no qualms in depicting envy as "the vice of human hate," "a moral incongruity" that delights in misfortune (*schadenfreude*) and ingratitude. He called envy a "hate that is the complete opposite of human love" and concluded:

> The impulse for envy is thus inherent in the nature of man, and only its manifestation makes of it an abominable vice, a passion not only distressing and tormenting to the subject, but intent on the destruction of happiness of others, and one that is opposed to man's duty towards himself as towards other people.[5]

Kant delineates a view of envy that is similar to popular ideas about evil. These presume that evil takes two forms: something 'sinful' that breaks the bounds of morality (the moral frame), and anything that causes harm, pain, misery or disaster. The marriage of the congruent concepts of evil and envy can be seen in primeval and universal fears of a crooked or blinking eye that carries a gaze imbued with hostility and wickedness, an expression said to be 'infected by the devil.' We refer, of course, to the ancient dread of the 'evil eye,' the *ayin ha'rah,* about which Rabbi Judah Loew of Prague, the famed sixteenth-century Kabbalist and 'creator' of the *Golem*, commented: "Know and understand that the evil eye concentrates within itself the element of fire . . . and so flashes forth destruction."[6]

This destructiveness may be inherent in a person's makeup, or may be a reaction to frustration or danger. Or, it could be situational, a reaction to an interpersonal event. Kleinian psychoanalysts see it as a derivative of primary aggressive impulses. Others assert it is a later derivative of character traits, interests and attitudes—in other words, a secondary motivating force that may even have adaptive functions. As neither idea is conclusive, it appears that the destructive impulse can be inherent and reactive. What does seem to be true is that envy, hence evil, is not just a curse, but a consequence of consciousness, an end that thrives on exaggeration and comparison. As many folk sayings attest: "Envy turns a blade of grass into a palm tree" and "The envious eye makes elephants of midgets."[7]

Intentionality, or direct willfulness, is another aspect of consciousness that impacts on evil. Consciously or unconsciously, evil demands 'malice aforethought.' Without such intentionality, the consequences of a particular event may be painful, destructive or even deadly, but not necessarily evil. The difference is between what has been called 'natural evil' and 'moral evil.'[8] The former does not involve human willfulness. It is an act of nature like a tsunami or hurricane. For humankind the consequences may be terrible, but unless one believes that natural events have conscious intentionality, they are not evil. A more appropriate term is 'tragedy.' A moral evil, however, demonstrates the direct hand of a human agent, such as the work of the infamous Dr. Mengele, who threw live children into fires, performed medical experiments and autopsies on conscious persons, cut off the body parts of female prisoners for tissue cultures, and so forth.[9]

In order to determine whether something is evil or not, one has to consider the act itself, the motivation and the consequences. 'Evil' involves human agency; it involves the direct influence of envy, jealousy and greed with related revenge and rivalry; and it leads to immense suffering, destruction and death. While evil breaks the bounds of morality, it is not always possible to know whether something is absolutely evil or not, because it may have redeeming features that do not become apparent for a long time afterward.

Evil is not the same as 'badness,' because the latter is more of a subjective reaction to pain and suffering, or simply dissatisfaction. Paradoxically, the persistence of evil is necessary for people to retain their humanity. This includes the freedom to be or not to be. Without such freedom of choice, as in the parable of Eve in the Garden of Eden, 'goodness' could not exist. This does not mean that good and evil are equal in power as the Manichaeans believed. But it does demonstrate some degree of the interconnection of the two phenomena, like light and dark or hot and cold.

The Kabbalistic perception of evil contains many elements that complement and potentially enhance psychoanalytic concepts. But there is a basic difference. Kabbalah is primarily addressing a spiritual universe. At the highest level there exists God, the infinite essence of all existence: omnipresent, omnipotent, omniscient and unknowable. Then, as we have already discussed, there exists an interacting chain of spiritual worlds, which directly involves man only at the lowest level. Hence, for Kabbalah, a discussion of good and evil touches upon the relationship between God the Creator, and his creations. But for psychoanalysis, considerations of evil are the province of man alone.

This being said, it is fascinating to explore what Kabbalah does mean by evil, and how it impinges upon man. Contemporary Kabbalists believe that evil is the result of creation itself. In order to bring the world into being—that is, for finite beings and finite environments to emerge from an infinite source—God contracts Himself. As we have previously described, this contraction or *tzimzum* brings into existence vessels, the *sefirot,* that represent the containing essence of God's qualities or characteristics. God uses his primary radiance to construct these vessels. He also utilizes the *sefirot* as a means to contain and shape and focus the *shefa* or flow of his radiance from above to below, that is, from 'emanation' to 'the actualization of human activity.' This situation is somewhat analogous to the attempts of contemporary physicists to contain a fusion reaction. In order to do so, they use energy—an intense magnetic field—to create an energy shield or flask to contain and shape another flow of energy, which takes the form of a plasma, a highly energized ionized gas.

When the *shefa,* or flow of God's radiance, cannot be contained by the *sefirotic* vessels, the 'lower' emotional ones shatter and thereby release a huge number of shards or fragments or shells, called *klipot.* These *klipot* pass from the upper spiritual realms to the lower world of materiality. Some *klipot* still retain a degree of goodness. Others are absolutely evil. The latter are remarkably similar to what the British psychoanalyst Wilfred Bion has termed 'bizarre objects,' little bits of reality enwrapping hatred. The shattering of the vessels (*Shevirat HaKelim*) destroys God's unity and brings forth *tohu* (chaos) into reality. This downchaining of the *klipot* or shards is another way of depicting the emergence of inherent and inherited envy.

Before proceeding further in our discussion of the *klipot* and how they materialize evil, we need to consider the opposite of evil: goodness. 'Good' and 'God' go together, for the sages say that goodness is a state of connection to God. Or, to put it another way, goodness is a state of idealization, acceptance and active connectivity to one's primary source. Spiritually and materially, Kabbalists insist that this source is God. Therefore, any thing, any person and any experience or any activity that establishes such a connection is good. Conversely, any disconnection is bad or evil, and denotes a state of alienation or exile (from God). Similarly, in human terms, the fifth of the ten commandments described in the Torah (the Old Testament) is to honor your father and mother, meaning, to acknowledge the source of your existence. In return, if you do this, you will then have a good and long life.[10]

The contemporary Jewish philosopher David Birnbaum adds to this picture by describing God and godliness in terms of the absolute potential to be what one can be, and to know what one can know. He notes that in the Torah, in the Book of Exodus, the name of God that was first proclaimed to Israel, *Eheyeh Asher Eheyeh,* means "I-Will-Be-That-Which-I-Will-Be."[11] From this he deduces that the name of God is essentially a statement that "the holiest state of the holy is God of Potential."[12] Birnbaum adds:

> God is the actualization of potential in its conscious holy form . . . holy potential within potential within potential *ad infinitum*. For the infinite God of Israel is a God of willed potential . . . [that] transcends time, space and the cosmos . . . rippling infinitely forward. . . .[13]

Birnbaum contrasts the 'Tree of Life' as in the Garden of Eden with the 'Tree of Knowledge.' While the 'Tree of Life' is associated with bliss and eternal life, he calls it a "gilded cage existence," a state of stasis with limited potential for growth or personal development, because life is predetermined. On the other hand he relates the 'Tree of Knowledge' to a life of challenge, freedom, responsibility, the pursuit of knowledge and infinite growth potential. Mankind comes into its own once it has tasted the fruit of the 'Tree of Knowledge.' Yes, this comes with pain, mortality and 'unleashed natural evil.' But it also releases joy, dignity and, especially, free will.[14]

Remaining attached, the 'Tree of Life' is akin to pre-birth, residing in the womb of God. But tasting the 'Tree of Knowledge' is akin to birth, with all the possibilities and difficulties that this entails. Far from committing a sin, by eating the apple of knowledge, Eve chose to choose life, the actualization of her potential as a woman and partner to Adam. Likewise Adam chose to be born with the potential for reaching for the infinite.[15] Birnbaum asserts, and many Kabbalists would agree, that this freedom to choose to reach for the infinite is the highest good and the ultimate purpose of 'man's' sojourn on earth.[16]

There exists a remarkable resemblance between the picture that the Kabbalists paint about good and evil, and the developmental theories of psychoanalysis. Although non-theistic and secular in orientation, Melanie Klein and her colleagues have delineated a point in the life of an infant, which they term 'the depressive position,' whereby the infant has to undergo an intense inner struggle between the forces of love and hate.[17] This occurs, in particular, when the infant realizes that the mother he loves (because she feeds him) and the mother he hates (because she is not available when he wants her) are one and the same. Then he fears that his hate will destroy the person he loves, or that he will not be able to repair the damage he has done to her or to others. Klein's theory provides the operational link between instincts and object relations. It demonstrates that 'bad' or 'evil' has to do with relationships that hurt people.

The depressive position parallels the conflict described by the Jewish sages, that is, between the *yetzer ha-tov* and the *yetzer ha-rah,* the force for goodness and the force for evil. The whole future life course of the infant depends on the outcome of this internal battle. If it fails, then the child is likely to grow up twisted, damaged and prone to severe mental instability. If it succeeds, the reward is sanity, that is, the capacity to love and work and engage in productive relationships. The latter issue is of paramount importance, for it implies a willing acceptance of the interpersonal roots of one's existence.

Failure to overcome 'the depressive position,' which in interpersonal terms means the failure to repair a person or relationship that one has damaged, is the moment when the forces of hate overwhelm the forces of love. In a worst-case scenario, an infant may revert to a state of paranoid terror. In order to overcome this terror, he divides himself into smaller and smaller bits, which ironically serves to bring about the very thing he fears: self-disintegration. His further intention is to interpose barriers between any remaining healthy parts of himself and his dreaded bits and pieces.

Alternatively the child may embrace power. Then a young person, or, future adult, tends to become suffused with envious and jealous hatred. He may refuse to recognize any source of supply: parents, friends, teachers, nature, or any relationship, any nourishment, which emanates from outside himself. On the contrary he seeks to triumph over all need by becoming his own source of nourishment, and to become God unto himself. This situation is a state of omnipotence called mania or the 'manic state.' This includes interpersonal ruthlessness and absolute denial of others' feelings.

In contemporary cultures, with values that emphasize materialism and self-sufficiency, the manic or hypo-manic (less severe) state of mind is the norm rather than the exception. The overactive pursuit of money, goods, food, drugs and status is culturally syntonic. That is why it is so hard to see. Harmful excesses also serve the self-defensive function of avoiding relationships, whether on secular or spiritual planes.[18]

The late Lubavitcher Rebbe, Menachem Mendel Schneersohn, has used the Biblical story of Moses and Pharaoh to depict such an inversion of reality. In this way he illuminates the nature of evil by chronicling an Egyptian king who knew no bounds.[19] The Rebbe addresses the question, how to do we transcend narcissism and manic infatuation?

He points out that the evil of Pharaoh is not promiscuity, which characterized the pagan cults of old Egypt; nor the enslavement and torture of millions; nor even his fondness for bathing in the blood of slaughtered children. On the contrary, the evil of Pharaoh is his own egocentrism, his insistence on regarding his own self as the source and standard of everything, like the deprecations of a dictator, or a narcissist, or a manic individual. This self-centeredness, a variation of absolute omnipotence encapsulated in the shape of a human, is the source of all depravity and cruelty. Like Pharaoh, the individual concerned believes that he (or she) is able to commit any act, any crime, that he regards as essential to his own definition of reality. Essentially he asserts: 'I have made myself. Good is what is good to me, evil is what is contrary to my will. I am the master of reality.'

In this regard, the prophet Ezekiel depicted Pharaoh as 'the great serpent who couches in the midst of his streams.' In other words, the Egyptian potentate was a beast who exclaimed, 'The river is my own, and I have made myself.'[20]

The Rebbe relates that Moses was frightened to meet Pharaoh for very good reasons. Moses knew that he was about to encounter a man in the role of a king with the delusion that he was God. In other words he was fated to face the essence of evil, the incarnation of unbounded narcissism, a man puffed up to mythic proportions, who, stripped of his disguises, behaved like a plethora of pythons that crush and devour everyone and everything in their path. Therefore God said to Moses:

> Come with me. We will go together into the serpent's palace, and penetrate the self-worship that is the heart of evil. Together we will discover that there is neither substance nor reality to evil—all that it is, is the misappropriation of the divine in man.[21]

The misappropriation of the Divine acts like an iron partition between man and God. This analogy is a further way of considering the Kabbalistic concept of the *klipot*. They act as intermediaries or barriers between a person and his source, and consequently, between one individual and another, as well as between a person and himself. In psychological terms the *klipot* subsume three degrees of alienation: *self from soul, self from others* and *self from self.*

The first, the alienation of the *self from the soul*, is equivalent to a person being cut off from his spiritual essence, or God. Another way to describe this state is to say that the individual lives in a state of alienation from his source, or as the Kabbalists put it, in a state of exile (*galut*). The fundamental reason for this condition is selfishness, which is the force or power of negativity, and which, in turn, leads to a break in the soul-self connection.

Writing in the *Tanya*, Shneur Zalman provides an elegant metaphoric explanation for the exile or alienation of the self from the soul.[22] The souls of men are like the flame of a candle. They naturally want to scintillate upwards. But if they soar too high, they detach themselves from their source, their wicks, and are soon extinguished. So they have to weave a delicate dance between scintillating upwards and remaining in contact with their wicks and the oils that flow through them. A flame that leaps too high is like a soul that disconnects from God. It becomes detached from its wick, from its essential oils, and therefore becomes 'wick-ed,' without a wick. Similarly when a person separates from his source, like a child from his parents or a politician from 'the people,' he becomes wicked.

The second degree of alienation concerns the *self from others* (family, friends, tribe, culture, tradition). When a person is in a manic state of mind, this involves a total denial of relationships. But for the hypo-manic person, there are less extreme ways of keeping oneself apart from friends or family. One way involves sulking, the petulant withdrawal from others. The other acts through ingratitude, an expression of envious resentment. In either case the paramount feelings are always hurt pride and an abiding sense of inferiority, while the precipitating issues invariably concern need and dependency. In this respect the denial of gratitude leads to 'grate-itude,' an endless negativity, where any hint of appreciation grates on the mind and tortures the self.[23]

The third degree of alienation separates *self from self.* By this we mean that a person creates divisions within his or her own personality in order to protect his good side from his bad side, or his passive side from his aggressive side, and so on. These divisions can operate just like divisions between people, whereby a diligent but weak child may choke up and hide away from the big bad bully around the corner. This process of subdividing the personality can be so haphazard that it resembles the chaotic mishmash of a person in the throes of a psychosis. However, it is more likely to be organized, as the psychoanalyst Donald Winnicott has described, in the manner of a non-defensive, receptive 'true self' and a grandiose, prideful, overly assertive 'false self.'[24] In either case the fault lines encompass libidinal issues. The person is concerned with wanting pleasure and avoiding pain.

A more ominous division of the mind occurs when an individual despairs of ever gaining basic necessities like love, care and attention. In consequence, he may reject his desires for life-affirming pursuits, and fall in love with death and destruction. The psychoanalyst Herbert Rosenfeld delineates this as a split between what he calls 'libidinal narcissism' and 'destructive narcissism.'[25] Initially a person's anger and negativity have to do with gaining goodies. He inflates himself and knocks others down in order to be the source of his own desires. But ultimately, he may deny goodness and idealize badness. Then his mind becomes taken over by destructive elements, which Rosenfeld argues can take the form of a gang of Mafiosi or a division of Nazi storm troopers. And when the person identifies with these figures, he becomes like these base elements onto others.

The identification with the aggressive forces in oneself can take various forms. The net result is that one part of the self gets bloated with hate and anger and does not allow any other feelings or considerations to be taken into account in internal or external relations. When this happens with the conscience or superego, an oversized, over-severe superego can follow. Then an individual who is so distorted becomes preoccupied with criticizing and persecuting his own life interests, or those of others. The character of Inspector Jarvis in Victor Hugo's *Les Miserables* typifies such a situation, whereby a man constricts his existence in order to pursue self-righteous vengeance.[26]

In the Jewish tradition the conflict between two great, equally knowledgeable sages, Hillel and Shamai, exemplifies the interplay between aggressive severity and loving acceptance. At best there is a balance between the two sides, representing the *sefirot* of *Chesed* (kindness) and *Gevurah* (severity). But if their conflict threatened to get out of hand, the rabbis tended to choose the side of Hillel because he represented love and moderation. However, there have been numerous periods when the spirit of Shamai has prevailed, leading to splitting, disunity, hatred and recrimination. This is a big problem today, two millennia after Hillel and Shamai competed for predominance. It is also an aftershock of the Holocaust, whereby the Nazis injected sadism and death into the collective body of the Jewish people, and indeed, the whole of mankind.

These splits and subdivisions between *self and soul, self and others* and *self and self* condemn people to live in a state of conflict and exile from God, from society and from their essential beingness. For the Kabbalists they demonstrate how a person can be imprisoned within another person or exiled within another part of himself, just as the Jews were imprisoned and exiled in Egypt before the revelation on Mount Sinai. In fact, on the deepest level of meaning, the recounting of the liberation from Egypt every Passover at the Seder table goes far beyond the narration of a common history. Most importantly, it conveys a journey that every person (Jew or non-Jew) has to make every year, in order to extricate himself or herself from the inner bondage of 'false selves' and 'destructive identifications.' These are all barriers that prevent one from overcoming foolishness and self-deception and interfere with his integrating or reuniting the upper spiritual and lower material aspects of existence.

The location of evil is another area in which the Jewish mystical tradition and psychoanalysis are in general agreement. According to psychoanalytic theory, evil is a manifestation of negative instinctual forces welling up from within which overwhelm the positive powers of love and life. Although this struggle may also reflect and be amplified by bad parenting and harmful circumstances, basically evil originates in destructive internal phenomena such as envy, greed and jealousy.

Similarly Kabbalah sees evil as an inner struggle between the Good Impulse (*yetzer ha-tov*) and the Bad Impulse (*yetzer ha-rah*). Or to put it another way, the relative balance between the Divine Soul (*Nefesh Elokit*) and the selfish Animal Soul (*Nefesh B'haimit*) determines the emergence of evil, or not. If the latter predominates, then evil—as manifested by a disconnection from one's essential source, arrogance, doubt, denial and pride—will predominate. So once again we see a personal confrontation with different parts of the self, where a particular individual represents an emotional and spiritual 'black box.' Lots of things go on inside the box. But an outside observer may only perceive an externalized result, such as a malicious quip.

In fact Kabbalah recognizes many connections to external events, especially within the processes of creation. We refer to shattering of the *sefirot* into tiny shards, the *klipot,* which in Kabbalistic thought are closely connected with the *yetzer ha-rah*, as well as the expulsion of Adam and Eve from the Garden of Eden, a cataclysm that is commonly associated with the origin of evil. Nevertheless, we can see that they are necessary for consciousness and the thrust for creation in all its forms. The psychologist Sanford Drob points out that for Freud, the existence of neurosis, with all its attendant problems, is the price of civilization and culture. But for the Kabbalists, splitting (*shvirah*) and evil are the price of creation.[27]

Both Kabbalah and psychoanalysis locate the immediate determinants of evil within the body and soul of the persons concerned. In contrast, Western culture as a whole has tended to identity evil with external agents and external events. In large part this has occurred because Western perspectives of evil have been heavily influenced by Persian (Zoroastrian), Greek, Roman and Christian sources. As we mentioned before, the ancient Persians considered evil to be a god, on a par with the spirit of good. So evil on earth was a consequence of the external interplay of these outside forces. The same is roughly true in Greek and Roman thought where many gods had the power to intervene, often for harmful and destructive purposes, in human activities. Eventually these outside interventions became known as 'cosmic forces,' which are really internal events projected onto 'stars and planets,' 'nature,' 'nationalism,' 'class struggle,' 'economic power,' and 'fate.'

Elaine Pagels points out in *The Origin of Satan* that pagan peoples believed that the gods could act directly, but also through spirit energies known as *daimones.* This was a Greek term. Later, under the influence of Christianity, these entities would become recognized under the notorious rubric of demons, evil spirits. Such spirits were considered to be agents of the Devil or Satan, the arch enemy and opponent of God and mankind.[28]

In Hebrew, the word 'Satan' simply means an adversary or opponent. The entity is not mentioned in the five books of Moses, the Torah. Satan is mentioned in three places in the Bible as a superhuman being who is obedient to God.[29] In the Book of Job, Satan emerges from his role as a supernatural messenger to challenge God's judgment and preeminence. In the Talmud, Satan is identified with the *yetzer ha-rah*, really a human rather than external force tempting people to sin.[30]

Pagels explains that Satan came into his own as the personification of evil, the Prince of Darkness, the leader of the fallen angels and arch-rebel against God's will in the books of the Apocrypha and the Chronicles of the early Christians. She also points out that Satan was initially a rhetorical weapon by which one group of Jews beat another. But this malevolence soon passed into the hands of the Apostles, who utilized the image to denounce Jews, pagans and dissident Christians with equal vehemence as agents of the Devil. So Satan was reborn and recast as a Demon, Devil, Lucifer and incarnation of the netherworld for political purposes. Clearly, Satan was a figure created in the imaginations of men crazed with hatred, a hatred amplified and then projected outwards into an external abode.[31] When this projection was denied, as it had to be in order to be effective, Satan took on an independent existence as a terrifying horned creature with claws, fangs, a razor-sharp tail and huge protuberant eyes, which could swoop down and bring disaster to anyone or anything that caught his gaze.

Within Judeo-Christian culture over the past couple of hundred years, there has been a marked decline in the kind of religious fervor that sustained the dread of Satan as an external emissary of evil. But this entity has not passed into oblivion. In contemporary culture Satan has become secularized. Karl Marx contributed to this process by claiming that capitalist economics were the root of all evil. Later liberal economists demonized the Marxists. At the same time Satan entered the political area, whereby the political left claimed Satan was an ally of the right and vice versa. As if to drive this point home, different leaders—Hitler, Stalin, Mao Zedong, Pol Pot and now, Bin Laden—have all managed to deify destructiveness and inflict demonic regimes at home and any other place they could invade or infiltrate.

In every one of these economic, political and social conflicts, 'Satan' personifies destructive omnipotence, created by human hatred and projected onto a cosmic tableau. The entity maintains its power by non-thinking, non-feeling and the continual turning of people into things, objects to be manipulated, controlled, broken and destroyed, all without any sense of morality or responsibility.[32] This is what is meant by the capacity of Satan to turn light into darkness.

The Baal Shem Tov emphasized the intimate connection between darkness and evil. He noted that darkness is necessary so light can exist.[33] Similarly, we need the wicked to distinguish the righteous, and the foolish to know the wise, suffering to appreciate pleasure and forgetfulness to discern memory. Interestingly, the *Zohar* emphasizes that we can speak of the 'divine dross,' the product of excretion, by which the Almighty purges itself of the forces of uncleanliness, and maintains its essential goodness.[34] This 'excretion' is very much akin to the process of envious projection. However, with envy the intention is to harm another, and here it is to purify the projector. Yet, the effects may be similar, the establishing of a Satanic counterworld, a darkness that conceals godly endeavors.[35] Drob adds that the waste products, the *klipot,* are completely infertile and parasitic on the divine traits of judgment and power. Therefore, we can see that the ". . . quest for power and the insistence upon severe judgment are hence the 'roots of all evil.'"[36]

Not unrelated, the Baal Shem's follower, Levi Yitzchak of Berdichev, commented on the beginning verses of the Book of Genesis.[37] He said that 'evening' represented the *tzimzum,* the primal constriction. In this way, God created the world by means of a void or darkened absence. 'Morning' represented the light, the primary radiance, by which God vitalized this void. Then Levi Yitzchak compared the development of man to the creation of the world. His first moments are full of darkness, replete with the Animal Soul (*Nefesh B'haimit*) and the Evil Urge. It takes the light of knowledge, right actions and loving relations to overcome the 'other side' (*sitrah achra*), all the deviltries that comprise the antithesis of Godliness. The implication of Rabbi Levi Yitzchak's commentary is that evil is a manifestation of ignorance. It is constricted consciousness, but because of the power of wisdom (sudden illuminations that dispel ignorance), it itself is never absolute or irredeemable.

Another distinguished disciple, Yaakov Yoseph of Polonye, added to these explanations after referring to the fourth verse of the Book of Genesis: "And God saw the light and it was good, and God divided between the light and the darkness."[38] He emphasized that once a person is able to distinguish between darkness and light, he must act to extract the light that may remain hidden in the darkness. By this he meant a person must recognize the darkness, the wickedness that lies within himself as well as outside himself, in order to bring the light, the goodness, the sparks of godliness that may be embedded in it, out into the open.[39] The light can then vanquish the darkness as goodness can dissipate evil, or selflessness can overcome selfishness.

Freud himself touched upon some of these issues in a paper entitled "The Antithetical Meaning of Primary Words."[40] Referring to the linguistic studies of the German philologist Karl Abel, Freud was struck by the fact that words develop by denoting a difference between two contrary states like dark/light or accursed/sacred. Concepts arise when there are distinct words to describe them. Before there were separate words for dark and light, there was an amorphous, indeterminate darkness/light, an ungraspable perceptual soup that carried the potential but not the actuality of darkness and light. And without words, memory, imagination, intellect, the whole of psychic reality cannot exist. Therefore, we can appreciate the profundity of the sages who declared that God created the world with a word.

In our paper "Antithetical Meanings of 'the Breast,'" we pointed out that Hebrew, a central member of the Semitic group of languages, is well placed to convey the complicated and contradictory meaning of words, especially due to its linguistic root system.[41] Most words consist of three consonant roots, although some have two, and others four. The addition of vowels determines the word's precise sense and function. Perhaps the most primary word of all is 'breast' because, for the infant as well as the adult, it denotes the source of everything life sustaining. In Hebrew the word for breast has a bilateral root with two consonants, *shin* and *daled,* Sh + D, and is pronounced

ShahD. If you add the letter *yod* after the *daled*, you get *ShahDi,* which is the possessive of ShahD, and means 'my breast' or 'my source.' But the same word also stands for one of the names of God. According to ancient Rabbinic distinctions, *sha* means 'who' and *dai* means 'enough.' Together the word signifies 'He who is self-sufficient,' which also conveys the idea of a primary being that is the cause of himself.

The ShahD, the breast, is both a part of the body and a function that is a center of desire and love and goodness. In turn it conjures forth good feelings and radiates them back, as a mirror returns a smile with an image of the smiler, smiling. But what happens when the ShahD is absent or envied or frustrating or functions inadequately? Then it is felt to be a focus of pain and badness and evil, and conjures forth fear and hatred. Hebrew clearly reflects this radical shift that is brought about by the projection of negative impulses onto the ShahD. The consonants remain the same. But the vowel changes. In this way the ShahD reverts to a ShaDe, a dark demon, a life antagonist, a dangerous entity suffused with rage and cruelty. Similarly the Hebrew word for evil is *Rah.* It consists of the consonants *resh* and *ayin.* But if one changes this vowel, then the word becomes *Ray'ah*, and its meaning is transformed from 'evil' to a source of help and goodness, that is, a 'friend.'[42]

If ShahD brings light and life into the world, then ShaDe brings darkness and death. From a psychoanalytic perspective, ShahD to ShaDe demonstrates the metamorphosis from the good breast to the bad breast, from good to bad, both in the object, which appears demonic and threatening, and in the subject, which feels demonic and threatened. The linguistic transformation also confirms the views of the Baal Shem Tov and his followers about the opposition of good and God with evil and darkness, light with night. Indeed, the Hebrew word for demon breast, ShaDe, is identical with the English shade, denoting a shadow or darkness that blocks the radiance of the sun and causes a person or thing to be cut off from its source.[43] In precisely the same way ShaDe is related to a shade, a devil or specter, equal to the dark, shadowy side of the self, which, like a shell or *klipah*, blocks the radiance to and from one's loved ones, and God.

For all of these reasons there appears to be a clear connection in Jewish thought between darkness and evil. And indeed, there are many references to the baleful effects of the loss of light and the power of darkness. Yet, there remains a considerable degree of uncertainty about the absolute consequences of darkness, or of evil. This is not because the sages have doubts about the relationship between darkness and evil, but because they do not see evil as a separate state of being.

The contemporary Hasidic scholar Adin Steinsaltz points out that good is real but evil is not, because it does not have an independent essence. Evil is not a co-partner with good, as the Persians believed *Ahriman* is with *Ormazd*, or as Thanatos is with Eros. Rather it is a perverted goodness, a goodness turned into a pale reflection of itself by the power of negativity.[44]

The Baal Shem Tov himself taught that evil is merely the lowest level of good. It is not a condition or power, rather a life direction. As the *Zohar* explains, evil is a downward direction (i.e., away from God). Evil exists in order to allow us to understand righteousness. It is not an absolute reality. Whether something is evil or not depends on the circumstances.[45] For example, consider the use of a broom. If it is used to beat a child, then it is evil. But if it is used to sweep dirt out of the house, then it is good.

Interestingly, psychoanalysis remains ambiguous about evil. In general, the main Freudian streams (classical, object relations, Kleinian) focus on Thanatos, the death impulse, envy, jealousy, greed, aggression, destructiveness, and so on, but do not tackle evil *per se*. Why? Probably because the concept of 'evil' has a theological or moral connotation, which Freud (or his translators) wished to purge from his writings.[46]

For Carl Jung, on the other hand, evil was a basic reality, and he wrote and maintained an extensive correspondence about it. In his autobiography, *Memories, Dreams, Reflections*, he narrated that as a boy he had come face to face with evil in the form of a vision of the dark, unclean side of God.[47] Yet, as he grew older, he took a more paradoxical approach. He agreed that evil has an absolute dimension that cannot be relativized, but he also insisted that evil was a matter of subjective value judgment.

One of Jung's major contributions was to delineate the shadow side of the self. In analytical psychology this subsumes darkness to the realms that one wants to hide. The 'shade' encapsulates everything in one's character that is nasty, hateful and primitive. Jung believed that the 'shadow' was far more than a reaction to circumstances. Rather it was an archetypal embodiment of evil and a fundamental focus of contention throughout the course of one's life.

Kabbalists would agree that everyone has to struggle with his or her darker impulses, but they do not accept that evil is a fundamental, independent principle of life. For them life comes from God and cannot be a source of evil. If this is the case, how does evil originate? Their answer is that evil is a nonentity, devoid of reality or substance. It is just the corruption of good, simply the shadow that conceals godliness in every thing and every person. Therefore, man has the power to choose to transform darkness into light and to redress this corruption though his own actions. For example, just as God creates the world with a word, man can transcend evil by rearranging the letters of our daily existence. What does this mean in practice? Let us give an example of this process from an episode in the life of a very disturbed young man who was a resident at the Arbours Crisis Centre in London.[48]

'Richard' had been severely wounded during the course of prolonged conflicts with an ostensibly loving but tyrannical family, as well as by his own inner demons. When his negativity predominated, he often affected a posture of psychotic withdrawal. Alternatively, he could also be warmly playful and communicative.[49] Joseph Berke was able to follow these emotional swings by observing his use of words. During up-periods Richard would doodle incessantly, emphasizing in particular the word EVIL. He liked to write and draw EVIL every which way.

Berke relates: "One day he cornered me in the kitchen and exclaimed, 'You know, Joe, EVIL spelled the other way is LIVE.' I had never previously thought of the reverse spelling of the word. Upon reflection, I observed that by playing with words one could turn evil to live, good to bad, not unlike the ancient Gods who could transform Furies into Eumenides or 'kindly ones.'"[50]

Richard nodded in agreement. Yes, he knew it was possible to turn bad to good, to transcend evil. That's why he doodled. It helped him to overcome terrible 'urges.' When EVIL returned, his rage gained the upper hand. But when LIVE appeared, his tension disappeared and the world became okay again. 'Richard' concluded:

> Joe, that's why I write. When I can't get away from EVIL, everything feels real bad inside. But when I change it 'round, to LIVE, then I feel good. I have to do this, Joe, turn EVIL to LIVE, and keep it there. For me, it's a matter of life and death.[51]

NOTES

1. The 'Way of the Great Dragon' is sometimes called the 'way of the left column' and among Kabbalists is known as 'the way of the shadow.' Mordechai Gafni, "Shattered Vessels, Stained Hands," *Wellsprings*, no. 48 (2001): 16.

2. A further intention of the 'Way of the Great Dragon,' that is, of Kabbalah, is to move from hiding from or killing the dragon, to befriending it, and using its powerful energies for good. Gafni, "Shattered Vessels," 15.

3. Sigmund Freud explicitly discussed the issue of the death instinct in a number of papers, including 1920, "Beyond the Pleasure Principle," in *Standard Edition*, ed. James Strachey, vol. 18; 1924, "The Economic Problem of Masochism," in *Standard Edition*, ed. James Strachey, vol. 19; and 1937a, "Analysis Terminable and Interminable," in *Standard Edition*, ed. James Strachey, vol. 23.

4. This is a dualistic philosophy, taught by the Persian prophet Manes, combining elements of Zoroastrian, Christian and Gnostic thought. The philosophical thesis is that the world is divided between good and evil principles. We see a parallel idea in one of the Dead Sea Scrolls: "The Scroll of the War of the Sons of Light

Against the Sons of Evil." See Yigal Yadin, *The Temple Scroll* (Tel Aviv: Maariv, 1990), 228–36.

5. *Schadenfreude* is pleasure derived from the misfortune of others. Immanuel Kant, "Metaphysik der Sitten" [in German], in *Samtliche Werke*, ed. K. Vorlander, vol. 3, 4th ed. (Leipzig: Felix Meiner, 1922), 26, quoted by Helmut Schoeck, *Envy: A Theory of Social Behavior* (New York: Harcourt Brace, 1970), 166.

6. Quoted by Joshua Trachtenberg, *Jewish Magic and Superstition: A Study in Folk Religion* (1939; New York: Atheneum, 1970), 56.

7. There exist hundreds of similar proverbs on the subject of envy, many of which are almost identical in different countries. These are quotes from the Russian genre. Schoeck, *Envy*, 20–21.

8. This is a distinction drawn by the philosopher David Birnbaum, *God and Evil: A Unified Theodicy / Theology / Philosophy* (Hoboken, N.J.: Ktav, 1989), 91.

9. Report in the *New York Times*, January 23, 1985, quoted by Birnbaum, *God and Evil*, vii.

10. Deuteronomy 5:14. This follows Aryeh Kaplan's (1981) translation, *The Living Torah: The Five Books of Moses* (Jerusalem: Maznaim Publishing, 1981), 894.

11. Exodus 3:13–14. Quoted in Birnbaum, *God and Evil*, 64, following Kaplan's *Living Torah*, 270–71.

12. Birnbaum, *God and Evil*, 65.

13. Birnbaum, *God and Evil*, 65.

14. Birnbaum, *God and Evil*, 61.

15. Birnbaum avers that by eating the apple of knowledge, Eve and Adam did not commit a crime (sin) as the Christian tradition (and parts of the Jewish tradition) assert. On the contrary they "contravened a caution," which is a crucial step below "sin." Birnbaum, *God and Evil*, 90.

16. Birnbaum, *God and Evil*, 77–78.

17. For a discussion of the depressive position, see Robert Hinshelwood, *A Dictionary of Kleinian Thought* (London: Free Association Books, 1991), 138–55.

18. Adults may blind themselves to the quest for absolute power, but children readily see it, for it is the gist of fairy tales and pantomimes. They love a well-played villain.

19. Menachem Mendel Schneersohn, *Week in Review,* vol. 9, no. 18, January 31, 1998.

20. Ezekiel 29:3. *Zohar*, 11:34a, quoted by Menachem Mendel Schneersohn, *Week in Review*, vol. 9, no. 18, p. 4.

21. Menachem Mendel Schneersohn, *Week in Review*, vol. 9, no. 18, p. 7.

22. Schneur Zalman of Liadi, *Likutei Amarim: Tanya.* Bilingual ed., trans. N. Mindel (1797; Brooklyn, N.Y.: Kehot, 1984), chaps. 17–19.

23. Joseph Berke will be exploring this condition in greater detail in a forthcoming paper on "Gratitude and Grateitude." See also Melanie Klein, *Envy and Gratitude* (New York: Delta, 1957).

24. Donald W. Winnicott, "Ego Distortion in Terms of True and False Self," in *The Maturational Processes and the Facilitating Environment* (1960b; London: Hogarth Press, 1972), 45.

25. Herbert Rosenfeld, "A Clinical Approach to the Psychoanalytic Theory of the Life and Death Instincts: An Investigation into the Aggressive Aspects of Narcissism," *International Journal of Psycho-Analysis* 52 (1971): 169–78.
26. Victor Hugo, *Les Miserables* (New York: Washington Square Press, 1977).
27. Sanford Drob, *Symbols of the Kabbalah: Philosophical and Psychological Perspectives* (Northvale, N.J.: Aronson, 2000a), 346.
28. Elaine Pagels, *The Origin of Satan* (New York: Random House, 1995), 120. 'Demon' means knowledge in Greek. See Carl Sagan, *The Demon-Haunted World* (New York: Ballantine, 1996), 116–18.
29. Zechariah 3:1–2, Job 1:2, 1 Chronicles 21:1.
30. Talmud Bava Bathra 16a.
31. Pagels, *Origin of Satan*, 149–53.
32. Discussed at length in Joseph Berke, *The Tyranny of Malice: Exploring the Dark Side of Character and Culture* (New York: Simon & Schuster, 1988), 250–51. In Jewish thought these 'leaders' and their regimes are the embodiments of Amalek, the paradigm of evil, rebel against God and source of every kind of deceit, treachery and destructiveness. Their descendants are identified with Haman (Book of Esther), Rome (Edomites) and Hitler (Nazi Germany). The Amalekites are considered to be the hereditary enemies of Israel. See Simon Jacobson, "A Cup of Vinegar," *Meaningful Life* 12(49) (2001): 1–4.
33. Baal Shem Tov (1698–1760). Discussed in Aryeh Kaplan, *Chassidic Masters and Their Teachings* (New York: Moznaim, 1984), 95.
34. Drob, *Symbols*, 333–34.
35. Drob relates this process of purification to the way that the Godhead is said (according to the *Zohar*) to be purged of evil by "cutting the hairs containing sparks from the *botzina di kardinuta* (Lamp of Darkness) on the head of Primordial Man." Drob, *Symbols*, 334.
36. Drob, *Symbols*, 347.
37. Kaplan, *Chassidic Masters*, 92.
38. Genesis 1:4. Aryeh Kaplan, *Living Torah*, 3.
39. Kaplan, *Chassidic Masters*, 97.
40. Sigmund Freud, 1910a, "The Antithetical Meaning of Primary Words," in *Standard Edition*, ed. James Strachey, vol. 11.
41. Joseph Berke and Stanley Schneider, "Antithetical Meanings of 'the Breast,'" *International Journal of Psycho-Analysis* 75 (1994): 491–98.
42. Gafni, "Shattered Vessels," 17. Gafni points out that "we need to befriend our *rah* to reveal our light."
43. Isaac Mosezson, *The Word: The Dictionary that Reveals the Hebrew Source of English* (New York: Shapolsky, 1989).
44. Adin Steinsaltz, *The Strife of the Spirit* (Northvale, N.J.: Aronson, 1988a).
45. Kaplan, *Chassidic Masters*, 94.
46. Bruno Bettelheim argues this point, in particular, in *Freud and Man's Soul* (London: Chatto & Windus/Hogarth Press, 1983), 49, 64.
47. Carl Jung, *Memories, Dreams, Reflections* (New York: Pantheon, 1963).

48. This is a unique mental health facility, founded by Joseph Berke and others, in 1973. See Joseph Berke et al., eds., *Beyond Madness: Psychosocial Interventions in Psychosis* (London: Jessica Kingsley, 2002). Also see the website www.arbourscentre.org.uk.

49. Joseph Berke, *Tyranny*, 283–84.

50. Joseph Berke, *Tyranny*, 284.

51. Joseph Berke, *Tyranny*, 284.

Chapter Five

The Container and the Contained

Whether 'evil' is illusory, as Kabbalists assert, or a basic reality, as psychoanalysts might reply, a sudden shattering of the fabric of existence is a common feature of their discussions. Thus Kabbalists, at least from the time of Isaac Luria (the Ari), have contemplated upon the *Shvirat HaKelim,* the breaking of the vessels. This occurred at the time at the creation of the universe when these vessels could not hold or contain the Divine radiance. The result was a multitude of shards or *klipot*, which are directly related to a state of disconnection from the Transcendent and the emergence of the *yetzer ha'rah* (the evil inclination). Concomitantly, psychoanalysts from Sigmund Freud through Wilfred Bion have described the dire consequences of intolerable psychic pressures. The mind 'blows apart' and little bits of fear and hatred ('beta elements') spew all over people and things.[1]

Both outcomes stem from a failure of containment, from vessels, from containers that cannot cope with whatever they had to contain, whether an excess of light or feelings or thoughts. According to the tradition, the container and its contents were initially one, the Divine radiance. Subsequently, as the Ari deduced, God concealed or contracted himself in such a way that His radiance created vessels from condensations of Himself. These held and gave shape to this radiance. We have alluded to a similar process when we referred to physicists who can create flasks of energy in order to contain bundles of energy (plasmas). Then there was a third state of differentiation whereby the vessels could interact between themselves and within themselves. This is the level of the *partzufim,* or 'archetypal personae,' which, as we shall soon detail, are equivalent to the attainment of 'whole object' relationships.

It appears that the mind goes through a similar period of development whereby at birth it is one with the body. Then somatic experiences rapidly differentiate as unconscious phantasies.[2] These mental representations of instincts, in turn, contribute to the construction of the tripartite structure of the mind, the ego, id and superego, by the mental mechanisms of projection and introjection. As with the creation of the *sefirot*, we can see here that psychic contents contribute to the construction of the psychic container.

Clearly, a rudimentary consciousness contributes to the development of mental boundaries, or a psychic skin.[3] This 'psychic skin' may be too thin or too thick or the phantasies that have helped to construct it may be too intense. Then the structure itself may split apart, only to be followed by further attempts to reconstitute itself.[4]

As the infant matures, so do his phantasies. These are not just to do with instinctive processes, but memories, perceptions and thoughts about actual events, internal as in dreams, or external as in relationships. Klein described these mental events as internal objects (emotionally charged images), as opposed to actual people and happenings, which are external objects.[5] The internal objects contribute to the creation of an internal object world of increasing sophistication. They also relate to external objects, first as things to be used or discarded (part objects) and secondly as people to be appreciated in their own right (that is, whole objects).

Depending on the responsiveness of the external environment, or not,[6] and how facilitating it is, or not,[7] and depending on the degree of intrinsic love or aggression,[8] these internal and external relationships will flourish or not. If these do flourish, they will allow the individual to construct worlds within worlds within worlds. We refer to a highly complex symbolic elaboration of what goes on in internal and external lives, as well as to the connections between them.

Similarly, every *sefira* includes within itself the ten other *sefirot*. Hence each vessel comprises and contains ten other vessels that comprise and contain ten other vessels and so on. This demonstrates that each *sefira* is both an infinite array of dynamic relations and a container of such relations.

The *sefira* is a container as well as the containing process. Evidently, the essential characteristic that allows the *sefirot* to function as a container of spiritual energies, and to convey these energies from the highest supernal realms to the lower incarnate worlds, is their capacity for receiving and giving. This allows the *sefirot* to engage in extended exchanges with each other, and ultimately with man.

It is remarkable that current psychoanalytic theory says the same thing about man's ability to serve as a container of his thoughts and feelings. We refer to 'object relations theory' as developed by Melanie Klein, Ronald Fairbairn, Donald Winnicott, Wilfred Bion and others, which points out that humans are inherently 'object seeking' to ensure their survival, development and maturation. In other words they don't just need, but crave relationships with each other in order to exist physically, mentally and emotionally. People are social beings. Such socializing allows them to contain themselves, to create themselves, and to construct reality itself. Conversely, a failure of containment, as we shall discuss in due course, will jeopardize all of these achievements.

Psychoanalysis considers this issue in two ways: 'holding' and 'containing.' The former was elaborated by Donald Winnicott, while the latter was advanced by Wilfred Bion. Both concepts are interrelated and ultimately try to address the same phenomena. But to begin they focus on different aspects of the problem.

Winnicott arrived at his theory of 'holding' during the course of exploring the parent-infant relationship.[9] He saw that at birth the mother and infant were bound together as a single unit, 'two in one.' Later they established a shared reality where they where both could exist as separate entities, before a third stage was reached when they could live independently. Winnicott contended:

> At first the individual is not the unit. As perceived from outside the unit is an environment-individual set-up. The outsider knows that the individual psyche can only start in a certain setting. In this setting the individual can gradually come to create a personal environment.[10]

> . . . of every individual who has reached to the stage of being a unit (with a limiting membrane and an outside and an inside) it can be said that there is an *inner reality* to that individual, an inner world which can be rich or poor and can be at peace or in a state of war.[11]

'Holding' is a very evocative word. It immediately conjures up an image of a mother holding a baby. Similarly we can speak of 'holding something up,' like the leg of a chair when it is glued back together and can stand on its own. But Winnicott meant more than basic support. His conceptualization denoted the total provision of physical and psychological care, both by the mother and by the whole family and social and material environment. These comprise all the spheres in which a child grows up, and from which he can construct his inner and outer worlds. The developmental aim is for the child to establish a thinking mind, a feeling heart, and a separate sense of self. Then he can relate as one whole person to other whole persons as part of a dynamic array of family, social and professional relationships.

Bion, on the other hand, concentrated on the intrapsychic processes and psychic structures that resulted from 'good' and 'bad' mothering, or, as he called it, 'containing.'[12] This is a kindred term to the one Winnicott used, but carries an important difference. 'Holding' suggests support coming from outside oneself, while 'containing' or 'containment' sets out the idea of a 'container,' or a vessel that encompasses or 'holds' or gives support from within itself.

Bion believed that at birth infants have an innate preconception and expectation of the breast.[13] By breast he did not just mean part of a mother's body, but a nurturing relationship. We would say that this includes mother's, and for that matter, father's willingness to feed, relieve pain and provide adequate stimulation.

The idea of an inborn disposition toward nurturing is very close to the Kabbalistic view that people carry within themselves sparks of the Divine. In this regard, Kabbalists note that everyone has an animal soul (*Nefesh B'haimit*) and a Godly soul (*Nefesh Elokit*). The animal soul is akin to the instinctual self or basic oral impulses to which Bion was referring. The Godly soul is a carrier of the sparks that impel a person toward spiritual experience. Although psychoanalysis remains ambivalent about transcendent perspectives, the presumption of sparks and dispositions accords with basic psychoanalytic principles and further illustrates the intriguing parallels between these two domains.

According to Bion, when an infant is hungry and the hunger is satisfied, then his expectations of feeding coincide with the actuality of being fed. This exchange, in turn, arouses a concept of nurturing, a sense of 'the good breast,' and feelings of satisfaction, which he is able to keep in and to himself. Bion's formulation suggests that the preconception of the breast is like an idea-in-waiting or an unperceived perception that exists in a state of potentiality.

The actual breast is the realization. Put together this realization with the preconception, and you get an actualized concept: 'breast,' 'feeding,' 'nurturing,' and so forth. This 'event' accomplishes several tasks, each of great importance. It not only allows for the creating of a concept, and for the storing or containing of this concept, but it also precipitates the process of conceptualization, which is akin to creating a mind or container in which the concepts will reside. In this analogy the process of conceptualization can be compared to an energy flask or vessel that both creates and contains concepts, the packets of bundled energy. Here Bion is demonstrating, like Winnicott, that the capacity for an interpersonal relationship, such as between an infant and mother, lies in the creation of both a psychic container and the contents of the container, that is, the contained.

This process has been described very well by Hanna Segal, a close colleague of Bion. Segal comments on what happens during a good mother-child relationship:

> When an infant has an intolerable anxiety, he deals with it by projecting it into the mother. The mother's response is to acknowledge this anxiety and do what-

> ever is necessary to relieve the infant's distress. The infant's perception is that he has projected something intolerable into his object, but the object was capable of containing it and dealing with it. He can then reintroject not only the original anxiety, but an anxiety modified by having been contained. He also reintrojects an object capable of containing and dealing with anxiety. The containment of the anxiety by an internal object capable of understanding is the beginning of mental stability.[14]

But what happens if an anxious infant is not comforted, or a hungry one is not fed? In Bion's terminology, what happens if a preconception does not meet a realization? Then you have the mating of a preconception with a frustration. This leads to a notion of 'no-breast-inside' or 'bad breast,' which includes an awareness of hunger, frustration and 'mother-absent.' This raises the question, can a 'no-breast' be inside an emptiness? It seems that 'emptiness' is a metaphor that stands for various degrees of anxiety and pain. Bion said that such events can stimulate the psyche to develop thoughts and thinking, or can turn it into a projector of unwanted experiences.

Before we proceed, it is worth mentioning that Bion does not believe that a 'concept' is a 'thought.' For him, a thought is more than a delineated awareness of something pleasant. It is a painful mental construct, or as he would say, 'a bad internal (mental) object' that either can make the thinking apparatus proliferate in order to tolerate itself, or collapse into concrete thinking. Then the mind does not distinguish between a thought and a physical object like urine or feces.

Of course, what transpires depends on the human environment. If the mothering is kind and generally available, then the infant will be more inclined to expand his thinking self and contain his upsets. If this is not the case, then the infant will use his mind like a hypertrophied intestinal tract in order to evacuate noxious experiences into others. This is a physicalized form of thinking like explosive vomiting or diarrhea. Bion called it projective identification.

Projective identification is both a mental mechanism and an interpersonal transaction. The mechanism involves a change in perception, whereby the infant denies his upset and forcefully attributes it to another person, thereby ridding himself of hated sensations. The transaction involves an action such as crying or screaming that serves to arouse the unwanted feelings in others. The result is a primitive form of communication whereby one person, the infant or projector, is able to evoke his experiences in another person, the parent or target. In addition, projective identification can be a means of avoiding separation (the two parties being bound together by a common state of mind), control (possession of another's being) or envious evacuation (by filling the object with concretized, hateful sensations).

This is not the place to go into an extended discussion of projective identification. Suffice to say that it is also a normal and necessary means of nonverbal communication. Projective identification is the operative mechanism of the transference relationship (when one sees and treats others as important figures in one's past or as aspects of oneself). Furthermore, it is the basis of the counter-transference relationship (when one unconsciously takes into oneself another's thoughts and emotions, and then feels and acts like the other). Transference and counter-transference occur during the course of every psychoanalytic relationship, but are also extensive aspects of everyday human exchanges.

Kabbalists would quickly recognize the process of projective identification under the rubric of *gilgul*, the transmigrations of souls. A similar notion first appeared in the *Bahir* (*Book of Illumination*), a formative text that was published in the twelfth century.[15] It subsequently was elaborated upon by Kabbalists in Gerona, Spain and elsewhere who spoke of "the concept of *ibbur*,"[16] which stood for impregnation. Their view was that the soul of another entered into a person during pregnancy or at the time of his birth. In the *Bahir* it is stated that a soul can transmigrate for a thousand generations. However, later Spanish Kabbalists believed that this could happen no more than three times. Interestingly, in the philosophic literature of the fourteenth century, the expression *ha'atakah,* which means displacement, was generally used in place of *gilgul*. But the word can also be translated as 'transference.'

During this period the concept of *ibbur* was refined and generally distinguished from that of *gilgul. Ibbur* indicates the entry of another soul into a person at any time of his life, not just before or at birth. Usually this soul would only dwell inside another for a limited period of time in order to accomplish a particular task. This definition is closer to what we would recognize as projective identification. Both transactions denote possession, and a transformation of the possessed into someone or something other than what he is. Here we are illustrating a Kabbalistic consideration of projective identification or *ibbur* from the point of view of the object.

However, from the point of view of the subject, the most serious consequences of the excessive use of projective identification are that the mind of an infant (or adult) who relies on it becomes increasingly impoverished and weak. It doesn't want, nor is it able to contain, what Bion called 'beta-elements,' which are raw, concrete bits of hated sensations and feelings.[17] Then this mind or self loses its containing function as well as its contents, and remains replete with emptiness. Unlike what takes place with the *sefirot* at the level of *nekudim* (spots or points), a primitive level where they receive and cannot give, here the self offloads but cannot receive. But the effect is similar. The impoverished self becomes extremely vulnerable to any further psychic or social pressures.[18]

We have dwelled at some length on the work of Winnicott and Bion because there are so many points of similarity between their ideas and related concepts in Kabbalah. Both emphasize the relationship between the subject and object and the content and their transactions. In our various psychoanalytic examples, the subject has been referred to as the mind or self or infant; the content as concepts and emotions; and the object as the vessel, or again as the mind or self or parent, which holds these contents. Although it is easy to deploy a common vocabulary to describe what holds things (a 'container') and what is held (the 'contained'), it is more difficult to find a word to describe the subject or originator of the containing process. The 'container-seeker' is a neologism and a somewhat tortuous term that at least has the merit of maintaining a common root and demonstrating the purpose of the interaction. So we shall use it to describe the subject, or whoever initiates the containing process.

The question is, can the subject or container-seeker put things into containers freely, or is there a reciprocity about this process that necessitates a particular kind of container for an exchange to take place? Bion and Winnicott have addressed this question, for they both note that for holding or containing to take place, there has to be a suitable container. In their eyes, this is 'a good-enough mother.'

As for projecting 'beta-elements,' Bion points out that there is something about the object that attracts the projective process, including, for example, 'the narcissistic mother,' who remains preoccupied with herself at the expense of her children. Certainly, among adults there are people who, by their voice or mannerisms, seem predisposed to attract others' evacuations or attempts to possess them.

Conversely Winnicott describes the mother, that is, the container, who can induce changes in her child, or as we put it, the container-seeker, by her capacity to survive his hatred. In so doing, the child feels less pressure to evacuate his mind, and learns to use his mother as a helpful partner in the containing process, so he too can become a container, and not an evacuator.[19]

Gedaliah Fleer, who lectures and writes extensively on Kabbalah, notes that the *sefirotic* vessels have a predisposition to contain a particular kind of radiance, and that this predisposition accounts for the spiritual flux that they can or cannot contain.[20] Such a perspective coincides with the observations of Bion and Winnicott. The container and the contained have special qualities that draw them to each other. So the container may attract the contained, but the converse is also true. The contents, whether emotions or radiances, also affect the vessels that hold them.

Fleer explains that at the time of the breaking of the vessels (*Shvirat HaKelim*), the Divine light (the *Ohr*) entered the vessels too quickly and with too much force. Consequently, they fragmented. But since the vessels were touched by the light (their contents) for a brief moment, part of the light clung to the shattered shards or pieces of the vessels. Thus, when these shards fell through the chain of worlds from *Atzilut* to *Beriyah,* they fell to a lower level than the light that they had previously contained. This happened because, metaphorically speaking, the vessels had a greater physical presence than the light. Therefore, when the vessels were reconstructed, they could never retrieve the original light, which remained in a higher (more spiritually elevated) world. However, they did retain a predisposition or longing for their original contents, since bits of the original light clung to them, and remained, even to the most minuscule extent, inside them. Fleer concludes that if the vessel is wholly other than the light it is supposed to contain—that is, if it does not possess clinging or embedded remnants—then it can never really contain that particular light. It can only do so if the predisposition or potentiality towards these contents exists. Or to put it another way, the secret of the 'vacated space' is that it bears the imprint of God's presence.

There is a further factor. The vessels 'feel' empty because the light they 'want' is somewhere else. That light is in a higher world, because it fell less far than the vessels that had contained it. For example, according to Kabbalah, when *Chesed* (the *sefira* identified with kindness) in the world of *Atzilut* was shattered, the original light fell to the level of *Yesod* (the *sefira* identified with foundation). However, the fragments of *Chesed* fell out of *Atzilut* and into the lower world of *Beriyah*. There it was reconstituted as *Binah* (the *sefira* identified with understanding). Yet, its original light was far away in *Atzilut*. This is the second reason for the longing. The first had to do with clinging traces, and the second had to do with spiritual distance.

The Kabbalistic account of breaking, falling and returning, but never totally finding, is analogous to the human drama of loss, separation and searching for someone or something that one knew but can never find or replace. This is an experience that extends from the heart, hence the Hasidic expression, *HaLev Mayvin*: "the heart understands." What does it understand? It understands that it once held powerful feelings—for example, love for a parent, child, friend or spouse, someone no longer close at hand. Maybe this heart broke, under the pressure of parting, and the love scattered as the vessel shattered. What remained? A few lingering traces: an aroma, a touch, a certain look, a piquant voice, embedded in memory, like a dream, real, but impossible to grasp.

Later, when this heart revives, it can hold love once again, but too often at a lower level, in a different context. A good analogy is a man transfixed by fleeting looks and sounds, who is continually searching for the love of his life. He sleeps with many women, he has many marriages, but never finds fulfillment. The love he seeks is always elsewhere beyond his grasp, while his yearnings remain stuck in a heart and mind that can't reach the object he wants to embrace. The same is true for a woman pursuing her soul mate.

Perhaps the tragedy, but certainly the paradox, of this dilemma is that these people, the container-seekers, may, in the end, find only others who cannot cope with their passions, as if they were internally programmed to respond to their narcissistic shadows, that is, to non-containing vessels. Such vessels permeate the history of mother-child relationships, at the period after birth, but before differentiation can take place. Then either the maternal container shatters from severe inner emotional pressure (a state that often manifests as a postpartum crisis) or the infant is unable to restrain his own powerful feelings, leaving him vulnerable to the vagaries of frustration and deprivation.

Bion, Berke and others have shown that the net result can be overwhelming envy, experienced as a world-destroying hatred, on the part of the infant toward the parents, or the parents toward their child.[21] A fairy tale like 'Snow White' or a myth like 'Oedipus Rex' are commentaries on the extreme aggression that lies just beneath the surface of our conscious thoughts.[22] Although most people don't act upon their violent impulses, they often collapse when confronted by mirror images of them, whether these dangerous images erupt from within themselves, or from without, as exemplified by primeval fears of the *ayin ha'rah*, the evil eye.

Then the mind stops being a receptacle for its impulses or thoughts and literally blows apart. Freud touched upon the blown mind during his discussion of dissociative states. Melanie Klein was more explicit in her description of schizoid mechanisms or splitting (of the ego) as a defense against envy, which she related to 'Thanatos,' the death impulse.[23] Bion was most explicit by delineating minds that fragment in the face of aggressive forces they cannot contain. This leads to extreme fears of annihilation and can presage a psychotic breakdown.[24] Heinz Kohut and Donald Winnicott have described comparable states under the rubric of 'disintegration anxiety' and 'annihilation anxiety,' respectively.[25]

The fragmented, disintegrated or annihilated mind, as well as the reasons for it, hold a surprising similarity to the Kabbalistic concept of the *Shvirat HaKelim.* In fact, the psychoanalytic views on fragmentation coincide with a fundamental perspective on the breaking of the vessels. One of the most famous allusions to this process was described in the beginning of the book of Genesis:

> The earth was without form (*tohu*) and empty (*bohu*), with darkness on the face of the depths (*tehom*).[26]

Aryeh Kaplan explains in *Innerspace* that the term *tohu* also means chaos.[27] In addition, *tohu* is related to *tehom,* which can be read as *tohu-m*, a word that indicates the 'depths' from which the original chaos of creation emerged. Kaplan points out that by rearranging the Hebrew letters of *tehom* (*THM*), you get *HaMavet* (*HMT*), which means 'death.' He concludes that *tohu* is the state that leads to the shattering of the vessels.

But *bohu*, which follows, has to do with the reconstitution of the vessels, because *bohu* can be read as two syllables, *bo* and *hu*. This literally means, 'it is in it.' Therefore, *bohu* refers to vessels that can hold light. Clearly, the process of *sefirotic* creation-shattering-reconstitution is comparable to the Kleinian idea of psychic creation-fragmentation-reparation. Perhaps it is not insignificant that the Chinese word for chaos, *luan,* also means 'envy.'

The Talmud tells of four great scholars who engaged in mystical contemplation ('entered the garden'): Ben Azzai, Ben Zoma, Elisha ben Avuyah and Rabbi Akiva. Of them all, Rabbi Akiva was the greatest. Before the four began their journey (traversing the highest states of mind), Rabbi Akiva warned them not to get stuck or distracted by what they saw. Nonetheless, Ben Azzai gazed and died, Ben Zoma went mad and Elisha ben Avuyah became an apostate. Only Rabbi Akiva entered and departed unhurt.[28]

The story is a parable about psychic containment and the consequence of contemplation that reaches levels that cannot be contained (advanced states of being). Three minds shatter: one dies (a total fragmentation), one 'goes off the rails' (and by implication, never gets back on) and the third gives up his mind (to others). But Rabbi Akiva remains safe, and his greatness grows, because he is able to encompass what he experienced (successfully assimilate mystical states of Divine connection and revelation).

Likewise, we have previously written about the personal struggles of one of the great Rabbinic figures who straddled the nineteenth and twentieth centuries, the fifth Lubavitcher Rebbe, Rabbi Shalom Dov Ber (the RaSHaB).[29] In 1903 the Rebbe left Russia and traveled to Vienna where he stayed for three months with his son Joseph Yitzhak (who eventually became the sixth Lubavitcher Rebbe). At that time the RaSHaB was forty-two years old and his son was twenty-two.

For some years the RaSHaB had been under great strain. He had suffered constant attacks on himself and his family by the Czarist police. And the Rebbe and his son had spent several periods in jail, often the result of denunciations by non-religious, assimilationist Jews. These same people (known as the '*Maskilim,*' adherents of secularism) had been trying, with some success, to undermine his work in establishing *Yeshiva Tomchei Temimim* (a center of Hasidic learning) in the town of Lubavitch (after which his followers were identified.)

These were external factors. There were also internal problems. Although the RaSHaB was a renowned Hasidic leader and a person of tremendous spiritual and intellectual accomplishment (known as the 'Maimonides' of his generation), he had become very dissatisfied with himself, because he didn't think he was living according to his own standards. In this vein, the Rebbe remarked to his son that he didn't understand even one concept in *Hasidut* (Hasidic thought) and found it difficult to concentrate on anything. His wife had remarked that he was very 'low in spirits.'

Around this time, the Rebbe heard about 'the famous Dr. Freud' and decided to seek a consultation with him. His son, Joseph Yitzhak, came with him. After listening to the Rebbe for some time, Freud concluded:

> Your head comprehends things your heart is unable to contain; your heart cannot assimilate what your mind comprehends.[30]

The word Freud used in German/Yiddish was *fartroght,* meaning 'to carry or to bear' (German: *fertragen*, 'to endure') or 'to hold or contain.' So the diagnosis can also be translated as "The head grasps what the heart cannot carry/bear," or "The head grasps what the heart cannot contain/endure."[31] Here Freud was describing a state of dissociation, presumably the result of the many pressures that the Rebbe had had to endure, which he felt were almost beyond endurance. Later we shall relate the advice that Freud gave the Rebbe, which may have helped him to reconstitute himself, a process known in Kabbalah as *tikkun*. Indeed, within a short time after seeing Freud, the RaSHaB began to write some of his greatest works.

The various examples we have cited denote a particular relationship between the vessel or container and its contents. For one reason or the other, the container may become too weak or its contents may become too strong, or there may be a combination of these two conditions. In consequence the container can no longer do its job and it fragments. As we have discussed, in Kabbalah this event is called the *Shvirat HaKelim,* the breaking of the vessels, while psychologically it is the moment when 'the mind blows' or the self falls apart.

However, there exists an alternative and much more constructive kind of relationship between the container and the contained: the reversal of roles. Then the container becomes the contents, and the contents become the vessel or container. The earlier quote in this chapter by Hanna Segal provides an excellent example of this process as a basic psychological transaction.

Intrapsychic reversal involves the projection (evacuation) of unwanted thoughts or feelings (contents) and their reintrojection (being taken back) in a modified form. As Segal points out, the reintrojection invariably includes an idea of the containing person (into whom the initial thoughts or feelings were projected), and which itself becomes a part of the modifications. These modifications may then be projected and reintrojected several times. The net result is that the person concerned, such as an infant or child or distressed adult, contains within himself a vessel that consists of multiple projections and reintrojections, a myriad of modified anxieties that themselves can serve as containers for future fears. The original container, such as a mother's mind, is always reintrojected or taken back, too. It not only merges with but actually becomes incorporated within modified, less toxic tensions. That is why we can say that the container (mind) has become the contained. At the same time, the modified anxieties, the prior contents, have become vessels that can hold further upsets, as well as for the containing process itself. The latter may then be symbolized, for example, by a kind heart or loving embrace.

These transactions mostly occur on an unconscious basis. But there are many examples of role reversal that occur with partial or full awareness on the part of the subject or container-seeker. Teenagers, for example, love to offload their insecurities on and into the mantle of powerful movie or sport or pop stars. Here we are not just referring to covert mechanisms of defense, 'identification with the aggressor,' as Anna Freud described.[32] But we refer to the almost endless array of conscious choices that people make to wear the strength and power of others. Then as Segal might show, hurt feelings get projected, strong identities get introjected, and after several steps, the feelings become the container, and their modifying vessels, the contained.

All this, of course, is context dependent. In the mother-child example we cited, the context is a maternal mind, able and willing to bear her child's anguish. In another situation, we refer to charisma-laden personalities who trade a willingness to be worn, like so many garments, in return for fame and fortune.

Personality or character traits represent different aspects of the self. People wear them like suits or dresses, and they often change according to fashion. For example, the 'hysterical character,' which was so fashionable during Freud's era, is less noticeable today, but the 'borderline personality' is much more prevalent. This confirms, as we have said, that character traits are the garments of the self.

In Hasidic teachings the garments of the soul are thought, speech and action. As Adin Steinsaltz points out, the term 'garments' signifies that which covers and conceals as well as that which expresses or reveals itself to the outside world.[33] It follows that 'thought' is the inner garment that 'reveals' the soul to a thinking person. When put into words, speech is the outer expression of such thoughts, and action is the manifestation of both thought and speech, the way the soul reveals itself in and through the physical world. But to begin, there is thought. As we discussed in our earlier chapter "The Self and the Soul," these garments also represent different aspects of a person's personality. So what Hasidut terms the garments (*levushim*) of the soul clearly delineate the self as well.

Thought is one of the basic 'self-garments' that originates in the mind or intellect. The first Lubavitcher Rebbe (the Alter Rebbe) wrote in the *Tanya* that when a person's intellect understands an idea, it also encompasses it. Then the concept is "grasped, enveloped and enclothed within that intellect which conceived and comprehended it."[34]

Later he came to a further conclusion. After the mind (the subject) grasps the concept, then the concept (the object) grasps the mind! Thus, the knower becomes the known, and the known becomes the knower. The context for this discussion has to do with man's attempt to apprehend God. Essentially the Alter Rebbe has described the reversal of roles as part of the process by which a person can grasp the ungraspable, God, and be grasped by Him. This is a basic thrust of Kabbalah, the need, the wish, to be close to God.

Thus Kabbalah is a manual, a handbook for discerning the Will and Wisdom of *El Shadi*, which is another name for God. The name *Shadi* literally means 'my breast,' and it refers to the primary source of everything. The Torah states that a Jew can become one with his source by carrying out the 613 *Mitzvot* (which means 'commandments' but can also be translated as 'connections'). They are set forth in the Old Testament (the written law) and in the Talmud (the oral law).

For observant Jews, these 613 *Mitzvot* are also garments. They clothe the Godly soul, the *Nefesh Elokit*, just as thought, speech and action enwrap the human soul, and as personality traits encompass the self. A person can use these garments to discover himself or to entrap himself; to liberate his life or to destroy it, as did Ben Azzai, Ben Zoma and Elisha ben Avuyah. They were too taken by abstract meditation and lost the focus provided by the garments of Torah, as *Hasidut* would recognize.

Steinsaltz reflects that learning about one's source involves far more than utilizing words. It is a union of minds, a mutual encompassing process by which Wisdom becomes a part of the thinker's mind and envelopes it. Concomitantly, the mind can become 'a divine mansion' when it comprehends, and thereby encloses, even the tiniest fragment of supernal Will. All this is very similar to the exchanges that Segal and Bion described. The containing-self becomes the contained, just as the contained becomes the containing-self. Through multiple reversals, the mind of the parent becomes a part of the mind of the infant, which becomes a part of the mind of the parent, and so on. Then the feelings and thoughts, the knowledge and desires of each, become a part of and support to the other.

Reversal, of course, is an ongoing process, a dynamic relationship between two bodies, parts, elements, call them what you will. At any moment one part contains the other, and vice versa. But there is a level of containment where the shifting back and forth between the vessel and its contents does not take place. The container simply contains. This is the level that Rabbi Akiva attained when he 'entered the garden.' And because he was able to contain his experiences and maintain this containment, his focus did not waver and he was able to ascend higher and higher through more and more advanced states of contemplation.

In Kabbalah, indeed, in all Jewish thinking, God is the ultimate container. God contains everything, but nothing can contain God. As Aryeh Kaplan narrates, this has to be the case because God is beyond all description. The moment you try to delineate God with words, you encompass what you are trying to delineate, and whatever that is, it is not God. Kaplan adds that we can certainly talk about God, but only by referring to our relationship with Him, or to God's relationship with man. We can never talk directly about God, Himself.

God is the Container of Containers, or, as modern mathematics describes, the 'set' that incorporates all sets but itself cannot be incorporated by any other set. As a basic prayer incants, "He knows the inclination of all creatures . . . He contains them all."[35]

Although we cannot describe God, Kabbalists can and do elucidate the characteristics or qualities of God, which we know as the *sefirot*. In the same way, it is possible to formulate certain qualities of the containing process and containment. One of the most important of these is the quality of atonement. This is the process of realigning the vessel with its contents. This denotes a situation whereby a vessel and its contents, the container and the contained, become in tune with each other.

We have already touched on this issue when we considered the 'need' of the container and contained to share some feature that draws them to each other. Thus the *sefirot* need previously embedded sparks to be able to hold a particular radiance, while people require prior love in order to activate new love. One might say that such vessels have retuning capacities, which allow them to retune themselves to certain radiances or feelings.

The authors still remember when radios had condensers attached to a knob that you turned to tune in certain stations. Nowadays digital circuits accomplish the same task. In either case a container-seeker (the listener) attunes to its object (music, for example).

Psychoanalysts call this the process of 'attunement.' This is a way of tuning into the thoughts, feelings, and, indeed, the whole gamut of inner conflicts felt by patients. It is an intense sensitivity which is also known as 'listening with the third ear.'[36] Eventually atonement can lead to at-one-ment, a state where the container and the contained are at one with each other, not merged, but where thinking and feeling align in the same direction. The experience is akin to the state of 'reverie,' which Bion believed was especially propitious for the psychic containment of one person by another.

Attunement is the opposite of splitting, fragmentation or dissociation. As we have seen, it is the moment when "my emotions agree with what my mind knows." In Kabbalah a quasi *sefira* designates this moment, the *sefira* termed *Da'at*. *Da'at* is often translated as 'knowledge,' although it means more than knowledge and is a quasi *sefira* because it is usually linked with *Keter* or crown, the preeminent of the ten *sefirot* that comprise the 'Tree of Life.' When this 'Tree' or constellation of *sefirot* includes *Keter* (Divine Will), then *Da'at* (which could comprise an 11th *sefira*) does not appear, or is indicated by a broken circle of dots below and between *Chochmah* and *Binah*. On the other hand, when Kabbalists do not refer to *Keter* on the 'Tree,' because *keter* is beyond human comprehension, then *Da'at* is included. Indeed, *Da'at* is the unifying principle that links together *Chochmah* and *Binah*, wisdom and understanding.

Da'at is an attunement that potentiates *Chochmah* and *Binah* and leads to a deep, intimate appreciation and knowledge about things. On a physical plane, for example, a person may know all about cigarettes, lung cancer and the effects of tobacco on the body. Still he may remain emotionally detached from the implications of this knowledge and continue to be a heavy smoker. But when his heart (emotions) coincides with what his mind (intellect) perceives, and he stops smoking, then he has attained *Da'at*.

On a spiritual plane *Da'at* involves multiple unifications of the *sefirot*. We have already explained that *Chochmah* and *Binah* are *partzufim* (anthropomorphized representations) representing *abba* and *ima*, father and mother. So *Da'at* is the unifying force between father and mother, the intimate knowledge that potentiates creation. This coincides with the original unification described in the Bible: "Adam knew Eve." Here *Da'at* or knowledge is an analogue of sexual union between a man and woman, the complete intertwining of selves. Similarly on an informational level, *Da'at* denotes the moment when the knower and known become a part of each other, joined and conjoined. Such conjoining has been described in diverse traditions. To cite but one, Eugene Herrigel in his book *Zen and the Art of Archery* delineates that moment when the archer, the arrow-in-flight and the target are one.[37] Although he did not use the term, that moment is *Da'at*.

Letter transformations reveal the innermost essence of this quasi *sefira* from another angle. Many Kabbalists assert that if you take the Hebrew letters of *Da'at*, and change them around, you get *aydoot* (AyDT), or 'witness.'

According to Jewish law, there always have to be two witnesses to substantiate testimony. Why two? Because an accurate testimony involves both intellect and feeling. When your mind (*Chochmah*) and your heart (*Binah*) are consistent with each other, that testimony or reality is true and consistent, without dissociation.

But *Da'at* can also mean differentiation or distinction as well as the ability to differentiate and distinguish one thing from another. How is this possible, since *Da'at* denotes unification? Really they are two aspects of the same coin. The act of unification demands prior differences—Adam and Eve, arrow and target, *Chochmah* and *Binah.* But as mathematicians point out, in order to 'know' distinctions, one first has to 'know' similarities. On a personal level, if a man or woman really has achieved a position of *Da'at,* if his or her heart and mind act in unison, then he or she is also in a position to differentiate what is like him or her, and what is unlike him or her. Such differentiation is also akin to containment.

We would like to conclude this discussion of the container and the contained by posing one further question: Is it possible to reach a state of being beyond containment?

In psychoanalysis the 'oceanic feeling' describes a mystical, cosmic state of being where a person feels at one with himself and the universe.[38] This experience denotes a point of conjunction between the container and the contained that lies beyond containment. Moreover, it is a way of being-in-the-world and being-beyond-the-world that links psychology and religion.

In *Civilization and Its Discontents*, however, Freud suggested that the oceanic feeling was a regression "back to an early phase of ego-feeling"[39] that recapitulated the experience of the infant at the breast. Essentially, Freud claimed that this was a pre-containing and pathological event. Since Freud's formulation, most analysts contend that the oceanic feeling is a form of psychopathology.

Andrew Samuels points out that analytical psychology describes similar experiences, but without the stigma or connotation of madness. To begin, he notes that the Jungian concept of the 'Self,' an archetypal image of man's fullest potential and internal unity, also contains what Jung called the 'God-Image.' This, in turn, is related to the experience of the 'Numinosum,' a state of transcendence where one feels totally connected to and a part of every aspect of the universe. Jung took pains to assert that such encounters with the 'God-like' were some of the most profound experiences a person could have, and were not inherently pathological.[40] Concurrently, contemporary humanistic or transpersonal psychology considers these occurrences under the rubric of 'peak experiences.'

Both the numinosic and oceanic feelings would be quite familiar to Jewish mystics, who consciously strive to achieve a state of *bitul*, or 'self-nullification.' This is comparable to ego-loss or the complete absence of egoic desires. Here 'ego' means not just pride, but any sliver of 'me-ness' or the subjective sense of self. The ability to reach such a point, to add a 'Y' to the 'I,' (the *Ani* in Hebrew), in order to achieve a state of nothingness (*ayin*), is the prerequisite for achieving an even higher state: *devekut,* or 'cleaving to God.' Various commentators have described *devekut* in terms of a merging with God, or an absolute attunement to God, or a condition of at-one-ness with the Infinite. The *Sefer Haredim*, a sixteenth-century book of spiritual teachings, sees *devekut* as "the most passionate love, [when] you are not separated from [The Infinite One] for even a moment."[41]

We can surmise that *devekut* denotes what Rabbi Akiva accomplished when he 'entered the garden.' It was the moment when he passed beyond personal containment and became at one with Him who "is all powerful and contains them all." By the same token, the fact that he had previously achieved *bitul* on the way to the 'garden' meant that he could later 'depart it' unharmed.

NOTES

1. Rafael E. López-Corvo writes: "There is no such thing as an impulse free of an object representation, therefore, even beta-elements as things-in-themselves, as the ineffable, endure the implicit presence of an object." Rafael E. López-Corvo, *The Dictionary of the Work of W. R. Bion* (London: Karnac, 2003), 45.

2. How this happens has been elaborated by Susan Isaacs in her seminal paper "On the Nature and Function of Phantasy," *International Journal of Psycho-Analysis* 29 (1948): 73–97. The spelling of the word phantasy is important. The 'ph' in phantasies refers to unconscious events. The 'f' in fantasies refers to conscious processes.

3. The importance of the skin, both as a physical boundary and a psychological boundary, has been described, in particular, by Esther Bick: "Notes on Infant Observation in Psycho-Analytic Training," *International Journal of Psycho-Analysis* 45 (1964): 558–66; "The Experience of the Skin in Early Object Relations," *International Journal of Psycho-Analysis* 49 (1968): 484–86.

4. Splitting of the ego is a defense against the extremely persecuting fears of bursting apart and annihilation. See Melanie Klein, "Notes on Some Schizoid Mechanisms," *International Journal of Psycho-Analysis* 27 (1946): 99–110.

5. Melanie Klein, "A Contribution to the Psychogenesis of Manic-Depressive States," *International Journal of Psycho-Analysis* 16 (1935): 145–74.

6. Wilfred Bion, "Attacks on Linking," *International Journal of Psycho-Analysis* 40 (1959): 308–315.

7. Donald Winnicott, "The Mentally Ill in Your Caseload," in *The Maturational Process and the Facilitating Environment* (1963; London: Hogarth Press, 1972), 223.

8. Melanie Klein, *Envy and Gratitude* (New York: Delta, 1957).

9. Donald Winnicott, "The Theory of the Parent-Infant Relationship," in *The Maturational Process and the Facilitating Environment* (1960a; London: Hogarth Press, 1972).

10. Donald Winnicott, "Psychoses and Child Care," in *Through Paediatrics to Psycho-Analysis* (1952; London: Hogarth Press, 1975), 221–22.

11. Donald Winnicott, "Transitional Objects and Transitional Phenomena," in *Through Paediatrics to Psycho-Analysis* (1953; London: Hogarth Press, 1975), 230.

12. Bion, "Attacks on Linking."

13. "The infant's experience of the breast as the source of emotional experiences (later represented by terms such as love, understanding, meaning) means that disturbances in relationship with the breast involve disturbance over a wide range of adult relationships." Wilfred Bion, *Transformations*, in *Seven Servants* (1965; New York: Aronson, 1977), 81.

14. Hanna Segal, "A Psycho-Analytic Approach to the Treatment of Schizophrenia," in *Studies of Schizophrenia*, ed. M. Lader (Ashford, Kent, England: Headley Bros., 1975b), 95.

15. Aryeh Kaplan, *The Bahir* (Newburyport, Mass.: Samuel Weiser, 1979).

16. Gershom Scholem, *On the Mystical Shape of the Godhead* (New York: Schocken, 1991), 222.

17. Wilfred Bion, *Attention and Interpretation*, in *Seven Servants* (1970; New York: Aronson, 1977).

18. Aryeh Kaplan, *Innerspace* (Jerusalem: Vagshal/Moznaim, 1990a), 78–80. This is based on Genesis 30:31–36, which gives us a clue as to how the *sefirot* were formed. Yechiel Bar-Lev summarizes the 'process': "In the first stage, the *sefirot* were not divisible at all in the sense of ten vessels. Rather, they were a single vessel made of ten. . . . In the next stage, the expansion began, and from the one vessel that included all ten, the ten *sefirot* became like spots. And this is what is called 'the world of the spotted.' In this stage, we speak of ten vessels that are separate from each other, but each and every vessel, i.e., every *sefira*, is like a spot which has not spread. . . . The world of the speckled is the next stage. Here the vessels changed from a single spot to a sense of inclusion or composition. In other words, every *sefira* became composed from ten, and this was repeated again and again. The world of the speckled is the world of emanation." Yechiel Bar-Lev, *Song of the Soul* (Petach Tikvah, Israel: Sefer ve Sefel, 1994), 173–74.

19. Colin James, "Bion's 'Containing' and Winnicott's 'Holding' in the Context of the Group Matrix," *International Journal of Group Psychotherapy* 34 (1984): 204–7.

20. Gedaliah Fleer, personal communication, June 1988.

21. Bion, "Attacks on Linking"; Joseph Berke, *The Tyranny of Malice: Exploring the Dark Side of Character and Culture* (New York: Simon & Schuster, 1988), 149–78.

22. Berke, *Tyranny*, 75–76.

23. Robert Hinshelwood, *A Dictionary of Kleinian Thought* (London: Free Association Books, 1991), 266–70.

24. Hinshelwood, *Dictionary*, 434–35.
25. Heinz Kohut, *The Restoration of the Self* (New York: International Universities Press, 1977), 103; Donald Winnicott, "The Theory of the Parent-Infant Relationship," in *The Maturational Process and the Facilitating Environment* (1960a; London: Hogarth Press, 1972), 41.
26. Genesis 1:2; Aryeh Kaplan, trans., *The Living Torah: The Five Books of Moses*, (Jerusalem: Maznaim Publishing, 1981), 3.
27. Kaplan, *Innerspace*, 82.
28. Talmud Haggigah 14b.
29. Stanley Schneider and Joseph Berke, 2000, "Sigmund Freud and the Lubavitcher Rebbe," *Psychoanalytic Review* 87 (2000): 1, 39–59.
30. Schneider and Berke, "Freud and the Rebbe," 44.
31. Schneider and Berke, "Freud and the Rebbe," 44.
32. Anna Freud, *The Ego and the Mechanisms of Defense* (1937; New York: International Universities Press, 1971), 109–21.
33. Adin Steinsaltz, *The Long Shorter Way* (Northvale, N.J.: Aronson, 1988b), 20–25.
34. Schneur Zalman of Liadi, *Likutei Amarim: Tanya*. Bilingual ed., trans. N. Mindel (1797; Brooklyn, N.Y.: Kehot, 1984), 17.
35. From the prayer "VeChol Ma'aminim" ("All Believe"), for the Jewish New Year (Rosh Hashanah), in the prayer book *Machzor for Rosh Hashanah* (New York: Merkos L'inyonei Chinuch, 1993).
36. This is a phrase used by a number of analysts, including Theodor Reik, who used it in the title of his biography, *Listening with the Third Ear: The Inner Experience of a Psychoanalyst* (New York: Grove Press, 1948).
37. Eugene Herrigel, *Zen and the Art of Archery* (New York: Vintage, 1974).
38. Stanley Schneider and Joseph Berke have written about the history of the concept of the 'oceanic feeling' in: "The Oceanic Feeling, Mysticism and Kabbalah: Freud's Historical Roots," *Psychoanalytic Review*, in press.
39. Sigmund Freud, 1930, *Civilization and Its Discontents*, in *Standard Edition*, ed. James Strachey, vol. 21, 72.
40. Andrew Samuels, *A Critical Dictionary of Jungian Analysis* (London: Routledge & Kegan Paul, 1986), 100. Numinosum refers to an awe-inspiring, mystical wonderment of religious experience whose source is perceived to be from outside of oneself. Derived from the Latin: *numen*, 'god,' and *nuere*, 'to beckon.' The term was first coined by Rudolf Otto in *The Idea of the Holy* (London: Oxford University Press, 1958) and used by Carl Jung.
41. Avram Davis, *The Way of the Flame: A Guide to the Forgotten Mystical Tradition of Jewish Meditation* (San Francisco: Harper, 1996), 79.

Chapter Six

Intimate Relations: From Infant to Adult

The *sefirot* are the containers and the contents of consciousness, a consciousness that ranges from the highest levels of spirituality to the most mundane reaches of materiality. In essence the *sefirot* communicate, filter and transmit cosmic intentionality and energy to the physical world. In this chapter we will refine and expand our prior discussion of these fundamental forces. We shall show how they develop and interact with each other. Moreover we shall consider how the basic structure of the *sefirot*, whether in the anthropomorphic shape of a man, or as a tree, relates to the parallel emotional development of the human being from infancy to adulthood.

The 'Tree of Life' (*Etz HaChaim*) is a holographic representation of the emanations or characteristics of the Creator.[1] The Bible tells us that God created man in His image. This does not mean that man looks like God. Rather, the intent, as understood in Rabbinic writings, is that man 'shares' many of His characteristics.[2,3] The doctrine of emanation presupposes a relationship and procession between higher and lower worlds whereby human terminology can be used to describe, as much as this may be possible, the Emanator. The *sefirot* are part and parcel of the language that has developed in order to accomplish this project.[4,5]

As usually portrayed, there are ten interconnected branches on the Tree of Life. Each of these is a *sefira* or Divine relational attribute. They are arranged in three longitudinal pillars or trunks: the right, the center and the left.[6] The central axis carries the Divine Will or Intentionality from its first unthought thoughts through a chain of events that lead to its implementation in the finite world. It is also concerned with centering, whereby man, in order to function, has to be centered. Any branching (orientation) too far to the right (softness) or too far to the left (severity) needs to be counterbalanced and emotionally rectified. When the 'right' is viewed as dominant, the 'left' is a necessary counterpoint, and vice versa.[7] What is clear is that Kabbalah views the world as needing a perfect balance of right and left. Too strong a polar stance will create an imbalance. The central *sefirotic* trunk is a way of maintaining order and balance in the world.

Kabbalah divides the ten *sefirot* into different groupings or constellations, depending on the issue at hand. One way of dividing them is to order them arboreally, as the Tree of Life. Another way is anthropomorphically—paralleling the human head and body. Still another way is to arrange them in order of their closeness to the Godhead. The higher-level *sefirot* represent internal intellectual processes, while the more lower-level *sefirot* represent the external expression of mental processes, particularly as emotions.

The *sefirot* are not only arranged longitudinally, but they are spiralic and concentric in that each *sefira* contains within it an entire developmental tree. And each *sefira* within that tree contains another tree. This has been described in the *Zohar* as the peels of an onion—one within another.[8] These *sefirot* are closely connected to infant, child, adolescent and adult developmental processes, including sexual and gender differentiation, cognitive thought, personality characteristics and interpersonal relationships—especially the capacity for intimacy.

We know that the human being develops through intimate relationships. As John Donne said: "No man is an island, entire of itself; every man is a piece of the Continent, a part of the main."[9] Developmental studies confirm this view, for they show that an infant deprived of close emotional bonds is at risk for retarded intellectual and emotional growth and may even physically pine away. Thus René Spitz made it clear in 1946, in working with Holocaust children in France, that the failure to thrive in the first years of life may lead to anaclitic depression and even death.[10] Depressions later in life can also be attributed to the emotional climate in the early years of life. As we have pointed out, current psychoanalytic theory emphasizes the importance of object relationships and projective processes on the emotional growth of the human organism. The same holds true for spiritual development as part of the unfolding of the *sefirotic* tree.

The derivation of the word *sefira* is unclear. It most probably does not derive from the Greek word for 'sphere.' It may have its root in the Hebrew for 'number,' as we learn from the *Sefer Yetzirah*: "Ten Sefirot of Nothingness; ten and not nine; ten and not eleven."[11] It may derive from the Hebrew for 'sapphire' (*sappir*), or for 'telling' (*sapper*). There are many names or synonyms for the *sefirot*. They include ". . . *ma'amarot* and *dibburim* ('sayings') . . . *orot* ('lights') . . . *midot*, in the sense of qualities . . . *mekorot* ('sources') . . . *sitrin* (i.e.,'aspects,' found mainly in the *Zohar*) and *ha-panim ha-penimiyyot* ('the inner faces of God')."[12]

The *sefirot* convey different aspects of the Ultimate and, therefore, create a radiance of overabundant light similar to that which emanates from the precious sapphire jewel. The theory of the *sefirot* is based on the Neoplatonic conception of God and the theory of emanation. He was defined as the Good, the One, an absolutely single and self-sufficient entity. All that exists has been produced not by any creative power, but rather through successive emanations from the Godhead. From the One, all forms of being have emanated or descended from Upper Spiritual Realms (of absolute revelation) to Lower Darker Domains (of absolute concealment). Thus, through this process of emanation of the Godhead, there appears an almost endless array of physical worlds. It is notable that the Kabbalists of the twelfth century needed to create a more Jewish view of this process of emanation, and utilized the term *sefira* in order to explain the multifarious manifestations of God's will.

From another angle, we can view emanation from the Source, the Godhead, as the filtering down of energy. The closer one is to the Source, the greater the power and intensity of the energy. The farther away one is from the Emanator, the Godhead, the more filtered or dissipated the energy becomes. The quest for spirituality is the innate desire that man has to reach ever-higher levels of spiritual sustenance. In other words, the more spiritual one becomes, the closer one reaches the Origin of energy and light. The *sefirot* provide pathways of transcendence.

One school of Kabbalistic thinking (as expressed by Menachem Recanati, a fourteenth-century Italian Kabbalist) sees the *sefirot* as God's vessels or instruments.[13] Another school of thought views the *sefirot* as God's tangible essence. This school of thought holds the seemingly paradoxical point of view that the *sefirot* are really God as well as representative of God. Yet, this latter view clearly shows the *sefirot* representing the procession from a higher source to lower manifestations or emanations. Aryeh Kaplan summarizes this philosophical argument in the following manner: "Are the *sefirot* essences of the Divine or are they vessels of the Divine? In other words, are the *sefirot* ten windows through which we can perceive the Divine, or are they ten tools that God uses to direct the world?"[14] The Ari (Isaac Luria) has written that both sides of this philosophical argument are correct.[15] A Judaic studies scholar, David Ariel, has labeled these two views as the *instrumentalists*, those who "explain that the *Sefirot* are God's vessels," and the *essentialists*, those who "believe that the *Sefirot* are God's essence."[16] These discussions demonstrate why we say that the *sefirot* are both containers and the contents of the containers.

The actual arrangement of the *sefirot* has been a subject of controversy among Kabbalists. Some have felt that the highest *sefira*, *Keter*, the one closest in proximity to the Godhead, was part of the Godhead and, therefore, not part of the ten *sefirot*. So another 'wisdom' *sefira*, called *Da'at*, was added in order to maintain the number of *sefirot* at ten. And there were others who disagreed and felt that the ten *sefirot* were all emanations from the Godhead and stood independently, with *Keter* remaining as the first of the ten *sefirot*.

The Biblical verse that alludes to these three Wisdom *sefirot* relates to the building of the Tabernacle (*Sukkah*) in the desert. God selected a gifted architect, Bezalel, and imbued him with ". . . wisdom, understanding and knowledge" (Exodus 31:3). Both *Chochmah* (wisdom) and *Bina* (understanding) are two aspects of the cognitive thinking process. The right channel, *Chochmah*, is viewed as a masculine energy force. And the left channel, the counterbalance, is *Bina*, a feminine energy source. Aryeh Kaplan states: "*Chochmah* is . . . associated with the nonverbal right hemisphere of the brain, while *Bina* is associated with the verbal left hemisphere."[17] Thus, *Chochmah* is more related to inspiration and creativity, while *Bina* is more analytical and focused. In a dyadic relationship such as the mother-child or therapist-patient relationship, both forces operate. There is the creative and inspirational aspect of *Chochmah* and the more analytic, directed, disciplined and focused *Bina*. While *Chochmah* may give the mother and therapist some understanding of the underlying thinking and emotional aspects, there is the need for *Bina* in order to take that inspirational part further by giving it direction. This embraces the feminine metaphor, the passive receptacle, that cloaks the active masculine.

The last *sefira* of mind and thought is *Da'at* (knowledge).[18] This *sefira* is the center spine that unites and integrates the right pole of *Chochmah* and the left pole of *Bina*. *Da'at* fuses the energies of the mind with deep feeling. This is the meaning of the translation of *Da'at*, 'knowledge' or 'knowing.' It is the direct experience of the lightning flash, the sudden illumination that conveys, "Ah, yes," the insights that a person can taste in his mind, so he can play with them and utilize them for further understanding.

There are several different schemata for viewing the *sefirot*. One way that we have already described is along three pillars or trunks. The *sefirot* on these axes can be further divided into three triangular groupings, according to their order of emanation. The first three form the world of thought, the next three the world of emotion, and the next three the world of corporeality. The last, or tenth, *sefira*, *Malkhut*, is the recipient of all the nine energy forces from above, while the top, or highest level of *sefira*, *Keter*, derives its source of light or energy from the *Ein Sof*, the Godhead.

In outline form, we can list these various groupings and then show the *sefirotic* Tree as the emanation process unfolds from the highest level, the One Godhead, to the lowest level of our world:

The Three *Sefirot* of the Mind (Mind and Thought)

Keter (the Crown of God, Will)

Bina (Intelligence / Understanding) *Chochmah* (Wisdom)

[*Da'at* (Knowledge)]

The Three *Sefirot* of Emotion

Gevurah (Justice / Severity / Power) *Chesed* (Mercy / Compassion)

Tiferet (Beauty / Splendor)

The Three *Sefirot* of Body

Hod (Glory / Majesty / Passivity) *Netzach* (Triumph / Eternity)

Yesod (Foundation)

The Tenth (Last) *Sefira*

Malkhut (Kingship)

These triangles can also be described in other ways, too: the top one as Spirit, the middle as Self / Soul and the third, as we have just said, as Body. Concurrently the process of emanation from the Godhead can be seen through the metaphoric representation of the *sefirotic* Tree (see Figure 6.1).

How can we reconcile these differing views? The highest order is also known by the acronym *ChaBaD*, which is a further name for Lubavitch Hasidism. They emphasize the 'higher' intellectual faculties that form the great triad of the *Ruach Ha-Kodesh,* the Divine spirit, which energizes everything. The middle triad is known by the acronym *ChaGaT*. This refers to an intensely emotional state whereby the person concerned yearns to reconcile opposites of love and hate, compassion and severity. If he or she succeeds, then he or she becomes confirmed in his or her humanity and reaches a milestone in achieving a firm sense of self. In Kabbalah this leads to *Tiferet*, the center of the Tree, a harmonious core, a uniting of opposites, the essence of beauty.

The integration of love and hate, *Chesed* and *Gevurah,* parallels the major developmental step that Kleinian analysts call the 'depressive position.' This means that the infant is no longer at the mercy of murderous rage if it

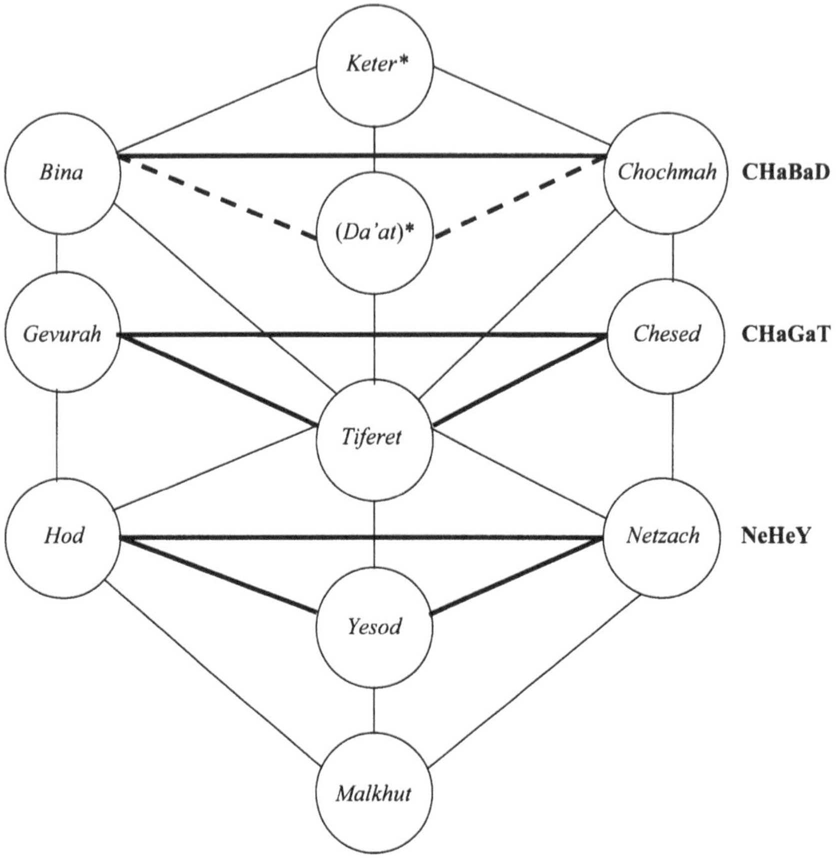

* Either *Keter* or *Da'at*—in order to leave the total number of *sefirot* at 10.

Figure 6-1. The Sefirotic Tree

can't get what he wants. On the contrary he recalls that the mother who deprives is also the mother who cares. So his mind mends, his heart heals and he begins to assume what can be called a moral sensitivity. No wonder that in Kabbalah the *ChaGaT* conveys the moral as well as emotional essence of a person. It is part of a continuum between the 'I' and the 'not-I'—one might say, between Being and Nothingness—and is featured strongly in the writings of Bratslav Hasidim.

In comparison the lower triad, *NeHeY*, represents vital psycho-biological processes, whether active, instructive and impulsive like *Netzach* or passive, cognitive and controlling like *Hod.* Again, the lowest member of this group, *Yesod*, is reconciliatory and reflective, but also generative, as in providing the physical means for another generation to emerge. Hence, the lowest grouping is akin to a foundation stone for the head and the heart (above) and *Malkhut,* the presence of God in the world (below).

Malkhut also encapsulates the four levels inherent within the Tree as a whole: root, trunk, branch and fruit. Interestingly, in some diagrams the *sefirotic* Tree is depicted upside down with its roots in heaven and its branches touching the earth. Moreover *Malkhut* embraces the *shefa,* or flow of Divine energies from Will to Mind to Heart to Body, as they move from a transcendent to an immanent or embodied reality.

Now let us look at the *sefirotic* Tree from yet another angle, from the perspective of its three trunks, or pillars: right, left and center. The right trunk consists of the *sefirot Chochmah, Chesed* and *Netzach*, and is known as the line of *Chesed*, lovingkindness. It also stands for action and expansion. The left branch or line consists of the *sefirot Bina, Gevurah* and *Hod,* and is known as the line of *judgment*. It also stands for passivity and constriction. The central branch or line consists of the *sefirot Da'at, Tiferet* and *Yesod*, and is known as the branch or line of *mercy*. The *Zohar* refers to the "right as representing perfection . . . and the left as engendering strife."[19] The two extreme poles of right and left temper each other. If one is too extreme, the other pole can overcompensate in order to arrive at some type of centering. The central pole represents a consensus or equilibrium that enables a mediation of both right and left.

If all this were not sufficient, within each trunk the conflicting qualities also constrain each other. In the same way that *Chesed* (compassion) can temper *Gevurah* (severity), and *Netzach* (thrust) can temper *Hod* (trust), the quality of compassion can also overcome the overactive, hyper-expansive side of *Netzach*, and the laid-back quality of *Hod* can help to overcome the excessive hate and vindictiveness of *Gevurah*. Hence we can say that each branch both mirrors and stabilizes the other. The complement of this process in man is the person who is able to live a well-balanced life—morally, mentally and emotionally

Although the analogy of a tree is widely used in the *seforitic* literature, anthropomorphic schemata are even more prevalent. Here the *sefirot* metaphorically represent the human head and parts of the body. Remember that we are describing states of consciousness here and how they appear to be concretized in or around the head, the torso, the arms and legs and the genitals.[20] This description is closely related to what the neurologist Antonio Demasio spoke to in the first chapter, when he strongly affirmed that both the body and emotions are important partners in the organization and development of consciousness.

There exist a great multitude of anthropomorphic representations of the *sefirot*. One schema is as shown in Figure 6.2, with *Keter* as the cranium and *Yesod* as the phallus.

Still others depict *Keter, Chochmah* and *Bina* as above the head and *da'at* at the level of the neck, or show the *sefirot* congruent with what Indian medical practitioners call the chakras or energy points of the body.

Interestingly, the Kabbalah refers to the six *sefirot* from *Chesed* to *Yesod* as masculine, while the seventh *sefira*, *Malkhut,* is feminine. This is because these six *sefirot* are conceptualized as energy channels that give and propel forward, while the seventh *sefira* of *Malkhut* is a feminine attribute, and it is the 'universal receiver.' *Malkhut* is also referred to as the womb. Aryeh Kaplan notes that *Malkhut* ". . . represents the power to receive, hold and eventually give back something more perfect and complete."[21] It also embodies the *Shekinah,* the female embodiment of the Godhead and the imminent presence of the Divine on earth.

As we noted earlier, the 'Primary *Sefirot*,' referred to as 'The First Three,' deal with the stages of thought.[22] The last seven *sefirot* deal with the stages of realization and actualization. Rabbi Isaiah Horowitz, known as the *ShLaH* after the initials of his major work, was a prominent Kabbalist in the Lurianic tradition. In *Shnei Luchot Habrit* (*The Two Tablets of the Covenant*), Horowitz gives the analogy of the building of a house.[23] First there has to be the *will* (*ratzon*), which is the *sefira* of *Keter*. Then an architect has to be employed to give concrete visual expression of the desire or will. This is the *sefira* of *Chochmah*. An engineer has to be employed to actualize the plans of the architect. This is the *sefira* of *Bina*. All three work together in order to bring into fruition will and the reality. *Bina* helps to contain and limit the architect's general plans that are represented by the *sefira* of *Chochmah*. These are the three *sefirot* of mind and thought. The last seven *sefirot* effectuate the realization and actualization of the thought and planning process.[24]

A less detailed description of this process can also be found in the writings of Rabbi Chaim Vital, which reflect the teaching of the Ari: "When a man desires to go to a particular place, he shall 'talk' to his legs so that they can move forward. As he thinks of where he wants to go, his legs move. The same holds true for the other limbs of the body."[25]

Before moving on to the psychological dimension of development, it is useful to review a further aspect of the internal process of the *sefirot*, which can serve as a bridge between the Jewish mystical literature and the psychoanalytic literature. Kabbalah asserts that the purpose of life is to effect change in the upper worlds so that their influence will be more favorable to man in the lower world. The emanations from the Godhead filter down through the upper worlds into the lower world. The process also includes a downward

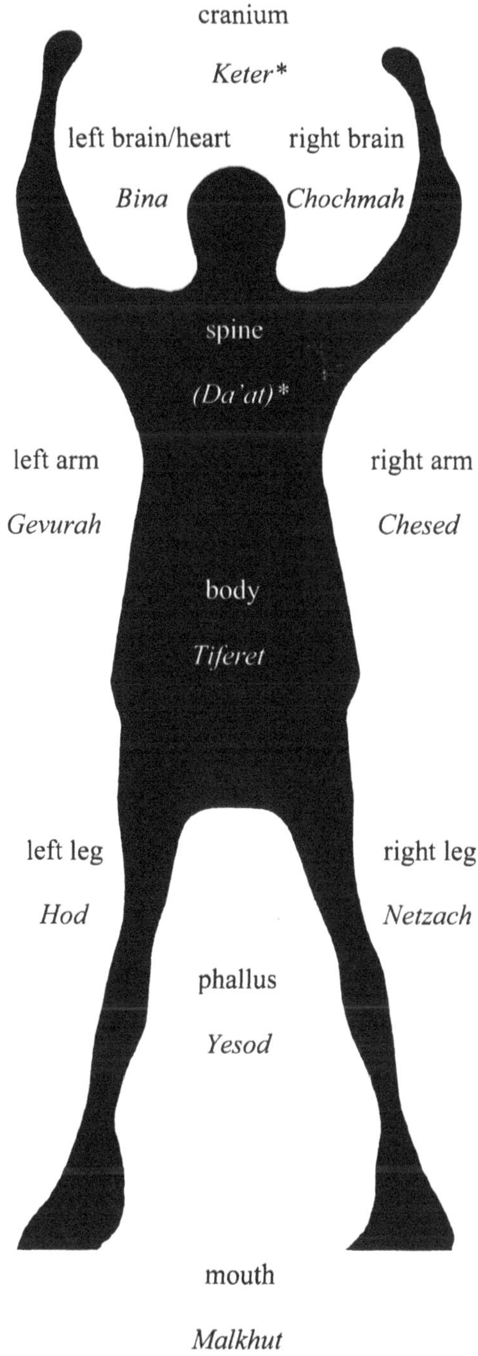

Figure 6-2. Anthropomorphic Representations

movement from the higher *sefirot* to the lowest *sefira* of *Malkhut*, the 'universal receiver.'

Conversely, the *Zohar* describes this as movement through various gates and passages that man passes through, reaching toward the Godhead, in order to try to reach as high a level as possible.[26] Here the movement to reach the Godhead is from lower to higher, whereas the emanations from the Godhead to man are from the higher to the lower. The analogy that the *Zohar* gives is the following: "An example can be given of the Supreme King, who is on-high, hidden and secretive, and this King made many gates, one leading into the other. At the end of all the gates was a gate with many locks, many openings, many halls—one after the other. Whoever wants to reach the King has to pass through this gate with all the locks and passages."[27] The metaphor is clear: to attempt to reach the Godhead, one has to traverse a convoluted process of worlds and *sefirot*, in order to achieve the highest possible levels of consciousness. Paradoxically, this may lead to a state of no-consciousness, no-thought and no-ego.

We can trace the origins of the internal workings of the self and of the soul to Freud's understanding of the mind as first described in "The Interpretation of Dreams."[28] In addition, his "Introductory Lectures on Psycho-Analysis" provide a remarkable resemblance to the *Zohar*'s description, above, of the movement through various gates and passages:

> Let us therefore compare the system of the unconscious to a large entrance hall, in which the mental impulses jostle one another like separate individuals. Adjoining this entrance hall there is a second, narrower, room—a kind of drawing-room—in which consciousness, too, resides. But on the threshold between these two rooms a watchman performs his function: he examines the different mental impulses, acts as a censor, and will not admit them into the drawing-room if they displease him.[29]

Here Freud conveys a clear description of movement from one level of consciousness to another with a censorship mechanism operating. In order for unconscious impulses to enter into consciousness, they need to pass the censor or 'watchman.' Significantly, the metaphor of movement from one room to another (larger to smaller or smaller to larger) is a familiar Talmudic expression that is used metaphorically in various descriptions of rooms—going from a larger to a smaller one and vice versa.[30] Even the description of a woman's gynecological system has an entrance room that leads into a larger room and to an upper attic.[31]

As the infant develops into the child, adolescent and adult, all previous life experiences and feelings are imprinted on the psyche. This means that the older person will have emotional aspects of the child within. It is the job of psychodynamic psychotherapy and psychoanalysis to try to uncover the earlier layers of feelings and experiences in order to connect to the emotional levels of the person's psychological self.

We have come a long way from Freud's initial understanding of the emotional life of the individual. Freud had defined his theoretical underpinnings as being based on drive theory: The impulses of the individual needed to find expression in discharge. This led to his identifying the drive impulses (libidinal and aggressive), primary and secondary process, instinctual processes (life and death instinct) and defenses to defend against the id impulses pressurizing the ego. However, he did not deal with the emotional relationships that occur in the very tight interactive dyad of self and object. That was left for others to define and refine.

The process of cognitive attunement now moved from a biologically determined one to a more psychologically attuned one, which gradually took into account all the personages and environmental factors that were involved in the rearing of the infant/child, and the unfolding of his thinking capacities and emotional responsiveness. In other words, we are talking about a much wider social network: parents, relatives, neighbors and friends. But the involvement could also be non-direct—as in the case of the adopted child. One did not have to personally or physically be present; the fact that there was an emotionally involved relationship *de facto* meant that the emotional engram (to use an Edith Jacobson simile) of the parent or significant person was engraved on the psyche of the infant/child.[32] It was not by coincidence that the Greek root for 'character' meant a lead letter used for printing—something that was unchangeable—because early on, personality traits were thought to be fixed and never changing, just like the immovable printed letter.

We have previously described the downward flow of spiritual energies through the *sefirotic* channels from the Highest Source to the lowest recipients in the material world. In order to further consider the emotional and cognitive development of the infant and adult, we shall now consider the upward flow of libidinal energies from the id (pleasure-seeking, impulsive, primary process thinking) and later the ego (reality-recognizing, logical, secondary process thinking) of the newborn being. By 'upward' we refer to the expansion of consciousness over time (growing up) and space (expanding relationships).

At birth, the neonate lives in a state of pure potential and undifferentiated consciousness. He is almost totally dependent on his mother for satisfying his instinctual needs such as feeding, the relief of discomfort and adequate stimulation. His main method of communication of these needs is by means of energetic crying. He does not recognize his mother (or caretaker) as separate from himself. She exists solely to do his bidding. So we can say that the baby exists in a state of fusion with his mother, and that she is the container of his

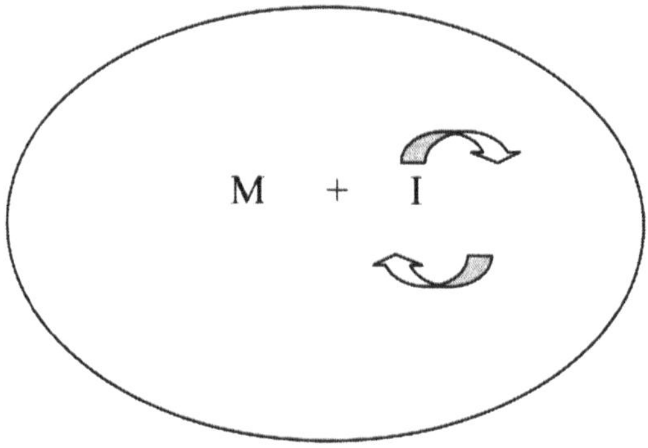

Figure 6-3. Parent-Infant Relationship

needs (the vessel). Concomitantly his mother struggles to contain and cope with his impulses and crying as well as his undifferentiated levels of awareness (the contents). This can be described by Figure 6.3.

This was the view of the parent-infant relationship (to paraphrase Winnicott) that prevailed among dynamic psychologists and psychoanalysts until the late 1970s to early1980s.[33] At that point, Robert Stolorow, Bernard Brandschaft and George Atwood formulated the concept of the 'intersubjective self.'[34] In some ways, this was an expansion of Winnicott's concept of the transitional object, potential space and therapeutic space. The infant was not only influenced by the mother, but he influenced the mother, as well as the space that impinged upon each of them. This meant that fantasies of the other could be 'felt' and affected by how the infant and/or the mother understood the cues of the other. Emotions were now able to be conceived as being conveyed by the shared space (potential or transitional space) of both infant and mother.[35] Figure 6.4 illustrates the concept of transitional or potential space.

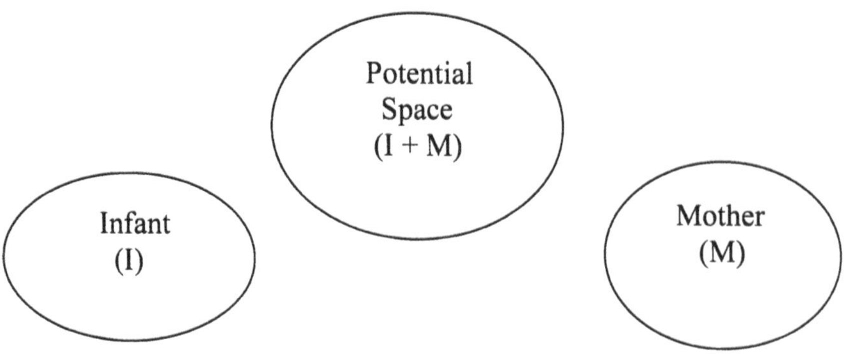

Figure 6-4. Transitional Potential Space

Mother and infant 'meet' in a shared space. This shared area becomes a mélange of shared affective and experiential material. The infant is not only affected by the interaction with the mother, but he also affects and impinges upon her. Winnicott referred to this shared space as the 'facilitating environment.' The implications for child rearing as well as the parallel to the therapeutic world of patient and therapist should be obvious.

This interaction of mother and infant is the moment when the infant begins to recognize other persons (father, siblings, relatives) who may impinge on his supposedly exclusive relationship with the mother. His libidinal wishes interact with external reality, to which he now responds not only with crying but with screaming, sounds, words, flailing about and other bodily activities. These communications flow upward and outward with intense energy and denote the beginning of the depressive position. His consciousness begins to differentiate as well as his thinking processes. The focus of this lower triangle (*Netzach*, *Hod*, *Yesod*) is the body. We can call it the Infant (mother-infant shared space).

The intersubjective theoreticians injected another notion. Not only was it possible to influence and be influenced by the other who shared a proximal spatial modality, but now one can conceptualize the interactions and interrelationships in a different vein. As shown in Figure 6.5, both the grown-up infant, the child and his parents 'deposit' their feelings and experiential parts of their selves into a 'middle' area called the intersubjective space. Both have input into that space. And both take from that space parts of each other that are mingled together.

The child now has a full range of emotional attachments to his parents and others, and experiences wild swings from intense love to extreme jealousy. Libidinal impulses are still very strong, but they are tempered by the capacity

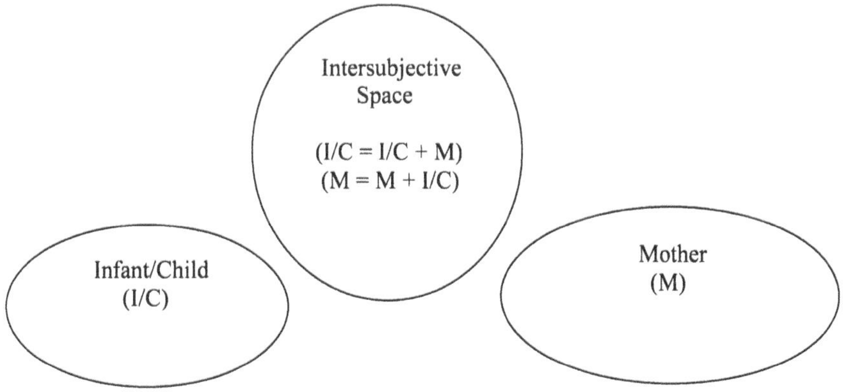

Figure 6-5. Intersubjective Space

for rational and symbolic thought and the creation of a panoply of internal and external worlds of relationships. The child develops a communicative armamentarium that includes a much wider use of language. This leads to a much greater differentiation of his thinking processes, which ranges from the pre-oedipal, to oedipal, to post-oedipal (latency) states. The focus of this middle triangle (*Chesed*, *Gevurah*, *Tiferet*) is emotionality. We can call it the Child.

The interpersonal/relational school of analysis gained momentum in the 1980s. The late psychoanalyst Stephen Mitchell borrowed heavily from the ideas of Harry Stack Sullivan in order to advance his ideas about intersubjective realities.[36] These not only concern the impact of infant on mother, or child on parents, but the impact of projective and introjective processes that adults have on each other. Notably, transference and counter-transference not only occur in the therapy room, but they impact on non-therapeutic relationships all the time. Such events are the grist of novels, films, plays and simple acts of falling in or out of love. Figure 6.6 attempts to illustrate this point.

As we can see from this diagram, the adult has an enormous range of attachments, not only to his parents, but to his peers, friends, acquaintances, colleagues, spouse, and so on. There is a great expansion of the capacity for intellectual accomplishment and symbolic creation. Emotionality is not lost, but secondary processes expand and include an enormous range of communicative tools. Here people can differentiate between personal and interpersonal awareness and beyond, into transpersonal and supra-personal realms (religious, mystical, meditative). The focus of this upper triangle (*Chochmah*, *Bina*, *Da'at*) is intellectual, and it is multifaceted. That is why we call it the Adult (adult relational space = others).

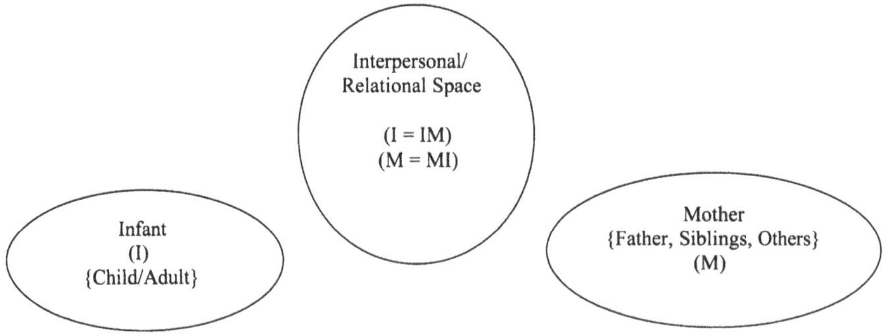

Figure 6-6. Interpersonal/Relational Space

Figure 6-7 illustrates the directions of life energies that we have been describing. The primary condition denotes the infusion of spiritual energies through the *sefirotic* tree from emanation to actualization. The complementary movement is the ascent, transformation and containment of libidinal energies as they pass from the infant to the adult.

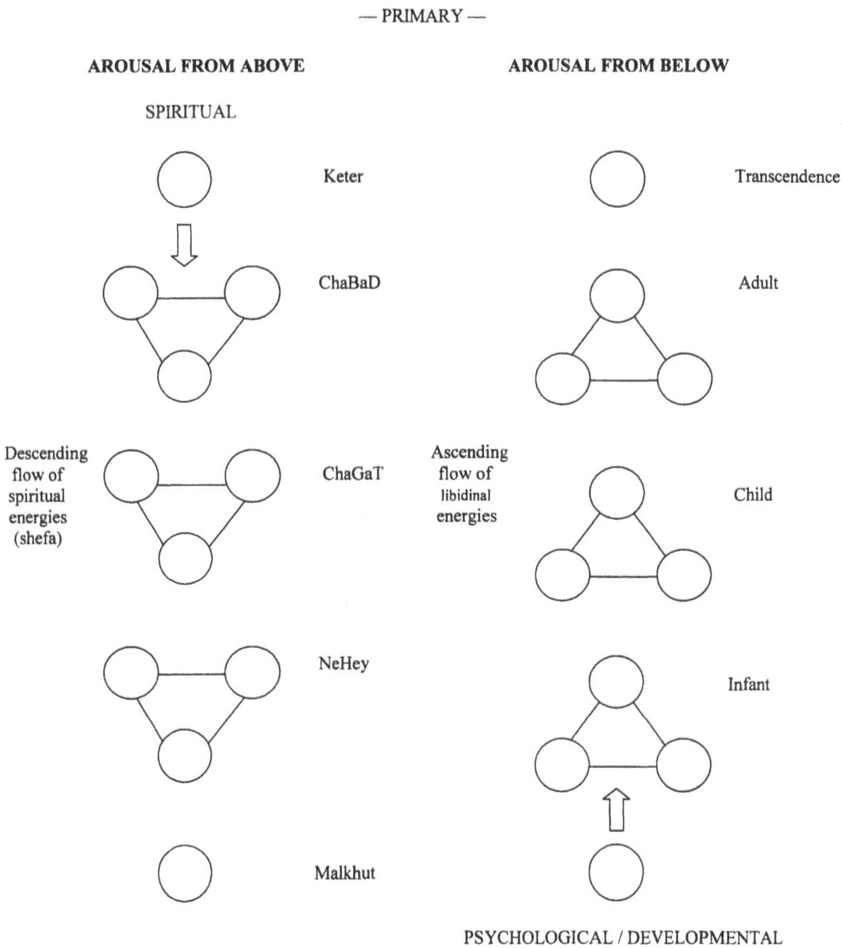

Figure 6-7. Directions of Spiritual and Life Energies

The converse process denotes the power of prayer to stimulate a cascade of spiritual arousal from the body though the heart to the brain and above. Concomitantly, once an adult has gained the capacity to reason or, as psychoanalysis postulates, has moved from primary to secondary process thinking, the downward reach of the intellect can enhance all aspects of a person's life and relationships.

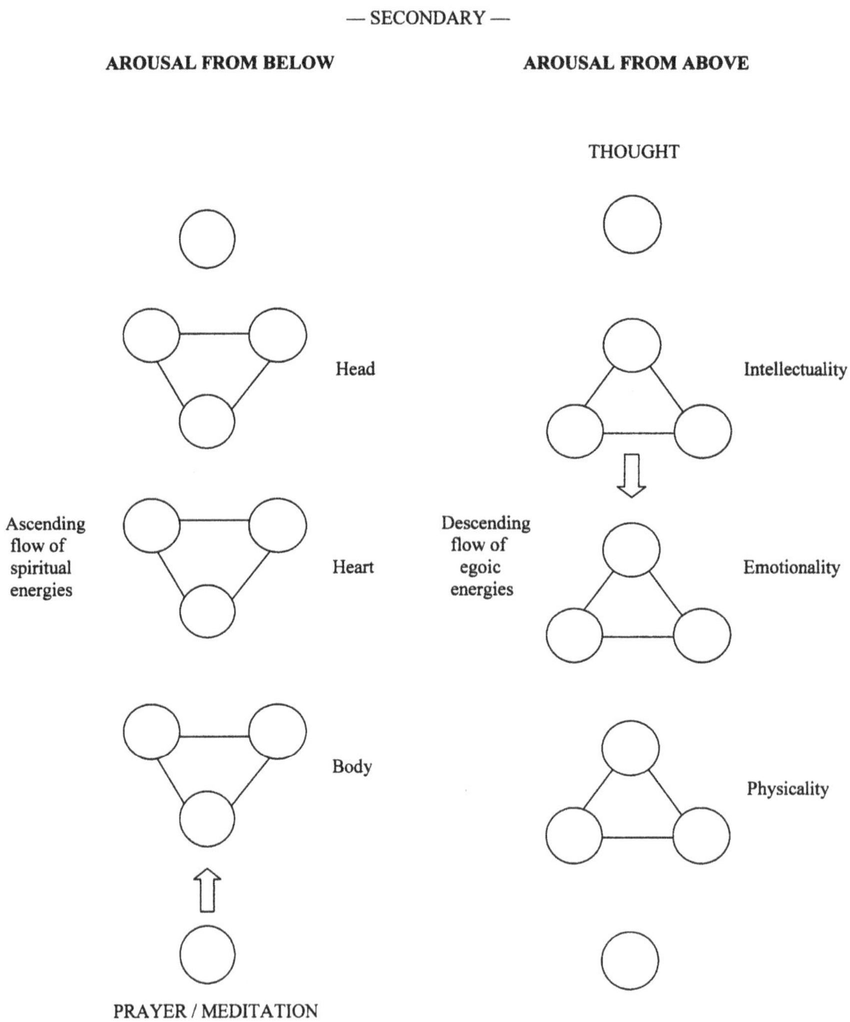

Figure 6-7. ***(continued)***

These movements are not neat. They stop, start, ascend and descend like the angels on Jacob's ladder. Similarly, psycho-physical processes can go forward, go backward or get stuck at certain levels of development. But, in general, they remain in a constant state of flux into and with each other. Truly an adult is *homo relations*, someone who can transmit and receive the widest array of communications, the most intense energies and the wildest thoughts. He can contain them, play with them and transform them, and live a life of actualized potential—spiritually, physically and emotionally.

In Kabbalistic terms this means he becomes both *Tiferet* and *Malkhut,* the giver and the taker. This is represented by the union of *Tiferet* and *Malkhut*—the uniting of the upper and lower, the masculine and feminine, the blending of opposites. Such joining also represents the state of peace prevailing in the world. We can see this as sundown of the seventh day marks the beginning of the Sabbath. Here the mystic can unite the bride and groom, day and night, the sacred and the profane. This is poignantly represented by the famous song, the *Lechah Dodi*, in the Sabbath liturgy. "The Sabbath is transformed into a cosmic wedding between the masculine *Tiferet* and feminine *Shehkina* of God."[37]

To understand this event analytically, one needs to relate to the nurturing mothering object that is the repository of all feelings and actions and serves as the Universal Receiver. Developmentally the mother has to be able, during early rapprochement (16 to 24 months of age), to allow the child independence with emotional support[38]—as Winnicott phrases it: ". . . the experience of being alone while someone else is present."[39] This is the hardest part for a parent, knowing when to 'let go' and encourage emotional independence. If the mother is too over-involved or too under-involved, then the essence and flow of *Malkhut* is not operating appropriately. Again we necessarily return to the theme of balance. For relationships to properly exist, there needs to be the right equilibrium that will enable *Malkhut* to avoid perversity and harmonize relationships without losing the unique identity of their component personalities.

NOTES

1. The phrase 'Tree of Life' comes from the Bible, Genesis 3:22: ". . . (man) must be prevented from putting forth his hand and also taking from the Tree of Life, eat from it and live forever." The Tree of Life is a parallel tree to the Tree of Knowledge of Good and Evil. The latter is the tree that God had commanded Adam and Eve not to eat from. Kabbalah scholar Gershom Scholem noted: "The two trees are fundamentally one: they grow from a common root, in which masculine and feminine, the giving and the receiving, the creative and the reflective, are one." Gershom Scholem, *On the Mystical Shape of the Godhead* (New York: Schocken, 1991), 70.

2. The image of a tree is also alluded to in the studying the Kabbalistic secrets in Ezekiel's vision of the Workings of the Chariot (*Ma'aseh Merkavah*). The Hebrew word for 'grafting' is the same root as for the word 'chariot.'

3. Rabbinic writings include the Talmud (Babylonian and Jerusalem versions) and all of the Midrashim (legal and homiletical explanations to the Bible).

4. The implication is that through disciplined study and meditation, one could be 'grafted' onto the Tree of Life through the various *sefirot* (Divine relational attributes). See Aryeh Kaplan, *Innerspace* (Jerusalem: Vagshal/Moznaim, 1990a), 126.

5. The eighteenth-century Kabbalist Moshe Chaim Luzatto has written: "The *sefirot* are God's traits that He made for himself to serve Creation. They are not traits in regard to His completeness and Primal true Being, but are created from His will and desire, for the sake of the beings that he desired to create. . . . They are not God's character, for 'character' is a concept that refers only to created beings, not to the Creator. These traits are types of Providence and illumination, that are brought to shine on His creation. . . . The *sefirot* are not something outside of Him. They are literally His traits: His compassion, grace, judgment, charity, and so on." From 'Kelalim Rishonim,' in *Da'at Tevunot*, p. 247. Quoted by Y. David Shulman, *The Sefirot: Ten Emanations of Divine Power* (Northvale, N.J.: Aronson, 1996), xix.

6. See Stanley Schneider and Joseph Berke, "Discovering Oneself: Kabbalah and Psychoanalysis," *Midstream* 51 (November–December 2005): 6, 24–27.

7. We can see this in the concept of placing a mezuzah "on the doorpost of your house and upon your gates" (Deuteronomy 6:9). The mezuzah must be on the person's right as he enters a room, as per the Talmud in Menachot (34a): "We enter the room on the right foot." However, as the *Zohar* (III:263b) points out, when we leave the room the mezuzah is on our left!

8. *Zohar* 1:19b–20a.

9. John Donne (1572–1631), "Devotions upon Emergent Occasions," Meditation 17 (1624). Quoted in R. Andrews, M. Biggs and M. Seidel, eds., *Columbia World of Quotations* (New York: Columbia University Press, 1996).

10. René Spitz, *The First Year of Life* (New York: International Universities Press, 1965). Spitz (1887–1974) worked with Holocaust children in France, paralleling Anna Freud's work in England at the Hampstead Clinics. Spitz pioneered in his studies on hospitalism and anaclitic depression. The former relates to institutionalized behavior and expectations, and the latter refers to depression that sets in because of the impairment of an infant's physical, social and intellectual development following separation from its mother or primary caregiver. From the Greek: *anaklisis*, 'a leaning back'; 'to lean on.'

11. A new translation and commentary on one of the oldest Kabbalistic books. Aryeh Kaplan, *Sefer Yetzirah (The Book of Creation)* (Newburyport, Mass.: Samuel Weiser, 1990b). This quotation is from 1:4.

12. Gershom Scholem, *Kabbalah* (Jerusalem: Keter, 1974), 100.

13. Quoted in David S. Ariel, *The Mystic Quest* (New York: Schocken, 1988), 68.

14. Kaplan, *Innerspace*, 40.

15. As the Ari notes: "The 10 *sefirot* are spherical, everything is contained within it . . . lights and vessels. The light is divided into: inner and comprehensive/encircling

light. The vessels are divided into: internal and external." In Chaim Vital, *Etz Chaim* [in Hebrew] (1587; Jerusalem/B'nai Brak: Videvsky, 1988), 1:3, vol. 1, p. 32. The Ari, Isaac Luria (1534–1572), settled in Safed and became the teacher of a large cadre of students who became part of an important school of mysticism. The Ari developed a systematic method of studying and understanding Kabbalah. His philosophical understanding and teachings were written down by his student Chaim Vital (1543–1620).

16. Ariel, *Mystic Quest*, 68.

17. Kaplan, *Innerspace*, 200, fn. 7.

18. The *Tanya*, the classical text of Lubavitch Hasidism, states that there are two types of *Da'at*: *Da'at Tachton* (the Lower Knowledge) and *Da'at Elyon* (the Higher or Supernal Knowledge). The latter unites *Chochmah* and *Bina*, at a higher spiritual level. The former creates the bridge between the *sefirot* of Mind and Thought and the *sefirot* of Emotion. See Yosef Wineberg, *Lessons in* Tanya (New York: Kehot, 1987), vol. 2, chap. 42.

19. *Zohar*, 1:17a.

20. *Tikuney Zohar*, 17a.

21. Kaplan, *Innerspace*, 42.

22. In Hebrew, *gimmel rishonot*, abbreviated as *g"r*.

23. Rabbi Isaiah Horowitz (1565–1630), known as the *ShLaH HaKadosh*, the Holy ShLaH, was a Kabbalist in the Lurianic tradition, and had a profound influence on the Hasidic movement and its leaders. This analogy is found in his famous work, *Shnei Luchot Habrit* ('The Two Tablets of the Covenant'), p. 8a, fn.

24. See Yechiel Bar-Lev, *Song of the Soul* (Petach Tikvah, Israel: Sefer ve Sefel, 1994), 88, for a similar analogy.

25. Rabbi Chaim Vital brings this down in *Etz Chaim*, 47:2, vol. 2, p. 359, which are the teachings of the Ari.

26. *Zohar*, 1:7b.

27. *Zohar*, 1:7b.

28. Sigmund Freud, "The Interpretation of Dreams," vols. 4–5 of *Standard Edition of the Complete Psychological Works of Sigmund Freud*, ed. James Strachey (1900; London: Hogarth Press, 1981). This *magnum opus* in two volumes traces Freud's beginning understanding of the workings of the mind as related to the unconscious and conscious elements.

29. Sigmund Freud, 1917, "Introductory Lectures on Psycho-Analysis—Lecture 19: Resistance and Repression," in *Standard Edition*, ed. James Strachey, vol. 16, 295.

30. Tractate Yoma 15b: "There were four rooms leading into [a room called] Beit HaMoked. Like small rooms leading into a large entrance hall." See also Tractate 'Eruvin 92b.

31. Tractate Niddah 116a: "The Sages used metaphoric terms with regard to a woman's internal gynecological organs: the room (uterus), the entrance/ante room (vaginal tract) and the upper room/attic (ovaries). . . ."

32. Edith Jacobson (1897–1978) was a psychoanalyst and psychiatrist who emigrated from Germany to the United States. She developed the concepts of self and object representation and also wrote on depression as it relates to loss of object love. She often referred to qualities of awareness of the felt experience and called

these 'memory traces' or emotional engrams of experience. Edith Jacobson, *The Self and Object World* (New York: International Universities Press, 1964), 52.

33. D. W. Winnicott, "The Theory of the Parent-Infant Relationship," in *The Maturational Process and the Facilitating Environment* (1960a; London: Hogarth Press, 1972).

34. R. D. Stolorow, B. Brandschaft and G. E. Atwood, *Psychoanalytic Treatment: An Intersubjective Approach* (Hillsdale, N.J.: Analytic Press, 1987).

35. The intersubjective approach seemed to include Winnicott's view with Heinz Kohut's understanding. Heinz Kohut (1913–1981), a psychoanalyst and psychiatrist, emigrated from Vienna to Chicago where he established a 'parallel' school of psychoanalysis called 'self psychology.' Kohut focused his theory on 'self states': one's sense of self-worth and well-being. Kohut emphasized the individual's need for positive relationships throughout the stages of the life cycle, and placed great emphasis on the importance of empathy. For an introduction to his theoretical formulations, see Heinz Kohut, *The Analysis of the Self* (New York: International Universities Press, 1971).

36. Stephen Mitchell, "The Intrapsychic and the Interpersonal: Different Theories, Different Domains, or Historical Artifacts?" *Psychoanalytic Inquiry* 8 (1988): 472–96. Mitchell borrowed heavily from the ideas of American psychoanalyst and psychiatrist Harry Stack Sullivan (1892–1949). Sullivan developed a theory of psychiatry based on interpersonal relationships, in which cultural forces have a major part to play in emotional disturbance. See Harry Stack Sullivan, *The Interpersonal Theory of Psychiatry* (New York: Norton, 1953).

37. Ariel, *Mystic Quest*, 105. See also Elliot Ginsburgh, *The Sabbath in the Classical Kabbalah* (Albany: State University of New York Press, 1989).

38. Margaret Mahler, *On Human Symbiosis and the Vicissitudes of Individuation* (New York: International Universities Press, 1968).

39. D. W. Winnicott, 1958, "The Capacity to Be Alone," in *The Maturational Processes and the Facilitating Environment* (1958; London: Hogarth Press, 1985), 30.

Chapter Seven

Faces, Guises and Roles: The *Partzufim*

Lurianic Kabbalah refers to the Kabbalistic teachings of Rabbi Isaac Luria, the Ari. In turn, it was built on the first systematized understanding of Kabbalah, which was perfected by his teacher and contemporary, Moshe Cordovero, in the sixteenth century. Cordovero's first major work was *Pardes Rimonim* (*The Orchard of Pomegranates*). In it he brought together the many disparate strands of Kabbalistic thought into a unified, coherent system. He further tried to delineate the bridge between the Divine and the less spiritual worlds below. He showed that this bridge is the *sefirot* and the relations among them. Under Cordovero, Kabbalah was set, for the first time, into a philosophical structure with organizing principles and an organic structure.[1]

Both Cordovero and Luria were teachers in the Upper Galilee city of Safed. Cordovero himself was a disciple of extraordinary men with the deepest understanding of spiritual and material reality, including Joseph Karo and Solomon Alkabetz. Similarly, many distinguished Kabbalists followed them. Therefore, Safed became a city famous as a center of mysticism, as it still is.

The Lurianic system of Kabbalah took the principles and philosophy of Cordovero and expanded them into an unusually complex and difficult philosophical order. While this may seem burdensome and unwieldy, it placed Kabbalah on the map as a true 'philosophical science' with a predictable direction and with clearly defined constructs, correlates and principles. Isaac Luria was gifted with the ability to experience mystical visions and insights as well as to articulate them into a vast array of metaphors, imagery and flowery descriptions. He is the only learned sage or teacher who had an extra letter added before his name, standing for *Elohi*, godly.

The Ari, who died at an early age, left a legacy that includes his mystic experiences, direct visions and communications with souls and spirits from 'other worlds' (and other times and places), as well as an extraordinary ability to describe imaginative symbolic thinking. In psychological parlance, the Ari possessed a special gift: the capacity to experience unusual, out-of-the-ordinary phenomena and translate this into a systematic philosophical system of understanding. One could even venture to describe this as a merger of the primary and secondary thought processes with both concrete and abstract expression. While the average person, at any point in time, is either in a concrete mode of thinking or an abstract mode of thinking, the Ari was able to simultaneously experience and transcend both the concrete and abstract modes. Thus, he could experience both modalities and merge them into a cognitive and emotional whole.

Luria taught us that there is no such thing as objective cognition; Kabbalah is a subjective discipline. One can learn and study Kabbalah, but the emotional aspect needs to be experienced. Theoretical book knowledge, without an experiential, subjective component, will give a distorted and incomplete picture as to what Kabbalah and the Jewish mystical tradition are all about. The object relations theorists also struggled with this issue in their move from a libidinal-seeking theoretical framework to an object-seeking way of understanding emotional development. This has been referred to in the psychoanalytic literature as the metaphor of 'being' and 'doing.'[2]

As we have been discussing, the basic elements of the Lurianic system of Kabbalah include the concept of contraction (*tzimzum*), the five universes, the five levels of the soul, the ten *sefirot* (Divine relational attributes), the breaking of the vessels (*Shvirat HaKelim*), the physiognomies or faces of reconstruction (*partzufim*), and restoration or reparation (*tikkun*). In this chapter we will introduce the concept of the archetype personae, or *partzufim*.

In order to enter the very complicated world of the *partzufim*, it is important to review some of the basic ideas in the Lurianic philosophy and understanding of Kabbalah. Before the creation of the world, the *Ein Sof*, or the One Godhead, entirely filled the infinite space. In order to allow room for the beings in the world that God wanted to create, space needed to be made available so that creation could take place and manifest itself. God constricted and contracted Himself (*tzimzum*) so that His pure radiance would not overwhelm or overpower that which was to be created.[3, 4] A beam of light remained, called the *reshimu* ('a residual trace'). In the vacated space ten circles or vessels, called *sefirot*, formed. The light entered the vacated space and filled the ten vessels (*sefirot*). The three circles closest to the Godhead (the *Ein Sof*) were able to contain this overpowering light; however, the other vessels were not able to contain the light and they burst. This is what is known in Kabbalah as the breaking or shattering of the vessels (*Shvirat HaKelim*).[5] From these shattered vessels, now called shells or shards (*klipot*), emanates the evil in the world. In order to reconstruct the shattered vessels and remove them from the intense light, they were transformed into figures or faces or physiognomies (archetype personae, the *partzufim*).

To explain this psychoanalytically, we would point out that emotionally charged issues can be so overwhelming to an individual that they generate within him an intense feeling of emotional flooding, an overload that exceeds his ability for self-absorption. In a therapy session, the therapist needs to be able to contain the intense tensions and pressures the patient is feeling. The psychoanalyst Wilfred Bion's term 'container-contained relation' succinctly sums up the necessity of a container function.[6] Either the patient is able to contain the internal turmoil or the therapist needs to fulfill that function. The 'containing' enables the patient to reconstitute himself and repair the damage that his psyche has sustained.[7]

One question that begs an answer is why God could not foresee the shattering of the vessels and either prevent it or go straight to the next stage and immediately create the *partzufim*. A simple answer would be that if God, in the beginning, had created the *partzufim* instead of the *sefirot*, there would have been no evil in the world, which came about as a result of the shattering of the vessels. Without evil, there would be no reward and no punishment, nor would there be free will.

Philosophically, one needs the dialectical polarity of good and evil. One cannot strive for good unless the possibility of evil lurks in the background.[8] This means that in reality, in the original 'world of chaos' (*tohu*), the *sefirot* were not interconnected but functioned independently. However, in the 'world of rectification and repair' (*tikkun*), which is the already created world that we live and work in, the *partzufim* work together as developmental archetypes. Moreover, they embody united masculine and feminine aspects of the self as well as generational personae (parents, grandparents). This situation mirrors the psychoanalytic conceptualization of object relations: personal strivings are always object seeking, that is, toward the forming and developing of relationships. In this respect we note that the original 'world of chaos' (*tohu*) is reminiscent of the part object world, as portrayed by Melanie Klein, and the incomplete object relations world of object and self and their representations, as advanced by Edith Jacobson.[9, 10]

A more convoluted, yet essentially important, answer to the existence of the *partzufim* is based on the principle of receiving and giving. In order to receive the light (energy, radiance) from God, a vessel must be closely connected to the Source, to God. However, God is the Ultimate Giver and the vessel is the ultimate receiver. In order for the vessel to express itself to the fullest, it must resemble God and, therefore, also have properties of giving. The only vessel that can give, receive and resemble the Divine is man. Man gives by leading a good life, striving for perfection and attempting to better the universe. Man resembles his Source by having free will, and this is only possible when both good and evil exist and man has to make choices.

After the shattering of the vessels, the 'leftovers' were reconstructed and rebuilt as the *partzufim*. Each of these *partzufim* has 613 parts paralleling the 613 commandments of the Torah and the 613 parts of the body (248 limbs and 365 nerves, veins and sinews). Therefore, theosophically, the *partzufim* resemble the Torah and mankind. They can now become receivers as well as givers. When man can truly become a receiver and giver, he gives and receives not only for himself but also for others—this is the striving for perfection by trying to perfect/correct the world order. The *partzufim* in this condition are the vessels that are now able to receive God's light. This corrected, end-result state is also a process called *tikkun*. In this process, the *partzufim* interact with each other in an anthropomorphic manner.[11] That is why the parts of the body as well as role differentiations within the family structure (father, mother, child), along with pregnancy, birth and development, play an important role in the Lurianic model. They all represent categories of intricate human relationships.

Relationships and developmental, hierarchical differentiation form the core in psychoanalytic theory. Ever since Freud's classic publication on stages of human development, theoreticians have studied how relationships are formed, develop and interact.[12] From a fused state of symbiosis that has developed *in utero*, immediately upon birth the infant begins a process of differentiation from the mother container. How the mother and infant allow this process to unfold will determine the normality or pathology of this relationship and of future relationships with others—since this primary relationship is paradigmic of other relationships.[13] The process of emotional separation involves progressing from symbiosis to part object to complete object differentiation. This, in turn, involves not only real objects but also object and self representations.

In the Bible and in rabbinic literature, God is very often described in humanlike terminology.[14] *Anthropomorphism*, as this attribution is called, consists of two aspects. In one, there is the ascription to God of human qualities such as human form (finger, hands, eyes, etc.). And in the other, known as *anthropopathism*, there is the ascription of every human emotion (God loves, God is angry, etc.). Many of the flowery anthropomorphic descriptions that may appear to be difficult and disconnected in different parts of the *Zohar* can be found in the more esoteric parts of the *Zohar*: the *Idrah Rabbah* and the *Idrah Zutah*. This is known as the Greater Assembly and the Smaller or Lesser Assembly, and refers to the gatherings and learning circles of Shimon Bar Yochai and his disciples at which highly mystical teachings were studied.

Another enigmatic work is the *Sifrah DeZeniutah* (*The Concealed Book*), which contains similar mysterious language.

While the Torah also describes God in such anthropomorphic terms, the Aramaic translator of the Bible, Onkelos (second century C.E.), as well as the Hellenic philosophers such as Philo, translated or explained this anthropomorphic imagery by qualifying or giving allegorical interpretations in order to avoid giving God manlike attributes. Mystics, Kabbalists and even Hasidim utilize various anthropomorphic descriptions in order to allow man to speak on two levels: through prayer *to* a God and theologically *about* a God. In Kabbalah, the ability to grasp the *partzufim* allows man to metaphorically understand his relationship to the Godhead and to become close to the Divine through performance of His commandments. This allows man to correct himself and correct the world. It is how Kabbalah preserves and integrates the infinity and non-knowing of God (the impersonal God) with the essential theological-religious relationship between man and God (the personal God). Thus, "the whole attempt of Lurianic Kabbalism to describe the theogonic process in God (i.e., His origins) in terms of human existence represents an effort to arrive at a new conception of the personal God."[15]

We need to now look at the *partzufim* in order to try to understand how the Ari utilized anthropomorphic symbolism, gender distinctions and developmental and generational roles in their various faces, guises and archetype personae in order to bring man closer to a mystical awareness and knowing of the essential elements of the soul.[16]

We are already aware that the basic purpose of the individual *partzufim* is to integrate disparate elements into a more coherent whole. This is accomplished by the associative and metaphoric descriptions accorded the *partzufim*. Through the *partzufim* there is an interactive and integrative relationship between the Godhead and man. This means that every emotion, feeling and action that man has is connected and anchored to a spiritual dimension. This, in effect, allows man a spiritual foothold in the upper worlds. Consequently, he is able to connect the lower realm with the upper worlds—through meditation and the quest for perfection.

As mentioned earlier, the *partzufim* arise out of the shattered vessels and are reconstituted *sefirot*. However, this reconstruction changes somewhat the original configuration of the ten *sefirot*, which are now divided into five groupings. The reason for the number five is that there is a mystical way that the Ari saw the Four-Letter name of God, as representing, either numerically or physically, a particular *sefira*. Out of this conceptualization, the ten *sefirot* were divided into five groups. The number five repeats quite often in Kabbalistic literature: five levels of soul, five worlds/universes, five *partzufim*.[17]

Each group represents a developmental progression in the family of man. The following is the division of the ten *sefirot* into the five groups:

Keter
Chochmah
Bina
Chesed, Gevurah, Tiferet, Netzach, Hod, Yesod
Malkhut

Each of these five groups of *sefirot* develops into a physiognomy or *partzuf* (singular of *partzufim*). We need to remember that each *partzuf* represents a specific stage in the process of reconstruction of man, and by extension, the universe.

Partzuf	*Sefira*
1. arikh anpin or *atik yomin*	*Keter*
2. abba	*Chochmah*
3. ima	*Bina*
4. ze'er anpin	*Chesed, Gevurah, Tiferet, Netzach, Hod, Yesod*
5. nukvah	*Malkhut*

Before proceeding further, we need to define our terms. Each of the *partzufim*, as mentioned earlier, represents an archetype or personage. Following is a brief description of each:

1. *arikh anpin*: It literally means 'the long-faced one' or 'the indulgent one.' This is a term from the *Zohar* and is the Aramaic translation of God described as 'slow to anger.' We see this clearly in the Biblical verses describing the 13 attributes of God: "God, God, Omnipotent, merciful and kind, slow to anger, with tremendous [resources of] love and truth. He remembers deeds of love for thousands [of generations], forgiving sin, rebellion and error. He does not clear [those who do not repent], but keeps in mind the sins of the fathers to their children and grandchildren, to the third and fourth generation."[18]

In developmental terms, this *partzuf* is the grandparent (grandfather). The implication here is that it is the grandfather (*sabah*) who carries the male voice. As we have explained, this *partzuf* is a reconstructed form of the *sefira* of *Keter*. Since the *partzufim* are described in role differentiation terms developmentally, the anthropomorphic description has the *partzuf* described in very human terms. So the grandfather in our developmental sequence is conceived of as having 'white hair.' Since this is a correction (rectification) of the *sefira* of *Keter*, and a *Keter* is a crown that is worn above the head, this *partzuf* can be visualized as consisting of two subparts: the crown above the head and the skull itself. One of the two subparts is called *arikh anpin* and the other is called *atik yomin* ('Ancient of Days'). The latter has as its source the verse in Daniel: "I saw the Ancient of Days sitting on a throne, His garment was white as snow, and the hair of His head was like pure wool."[19] The first subpart (*arikh anpin*) is mentioned in the Torah and the second subpart (*atik yomin*) is mentioned in the Prophets, which should technically place the first subpart on a higher plane—closer to the source of God. However, Italian mystic and Kabbalist Moshe Chaim Luzzatto noted that the *partzuf* of *atik yomin* guides the *partzuf* of *arikh anpin*.[20] Interestingly, in 1727, while in the throes of a deep meditative trance, Luzzatto heard a Divine voice, which he believed to be that of a *maggid* (a Divine power that reveals heavenly secrets to chosen human beings). For the next several years, Luzzatto was influenced in his writings and teachings by the *maggid*. These 'magical' revelations eventually led leading rabbis and scholars to threaten to brand Luzzatto as a heretic. To avoid this, he had to refrain from committing to writing the words of the *maggid*.[21]

2. *abba*: It means 'father.' This is the restoration of the *sefira* of *Chochmah*. This is the male parent, as opposed to the female parent *ima* (which is the next *partzuf*). These two parental figures are mentioned in the *Zohar* as "God our Lord, this is father and mother."[22] We will elaborate more on the parental figures of father and mother in the next *partzuf* of *ima* (mother). Father (*abba*) and mother (*ima*) are both on equal footing; they are on the same plane. One is right (male, father) and one is left (female, mother).[23] Thus, there is a 'centering' that needs to take place which takes into account both the male and female aspects of the personality.

3. *ima*: It means 'mother.' This is the restoration of the *sefira* of *Bina*, and it is the female parental figure. Both father and mother ". . . function in a dual capacity: they exist as a medium for the re-individuation and re-differentiation of all the emanated beings into transmitters and receivers of influx, and they also serve as the supreme archetype for that procreative 'coupling' (*zivug*) which, in its metaphorical aspect of 'looking face-to-face' . . . is the common root of all intellectual and erotic unions."[24] The first function is quite similar to the neurological concept of afferent and efferent neuronal pathways. Impulses that travel toward or into the central nervous system are sensory or afferent. Those that leave are motor or efferent. Nearly all nerves contain both afferent and efferent fibers and are known as mixed nerves. The father and mother are, in a sense, the procreators who also temper the impulses and feelings that come in and go out. They are both transmitters as well as receivers. They provide more 'brain power,' all of which is known as *mochin* (small brains). And they create more light and energy by their sexual proclivity.

Father and mother are representative of the two intellectual systems of wisdom (*Chochmah*) and understanding (*Bina*). They can be expansive or constricted in their thinking prowess. This follows the cognitive thought processes of concrete and abstract thought. The *mochin* (brains) also allude to the personality characteristics. There is a blend of cognitive and emotional characteristics. Father and mother are descended from the grandfather (who planted the seed, i.e., the sperm) and couple in order to procreate and bring forth offspring. This sexual union is the second function. The offspring or children that ensue from the coupling relationship (*zivug*) are the next two *partzufim*.

4. *ze'er anpin*: It equals 'the short-faced one' and can also be translated as the 'impatient one.' This *partzuf* is the reconstruction of the six lower *sefirot*: *Chesed, Gevurah, Tiferet, Netzach, Hod, Yesod*. In this new configuration, there is a mitigation of the harsh powers of God's judgment (*din*). This is done through sexual coupling (*zivug*), gestation or embryonic development (*ibbur*), birth (*laydah*), nursing (*yenika*) and growing into maturity (*gadlut*) from immaturity (*katnut*). One can see the anthropomorphic descriptions of sexual intercourse and the development and growth of the fetus through birth, nursing and developing maturity. This *partzuf* is the male child of the father and mother coupling. The female child, we will see in the next (and last) *partzuf*, is known as *nukvah*. The essence of the Guiding Power of God in this world is rooted in *ze'er anpin* (the male aspects) and in *nukvah* (the female aspects). As Luzzatto remarks: "In the *partzufim* of *ze'er anpin* and *nukvah*, there are parallel concepts to everything in man below. If they were not in these *partzufim* they would not exist below."[25] By this he means that the reconstituted six *sefirot* are the root of all created things. But we can find the emotional attributes for God's Divine light and power in this *partzuf*.

5. *nukvah*: It means literally 'an orifice,' 'a repository.' This is the female part, the complementary feminine aspect of the previous *partzuf*, *ze'er anpin*. This *partzuf* is the correction of the *sefira* of *Malkhut*. Again we find the metaphoric descriptive concept of *zivug* (coupling, attachment) when the previous *partzuf*, *ze'er anpin* (the masculine aspect) couples with *nukvah* (the feminine aspect). As Aryeh Kaplan writes: "Whereas *abba* and *ima* are the masculine and feminine forces of creation, the information and logic with which God created the universe, *ze'er anpin* and *nukvah* are the masculine and feminine forces of providence, or of God's presence in the world."[26] This means that there is a dyadic interactive process between God and man. Just as God can influence man, so too can man have a hand in the process. All of man's actions involve a response by God to what we do, do not do, intend to do, etc. The forces of providence refer to God's actions and responses to man's actions.

Kaplan, quoting the *Zohar* and the writings of the Ari, notes that the ineffable name of God, the Tetragrammaton, as represented by the four Hebrew letters *yod, heh, vav, heh*, can be divided into two parts.[27] The first two letters (*yod, heh*) are never separated, as they represent the forces of creation. That is why the name of God is often abbreviated by these two letters. The latter two letters (*vav, heh*) are related to the forces of providence. Here, depending upon how man interacts with God, God is either revealed and both letters are together, or God hides His face because of evil in the world and the letters are separated. The Ari devised special meditative practices in order to try to unite these last two letters. *Nukvah* is also referred to as the Community of Israel, because she is the assembly of all their souls. She unites the entire Community as well as the Kingdom of God. *Malkhut* is the last of the *sefirot* and the end source of all of God's emanation. But this last *partzuf* is only complete with the coupling with *ze'er anpin*.

The *partzufim* are the rectification and reconstruction of the *sefirot* after the shattering of the vessels, and this new cosmic order is called the World of *Tikkun* (rectification). The *partzufim*, or archetypes, are the new 'vessels' for the Infinite Light of God. The Ari conceived of the *partzufim* as separate personalities. The *partzufim* themselves help us to understand the Kabbalah's conceptualization of role differentiation on a developmental level, as well as sexual and gender role differentiation. This can be graphically drawn as follows:

Partzuf	Developmental Correlate
1. *arikh anpin* or *atik yomin*	grandfather
2. *abba*	parent: father
3. *ima*	parent: mother
4. *ze'er anpin*	child: boy/male/brother
5. *nukvah*	child: girl/female/sister

In effect, we now can see a progression of the nuclear family from the grandfather (who starts the cycle of procreation), to the father who couples with the mother. The mother then becomes pregnant and the fetus gestates within her, until we have the birth of the male.[28] The infant is nursed and grows to maturity. The mother then becomes pregnant a second time and a sister is created. At the same time, the personality of each is cultivated (referred to in Kabbalah as *mochin*, the 'brains') and matures as does the body. While *ze'er anpin* and *nukvah* are brother and sister, after they mature they become a couple, a bride and groom. We find parallels for this transformation in the Song of Songs, an allegorical and symbolic exposition—for example, ". . . my sister, O bride . . ." and ". . . my sister, my love. . . ."[29] While incest, in this case sexual relations between a brother and sister, is not permissible, on a metaphoric spiritual level, this coupling is permitted. We see this in the Torah, where it is reported that both Abraham and Isaac called their wives 'sister.'[30] According to the Kabbalists, both Abraham and Isaac had relationships with their wives that were akin to relationships on a higher spiritual level—like the coupling relationship between *ze'er anpin* and *nukvah.*[31] This is a special type of intimacy.

Relationships are very complicated and convoluted. Not all relationships can reach a high level of intimacy and 'spirituality.' In order to better understand how relationships develop and endure, we need to look at how the child develops emotionally, in stages that are similar to the developmental progression of the *partzufim*. In addition, we will need to understand more fully the concepts of love and intimacy. We will start by investigating the concept of developmental stages.

In *Midrash Rabbah*, we find the following description of the developmental stages of man:

> 'Futility of futilities, said Kohelet, futility of futilities! All is futile.' The seven 'futilities' that Kohelet said [seven times the word 'futile' appears] parallel seven worlds that man goes through. [The first world] at age one, he is like a King, carried around in a canopied chair, asked by everyone how he is, kissed and hugged by all. [The second world] ages two and three, he is like a pig, his hands touching all types of filth and excrement. [The third world] at age ten, he jumps like a goat [always playful]. [The fourth world] age twenty, he is like a young stallion, neighing loudly and looking for a mate. [The fifth world] until age forty, he marries a woman and is like a mule, constantly procreating and working diligently to make a living, carrying on his back the responsibility of family. [The sixth world] he has many children and the responsibility of providing for them makes him act, at times, like a dog, barking and wondering from where will come money and food. [The seventh world] he is now old and is like a monkey, his physiognomy has changed, he is constantly asking questions, reverts back to playing like a child, is made fun of by his children and other family members, cursed and hated.[32]

Sigmund Freud, who, we believe, was very knowledgeable of Jewish sources, may have been aware of this interesting developmental survey of the age of man. In 1905, Freud delineated five developmental stages in the emotional development of the child[33]:

ages 0–2 years: the oral stage
ages 2–4 years: the anal stage

ages 4–6 years: the phallic and oedipal stage
ages 6–11 years: latency
ages 11–18 years: adolescence

Freud showed how the child needs to work through certain emotional issues or conflicts in order to progress to the next stage. If there were problems as a result of frustration or overindulgence that occurred at a specific age, these could lead to fixations (stuckness) and could have a deleterious effect on the child's emotional development and progression to the next stage. Freud was interested in the intrapsychic development of the child; relationships to the 'other' were implied although not specifically stated. So, the parallel to our understanding of the *partzufim* is not realistic, since *partzufim* take us on a journey through the world of relationships. In following an in-depth understanding through our understanding of *partzufim*, we would explore the familial hierarchical relationships from grandfather to parents to children. We need to more fully appreciate the gender issues and see the relative strengths of both the male and the female aspects of our personality structure.

The concept of inter-psychic development was more completely elaborated by the neo-Freudian Erik Erikson in his epic work *Childhood and Society*.[34] Following Freud's developmental stages and building upon them, Erikson added the psychosocial component: parents, siblings, relationships, school and work. Erikson's developmental stages were constructed in such a way that the theoretical framework had eight stages and ended at death—old age. Each stage poses a unique developmental task, and confronts individuals with a crisis that they need to struggle with. The crisis becomes a 'turning point,' a period of increased vulnerability and heightened potential. The interaction that takes place between the individual and society during each stage can change the course of personality in either a positive or negative direction. The stages are constructed as valences, vacillating between a more positive and a more negative pole. Both poles are important, and the individual needs to incorporate a bit of both with the ascendancy going to the more positive pole. The following are the eight stages as delineated by Erikson, with the polar opposite valences:

ages 0–2 years: basic trust versus mistrust
ages 2–4 years: autonomy versus shame and doubt
ages 4–6 years: initiative versus guilt
ages 6–11 years: industry versus inferiority
adolescence: identity versus role confusion
young adulthood: intimacy versus isolation
adulthood: generativity versus stagnation
old age: integrity versus despair

Erikson's stages correspond with the developmental process as found in the *partzufim*, but in reverse order. Instead of beginning with the grandfather, as in the *partzufim*, we end in Erikson's stages with the grandfather (stage eight). The *zivug*, or coupling, takes place around stage six, and procreating and having offspring continues into stage seven. Stages one through five are the stages of childhood and adolescence.

It is useful to look at Erikson's stage five (adolescence) and stage six (young adulthood), in order to understand the concepts of identity, love and intimacy. The *partzufim*, as they mature, differentiate into clear identity roles and become intimate and couple in sexual relations in order to express love for one another as well as to become emotionally intimate with each other.

Love, in the intimate sense, is not only a physical expression of emotion, but also a spiritual one. When Erikson talked of intimacy in the young adult stage, he was referring to the ability to have two people emotionally connect to each other without each one losing his or her own individuality. This contrasts with the Kabbalistic way of thinking (as articulated metaphorically and symbolically in the Song of Songs) whereby the person who truly loves God negates his own existence in the service of God.

The human emotion of love is an elevated emotion in that the more genuine the love is, the more the lover abandons any thoughts of personal gain. True love is not based on reciprocity ("What will I gain from this?"), but is selfless. In Hebrew the word for love is *ahavah*. The two-letter strong root in that word is *HaV*, to give. An intimate relationship based on true love is the ability for each partner in the relationship to give to the other without losing his or her individuality. If we place both stage five (identity) and stage six (intimacy) together, the true definition of intimacy is the ability to give and receive without losing one's identity or individuality.

Let us now consider the issue of sexuality, identity and gender. In the Freudian paradigm, the child achieves his or her first understanding of 'identity' at the conclusion of the oedipal stage. This follows a period (the phallic phase—the precursor of the oedipal stage) where the child begins to first emotionally connect with the opposite-sex parent. By the age of five or six years, the child has begun to identify with the same-sex parent.[35] This means that there is now an awareness on the part of the little boy that he wants to grow up and be like daddy, while the little girl wants to grow up and be like mommy. That is the child's first conceptualization of sexual identity. Ten years after Freud described the stages of development (from birth until late adolescence), he added a 'footnote,' and stated: ". . . the concepts of 'masculine' and 'feminine,' whose meaning seems so unambiguous to ordinary people, are among the most confused that occur in science . . . in human beings pure masculinity or femininity is not to be found either in a psychological or biological sense."[36]

Freud was correct. Every male has a smattering of female hormone, as each female has a small amount of male hormone. This is a biological fact. The Biblical verse ". . . male and female, He created them . . ." occurs before the creation of Eve.[37] Commentators on this verse describe the creation, at first, of an androgyny that was later separated into a male and a female part. So there are male and female within each of us.

Probably around the same time, at the conclusion of the Freudian oedipal stage, the child begins to understand that there are sexual identities and gender roles. The former is the conception that people have of themselves of being male or female. The latter are sets of cultural expectations that define the ways in which the members of each sex behave. Freud's early theory of psychosexual development lacks the concept of gender identity.[38] While Freud does talk of masculinity and femininity, he does not take into account the individual's conceptualization of self or object relations development and the inner world of representations. This was a much later development, after Melanie Klein's groundwork in describing part objects and the unfolding of object relations theory.

Importantly, the Kabbalists had a very highly developed understanding of gender roles and identities. As we have seen in our review of the *partzufim*, there is a developmental progression: grandfather > father > mother > son > daughter. In addition, the *partzuf* of *ze'er anpin* is the masculine identity and at maturity couples with the last *partzuf* of *nukvah*, as mentioned earlier. God's manifest presence, the *Shekhinah*, is channeled through the last of the ten *sefirot*, *Malkhut*. This, later reconstructed and rectified, becomes the *partzuf* of *nukvah*. *Malkhut*, the last vessel, and in its new form, the *partzuf* of *nukvah*, gathers the essence of all that has preceded (the other nine *sefirot* and the other *partzufim*) and channels it outward.

While gender identities are stable in that they are either masculine/male or feminine/female, there is, at times, an interchange as well as overlap. While the *Shechinah* (God's Divine presence) is generally female, there are interspersed masculine parts.[39] We have an interesting example in the *Zohar* of the switching of gender identities:

> This is the angel who is sometimes male and sometimes female. When he channels blessings to the world, he is male. . . . But when his relationship to the world is that of judgment, then he is called female. . . .[40, 41]

This is very similar to Harvard psychologist Carol Gilligan's concept of 'male voices' in females and 'female voices' in males.[42] Sometimes the role determines the voice (whether one will be more masculine or feminine) and sometimes the voice determines the role. An entire book has been written by

Elliot Wolfson, a prolific writer on Kabbalah studies, on gender in Kabbalistic symbolism; it discusses the interrelationship of male and female aspects in order to bring the *Shekhinah* (God's Divine presence) to mankind.[43] The importance of the developmental and gender identity aspects of the *partzufim* is in order for the world to have both male and female elements joined together to work for the betterment of mankind, as well as for the rectification and reconstruction of the world—*tikkun ha'olam.*

Significantly, Sholem Dov Ber Schneerson, in a Hasidic discourse that he gave on the Jewish New Year (Rosh HaShanah) in 1898, remarked on the 'feminine capacity,' as different from the male's essence.[44] He noted:

> Just as the male bestows the seminal drop, the female contributes the ovum. The ovum, however, serves as a receptacle to receive the seminal drop from the male . . . both male and female elements are necessary. . . . In summary, the actual existence of the child is due to the power of the female [*Malkhut*], and this capability comes from the superiority of her origin over the male [*ze'er anpin*], i.e., her source in the essence.[45]

A child cannot be formed without the male and the female working together in tandem.

Comparatively, Joseph B. Soloveitchik, the philosopher and theologian, noted the metaphysical and personality differences inherent in males and females.[46] Soloveitchik went way beyond the standard 'active-passive' paradigm and described how the male and female need each other not only in order to produce life, but also to grow emotionally, one through the other. We grow through our spiritual development, which raises us to a higher plane that enables us to blend both male and female aspects together. According to Soloveitcik this is the merger of the 'male' with the 'female' aspect. This is the final *partzuf* of *nukvah* that, after maturing and coupling with *ze'er anpin*, produces God's manifest bounty for our rectified and reconstructed world.

Psychoanalysts Joseph and Anne-Marie Sandler investigated the concepts of construction and reconstruction.[47] Since psychoanalysis, as advanced by Freud, attempted to help patients understand themselves better and relate better to the 'child within,' the question that arose was whether the patient would 'return' back to his earlier lifespace, prior to the conflicts or trauma (reconstruction). Or, was there to be a new construction, based on what transpired in the therapeutic encounters? Put another way: the parental and authority imagoes need to be re-worked into non-threatening objects that can be handled and integrated within the self. In Kabbalistic terminology, these are the 'part objects'—the *sefirot*—and 'whole objects'—the *partzufim*, which convey the wide array of relationships that help build satisfying family and social circles.

Finally, it is fascinating to note that there are 22 connections between the *sefirot*, which correspond to the 22 letters of the Hebrew alphabet. This fact further intertwines the work of Luria and Luzzato with Fairbairn and Bion. Therefore, we can see why the mystics state that the diversity of relationships creates the building blocks of language, and through language the world came into being.

NOTES

1. Rabbi Moshe Cordovero (1522–1570), is known by his acronym, the ReMaK.
2. John Sutherland has reviewed the classical object relations theorists and their ways of understanding the mother-infant / therapist-patient relationship, with an analysis of the 'being' and 'doing' metaphor. See John Sutherland, "The British Object Relations Theorists: Balint, Winnicott, Fairbairn, Guntrip," *Journal of the American Psychoanalytic Association* 28 (1980): 829–60.
3. Various metaphors are used to describe the radiance of God; 'energy' and 'light' are two examples. While radiance may have a theological connotation to some, energy and light are symbolic representations that transcend theology and accentuate the physical and metaphysical aspects of a vibrant energy system. Quantum physics is built upon an energy system that can be metaphorically described as light and energy.
4. The physicist Michio Kaku, writing about the universe as being created *ex nihilo* (the "universe-from-nothing theory"), describes a system of positive and negative electrical charges that balance each other out exactly. Michio Kaku, *Parallel Worlds* (London: Allen Lane/Penguin, 2005), 94–95. The Kabbalistic concept of *tzimzum* ('constriction,' 'contraction'), utilizing Kaku's electrical charge theory, would label the Creator as the positive charge, the energy/light source, which needs to contract/constrict to the point of allowing other beings in the world to be created and to survive. These beings would be the 'contra' or negative valence. Both the positive and negative are necessary.
5. In modern Hebrew, when one feels overwhelmed and cannot contain what is happening, the expression that is used is: 'my container/capacity is broken.'
6. Wilfred Bion, *Attention and Interpretation*, in *Seven Servants* (1970; New York: Aronson, 1977).
7. The Kabbalistic term *tikkun* describes similar processes and will be more fully discussed in a later chapter.
8. The Danish philosopher Søren Kierkegaard (1813–1855), in his famous work *Fear and Trembling* (1843; Harmondsworth, Middlesex, England: Penguin, 1985), developed a method of understanding through dialectical machinations. Through the use of polar opposites, one could understand more fully each of the extreme views or positions. This laid the groundwork for existential philosophy and Jacques Derrida's deconstruction theory. See Jacques Derrida, *The Gift of Death*, trans. David Wills (Chicago: University of Chicago Press, 1995).

9. Melanie Klein, "A Contribution to the Psychogenesis of Manic-Depressive States," *International Journal of Psycho-Analysis* 16 (1935): 145–74.

10. Edith Jacobson, *The Self and the Object World* (New York: International Universities Press, 1964).

11. Anthropomorphism is the attribution of human motivation, characteristics or behavior to inanimate objects, animals or natural phenomena.

12. Sigmund Freud, "Three Essays on Sexuality," in *Standard Edition of the Complete Psychological Works of Sigmund Freud*, ed. James Strachey (1905a; London: Hogarth Press, 1981), vol. 7.

13. See the classic text on developmental theories: Phyllis Tyson and Robert Tyson, *Psychoanalytic Theories of Development* (New Haven, Conn.: Yale University Press, 1990).

14. Rabbinic literature refers to explanations, commentaries and homiletical elaborations of Biblical texts.

15. Gershom Scholem, *Major Trends in Jewish Mysticism* (1941; New York: Schocken Books, 1995), 269.

16. We use the term 'knowing' rather than 'knowledge.' The latter is technical and theoretical. The former includes experiential and emotive aspects.

17. A source for this is found in the *Zohar*, 3:228a. See also Aryeh Kaplan, *Innerspace* (Jerusalem: Vagshal/Moznaim, 1990a), 93.

18. Exodus 34:6–7.

19. Daniel 7:9.

20. Rabbi Moshe Chaim Luzzatto, known by his acronym: RaMCHaL (1707–1747).

21. Yechiel Bar-Lev, *Song of the Soul* (Petach Tikvah, Israel: Sefer ve Sefel, 1994), 245.

22. *Zohar* 1:26 a.

23. *Zohar* 3:290 a.

24. Gershom Scholem, *Kabbalah* (Jerusalem: Keter, 1974), 141. See also Moshe Idel, *Kabbalah and Eros* (New Haven, Conn.: Yale University Press, 2005).

25. Quoted in Bar-Lev, *Song of the Soul*, 378.

26. Kaplan, *Innerspace*, 104.

27. Kaplan, *Innerspace*, 210; *Zohar* 2:14a.

28. The fetus, *in utero*, exists in a world where all knowledge and learning has taken place. This fetus 'sees the light,' the energy source. According to the Talmud Niddah 30b, a light is constantly illuminated, and the fetus can see from one side of the world to the other. When the fetus exits in the birth process, an angel strikes the infant on the upper lip (hence, the indentation) and all learning and understanding is forgotten.

29. Song of Songs 4:9; 5:2.

30. Genesis 12:13; 26:7.

31. *Zohar* 1:140 b.

32. Midrash Rabbah is part of the vast Rabbinic literature (see note 14, above) of discourses and anecdotal tales based on the verses in the Bible. This particular elaboration was written around the twelfth century, and is based on the Biblical verse, Ec-

clesiastes 1:2. The bracketed words are not directly written in the text but are 'implicitly' derived.

33. Freud, 1905a, "Three Essays on Sexuality," in *Standard Edition*, ed. James Strachey, vol. 7.

34. Erik Erikson, "The Eight Stages of Man," in *Childhood and Society* (New York: Norton, 1950). There has always been a clouded historical understanding of the identity of Erikson's father. Historian Lawrence Friedman, in his book *Identity's Architect: A Biography of Erik H. Erikson* (Cambridge, Mass.: Harvard University Press, 2000), makes a convincing case for Erikson's mother becoming pregnant with Erik by another (not-named) man, while still legally and Jewishly (Halachically) married. This, in effect, could make Erikson a *mamzer*, a bastard, by Jewish Halachic Law. And this man was 'Identity's Architect.'

35. The ages given are 'correct' according to Freud in 1905, but the stages probably occur at an earlier age today.

36. Freud in his "Three Essays on Sexuality" added this footnote in 1915 to his sub-section on "The Differentiation Between Men and Women." Freud, 1905a, "Three Essays on Sexuality," in *Standard Edition*, ed. James Strachey, vol. 7, 219–20.

37. Genesis 1:27.

38. Freud, 1905a, "Three Essays on Sexuality," in *Standard Edition*, ed. James Strachey, vol. 7.

39. Gershom Scholem, "Shekhinah: The Feminine Element in Divinity," in *On the Mystical Shape of the Godhead* (New York: Schocken, 1991), chap. 4.

40. The 'redeeming angel' in Genesis 48:16.

41. *Zohar* 1:232 a.

42. Carol Gilligan, *In a Different Voice* (Cambridge, Mass.: Harvard University Press, 1982).

43. Elliot Wolfson, *Circle in the Square: Studies in the Use of Gender in Kabbalistic Symbolism* (Albany: State University of New York Press, 1995a).

44. Known by his acronym, the RaSHaB (1860–1920), the fifth Lubavitcher Rebbe.

45. Shalom Dov Ber Schneersohn, *Forces in Creation* (New York: Kehot, 2003), 40, 42.

46. Joseph B. Soloveitchik, *Family Redeemed: Essays on Family Relationships* (New York: Toras HoRav Foundation, 2000).

47. Joseph Sandler and Anne-Marie Sandler, *Internal Objects Re-Visited* (New York: International Universities Press, 1999).

Chapter Eight

The Language of Creation

Before time and space began, there was a dark nothingness. Then God created existence with a word.

> God said, 'Let there be light,' and there was light. God saw that the light was good, and God separated between the light and the darkness. God called the light, 'Day,' and to the darkness, He called 'Night.' . . .[1,2]

Like a 'young God,' a baby also creates reality. Through the use of words, he names things, and they exist. And as he develops, words help him grow, change, be hurt ('curse words'), be saved ('sticks and stones can break my bones but words can never harm me'), be healed (psychoanalytic interpretations) and become one with the universe (religious revelation).

Language is the organized application of words, not just for the purpose of description or for communication, but for creation. Language lays the basis for society and culture—in other words, more worlds.

Interestingly, in English a 'word' is just one letter away from a 'world.' It is only missing the letter 'l,' which one might aver stands for 'life.' In this regard, a 'word' plus an 'l' equals a 'world.' Or to put it another way, the created *world* contains an infinite array of generative words.

We can see the same process at work in the Hebrew language. The Hebrew for word is *milah* (MiLaH). And the Hebrew for world is *olam* (OhLaM). Both share the same consonants, M and L. The letters, o and h (*vav* and *heh*), are quiescent letters or semi-vowels, not part of the root. In contrast the O (*ayin*) is a guttural, a silent letter, which according to Kabbalah denotes Divine providence, or the will of God.[3] This enables us to better understand the first book of the Bible, Genesis, whereby a word that encompasses the will of God creates the world.

This unfolding of reality can be approached from another, human perspective. We can observe what happens in certain circumstances when a person inhabits a state of meaninglessness, bereft of words, before language exists. This was the case with the 'wild child,' Helen Keller, who became blind and deaf as an infant and lapsed into a state of inchoate darkness. Helen Keller's entry into language permitted her to actualize not just the world outside herself, but inwardly as well.[4]

According to Helen's story, a few months before her seventh birthday she began to make contact with a new teacher, Miss Annie Sullivan, whom her despairing parents had engaged in order to socialize her. Miss Sullivan proceeded to spell words into Helen's hands. At first, the little girl did not understand what Miss Sullivan was doing, although she enjoyed the physical sensations. Then she became frustrated, and at one point smashed a doll that Miss Sullivan had given her along with the word 'd-o-l-l.' Helen relates,

> Neither sorrow nor regret followed my passionate outburst. . . . In the still dark world in which I lived there was no strong sentiment of tenderness . . . I (just) had a sense of satisfaction that the cause of my discomfort was removed.[5]

This procedure was repeated many times, especially with water. Finally the wild little girl realized that there was a connection between the word 'w-a-t-e-r' and the substance she felt running over her hand. It is worth quoting from Helen Keller's description of this event at some length, because it so movingly denotes the moment when she could apprehend external reality, and expand her psychic life as well.

> Suddenly I felt a misty consciousness as of something forgotten—a thrill of returning thoughts; and somehow the mystery of language was revealed to me. I knew then that 'w-a-t-e-r' meant the wonderful cool something that was flowing over my hand. That living word awakened my soul, gave it light, hope, joy, set it free! I left the well-house eager to learn. Everything had a name, and each name gave birth to a new thought. As we returned to the house every object which I touched seemed to quiver with life. That was because I saw everything with the strange, new sight that had come to me.[6]

Helen learned that a concrete pattern of physical sensations could be the equivalent of a thing or object. Later she extended this realization to emotions and actions. The sensations served to 'name' the object and separate it from the amorphous night that she had previously inhabited.

Perhaps an even greater breakthrough occurred when she was able to relate the sensations with the idea of a letter, and then the sequence of letters with a word. Therefore, Helen learned that such abstractions, a letter, or specific grouping of letters, a word, could act as a designator or pointer to what existed outside herself. In this way the world literally came into being. As she herself exclaimed, darkness became light, and she began 'to see.'

In linguistics, designators are called 'signs.' Signs point to things and are the literal equivalent of what they point to. As the philosopher Ernst Cassirer notes, signs convey meaning, but in a very limited, rigid, inflexible manner.[7] Nonetheless, for Helen the act of naming, or learning to use signs, denoted a major expansion of her thought processes. Before the breakthrough with Miss Sullivan, her awareness had been roughly limited by sensations that gave pleasure or pain. Afterward, the rapid increase in her vocabulary helped her to learn how to learn, and to master increasing levels of abstraction.

What followed was that words began to take on an independent existence. Helen could play with them and generalize from one word, or idea, to another. She could connect words with feelings, words with people, words with relationships, and, in so doing, not only grasped the outside world, but also gained an inner world, her mind.

Cassirer argues that consciousness begins when 'signs' become 'symbols.' By consciousness he means the capacity to enter into larger and larger spheres of human meaning, or interconnectiveness. All this, in turn, is implicit in our mastery of making and using symbols, or the process of symbolization. Symbols, which include the domains of words, pictures and body movements, differ from signs in that they do far more than designate or identify things. Symbols are variable, plastic and versatile, and move from the particular to the universal and back. While signs point, symbols carry meaning, as a poem, on not one but many levels. They are the basis of self-reflection, self-awareness and self-realization. In other words, symbols are what make us human, while they also allow us to extend ourselves far beyond the bounds of human limitations. Signs keep us tied to the ground. Symbols allow us to soar.

The story of Helen Keller is so rich because it delineates the passage from a pre-primitive state of mind (chaotic darkness), to one replete with concrete signs (literal designators), to a profound creative consciousness (symbolic imagination). Indeed, these accomplishments led her to graduate *cum laude* in the German and English languages from Radcliffe University in 1904, and then to embark on a career as a successful writer and lecturer. Therefore the story serves as a useful prologue to both the psychoanalytic and Kabbalistic conceptualization and use of language. While psychoanalysis denotes the language of the self, Kabbalah conveys the language of the soul.

During the course of helping his mentally and emotionally crippled patients, Freud elucidated a vast area of human experience that became known as the 'unconscious.' The 'unconscious' and the associated 'preconscious' are areas of consciousness to which a person normally does not have access, but which greatly influence the course of his or her life. In his early works, especially *Studies on Hysteria* (with Josef Breuer),[8] and *The Interpretation of Dreams*,[9] Freud demonstrated that the unconscious mind has its own way of thinking, its own language, so to speak, which is invariably concealed. Like an accomplished archaeologist, he uncovered a forgotten civilization and discovered the means to access or translate its long-lost literature.

The 'letters' of the unconscious are symbols that represent basic instinctual processes, while symbolization denotes the organization of these letters into a comprehensible 'speech.' Essentially Freud opened a new branch of linguistics, the study of symbols and symbolization. The discipline he created, psychoanalysis, is the systematic exploration and elaboration of this unconscious vernacular with all its concealed manifestations and communications.

One of Freud's most significant accomplishments was to see that the mental, physical and behavioral peculiarities that drive people 'mad' and that others consider signs of 'madness' are attempts to reveal 'unconscious' forces. The task of the psychoanalyst is to make the unconscious conscious, that is, to translate the hidden or coded texts of the self, and to register people's symbolic expressions. Psychoanalysts call these translations 'interpretations.' A skillful interpretation can illuminate dark zones of the interior and thereby bestow profound insights, not only into the self, but into the soul as well. Perhaps that is why Freud's biographers point out that if he had not been a great 'linguist,' he could have been one of the world's greatest novelists. Similarly, if he had not lived and defined himself as a *fin de siècle*, secular Jewish intellectual, Freud might have found a home as a student of Kabbalah, as we touched upon in our study of Freud and his meeting in 1903 with the fifth Lubavitcher Rebbe.[10]

Many of Freud's immediate colleagues expanded his study of the language of the self. Ernest Jones distinguished between what he called the expression of 'true symbolism' and 'symbolism in its widest sense.'[11] The former was always unconscious and was the result of internal psychic conflict. The latter concerns ". . . almost the whole development of civilisation. For what is this other than a never ending series of evolutionary substitutions, a ceaseless replacement of one idea, interest, capacity or tendency by another?"[12] This theme was enriched by the 'anthropological work' of Otto Rank and, of course, by Carl Jung, who propounded the idea of a 'collective unconscious' and symbolic 'archetypes.' For Jung the 'collective' was a huge reservoir of phylogenic experiences, a transpersonal template that could serve as the counterpoint to personal, instinctual desires. For a person to find himself, he has to extract himself from the grasp of the collective.

Paradoxically, after individuation has taken place, the same person has to dive into the collective in order to taste beyond-the-self or transcendental realms. In either case, Jung stated that the language of the self was mediated by intrinsic patterns or images that he called archetypes.[13] These were symbols—but more than symbols. If a Freudian dream-symbol was akin to a word in the language of the self, then an archetype was more like a sentence in the service of the psyche. Jung showed how these building blocks ('the anima,' 'the animus,' 'the shadow' and so on) contributed to the innate structure of the self, as well as to the possibility of surpassing one's limitations.

Succeeding generations of psychoanalysts have also focused on the power of language to enhance positive or negative psychic and social processes. Melanie Klein emphasized the destructive consequences when numbers, letters and words or the connections between them got stuck at the level of primal aggression and sadism. She showed that disturbed children with whom she worked became tormented by reading, writing, speaking or relationships of any kind. This occurred because they could only use numbers, letters and words as weapons to cut, burn or tear up their parent's insides or body parts.[14]

Thus one little girl could not use the word 'scissor.' As far as she was concerned, to say it, or even to think it, meant that she was literally cutting her mother's body to pieces. Another child was terrified by the number two, because it signified attacks on his parents' relations, to cleave them into 'two.' As a result these children could not create a psychic structure in themselves. They functioned as evacuators, but not containers. Klein noted that adults act in a similar manner during a psychotic regression.

Klein's descriptions were more fully elaborated by her student and colleague, Hanna Segal. She differentiated between what she termed a 'symbolic equation' and a 'symbol.'[15] With the former, there was no separation, no difference between the letter or number or word and its intention or function. That is why Klein's patient felt that the word 'scissor' equaled a scissor, or the number two equaled an ax. In this instance, just to use the word brings about the frightening intention. Such concrete or robotic thinking leaves no space for a psychic interior or self to grow. The child remains preoccupied with not seeing and not thinking, and with retaining absolute control over 'pseudo-linguistic' events.

On the other hand 'symbols' represent but are not the same as the intention or object. They have a separate existence that the symbolist can recognize, respect and utilize. As Segal confirms, symbols allow us to be human. Moreover, they allow us to think, to play, to create our interior as well as exterior worlds. Scientists would say that true symbolization enables us to reach towards the stars. As we shall soon see, Kabbalists would add that letters create the universe.

Perhaps the most influential post-Kleinian was Wilfred Bion. He concluded that a newborn child has an inborn knowledge or expectations of basic experiences like the breast. Here 'the breast' means all the psychological and emotional feelings involved in being fed and not being fed. Bion called this a 'pre-conception.' When this pre-conception (of feeding) met actual feeding, then contact of one with the other gave rise to a 'conception' and emotional satisfaction.[16]

In a related way, Kabbalah discusses how humans are born with an animal soul and a Divine soul. Clearly the animal soul is concerned with physical sustenance, just as the Divine soul is concerned with spiritual nourishment. Both entities are mediated by the breast. In Hebrew the combination of two consonants, SH (*Shin*) and D (*Daled*) describes desires, as well as the object of these desires, and makes the word *SHahD*, which means 'breast.' But the same letters also create the basis for one of the words for God, *SHaDi,* which literally means 'my breast' or 'my primary source.'[17] As Bion might point out, both *SHahD* and *SHaDi* first emerge as 'pre-conceptions.' On a spiritual plane, such an idea helps to explain why Jewish as well as other mystical traditions clearly state that knowledge of God is inborn or inherent in every person.

When such a 'pre-conception' is actualized, or, as Bion puts it, a 'pre-conception' meets a realization (a mouth finds a breast, a seeker intuits the Godhead), the product is an emotion—satisfaction, for example—but not a thought. Thoughts, which can be defined as definite mental units of awareness, come about from a negative, rather than a positive, experience, from the union of a 'pre-conception' with a frustration. In other words something, a specific state of consciousness, arises from nothing. By implication, the thought or idea 'breast' arises from the absence of 'the breast.' Jewish tradition states a similar idea more succinctly, *yesh m'ayin,* which means 'something from nothing.' Words, worlds, the whole conceptual as well as material universe, they all arise from absence, from a state of nothingness.[18]

These ideas resonate with the work of French psychoanalyst Jacques Lacan, for whom language was of central importance in discerning consciousness as well as the interplay of consciousness from person to person. By 'consciousness' we include, of course, all of Freud's triadic distinctions: unconscious, preconscious and conscious mental processes. Following Freud, Lacan's basic dictum was that "the unconscious is structured like a language."[19]

In formulating these ideas, Lacan was immensely influenced by the work of the French social anthropologist Claude Levi-Strauss, who developed structural anthropology, and the Swiss linguist Ferdinand de Saussure, who pioneered structural linguistics. Both thinkers sought to describe fundamental, scientifically rigorous rules of kinship and communication. Lacan expanded their models of linguistic analysis to explore many of the issues we have just touched upon, such as the nature of 'the self' ('subjectivity') and social relations ('intersubjectivity').

It is worth noting that Lacan considered himself to be an atheist and disavowed his Catholic roots. Like Freud, he fought to replace religion with science, and to embrace psychoanalysis with methodology. But also like Freud, his discourses abound with religious allusions. In 1954, for example, he referred to St. Augustine's *De Locutionis Significatione*, in the course of discussing speech ('parole'). Lacan wrote that speech is like the words declaimed by God in the book of Genesis. It is a 'symbolic invocation' that creates, *ex nihilo,* "a new order of being in the relations between men," a point of view which would not do an injustice to Bion or to Kabbalah.[20]

Like Cassirer, Lacan was fascinated with the way that people express varying degrees of meaningfulness ('signification') through language, especially by deploying signs and symbols. Thus Lacan's work was closely connected with semiotics, or the systematic study of these two linguistic modalities. He especially focused on the relationship between subject and object, or signifier and signified. But in doing so, he defined these terms differently from Saussure and other theoreticians and also maintained views about symbols and the process of symbolization that conflicted with Freud.[21] We will not delve into these distinctions here. However, what is very relevant is the transcendent conclusion to which Lacan comes: that through symbolic language man can create a new order of reality not dependent on biology or genetics, rather a 'universe' onto itself. As Lacan writes:

> The symbolic order from the first takes on its universal character. It isn't constituted bit by bit. As soon as the symbol arrives, there is a universe of symbols.[22]

In his latter years, Lacan shifted from a linguistic to a mathematical approach in order to more precisely describe the process of signification, and as a means of formalizing psychoanalytic theory. He was fascinated by algebraic algorithms (sets of instructions as in computer programs) and by topology (the study of certain geometric figures and the spaces they generate). Thus he used the möbius strip, a strip of paper twisted and joined so it only has one edge,[23] to query opposites like inside/outside, love/hate or signified/signifier.

Lacan studied one figure, the torus, in particular detail. This is a three-dimensional object akin to a bagel. Lacan saw in the torus many human characteristics. For example, in a torus the center of gravity falls outside itself. Similarly, many people tend to locate their experiences in others, outside themselves. When this happens, we can say that they are uncentered and liable to become unbalanced. In similar ways, Lacan delighted in extending

Freud's topographic (conscious, preconscious, unconscious) and structural (ego, id, superego) theories, by delineating psychic space in terms of mathematical space.

But for our purposes the figure of the torus holds a special significance. It is a mathematical entity that may serve as a bridge between the language of psychoanalysis and the language of Kabbalah. Before explaining this further, we want to return to Kabbalah and consider how different texts describe the Hebrew language as channels of consciousness and agents by which God created the world with a word.

The *Sefer Yetzirah* (*Book of Creation*) is the oldest and one of the most mysterious Kabbalistic texts. It has no known author, but according to Aryeh Kaplan, who translated and provided a beautiful modern commentary on the work, many of its ideas may date to biblical times. The particular importance of this wisdom has to do with the inner essence and meaning of the 22 letters of the Hebrew alphabet and the use of these letters to bring about the process of creation. The book begins with the statement "With 32 mystical paths of Wisdom engraved God. . . ."[24] According to Kaplan, the 32 paths refer to the 22 alphabet letters and the 10 *sefirot*, or basic qualities of existence. They are the channels by which the Mind or Will of God controls creation. But they are also the means by which man can exert his mind to experience the Mind of God, and to know his Will. How is this Will revealed? Most tangibly, through the alphabet. It is the carrier of transcendence, as well as being the necessary link with the physical universe.

A noted contemporary Kabbalist, Yitzchak Ginsburgh, has provided a detailed exposition of the mystical quality of the Hebrew letters.[25] He sees these letters as 'channels of creative consciousness,' and describes how the letters, or more specifically, particular permutations of letters, such as in words, contain the 'Divine Force.' They are the instruments by which God creates *yesh m'ayin,* something from nothing.

Similarly, the late Lubavitcher Rebbe, Menachem Mendel Schneerson, wrote that the letters of the *aleph-bet* (Hebrew alphabet) are "the building blocks of creation."[26] These are the generative units that comprise the names of creatures, objects, concepts and so forth. From a Kabbalistic perspective, such names serve as channels by which higher spiritual forces imbue 'things' with their existence and vitality. Concomitantly, names are the means by which God reveals himself in the lower world (concrete reality)

The 'Divine Force' is also known as the 'Life Force.' The reason why the Hebrew letters contain the 'Life Force' and are channels for it, is because they also represent the 22 different connections between the *sefirot.* These are responsible for 'downpouring' of the life energies. According to Kabbalah, this 'downchaining' starts at the top, at the Godhead, and is channeled through the *sefirotic* trees associated with each of the four Worlds or Universes: Emanation, Creation, Formation and finally Action, the domain of humankind. In fact, what we are describing is the 'downchaining' of a never-ending, holistic array, for each *sefira* in itself contains the whole *sefirotic* tree, repeated *ad infinitum*.

Classical Freudian psychoanalysis also postulates a 'Life Force' called the 'Life Instinct.' This also known as 'libido,' 'libidinal energy,' 'free energy,' and 'Eros.' Unlike Kabbalah, it flows 'upward' from the unconscious 'id' to the conscious 'ego,' that is, through the psychic structure or topology of the mind.

In Jungian theory (analytical psychology), the 'Life Force' has been known at different times by the terms 'life instinct,' 'life energy,' '*élan vital*' or 'animation.' This is a more generalized energy than the Freudian 'Life Instinct,' with its emphasis on self-preservation and sexuality. The Jungian 'life energy' is concerned with unity and progress, and also spurts 'upward' from the unconscious part of the psyche. But the Jungian 'unconscious' is a much more broadly based progenitor than its Freudian counterpart. It does not simply refer to a part of the mind that is unconscious—that is, not amenable to conscious awareness. Rather, the Jungian 'unconscious' is a personal and collective wellspring, a dynamic entity straddling time and space. In this sense it is more akin to a Divine-driven transcendental source.

Another major difference is that in Freudian and Jungian thought the analogues of the 'Life Force' are themselves opposed by an equal and opposite energy called the 'death instinct' or 'Thanatos.' Judaism does not hold such a rigid view, which is more akin to the old Zoroastrian idea of the fight between good and evil. Evil is the concealment of Godliness. Or, to put it in modern terms, evil is ingratitude: hatred of 'the giver' and denial of 'the source.' This dual instinctual system of the good impulse and the bad impulse comprises a dialectic. It exists in order to prod 'man' to choose good, or 'life.'

There is, however, an important area where Kabbalah and psychoanalysis do agree. Many of the basic structures of the mind, like the building blocks of the soul, can be conceived both as units of energy and as carriers of energy. Thus in Kabbalah the Hebrew letters are both packets of energy and channels for the 'Life Force.' Similarly 'Eros' is both a force and a container of the force. This situation is akin to quantum theory, where elementary physical particles can be seen as both particles or waves, depending on how one is accessing them.

Ginsburgh explains that each of the Hebrew letters exists in three dimensions. These are 'Worlds,' 'Souls' and 'Divinity.' 'Worlds' refer to the physical, moral, personal and material aspects of existence. 'Souls' refers to the religious and spiritual aspects, while 'Divinity' has to do with God and His interplay with man. These distinctions had been delineated by the Baal Shem Tov, the father of Hasidism, in a famous letter of 1746 to his brother-in-law, in which he recounted his 'ascent' to the highest heavens and what he had learned.[27]

> With every word and expression that leaves your lips, have in mind to bring about a unification. Every single letter contains universes, souls and Godliness, and as they ascend, one becomes bound to the other, and they become unified. The letters then become unified and attached to form a word. They are then actually unified with the Divine Essence, and in all these aspects, your soul is included in them.[28]

Here the Baal Shem Tov revealed the power of letters and words to create and integrate various states of consciousness and 'being' between man and God. This is on a 'Soul' or spiritual level.

Comparably, on the level of 'Worlds' or substantive reality, Melanie Klein has shown that words have the power to act emotionally and psychologically to resolve inner conflicts between love and hate, and to bring about the integration of the self. This begins during what Klein termed the 'depressive position.' This process is part of a reparative thrust to 're-pair' the self, and to bring about unifications both internally and externally with friends and family.

The power of the Hebrew letters to bring things into existence and unify relations also depends on their possessing three different facets or representations of the Worlds of *Asiyah* (Action, the earthly plane), *Yetzirah* (Formation) and *Beriyah* (Creation). These Worlds are the four universes of Godly reality ranging hierarchically from the earthly plane to the higher levels of spirituality (which encompasses *Atzilut*, or Emanation). While these different facets of physical and spiritual existence are often translated or referred to as 'worlds,' the term is different from and much more encompassing than the same word used to describe the dimension of letters. So, in order to avoid confusion, at this moment, we shall refer to these 'Worlds' or *Olamot* as 'Universes.'

According to Ginsburgh, there exist three additional facets of the letters. 'Form,' also known as 'shape,' is the representation of the letters at the earthly level of *Asiyah*, and refers to the visual aspects of the letter. 'Name' is the representation of the letters at the higher level of *Yetzirah*, and yields its auditory properties as well as its direct and symbolic significances. 'Number' is the representation of the letters at the highest embodied level of *Beriyah*, and includes the pure abstract thought or 'wisdom' of the letter. Each of these facets contains specific powers or energies and reflects three degrees of dimensionality. Thus, the Kabbalist describes form in Worlds, form in Souls and form in Divinity, with corresponding categories for name and number. So each letter contains nine categories of meaning and acts as a code to engender creation.

The genetic code provides a useful analogy. It utilizes combinations of four amino acids known by the letters A, C, G and T and controls physical inheritance. In contrast, it is said that the 22 Hebrew letters subsume a code for TOE, the 'theory of everything,' and its associated COE, the 'creation of everything.' Conceivably the equivalent, in cutting-edge physics, is a unified field theory, which, according to the physicist Michio Kaku, is an equation in 10-dimensional hyperspace that will allow us to "read the mind of God."[29]

From a further perspective, the study of the Hebrew letters is an exercise in spiritual semiotics. This parallels the work of linguists such as Saussure, with his intense interest in signs, symbols and syntax, and psychoanalysts like Lacan, who used semiotics to elucidate consciousness.

Comparably the Kabbalist not only focuses on the look of the letter—its visual structure—but on its sound, and the way a particular sound arises from a part of the mouth: lips, tongue, teeth, palate and throat. This determines its energy and impact. As the Australian psychologist and hasid Laibl Wolf details:

> . . . the Kabbalah places great emphasis on the analysis of words and letters, their numerical equivalence, interchangeability, shapes, and the end-of-word final letters. Each nuance opens up a panorama of spiritual depth, far more complex than any grammatical construct might suggest.[30]

In English and other languages, the recombination of letters does not usually generate kindred meanings. However, in Hebrew it does. According to Kabbalah, the fact that words possess the same root letters, even if in different combinations, indicates that they are inherently linked. For example, the Hebrew letters tz-h-r (tzaddi-heh-resh) spell the name *tzohar* and mean 'radiating Divine Light.'[31] But if we take the same letters and rearrange the order to r-tz-h, we have the word for 'desire' or 'wanting.' Alternatively, h-tz-r means 'adversary,' someone who is coming after you. Similarly, tz-r-h, yields 'trouble.'[32] From all this we can learn that if we misdirect our desires, we will create adversaries and troubles, within ourselves and without. But if we direct them appropriately, then we are likely to realize an inner radiance and personal enlightenment.

Even without touching on the dimensions of shape (form) and number, this exercise demonstrates to a small extent the complexity and power of Kabbalah to generate universes of meaning. Let us explore in greater detail the first two letters of the Hebrew alphabet, *aleph* and *bet*. They are intimately involved with the nature of the Godhead and the enigma of creation. Moreover, they share some symmetry with the work of Wilfred Bion and his conceptualizations of psychoanalytic theory and practice.

Aleph is the first letter of the Hebrew alphabet, and the numerical equivalent of *aleph* is one. According to the *Zohar*, *aleph* is 'the image of God' by which man was created. It is the starting point or original cause of all natural processes. It is the nothing, *Ayin* ('no-thing-ness'), and the everything, *Ein Sof* ('without end'). No doubt for this same reason, the German mathematician Georg Cantor chose *aleph* to be a symbol for infinity.[33] Without an accompanying vowel, the *aleph* has no sound. It is a glottal stop, a position taken by the larynx in preparation for speech. The letter is pure potential, the essence that cannot be grasped, but paradoxically it is also the "timbre of revelation: the sound of sheer silence."[34]

For Daniel Matt, a leading authority on Jewish mysticism, *aleph* is "the uncarved block, preceding the shaping of words."[35] This idea refers to the tradition that the Torah was written with letters of black fire on a background of white fire.[36] Since white contains all colors and all light, we can say that it is the 'absolute all' that precedes both words and worlds, just as the Creator precedes his creations. Consequently some mystics, in their attempt to unite with the infinite, prefer to 'read' the whiteness of the Torah parchment, rather than the black ink of the letters.

Surely this was Bion's aim, not to focus on his patient's symptoms and statements, their blacknesses, but to listen to their hidden silences, in order to 'read' the white ambiguity of their total personality. This was their 'O,' the term Bion coined to express the changeless, the eternal, the infinite, the ineffable. As the psychoanalyst Michael Eigen points out, 'O' was the alpha and the omega, nothingness and everythingness of a session, but especially, its unknowable reality. This included emotions and thoughts so intense, so rapturous, that they could not be contained or represented in language.[37]

Bion was conversant with, and made use of, both the Eastern and Western mystical traditions. He was certainly familiar with Kabbalah. Eigen recalls that when they met in 1977, Bion startled him by referring to Kabbalah at length.[38] Perhaps he was also familiar with the Torah codes represented by the Hebrew acronym, PaRDeS, or 'orchard.' PaRDeS subsumes four levels of understanding the Torah, which Kabbalists see as the blueprint of existence. As we have described above, P stands for *pshat*, the literal significance of things. R indicates *remmez*, a hint of, or homiletical allusion to, deeper meanings. D conveys *drush*, or the metaphorical and allegorical explanations. Finally, S stands for *sod,* or secret, most hidden levels of reality. Clearly Bion liked to use biblical stories and expressions to portray psychoanalytic processes on the level of D and S, their deepest, formless essence. He may even have heard, and certainly would have agreed with the aphorism that R. D. Laing was fond of quoting, "You canna avoid the Void."[39]

The second letter of the Hebrew alphabet is *bet.* This letter looks like a house lying on its side. The letter literally means 'house,' and Kabbalists assert that this letter contains God's 'wish' to create a dwelling place in the physical world.

How does this occur? According to Yitzchak Luria, God contracts himself and allows a void (vacated space) to endure where previously there had only been His radiance. After many such contractions (*tzimzumim*), 'otherness' came into being. By 'otherness' we mean finitude in place of infinity and multiplicity in place of singularity. This was accomplished by carving a black fire on white fire, whereby the black fire is the void and the progenitor of words.

If *aleph* is the uncarved black, then *bet* is the carved black, and the basic tool by which existence was created. It is the first letter of the Torah and the first letter of 'in the beginning,' *B'reishit* as well as *Baruch,* meaning blessing. God's blessing is to speak and be separate from his creation, thereby establishing duality in the world: male and female, good and evil, the upper realms and the lower realms, the unconscious and consciousness, concealment and revelation. In all this, God's agent is the letter *bet*, whose numerical equivalent is two.

Significantly, one of Bion's most important contributions to psychoanalysis was to distinguish between *aleph* and *bet*, what he called alpha functioning and beta elements. The former had to do with a state of mind prior to the existence of meaning, as well as the process of acquiring meaning from sense impressions. Like *aleph*, alpha functioning is a condition of undifferentiated potentiality awaiting realization. If successful it yields alpha elements, which provide "the furniture for dreams and for thinking."[40] In contrast, beta elements are chaotic bits of unprocessed thinking and undigested sense data. They represent the results of unsuccessful alpha functioning that are felt to be only suitable for evacuation into the world. Bion's 'betas' also yield dualities and multiplicities, but unlike the letter *bet*, which is a blessing for creation, beta-elements are crazy-making, destructive and very far from 'O.'

Ultimately Bion located alpha, beta and other elements as coordinates on a matrix or 'grid,' in order to provide a systematic map of the mind. It is clear that Bion, along with his French counterpart Jacques Lacan, turned to mathematics to facilitate psychoanalytic thinking and the exchange of ideas.

For parallel reasons, linguistics often reads like a branch of mathematics. Concomitantly, many prominent Kabbalists and scholars of Kabbalah, including Aryeh Kaplan, Adin Steinsaltz and Yitzchak Ginsburgh, began their careers as physicists and mathematicians. This overview brings us to the work of Stan Tenen, an American mathematician, linguist and student of Kabbalah.[41] His investigations of the Torah, beginning with the topology of *B'reishit* ('in the beginning'), confirm that the Hebrew letters have "intrinsic geometric and mathematical properties," akin to the figures that Lacan explored and the channels that Ginsburgh described. He asserts that their analysis can yield a "true science of consciousness."

Tenen likes to quote the Rabbinic dictum that the secret of the Torah lies in the first letter. But if you don't 'get it,' the message can be found in the first word, or the first phrase, or the first paragraph. He is not referring, of course, to the controversial 'Bible Codes,' popularized by Michael Drosnin,[42] but to a much more profound understanding of the shape (sequence of geometric forms and topological relationships), name (inner meaning) and number (*gematria*) of the Hebrew letters as expounded in the *Sefer Yetzirah*.

One of Tenen's initial discoveries was that the first verse of Genesis generated the spatial configuration of a torus or a bagel. Tenen, who was self-taught in Hebrew, came to this conclusion after months of meditating on and playing with the letters. One day it occurred to him to write each letter on a bead and then string them together. This resulted in 27 beads corresponding to the 22 letters of the alphabet (*aleph-bet*) and 5 final letters. Another creative leap led him to wrap the string of beads around so that the letters autocorrelated or paired up, *alephs* with *alephs, bets* with *bets,* and so on. From the topology of the ensuing pyramid, "a beautiful, toroidal pattern emerged." Eventually he realized that the patterns had a particular meaning:

> The text literally folds itself up into a model which generates the letters in which it is written, and does so in such a way that you can read the text as a meditational dance.[43]

For a long time Tenen pondered on the torus and the boundary figure or model inside it. He could see that the model changed shape as he surveyed it from different angles. He also knew that the torus was, as we have just mentioned, the topological equivalent of the original pyramid or tetrahedronal structure. Eventually he saw that this structure was like a tent, and the changing figure inside it was like a 'vortex' or flame. He didn't have to shine a light on the twirling model to generate letters. Just by looking at the vortex, he 'found' all 27 Hebrew letters (22 plus 5 'final' letters which complete a word), which he noted were commensurate with the 27 'preferred' pointing directions used in hyper-dimensional space.

Essentially Tenen discovered what Yitzchak Ginsburgh and other Kabbalists had long established, that the Hebrew letters represent gestures and movements, all the dynamic activities involved in creation. As Tenen points out:

> Kabbalah is not about things. It is about relationships, and projections. Structure and process are complements, like wave and particle, like the Light (vortex) in the meeting tent.[44]

The language of consciousness, in all its combinations and permutations, is the common thread that unites Kabbalists and psychoanalysts, linguists and mathematicians. As we have seen, the torus is a particularly useful figure to show where consciousness is located (Lacan) or how it comes about (Tenen). Both thinkers have studied the topology of external space, in which letters are generated, and inner space, to delineate mental structures (following Freud's topographical and structural theories). Similarly, Bion postulated a spatial grid to demonstrate mental processes.

In contrast, Kabbalah uses numerical analysis, called *gematria,* to link letters and words in time and space. In Hebrew this is easy because every letter has a numerical equivalent, *aleph* = 1, *bet* = 2, and so on until the last letter, *tav* = 400. This value is an intrinsic facet of every letter and represents the power of *chochmah* or wisdom in that letter. This is a form of 'revealed *gematria*,' which has been used since Talmudic times to demonstrate the correspondence between words and ideas. Thus, in the Torah, after Jacob had his wondrous dream about angels ascending and descending on a ladder, he exclaimed, "There is God in this place." In Hebrew the numerical value of this phrase is 541. But if you look up the numerical value of all words with the value of 541, you find that one of the words is Israel. So scholars have concluded that the place to which God refers is Israel.[45] Another example comes from the Ari. He advised that when eating bread one should dip the bread in salt three times. Why? Because in Hebrew the *gematria* for God's four-letter name is 26. Three times 26 is 78, which is the *gematria* for bread (*lechem*) as well as salt (*melach*).[46]

Gutman Locks has written an entire book that gives the *gematria* or numerical equivalent for every word in the Torah.[47] It may seem odd to equate words or ideas on this basis. But in an introduction to the book, the renowned Kabbalist and philosopher Immanuel Schochet points out that these equations are no less than the garments of the soul that the seeker uses to climb the heights of spiritual reality.[48] By the same token we have already touched on a further discipline, 'mystical *gematria*,' which recognizes the correspondence between the 10 *sefirot* and the 22 letters of the Hebrew alphabet. This is a system that has been elaborated on in many Jewish mystical writings, including the *Zohar.*

Gematria comes from the Greek word for 'geometry.' Whether geometrical or numerical, these analyses demonstrate the dual nature of language, as the energy of creation (vortex, light, divine force, life force, libido) and carrier of the energy (channels, vessels, symbols, structures). What matters is creation itself, an unfolding that needs both the text and the textbook, both the 'black fire' and the 'white fire.' Psychoanalysis and Kabbalah show how letters and words, indeed, everything that follows from them, must be used in an ongoing 'dance' to germinate reality. Without this continuing process, as we saw from the story of Helen Keller, reality itself would collapse.

NOTES

1. Genesis 1:3–5; *The Chumash: Stone Edition* (New York: Mesorah Publications, 1998), 3.

2. This is related to the statement "With ten utterances the world was created. . . ." *Pirkei Avot* (Sayings of the Fathers), 5:1. Ten times "God said" (ten utterances) occurs. *Siddur Tehillat HaShem*, trans. Rabbi N. Mangel (New York: Merkos L'inyonei Chinuch, 1978), 286.

3. This is discussed by the Kabbalist Yitzchak Ginsburgh in *The Hebrew Letters: Channels of Creative Consciousness* (Jerusalem: Gal Einai Publications, 1990), 238–39.

4. Keller became blind and deaf at 19 months of age. Presumably she retained a memory of many of the sights and sounds she had experienced before then. Nevertheless, before she discovered or rediscovered words, she had regressed into a raging void and had become unmanageable. What had not been lost, however, was intelligence, will power and potential. See Helen Keller, *The Story of My Life* (1903; New York: Bantam, 1990).

5. Quoted by Robert Young, *Mental Space* (London: Process Press, 1994), 18.

6. Young, *Mental Space,* 18–19.

7. Ernst Cassirer, *An Essay on Man: An Introduction to a Philosophy of Human Culture* (Garden City, N.Y.: Doubleday Anchor Books, 1954), 48–61.

8. Josef Breuer and Sigmund Freud, "Studies on Hysteria," in Sigmund Freud, *Standard Edition of the Complete Psychological Works of Sigmund Freud*, ed. James Strachey (1895; London: Hogarth Press, 1981), vol. 1.

9. Sigmund Freud, 1900, "The Interpretation of Dreams," in *Standard Edition*, ed. James Strachey, vols. 4–5.

10. Stanley Schneider and Joseph Berke, "Sigmund Freud and the Lubavitcher Rebbe," *Psychoanalytic Review* 87 (2000): 39–59.

11. Ernest Jones, "The Theory of Symbolism," in *Papers on Psycho-Analysis*. (1916; London: Tindall & Cox, 1948), 93–104.

12. Quoted in Charles Rycroft, *A Critical Dictionary of Psychoanalysis* (Harmondsworth, Middlesex, England: Penguin, 1972), 162.

13. Andrew Samuels, *A Critical Dictionary of Jungian Analysis* (London: Routledge & Kegan Paul, 1986), 26–27, 31–32. See also Carl Jung, *Man and His Symbols* (London: Aldus, 1964).

14. Melanie Klein, "An Obsessional Neurosis in a Six-Year-Old Girl," in *The Psycho-Analysis of Children* (1924; New York: Delta, 1975), 35–57.

15. Hanna Segal, "Notes on Symbol Formation," *International Journal of Psycho-Analysis* 38 (1957): 391–97.

16. Colin James, "Bion's 'Containing' and Winnicott's 'Holding' in the Context of the Group Matrix," *International Journal of Group Psychotherapy* 34 (1984): 208–9.

17. Joseph Berke and Stanley Schneider have amplified these ideas in their paper "Antithetical Meanings of 'the Breast,'" *International Journal of Psycho-Analysis* 75 (1994): 491–98.

18. In this regard it is significant that the ancient Greeks also conceptualized the creation of the world as *ex nihilo*.

19. Jacques Lacan, *The Seminar, Book XI. The Four Fundamental Concepts of Psychoanalysis*, trans. Alan Sheridan (1964; London: Hogarth Press and the Institute of Psycho-Analysis, 1977), 20. Quoted by Dylan Evans in *An Introductory Dictionary of Lacanian Psychoanalysis* (London: Routledge, 1996), 97.

20. Evans, *Introductory Dictionary*, 191.

21. Evans, *Introductory Dictionary*, 182–85, 202–3.

22. Jacques Lacan, *The Seminar, Book II. The Ego in Freud's Theory and in the Technique of Psychoanalysis*, ed. J. A. Miller, trans. S. Tomaselli (1954–1955; Cambridge: Cambridge University Press, 1988), 29. Quoted in Evans, *Introductory Dictionary*, 202.

23. The Möbius strip is named after the German mathematician August Ferdinand Möbius (1790–1868). The artist M. C. Escher based several of his lithographs on this strip.

24. Aryeh Kaplan, *Sefer Yetzirah (The Book of Creation)* (Newburyport, Mass.: Samuel Weiser, 1990b).

25. Yitzchak Ginsburgh, *The Hebrew Letters: Channels of Creative Consciousness* (Jerusalem: Gal Einai Publications, 1990).

26. Menachem Mendel Schneerson, quoted in *Week in Review* 10 (39), 10 June 1999.

27. Also known by the acronym the BeSHT. His name means the 'Master of the Good Name.' The Baal Shem Tov had a profound knowledge and understanding of Kabbalah as well as sharing many characteristics of a healer. For a detailed discussion of the Baal Shem Tov, see Moshe Rosman, *Founder of Hassidism: A Quest for the Historical Ba'al Shem Tov* (Berkeley and Los Angeles: University of California Press, 1996).

28. Aryeh Kaplan, *Chassidic Masters and Their Teachings* (New York: Moznaim, 1984), 14.

29. Michio Kaku, "It's All So Clear in 10-Dimensional Hyperspace," *London Independent*, January 19, 2000.

30. Laibl Wolf, *Practical Kabbalah* (New York: Three Rivers Press, 1999), 27.

31. The Zohar (Z=*zayin*) is the most important text of Kabbalah; the name can be translated as The Book of Radiance. The word *tzohar* is the name of the skylight or luminous stone that Noah had in his ark. The Hebrew letters *zayin* and *tzaddi* are from the same family root, and can switch.

32. *r-tz-h* gives *RaTZaH* for wanting, desiring; *h-tz-r* gives *HaTZaR* for adversary; *tz-r-h* gives *TZaRaH* for trouble.

33. Daniel Matt, *God and the Big Bang: Discovering Harmony between Science and Spirituality* (Woodstock, Vt.: Jewish Lights, 1996), 109. Matt pointed out that Cantor used a variation of the written *aleph*. See also discussion in Amir Aczel, *The Mystery of the Aleph: Mathematics, the Kabbalah, and the Search for Infinity* (New York: Four Walls Eight Windows, 2001).

34. Matt, *God and the Big Bang*, 111.

35. Matt, *God and the Big Bang*, 109.

36. *Midrash Tanchuma*, chap. 1.

37. Michael Eigen, *The Psychoanalytic Mystic* (London: Free Association Books, 1998), 39–40.

38. Eigen, *Psychoanalytic Mystic,* 64.

39. Personal communication.

40. Robert Hinshelwood, *A Dictionary of Kleinian Thought* (London: Free Association Books, 1991), 229.

41. Stan Tenen is the director of research of the Meru Foundation, which was established in 1983 to study ancient alphabets and texts from a modern mathematical perspective. Although he has published many papers, his work is best accessed through the website of the Meru Foundation: www.meru.org.

42. Michael Drosnin, *The Bible Code* (New York: Simon & Schuster, 1997).

43. *Living Letters*, lecture by Stan Tenen, video ed. (Sharon, Mass.: Meru Foundation, 14 July 1992). This 'bagel' was divisible into seven regions. Tenen realized that when he made a model of the boundaries between these regions, he generated a shape that mirrored the human hand. More surprising, by slowly rotating this model on a string after focusing a coherent light on it, he was able to create shadowgrams of all the Hebrew letters. It seemed that the letters were intrinsic to the original torus, and represented various forms of differentiation of self from other, inside from outside. As we have previously noted, the first letter of the Torah, *bet*, means house. So the letter emphasizes the importance of dichotomy because a house is a structure that establishes inside and outside, as well as separates the Creator from His creations. See also Stan Tenen, *The Alphabet in Genesis* (Sharon, Mass.: Meru Foundation, 2006).

44. Tenen/Meru postings to Jack Sarfatti's "Kabbalah" discussion, September–October 1998.

45. Gutman Locks, *The Spice of Torah: Gematria* (New York: Judaica Press, 1985), i.

46. Locks, *Spice of Torah*, ii.

47. Locks, *Spice of Torah*.

48. Immanuel Schochet, "Gematriya: The Principles of Numerical Interpretation," in Locks, *Spice of Torah*, v–vii.

Chapter Nine

States of Mind

Historically, as we follow Freud's 'discovery' of psychoanalysis, we can see an interesting developmental paradigm. Early in his medical career, in 1883, Freud spent five months working in the Psychiatric Clinic of Theodor Meynert, the greatest brain anatomist and neuropathologist of that time.[1] Here began Freud's *mechanistic* understanding of mental structures. Later, in 1885–1886, Freud spent nineteen weeks studying under the tutelage of the world-famous neurologist and director of the Hospice de la Salpêtrière, Jean-Martin Charcot.[2] Freud's teacher was a mechanist, combining his studies of hysteria with hypnotism, and he tried to limit his students to strictly physical observations. Freud, however, began to ask psychological questions.

Upon his return to Vienna, Freud began his professional association with a Viennese physician, Josef Breuer, the son of Leopold Breuer, who was a student of Moses Schreiber, the Chatam Sopher, the renowned Rabbi of Pressburg.[3,4,5] The Breuer family lived in the same apartment building as the Hammerschlag family. Paul, the son of Samuel Hammerschlag, married Bertha, the eldest daughter of Josef Breuer. The Freud, Breuer and Hammerschlag families were very close, having all been raised in Orthodox Jewish traditions. Samuel Hammerschlag was a professor of religious knowledge and Hebrew, and a teacher of Freud.[6] Freud's daughter Anna was named after Prof. Hammerschlag's daughter Anna, who was 'Irma' in Freud's famous dream.[7] Therefore, we cannot dismiss the importance of the influence of family teachings and tradition—developmental history—upon the origins and underpinnings of psychoanalysis.

Freud slowly moved from a mechanistic, physical way of perceiving and understanding behavior to a more emotional questioning and psychological understanding. Upon his return from Charcot, Freud first worked with hypnosis and then later with the pressure technique. This latter technique was Freud's bridge from mechanistic to psychological understanding. In the pressure technique, Freud had his patient lie on a couch and pressed his hand on the patient's forehead while asking questions and expecting his patients to free-associate. In *Studies on Hysteria*, written with Breuer, Freud began to abandon the use of hypnosis and the pressure technique, and focus more on the psychological etiology of the patient's emotional difficulties.[8] He found that his active role in asking questions and physically 'manipulating' the patient were impediments to the abreactive and cathartic process developed by Breuer and expanded by Freud, and to Freud's own free-association technique. Psychoanalysis would try to help the patient discover through free association what he had failed to remember.[9] The analytic technique would allow the therapist to work with the patient's associations and resistances to understanding.

In tracing the history of Kabbalah, we can also see a dichotomy between a theoretical and philosophical understanding of human existence and a more physical, hands-on, practical way of action and understanding. These seemingly polar opposites are viewed differently by scholars, and we are led to speculate that this strong distinction may not have been so sharp. Understandably Rabbinic tradition was fearful that hands-on, practical Kabbalah would become a pastime and vocation of and for the masses, and this posed many ideological problems. After all, Kabbalah as an esoteric philosophy was kept under wraps for so many years precisely because of this fear. Yet, Kabbalah could not just be kept to a pure philosophical and theoretical understanding. In order to understand God's 'game-plan' for the world, see man's role in the 'game of life,' and do actions that can bring *tikkun ha-olam* ('repair and restoration of the world'), there needed to be some hands-on, practical actions that can bring man closer to God and to the spiritual realm.

In the twelfth and thirteenth centuries, when Kabbalah as a doctrine and system surfaced in southern France and Spain, there arose the need to distinguish between what was called 'Kabbalah *iyyunit*' (theoretical or esoteric Kabbalah) and 'Kabbalah *maasit*' (practical or magical use of Kabbalah). The study of theoretical Kabbalah included the meditation on Divine mysteries (creation, the fiery chariot, angels, etc.) and utilized proper states of devotion (*kavanot*) in order to influence the heavenly spheres (upper worlds) and the soul of man. This form of Kabbalah was the one advocated by the Lurianic school.[10] The more magical side of practical Kabbalah flourished in North Africa, Yemen and Eastern Europe (through the developing Hasidic school), and utilized amulets, magical incantations, mystic formulas and permutations on God's name.

This particular brand of Kabbalah deals with 'white' magic.[11] This is an area whereby one adjures in God's name or permutations of God's name, utilizes numerology, chiromancy, ideas and practices connected with the concept of the *Golem*, and so on. These types of practices can easily overstep into the area of 'black' magic, which is the use of "dark, demonic powers . . . and various forms of sorcery that were designed to disrupt the natural order of things. . . ."[12] This sounds similar to Jung's concept of the 'shadow,' that dark side of human nature. However, it is one thing to be able to be 'in touch' with the dark side of one's nature, but it's altogether different to confront and utilize evil for personal gain. As Gershom Scholem states: "Activity of this sort was considered a rebellion of man against God and a hubristic attempt to set himself up in God's place."[13] And in Jung's words: "It is quite within the bounds of possibility for a man to recognize the relative evil of his nature, but it is a rare and shattering experience for him to gaze into the face of absolute evil."[14]

In the writings of Hasidei Ashkenaz ('the pious men of Germany'), there are many references to 'white' and 'black' magic. They were a school of mystics in thirteenth-century Germany who 'specialized' in the cultivation of inner piety through asceticism, humility and strict morality, and the meticulous establishment of correct prayer formulas.[15] This was not a formally organized movement, but many of its characteristics were incorporated by Israel Baal Shem Tov and eighteenth-century Hasidism: ecstasy, piety and the "doctrine of the Shekhinah."[16]

One of the most influential figures in the establishment of Kabbalah as a non-esoteric theosophy was Abraham Abulafia.[17] Abulafia's main interest was to find a way to experience a more intimate connection to the spiritual and divine. By contemplation and focusing attention on the letters of the Hebrew alphabet, he felt he could obtain a pseudo-prophecy. His theory was that the configuration of letters that constitute God's name was the true path to ecstasy. Meditations upon the Divine name via the 'science of letter combination' (*chochmat ha-ziruf*) were the path to pure thought and expressive emotionalism. This is Abulafia's 'music of the alphabet.'

According to Moshe Idel, professor of mysticism and Kabbalah at the Hebrew University in Jerusalem: ". . . the knowledge of the Names . . . enabled Abulafia to free himself of the bonds of the material world; only thereafter was he graced with revelation. Within this revelation lies the mystical experience Abulafia termed *prophecy*."[18] Abulafia followed the instructions he found in the *Sefer Yetzirah* (*Book of Creation*) in order to perform letter permutation. Since God created the world with letters and words, Abulafia sought to imitate this.[19] He tried to "gain access to the profoundest secrets of mystical cosmology and theology by the three methods of Kabbalah, being

Gematria, Notarikon, and *Temurah.*"[20] These terms refer to the calculation of the numerical value of letters and words (*gematria*), interpretations of the letters of a word as abbreviations of sentences (*notarikon*) and interchange of letters (*temurah*). Abulafia's purpose was to lose oneself in meditative contemplation and concentration on letters and words that dance as musical notations in order to enter an ecstatic trance. This enabled him to enter within his own self and ascend the meditative ladder to contact with the spiritual and Divine.

Abulafia was radical in his thinking that one could lose consciousness for a while by trying to focus and concentrate on something intense. This paradoxical thinking is reflected in meditative trances. But Abulafia knew that he had to find a method that would circumnavigate resistance while still attempting to reach a higher spiritual goal. Abulafia called this "untying the sealed knots."[21] Scholem offers an interesting metaphor to explain untying the sealed knots:

> There are certain barriers which separate the personal existence of the soul from the stream of cosmic life . . . there is a dam which keeps the soul confined within the natural and normal borders of human existence and protects it against the flood of the divine stream, which flows beneath it or all around it; the same dam, however, also prevents the soul from taking cognizance of the Divine. The 'seals' which are impressed on the soul, protect it against the flood and guarantee its normal functioning.[22]

In order to achieve pure concentration and understanding, Abulafia recommended meditating on something abstract (a flower, a bird, etc.). This had some positive effects but the object was divorced from the desire to concentrate on a higher spiritual plane. It is here that Abulafia turned to the Hebrew alphabet; this is the 'science of letter combination' (*chochmat ha-ziruf*) mentioned above.[23] One could meditate on a specific idea and 'jump' (*dillug*) or 'skip' (*kefitzah*) from one idea to another. This is 'free association' as a type of concentration within meditation. Freud later utilized the concept of free association as part of his dream interpretation.[24]

Psychoanalysts Jean Laplanche and Jean-Bertrand Pontalis defined Freud's 'Rule of Free Association' as a "method according to which voice must be given to all thoughts without exception which enter the mind, whether such thoughts are based upon a specific element (word, number, dream-image or any kind of idea at all) or produced spontaneously."[25] The mind would 'jump' and 'skip' from one associative link to another, and it is the task of the therapist to be able to follow the thread that connects these associative links.

This is the key to the unconscious. "[Freud] . . . discovered a process of demystification and de-alienation facilitated by the free association of thoughts and feelings . . . through encouraging his patients to free associate, Freud was able to initiate a process of de-repression."[26] And through the release of repressed thoughts and feelings, his patients were relieved of their troublesome symptoms.

One of the most famous of these patients was a young woman (called Anna O.) who suffered from hysterical paralysis. She was treated for this by Joseph Breuer, Freud's mentor and older colleague. Anna discovered that she could alleviate her symptoms by talking frankly and spontaneously about them with Breuer, an occurrence that became known as 'the talking cure.' Subsequently Breuer and Freud described this treatment in their joint work, *Studies on Hysteria*.[27] Although they eventually had a falling-out, Freud did credit Breuer with the discovery of psychoanalysis.[28] Years later it became known that 'Anna O.' was Bertha Pappenheim, a very successful poet and social worker in Vienna.[29] Remarkably, it transpired that Bertha's grandfather, Wolf Pappenheim, had been a wealthy merchant in Pressburg (now Bratislava, Slovakia), and had benefited from the 'the talking cure' two generations beforehand. Wolf used to suffer from depression. As he was a benefactor of the Yeshiva of the Chatam Sopher, he had the privilege of going for weekly walks with the eminent scholar, at which time he would freely discuss his problems. Invariably these walks lifted his moods. Turning to him, he exclaimed, "I feel better just talking to you. I return from our walks with a cleansed soul. Talking with you is the best cure for melancholy."[30] Previously the Chatam Sopher told him, "You are fabricating the reasons for your feelings of guilt . . . you expect them to have a rational cause. . . . But I have an idea that your sentiments would not be much altered if you gave away your money and your houses. . . . If you want to discover the roots of such feelings, you have to travel deep and far. There are ways."[31]

The process of free association can be seen as a form of meditation. Aryeh Kaplan has explored how we can understand the importance of meditation in the lives of the prophets by tracing through Biblical, Midrashic and Talmudic sources the method of meditation and self-introspection that focuses on a specific idea, name, number or object, in order to enter into a meditative state.[32, 33] This enables the initiate (today we would call him or her a patient or client) to attempt to understand the self. After all, the purpose of psychotherapeutic relationships is for the patient to better understand himself or herself. One of the Biblical words that corresponds very much to Abulafia's accentuating the need to concentrate on something in order to enter a self-introspective, contemplative stance is *siyach* ('inner conversation, meditation'). Interestingly, it seems as if there is a bit of a paradox here. On one hand, there is the importance of focusing on something, and yet this intense focusing enables one to 'free float' attention in order to arrive at the focused object!

Freud struggled with this seemingly similar paradox. It is clear from his "Papers on Technique" that the patient has to allow anything that comes into his or her head to be reported: ". . . say whatever goes through your mind . . . never forget that you have promised to be absolutely honest. . . ."[34] The patient is 'unfocused' on anything specific because the mind is 'wandering' until it yields the hidden treasure of the unconscious—the real repository of understanding and meaning. And, it is precisely this unfocused attitude that allows the truth to emerge. What is really happening is that by allowing the mind to seemingly wander, it is seeking its own real level of truth. Abulafia's beginning by focusing on 'something' allows the mind to wander until it reaches the 'ultimate' truth for the particular person at the present spatial and temporal point.

The therapist has to undergo a parallel transformation. No note-taking, no planning of theoretical or research papers based on the material that emerges in the therapeutic sessions—"It is not a good thing to work on a case scientifically while treatment is still proceeding"[35]—only an ability to suspend thinking and judgment. As Freud specifically notes: "The technique . . . consists simply in not directing one's notice to anything in particular and in maintaining the same 'evenly-suspended attention.' . . ."[36] By concentrating too much on what is being said (or implied), the therapist loses track of connecting to the patient and his or her material on an unconscious level. While paying direct attention will focus, the purpose of therapy, as in meditation, is not to focus directly but to let the unconscious elements direct us. Freud continues: ". . . [the therapist] must turn his own unconscious like a receptive organ towards the transmitting unconscious of the patient."[37]

In order to better understand the various levels of the unconscious and conscious, which we term altered states of consciousness, we will now focus our attention on one of the more colorful and profoundly systemic Kabbalistic thinkers, Moses Cordovero, a disciple of the famous Joseph Karo, the author of the *Shulchan Aruch* (*Code of Jewish Law*).[38] Karo himself wrote about his many mystical revelations and conversations which usually took place at night. This diary is written as an ongoing conversation with a heavenly voice, angel, spirit, who communicated supernatural illumination to the 'sleeping' mystic.[39]

Cordovero was an expert in both meditative and practical Kabbalah. One of his methods of meditation was called *gerushin* (literally, 'divorces'). One meditated upon a word or part of Scripture and kept repeating it—like a mantra—until a higher meditative state was reached. One could then gain insight into that word or Scripture without having to delve into a contrived analysis. The *gerushin* or 'divorce' implied a divorcement from the surrounding world and concentrating on the word, thought or Scripture.

Earlier we had alluded to Cordovero as being 'colorful.' This was a double entendre. No doubt his brilliance, innovativeness and originality were such that he stood out among even his Kabbalistic peers. His uniqueness gave him a certain 'colorful' status. But even more than this, he added the ability to utilize colors to his meditative contemplative scheme. Therefore, when he meditated on one of the names of God, he could enhance and intensify this meditation when adding various vowel permutations.[40] In addition, Cordovero added the possibility of binding the name and vowel permutation with a color. This color usually had some significance that was related to an association with one of the *sefirot*.[41] For example, since the *sefira* of *Gevurah* (strength) is related to wars, bloodshed and aggression, it is easy to understand why the color red is identified with this *sefira*. As Aryeh Kaplan noted: "The colors are used allegorically to allude to their functions and results."[42] The color not only aids in meditative contemplation, but it also helps to awaken in our psyche associative thoughts that relate to our emotional, internal world. It's not just running water that makes a young child want to urinate, it also conjures up within the child's psyche the associative and emotional elements connected to water.

Kabbalah advanced the notion of becoming 'in touch' with various states of the mind through active techniques. Yigal Arica, a secular Israeli writer of popular books on mysticism, recently published a book on practical Kabbalah.[43] In it he describes various activities and methods that can bring one to a state of mystical contemplation, thought or even ecstasy. He discusses dreams, amulets, meditation, the study of physiognomies (facial expressions and formations) and chiromancy (the study of man's fate and character through an analysis of fingers, palms, hands and palm lines). Arica, who comes from a family of Kabbalists, wrote a 'how-to-do-it' book that aroused the ire of the scholarly community. In contrast, when Scholem wrote about such topics as chiromancy, demonology, meditation and *gematria* (explaining a word or groups of words according to the numerical value of the letters), it was clear that this was only an academic and scholarly exercise, devoid of practical implications.[44] Arica, on the other hand, makes it clear that his purpose in writing this book was to encourage laymen to learn more about Jewish mysticism through the various practical methods available.

E. A. Wallis Budge and Joshua Trachtenberg were two scholars of folk religion who wrote about the practical aspect of communication with one's own inner self and soul through amulets, talismans and other methods of belief, magic and superstition.[45] They wrote about dealing with incantations, amulets, use of names and other techniques in order to ward off the evil eye, to conjure up spirits and to enable the user to reach various states of mind. Their studies are socio-historical in nature, but they do point out how Kabbalistic methods were 'translated' into laymen's terms so that the 'common man' could reach different levels of consciousness in the quest for communion with the Godhead—religiously, culturally, anthropologically and emotionally.

Moshe Idel describes several mystical techniques that "Kabbalists used . . . in order to induce paranormal states of consciousness."[46] Moshe Hallamish, a professor of Kabbalah and prolific writer on Kabbalah and mysticism, called these "techniques to understanding secrets."[47] Idel distinguishes between two main types of techniques: *nomian* (mystical techniques that involve some aspect of Halachic or Jewish Law practice) and *anomian* (mystical activity that doesn't involve Halachic practice). Some of the techniques that Idel describes include "weeping as a mystical practice," "ascent of the soul," "combinations of letters of the Divine Name" and "visualization of colors and Kabbalistic prayer."[48] We can see that there are numerous techniques that can be used to induce mystical contemplative states. How would psychoanalysis explain this?

Consider the *Interpretation of Dreams*, which was Freud's *magnum opus*. Written in the period 1899–1900, it was a book most probably influenced by his Jewish cultural upbringing and religious roots.[49] In his preface to the first edition Freud wrote: ". . . the dream is the first member of a class of abnormal psychical phenomena. . . ."[50] Freud recognized that dreams come to inform us of something that we sense through an unconscious mode. Since it doesn't conform to everyday waking life, Freud called it 'abnormal.' But, in reality, as Freud wrote: "*The interpretation of dreams is the royal road to a knowledge of the unconscious activities of the mind.*"[51] Kabbalists relate to dreams as man's connection to the upper celestial spheres. When a person is asleep, his conscious mind is resting. When he dreams, symbolic ideas, thoughts and 'stories' arise fleetingly and haphazardly.

A hundred and fifty years earlier, Moshe Chaim Luzzato wrote: "As one sees in a dream, where the topics rapidly fluctuate in a moment . . . the actual items seen in the dream aren't really seen, only the imagination is functioning and showing what the soul is experiencing. . . ."[52,53] Interestingly, the Kabbalists, Freud and the neuroscientists all agree that something is occurring within the brain during dreaming that 'loosens up' everyday thoughts and allows the mind/soul to connect to something outside of the normal, regular experience.[54]

Returning to our discussion of 'active' and 'passive,' we can further our understanding regarding states of mind. In order to parallel our understanding of Kabbalistic thinking on meditation, self-reflection and 'activity' from a psychoanalytic vantage point, we need to look at the differences between a passive and an active attitude on the part of the psychoanalyst. Does psychoanalysis advocate a passive role to be played by the therapist, or is activity at worst tolerated and at best advanced? Freud, in his famous paper before the Budapest Psycho-Analytical Conference in 1918,[55] made a strong case for psychoanalysts to posture for a more passive attitude in their treatment. Basing himself on Ferenczi's paper, Freud carefully avoided attacking Ferenczi, but made it clear that active therapy was not a preferred method for psychoanalytic treatment.[56] Ferenczi had written: "I was compelled in this case to give up the passive part that the psycho-analyst is accustomed to play in the treatment, which is confined to the hearing and interpretation of the patient's ideas, and had by active interference in the patient's psychic activities to help over dead points in the work of the analysis."[57]

Freud made a strong case for a passive analytic stance by noting that ". . . it was a *frustration* that made the patient ill, and that his symptoms serve him as substitutive satisfactions. . . . Cruel though it may sound, we must see to it that the patient's suffering . . . does not come to an end prematurely . . . we must re-instate it elsewhere in the form of some appreciable privation."[58] Freud's famous principle "*Analytic treatment should be carried through, as far as is possible, under privation—in a state of abstinence*"[59] stated quite clearly his desire that analysis be a passive treatment on the part of the therapist—forcing the patient to utilize the therapist in the transference as a wellspring of support that would enable the patient to actively pursue his or her own treatment.

Ferenczi, writing in 1920, owed a debt to his patron and professor. He felt that "in general, the treatment must be carried out in a condition of *abstinence*. . . ."[60] The meaning of this ("in general") was clear: Ferenczi thought that there are times that a more active approach may be desirable. But he qualified his point and emphasized: ". . . the activity roused in the patient is only means to the end. . . ." And: ". . . active technique only plays the part of *agent provocateur*; its command and prohibitions assist in obtaining of repetitions that must then be interpreted or reconstructed respectively into memories."[61]

The social historian Peter Gay,[62] in his biography of Freud, notes in his paraphrasing of the Freud-Ferenczi correspondence that "Ferenczi's way with his patients struck Freud as an invitation to disaster. 'You have made no secret of the fact that you kiss your patients and let them kiss you.' To be sure, a kiss may be perceived as harmless. People in the Soviet Union were very free with such salutations. 'But that does not alter the fact that we are not living in Russia, and that with us a kiss signifies an unmistakable erotic intimacy.'"[63]

An attempt to synthesize both Freud's and Ferenczi's ideas was tried by a radical psychiatrist, John Rosen, in the early 1950s.[64] Rosen, in his discussions with the psychoanalyst Paul Federn, coined the term 'direct analysis' in his work with regressed, schizophrenic patients.[65] Rosen felt that, at times, there was a need to modify the existing psychodynamic understanding and treatment of difficult patients by becoming more active in the therapeutic engagement. This active treatment promoted emotional growth in the patient and allowed the dormant state of mind of the patient to emerge into proactive movement.

We also think that the bridge to understanding the activity-passivity paradigm can be found in our understanding of altered states of consciousness. This will also help us to better understand the two types of Kabbalah: speculative/esoteric and practical/magical (in simpler terms, the difference between theoretical and practical ways of understanding mysticism and the 'hidden,' as opposed to the 'revealed'). Passivity is similar to theoretical and activity is similar to practical.

In our paper on an altered state of consciousness that occurred to the Fifth Lubavitcher Rebbe (known as the RaSHaB) in 1903, we wrote that altered states of consciousness, "in Kabbalistic-mystical terms, . . . is communication with the upper worlds."[66] Or, as the physician *cum* philosopher and psychologist William James wrote: "Mystical states . . . are states of insight . . . they are illuminations, revelations."[67] There are methods that enable one to reach a different level of feeling, insight and understanding. This 'state of mind' is found in Kabbalah and other mystical systems and is mirrored in the therapeutic realm of psychoanalysis.

Words play a major role in prayer, in meditation and in psychoanalysis and psychotherapy. Freud, quoting Goethe, writes: "No doubt 'in the beginning was the deed' and the word came later; in some circumstances it meant an advance in civilization when deeds were softened into words. But originally the word was magic. . . ."[68]

Before looking at this in further detail, it is significant that Freud returned to Goethe, in a seeming reversal of the original quotation that appears in the Talmud: "'In the beginning' is also a statement."[69, 70] Freud chose to quote a secondary source, rather than the well-known Talmudic saying, which also finds echoes in other Jewish primary sources. Freud, clearly cognizant of his (Hasidic) Jewish roots and upbringing, even gives his *Question of Lay Analysis* the subtitle *Conversations with an Impartial Person*. This is clearly related to the classic Hasidic text, the *Tanya*, which is subtitled *The Book of Intermediates*.[71]

Words are powerful tools, as we described in the last chapter on the language of creation. Indeed, Freud stated: ". . . do not let us despise the *word*. After all it is a powerful instrument; it is the means by which we convey our feelings to one another, our method of influencing other people."[72] As we have seen in the last chapter, Kabbalah places major emphasis on the power and strength of words. Words said in this world can influence the upper spheres and control the destiny of man and mankind. As the *Zohar* states: "A word that exits man's mouth goes upward and can influence for good or for bad." And: "Even a small [insignificant] word has a place, and is never lost."[73] This is echoed in the *Mishnah*: "The world was created with ten sayings/statements. . . ."[74] The meaning here is that the Biblical phrase "And God said" appears ten times in the early sections of Genesis. We see, therefore, that God's handiwork was preceded by the letters of creation—again stressing the importance of the word in creating, influencing and repairing reality.

In discussing 'active' and 'passive,' we also need to relate to the notion of control. Freud was careful to avoid any influence upon the patient, allowing the patient to slowly come to grips with the unconscious forces controlling thinking, feeling and action. Anthropologically, Freud was influenced by Sir James Frazer, the Scottish social anthropologist: "Frazer's first psychological theory . . . was based on the belief in an 'external soul.' The totem, according to this view, represented a safe place of refuge in which the soul could be deposited and so escape the dangers which threatened it. . . . Frazer himself subsequently abandoned this theory that totemism was derived from a belief in souls. . . ."[75] For Frazer, and Freud, the real issue was man's need to control the world around him. Some theorists called this mastery animism, totemism, sorcery or magic. Freud called this "body of instructions upon how to obtain mastery over men, beasts and things—or rather, over their spirits . . . technique."[76] But the issue of control is of paramount importance. Influence and control can be subtle and can have an almost 'uncanny' way about them. They tend to 'creep up' upon you and influence you. We need to look at the philosophical systems of mysticism and spiritualism in order to understand more fully our topic of 'states of mind.'

Freud, the scientist, noted: "I cannot discover this 'oceanic' feeling in myself. It is not easy to deal scientifically with feelings . . . it is very difficult for me to work with these almost intangible qualities."[77] Since these amorphous feelings could not be defined objectively, Freud did not investigate the intangible. He never stated that these feelings did not exist, they just weren't part of his *Weltanschauung* . It seems as if Freud was fearful of entering the mystical 'orchard'[78] because of its association with organized religion, which Freud had rejected.

In 1936, Freud dedicated a paper to Romain Rolland, the philosopher and author, on his seventieth birthday, in which he related a recurring psychical situation which appeared to him as confusing. Freud had a momentary feeling that "'*What I see here is not real.*' Such a feeling is known as a 'feeling of derealization.'" As Freud notes, they are "'sensations' . . . attached to particular mental contents and bound up with decisions made about these contents." Defensively operating, "they aim at keeping something away from the ego. . . ."[79] One can attempt to make a strong case for understanding derealization as a psychological mechanism that operates in a mystical sort of way. Freud alluded to this, but wasn't willing (or able?) to pursue it any further. The closest Freud came to this was his brief notation in 1938: "Mysticism is the obscure self-perception of the realm outside the ego, of the id."[80] In the *Zohar* we find the following: "During the time that man is sleeping, there is the taste of death as the soul ascends upwards . . . and is judged by [that] man's actions and words. . . ."[81] There is something that is 'felt' during dream and 'floating' states. We need to explore this further as we try to put forward a working definition of the 'oceanic feeling' or mysticism.

Freud stated that the 'oceanic feeling' is bound up with the concept of ego boundaries: ". . . the ego detaches itself from the external world." It is precisely this regressive state of the ego that gives one the 'oceanic feeling.' This is the feeling "of limitlessness and of a bond with the universe."[82] It seems that the 'oceanic feeling' is bound up with our understanding of consciousness. When one attends to something and is aware (Freud's attention cathexis), this is consciousness. Any change from that attention to another state can be referred to as an alternative or altered state of consciousness. The parallel for this is in the *Zohar*, where there is a discussion on the difference between a dream and prophecy. The *Zohar* notes that there are gradations or steps that are built one upon the other.[83] In other words, there is a progression from the more revealed to the more hidden. It is the mystical quality of 'unrealness' that enables us to connect from a more disconnected state. This is the 'free floating attention' that Freud had coined as "evenly-suspended attention."[84] If we concentrate too much on something, we censor and selectively edit in or out whatever is relevant at that particular moment in time. Kabbalah and psychoanalysis both inform us that one needs to 'freely float' in order to connect to the real meaning and understanding.

William James has commented: ". . . Mystical states . . . [are] also states of knowledge. They are states of insight . . . they are illuminations, revelations. . . . The mystic feels as if his own will were in abeyance, and indeed sometimes as if he were grasped and held by a superior power."[85] And the Anglican writer on mysticism, Evelyn Underhill, in a classic definition of mysticism wrote: "mysticism [is] the art of establishing one's conscious relation with the Absolute . . ."[86] It appears that mysticism oftentimes was identified with religious practice, and one can readily understand why many shied away from any identification or association with religious feelings or practices. Spirituality and religion became theosophical systems to be avoided. Anything that was related in any way to organized religious feelings or practices was shunned and rejected. This situation didn't allow spirituality or mysticism to develop in psychological contexts as divorced from any religious connotation. In effect, we were left with two similar philosophical systems perceived as vastly dissimilar: mysticism and psychology.

Jung, who tried to place a strong emphasis on the occult and spirituality, wrote: ". . . the various forms of religion no longer appear to come from within, from the psyche; they seem more like items from the inventory of the outside world."[87] This is reminiscent of Frazer and Freud's discussions on the 'external soul.' Jung was alluding to the fact that something was missing in modern man—something 'spiritual' or 'mystical.'

Bion tried to relate to this *feeling* quality by creating a distinction between knowing (K) and being (O). As he states: "Reality has to be 'been.'"[88] In 1970, he referred to O as the experience or 'thing-in-itself.' Bion then continues:

> I shall use the sign O to denote that which is the ultimate reality represented by terms such as ultimate reality, absolute truth, the godhead, the infinite, the thing-in-itself. O does not fall in the domain of knowledge or learning save incidentally; it can 'become,' but it cannot be 'known.' It is darkness and formlessness but it enters the domain K when it has evolved to a point where it can be known, through knowledge gained by experience, and formulated in terms derived from sensuous experience. . . .[89]

This echoes the famous Talmudic story of the "four who entered the orchard."[90] The story seems to be relating to a venture into the world of mysticism through contemplative meditation. Some of the participants allowed themselves to 'float' and experience the Godhead. Others were too caught up with 'doing' and became absorbed in themselves and were unable to divorce themselves to the point of just 'being.' They missed the essence of the mystical experience, which was to 'be' rather than to 'do.'

Bion, unlike Freud, was able to go beyond the purely scientific and allow himself to 'float' and pick up mystical cues. In 1933, Freud made a statement that brought his public coolness toward the occult closer to his private interest and desire for further understanding: "No doubt you would like me to hold fast to a moderate theism and show myself relentless in my rejection of everything occult. But I am incapable of currying favour and I must urge you to have kindlier thoughts on the objective possibility of thought-transference and at the same time of telepathy as well."[91] Freud explained his earlier fear of not wanting to recognize the validity of such paranormal phenomena in the following manner: "When they first came into my range of vision more than ten years ago, I too felt a dread of a threat against our scientific *Weltanschauung*, which, I feared, was bound to give place to spiritualism or mysticism if portions of occultism was proved true. Today I think otherwise."[92] The need to protect the scientific discipline of psychoanalysis even at the expense of avoiding potentially conflictual issues is the central theme. Mysticism and Kabbalah need not be wary of the unknown and undefineable.

An overview of psychotherapeutic principles and methods runs the gamut from Freud's earliest drive theory conceptualizations to object relations and intersubjective theoreticians. The study of intersubjectivity seems to be another medium or way to try to understand interactive processes, as they focus on the analytic work that takes place within the realm of ". . . *subjective reality*—that of the patient, that of the analyst, and the psychological field created by the interplay between the two."[93]

Bion tried to find the 'right word' to describe the transcendental, mystical feeling that somehow gets conveyed between patient and therapist. Again, we see the importance of 'the right word.' As Bion wrote: ". . . I propose to use the term 'intuit' as a parallel in the psychoanalyst's domain to the physician's use of 'see,' 'touch,' 'smell,' and 'hear.'"[94] This is similar to a comment by Christopher Bollas, a psychoanalyst and English professor: ". . . psychoanalysis . . . the reliving through language of that which is known but not yet thought (what I term the unthought known). . . ."[95] Something very mystical occurs within the therapeutic experience—an unusual and spiritual experience. The essential point here is for the need to 'float' and connect to the unconscious floating elements 'in the air.' Kabbalists in meditative contemplation via prayer, word manipulations and other techniques are able to achieve this 'evenly-suspended attention' that psychoanalysts try so hard to reach. As Michael Eigen remarked: "There are mysticisms of emptiness and fullness, difference and union, transcendence and immanence."[96]

The psychoanalyst Trigant Burrow, a man 'ahead of his time,' began innovative explorations of the psyche in order to search for the underlying reasons why people behave as they do. These explorations, starting in the 1920s, cost Burrow his university appointment and led to his being excommunicated from the American Psychoanalytic Association. This was connected to Burrow's wanting to investigate what fueled societal behavior, and what he called the "preconscious foundation of human experience."[97] Burrow was talking about a personality template that influenced the individual and society. As he wrote, ". . . this preconscious matrix of personality persists as a sort of background of consciousness, representing a biologically permanent mode that is inherent in human development. . . . The preconscious type of personality is sensitive, inspirational, intuitive and creative." If we aren't cognizant of this preconscious element in the human personality, it's like having an unanalyzed person 'on the loose.' There will be a tendency to act out, respond symbolically or metaphorically—not be rooted in the actual 'here and now.' Burrow called this "a flight toward the mystical."[98] The French psychologist and sociologist Gustave Le Bon, a major primary reference for Sigmund Freud's understanding of group behavior, termed this "a religious shape assumed by all the convictions of crowds."[99]

It is important to point out that the terms 'mystical' and 'religious' do not necessarily have a religious-as-religion connotation. Rather, we are dealing with concepts and ideas that relate to the underlying, unconscious emotional receptivity and awareness that enable us to pick up on unconscious cues, affect and behaviors. The psychoanalyst James Grotstein has commented: "I posit that the unconscious is perhaps as close to the 'God Experience' as mankind can ever hope to achieve"[100]—not religious experience *per se*, but a spiritual, mystical, unconscious perception. This is probably the main reason why Freud and many others were afraid to connect to the unconscious mystical threads in-the-air.

Mysticism is an attempt to transcend ordinary understanding to try to 'know' on an experiential and cognitive level the 'inner reality' of the Divine Majesty—the spiritual. This can be done on a religious or non-religious plane. The mystic endeavors to attain this state of union without getting lost in the Divine abyss, without losing a sense of presence. *Mystic* comes from the Greek *mystikós*, 'to reveal only to the initiates into the mysteries.' In our terminology, mysticism is a type of 'floating' whereby the group members connect to a spiritual, mystical unconscious. There evolves an unconscious union in the here and now, which connects *all* group members on a subliminal level.

In the Zen mind, "when you try to understand everything, you will not understand anything. The best way is to understand yourself, and then you will understand everything. . . . So we say that true understanding will come out of emptiness. . . ."[101] We often feel like we are in the midst of a chaotic process that seems to force us to deviate from knowing what is going on. We need to understand that this chaos is an important part to our connecting on a preconscious/unconscious level to what is really happening around us. The mystical or spiritual dimension has to be subliminally connected to; we cannot allow ourselves to be shifted away from unconsciously connecting to the underlying themes and feelings. As the Buddhist scholar and teacher Chögyam Trungpa writes: ". . . chaos helps us to see what is underneath all these thought patterns. . . ."[102] We need to allow ourselves to be unfettered so that we can connect to the underlying themes and affects.

Concomitantly, in the Kabbalistic system, there is a connection between our present or lower world and supernal upper worlds. This explains the underlying unconscious feelings that are floating 'in the air.' Man has cosmic influence—lower and upper worlds have a symmetrical correspondence. The Talmud states: "No drop comes down from above without having two drops come from below."[103] Kabbalah is a mystical search that uncovers the hidden and the revealed. One needs to allow the process to occur.

The 'oceanic feeling' and the mystical quality that is 'felt' parallels the movement from one world to the next in Kabbalistic thinking—especially movement within the last two worlds. However, Freud had great difficulty accepting the fact that there was a deeper nature to the soul, as we stated earlier, and this was probably one of the reasons that Freud and Jung separated. Jung's early works contained within their titles the words 'so-called occult,' 'spiritualistic medium,' 'symbols of rebirth,' 'the collective unconscious' and 'the soul and death,' to name a few. Jung was willing to extend his observations to the parapsychological world, which allowed him access to the realms of the hidden, unconscious worlds.

In a not-too-dissimilar vein, Freud showed that one could live in two spheres simultaneously.[104] On the conscious level, we live our lives in thought and action that we are aware of: the manifest content. But there is another level, the unconscious level or latent content. The unconscious level, likened metaphorically by Freud to that part of the iceberg that is beneath the surface of the water, has major influence in both thought and action over the conscious level, the above-the-water part of the iceberg. We are constantly influenced by the latent content, by the unconscious. In Kabbalistic terms, we are constantly influenced by the interplay between our present world and the other worlds impinging above us. Just as the upper worlds can influence our world, so too can we influence upper worlds for our own benefit as well as for rectification and reparation of mankind.

NOTES

1. Theodor Meynert (1833–1892) was the first scientist to perceive brain research as a systematic discipline; he wanted to establish psychiatry as an exact science based on clinical-pathological observations, anticipating today's modern biological psychiatry.

2. Freud received a traveling bursary from the University Jubilee Fund in order to study with Jean Martin Charcot (1825–1893). Sigmund Freud, 1886, "Report on My Studies in Paris and Berlin," in *Standard Edition of the Complete Psychological Works of Sigmund Freud*, ed. James Strachey (1886; London: Hogarth Press, 1981). Mechanistic thinking and understanding is a throw-back to the nineteenth-century Newtonian paradigm, in which things in the environment are seen as more machine-like. They, therefore, deny free will and explain human behavior as a function of biology.

3. Josef Breuer (1842–1925).

4. Leopold Breuer (1791–1872) was a teacher of Hebrew and was succeeded at the Jewish School of Vienna by Samuel Hammerschlag. See Tom Keve, *Triad: The Physicists, the Analysts, the Kabbalists* (London: Rosenberger & Krausz, 2000).

5. Rabbi Moses Schreiber (1762–1839), a Hungarian Rabbinical authority who was Rabbi of Pressburg (Bratislavia) and a strict Orthodox personality. He fought vig-

orously against any eroding of the Orthodox liturgy or religious practices. He was the author of a six-volume work that he called "Novellae and Responsa of Moses Sopher," and he became known by the Hebrew acronym ChaTaM Sopher.

6. Samuel Hammerschlag (1826–1904). Freud wrote an obituary of his former teacher, without mentioning that Prof. Hammerschlag was his teacher. Sigmund Freud, 1904, "Contributions to the *Neue Freie Presse*: Obituary of Professor S. Hammerschlag," in *Standard Edition*, ed. James Strachey, vol. 9, 255–56.

7. The 'Irma' dream is the first dream that Freud analyzed one line or thought at a time. At the end of his interpretation, Freud made his famous statement: "*When the work of interpretation has been completed, we perceive that a dream is the fulfillment of a wish*" (italics original). Sigmund Freud, 1900, "Interpretation of Dreams," in *Standard Edition*, ed. James Strachey, vol. 4, 106–21.

8. Josef Breuer and Sigmund Freud, 1895, "Studies on Hysteria," in *Standard Edition*, ed. James Strachey, vol. 2.

9. Sigmund Freud, 1914a, "Remembering, Repeating and Working-Through," in *Standard Edition*, ed. James Strachey, vol. 12.

10. Developed by Isaac Luria (the Ari) (1534–1572).

11. Section on practical Kabbalah in Gershom Scholem, *Kabbalah* (Jerusalem: Keter, 1974), 182–89.

12. Scholem, *Kabbalah*, 183.

13. Scholem, *Kabbalah*, 184.

14. C. G. Jung, *Aion,* in *The Collected Works of Carl G. Jung*. Bollingen Series XX (Princeton, N.J.: Princeton University Press, 1951), vol. 9, p. 83.

15. Scholem, *Kabbalah*, 31–42.

16. Scholem, *Origins of the Kabbalah* (1962; New York: Jewish Publication Society and Princeton University Press, 1987), 186.

17. Abraham Abulafia (1240–1292) was a Spanish mystic and Kabbalist. He founded a new school of mysticism called Prophetic Kabbalah. He instructed initiates how to obtain the spirit of prophecy through contemplation and meditation on the letters of the Hebrew alphabet. Some of the more strict Rabbis looked upon his new theosophy as heretical because of what they thought were messianic pretensions, and he was attacked in writings and speeches.

18. Moshe Idel, *Messianic Mystics* (New Haven, Conn.: Yale University Press, 1998), 62.

19. See Aryeh Kaplan, *Sefer Yetzirah (The Book of Creation)* (Newburyport, Mass.: Samuel Weiser, 1990b), chap. 2.

20. Gershom Scholem, *Major Trends in Jewish Mysticism* (1941; New York: Schocken Books, 1995), 127.

21. Abraham Abulafia, *Otzer Eden Ganooz (*Hidden Eden*)* [in Hebrew], ed. Amnon Gross (1286; Jerusalem: Barazani, 1999), esp. 34, 66.

22. Scholem, *Major Trends*, 131.

23. The 'science of letter combination' is also found in two other works by Abulafia: *Chayei HaOlam HaBah* (Life in the World to Come) [in Hebrew], ed. Amnon Gross (1280; Jerusalem: Barazani, 2001) and *Imrei Shefer* (Beautiful Words) [in Hebrew], ed. Amnon Gross (1291; Jerusalem: Barazani, 1999).

24. Freud, 1900, "Interpretation of Dreams," in *Standard Edition*, ed. James Strachey, vols. 4–5.
25. Jean Laplanche and Jean-Bertrand Pontalis, *The Language of Psycho-Analysis* (London: Hogarth Press, 1980), 169.
26. See Joseph H. Berke, "Psychoanalysis and Kabbalah," *Psychoanalytic Review* 83 (1996): 852.
27. Josef Breuer and Sigmund Freud, 1895, "Studies on Hysteria," in *Standard Edition*, ed. James Strachey, vol. 2.
28. Breuer was originally credited by Freud with having discovered psychoanalysis. In Freud's first lecture on psychoanalysis at Clark University, in 1909, Freud remarked: "If it is a merit to have brought psycho-analysis into being, that merit is not mine. I had no share in its earliest beginnings. I was a student and working for my final examinations at the time when another Viennese physician, Dr. Josef Breuer, first (in 1880–2) made use of this procedure on a girl who was suffering from hysteria." Sigmund Freud, 1910b, "Five Lectures on Psycho-Analysis," in *Standard Edition*, ed. James Strachey, vol. 11, 9. This declaration in the Clark University lectures was later retracted, when Freud stated: "For psycho-analysis is my creation. . . . Since I gave those lectures, however, some well-disposed friends have suggested to me a doubt whether my gratitude was not expressed too extravagantly on that occasion." Sigmund Freud, 1914b, "On the History of the Psycho-Analytic Movement," in *Standard Edition*, ed. James Strachey, vol. 2, 7–8.
29. Keve, *Triad*, vi.
30. Keve, *Triad*, vi, 123.
31. Keve, *Triad*, 123–24. This is a reconstructed exchange between the Chatam Sopher and Wolf Pappenheim.
32. Aryeh Kaplan, *Meditation and the Bible* (Newburyport, Mass.: Samuel Weiser, 1978).
33. Midrash is the literature that interprets Biblical Scripture. Talmud, based on Biblical Scripture and Midrashic literature, is a record of eight centuries of discussions on points of law and lore.
34. Freud, 1913, "On Beginning the Treatment," in *Standard Edition*, ed. James Strachey, vol. 12, 135.
35. Freud, 1912b, "Recommendations to Physicians Practising Psycho-Analysis," in *Standard Edition*, ed. James Strachey, vol. 12, 114.
36. Freud, 1912b, "Recommendations to Physicians Practising Psycho-Analysis," in *Standard Edition*, ed. James Strachey, vol. 12, 111.
37. Freud, 1912b, "Recommendations to Physicians Practising Psycho-Analysis," in *Standard Edition*, ed. James Strachey, vol. 12, 115.
38. The works of Cordovero (known by his acronym, ReMaK) describe a well-thought-out, systematic, theosophical and mystical philosophy with practical (which he called 'devotional') applications. The Ari's philosophical and theoretical understanding was built upon the ReMaK's system. One of the ReMaK's disciples was Hayim Vital, who later became the Ari's major disciple and interpreter of the Ari's philosophy, which he later committed to writing. The Lurianic (Ari) Kabbalah system was based on Cordovero's original philosophical system.

39. Joseph Karo wrote a diary recording the mystical revelations that he experienced at nighttime. Joseph Karo, *Magid Meisharim* [in Hebrew], ed. and trans. Y Bar-Lev (1875; Petach Tikvah: privately printed, 1990).

40. Cordovero, *Pardes Rimmonim* (Orchard of Pomegranates) [in Hebrew] (1548; Jerusalem: Yerid Hasefarim, 2000), 19:3.

41. Cordovero, *Pardes Rimmonim*, Gate 10.

42. Aryeh Kaplan, *Meditation and Kabbalah* (Newburyport, Mass.: Samuel Weiser, 1982), 180.

43. Yigal Arica,1998, *Practical Kabbalah.* This is a popular exposition of a serious topic that has been debated by Kabbalah scholars for centuries: should Kabbalah be studied theoretically or with practical applications on how to harness the Kabbalistic energies?

44. Scholem, *Kabbalah*, 337.

45. E. A. Wallis Budge was in charge of the Egyptian and Assyrian antiquities in the British Museum. Dr. Joshua Trachtenberg, who was born in London, served as an American pulpit rabbi for nearly 30 years.

46. Moshe Idel, *Kabbalah: New Perspectives* (New Haven, Conn.: Yale University Press, 1988), 74.

47. Moshe Hallamish, *Introduction to the Kabbalah*, 65.

48. Idel, *Kabbalah: New Perspectives*, 75, 88, 97, 103.

49. Freud, 1900, "Interpretation of Dreams," in *Standard Edition*, ed. James Strachey, vols. 4–5.

50. Freud, 1900, "Interpretation of Dreams," in *Standard Edition*, ed. James Strachey, vol. 4, xxiii.

51. Freud, 1900, "Interpretation of Dreams," in *Standard Edition*, ed. James Strachey, vol. 5, 608 (italics original).

52. Moshe Chaim Luzzato, RaMCHaL (1707–1747), was an Italian mystic and poet. In his states of mystical trance, he claimed to have heard angels who communicated to him heavenly messages that enabled him to compose Kabbalistic works. In 1743–1744 he settled in Acre (Acco), Palestine, and died with his family in the plague of 1747.

53. Moshe Chaim Luzzato, *Kalach Pitchei Chochmah* (138 Windows to Wisdom) [in Hebrew], ed. C. Friedlander (Bnai Brak: Gittler, n.d.), 27.

54. Mark Solms, a neuropsychologist and psychoanalyst, and Oliver Turnbull, also a neuropsychologist, referred to dreams as ". . . hallucinations that we *all* experience—hallucinations that have been regarded by many as a 'normal' form of psychosis." Mark Solms and Oliver Turnbull, *The Brain and the Inner World* (London: Karnac, 2002), 181.

55. Freud, 1919c, "Lines of Advance in Psycho-Analytic Therapy," in *Standard Edition*, ed. James Strachey, vol. 17.

56. Sandor Ferenczi, "Technical Difficulties in the Analysis of a Case of Hysteria," in *Further Contributions to the Theory and Technique of Psycho-Analysis* (1919; New York: Brunner/Mazel, 1980).

57. Ferenczi, "Technical Difficulties," 196.

58. Freud, 1919c, "Lines of Advance in Psycho-Analytic Therapy," in *Standard Edition*, ed. James Strachey, vol. 17, 162–63.

59. Freud, 1919c, "Lines of Advance in Psycho-Analytic Therapy," in *Standard Edition*, ed. James Strachey, vol. 17, 162.

60. Sandor Ferenczi, "The Further Development of an Active Therapy in Psycho-Analysis," in *Further Contributions to the Theory and Technique of Psycho-Analysis* (1920; New York: Brunner/Mazel, 1980), 202.

61. Ferenczi, "Further Development," 212, 217.

62. Peter Gay was born in Berlin as Peter Joachim Fröhlich. He escaped from Nazi Germany in 1939 and came to the United States, where he received his education and eventually became a professor of history, teaching at Columbia University and Yale University.

63. Peter Gay, *Freud: A Life for Our Time* (New York: Norton, 1998), 578.

64. John Rosen, *Direct Analysis* (New York: Grunne & Stratton, 1953). Rosen was known as a radical psychiatrist in that he physically and verbally 'attacked' his severely regressed schizophrenic patients, in order to pull them out of their apathy and stupor. He was known as an active and direct psychotherapist. By today's standards, his active treatment would be viewed as aggressive and possibly abusive.

65. Paul Federn was one of the original eight followers of Freud who met in weekly scientific meetings at Freud's home. Federn eventually became head of the Viennese Psychoanalytic Society. He escaped Vienna in 1938 and settled in New York. In the late 1940s, he was helpful to John Rosen in understanding Rosen's psychotic patients and, according to Rosen, "became sufficiently interested to attend actual treatment sessions." Rosen, *Direct Analysis*, 2.

66. Joseph. H. Berke and Stanley Schneider, "A Tale of Two Orphans: The Limits of Categorization," *Mental Health, Religion and Culture* 4 (2001): 87–88.

67. William James, *The Varieties of Religious Experience* (1901; New York: Mentor Books, 1958), 293.

68. Freud, 1926b, "The Question of Lay Analysis," in *Standard Edition*, ed. James Strachey, vol. 20, 188.

69. This is also the last line in Freud's 1912–1913 "Totem and Taboo," in *Standard Edition*, ed. James Strachey, vol. 13, 161. In this citation, 'Deed' is capitalized.

70. Talmud Rosh HaShannah, 32a.

71. Schneur Zalman of Liadi, *Likkutei Amarim: Tanya.* Bilingual ed. Trans. N. Mindel (1797; Brooklyn, N.Y.: Kehot, 1984), title page.

72. Freud, 1926b, "The Question of Lay Analysis," in *Standard Edition*, ed. James Strachey, vol. 20, 187–88.

73. The *Zohar* teaches that there is a correspondence between the 'lower' and 'upper' worlds. Therefore, man's deeds have cosmic influence. These quotations come from 2:47b and 2:99b.

74. *Ethics of the Fathers*, 5:1.

75. Freud, 1912–13, "Totem and Taboo," in *Standard Edition*, ed. James Strachey, vol. 13, 116–17.

76. Freud, 1912–13, "Totem and Taboo," in *Standard Edition*, ed. James Strachey, vol. 13, 78.

77. Freud, 1930, "Civilization and Its Discontents," in *Standard Edition*, ed. James Strachey, vol. 21, 65, 72.

78. The mystical 'orchard' refers to the famous story that appears in the Talmud Haggigah 14b: "Four entered the orchard. . . ." They were part of a meditative experience and overstepped the boundaries and 'entered' into the upper sphere of the Godly Throne. Three were stricken and only one escaped unscathed.

79. Sigmund Freud, 1936, "A Disturbance of Memory on the Acropolis," in *Standard Edition*, ed. James Strachey, vol. 22, 244–45.

80. Published posthumously in 1941: Freud, 1938/1941, "Findings, Ideas, Problems," in *Standard Edition*, ed. James Strachey, vol. 23, 300.

81. *Zohar* 3:121b.

82. Freud, 1930, "Civilization and Its Discontents," in *Standard Edition*, ed. James Strachey, vol. 21, 68.

83. *Zohar* 1:183 a, b.

84. Freud, 1912b, "Recommendations to Physicians Practising Psycho-Analysis," in *Standard Edition*, ed. James Strachey, vol. 12, 111.

85. James, *Varieties*, 293.

86. Evelyn Underhill, *Mysticism* (London: Methuen, 1912), 97. Underhill was initially an atheist who became increasingly drawn to religion (Catholicism). Over the years she became interested in mysticism in general, and practical mysticism, specifically. She organized ecumenical retreats, and upon her death in 1941 was recognized as an outstanding expert on theology.

87. C. G. Jung, "The Spiritual Problem of Modern Man," in *The Portable Jung*, ed. J. Campbell (1928; New York: Penguin, 1976), 466.

88. W. R. Bion, "Transformations," in *Seven Servants* (1965; New York: Aronson, 1977), 148.

89. W. R. Bion, *Attention and Interpretation*, in *Seven Servants* (1970; New York: Aronson, 1977), 4, 26.

90. Talmud Haggigah 14b.

91. Freud, 1933, "New Introductory Lectures on Psycho-Analysis—Lecture 30: Dreams and Occultism," in *Standard Edition*, ed. James Strachey, vol. 22, 54.

92. Freud, 1933, "New Introductory Lectures on Psycho-Analysis—Lecture 30: Dreams and Occultism," in *Standard Edition*, ed. James Strachey, vol. 22, 54.

93. Over the past one hundred years, clinicians have been grappling with trying to understand how and why emotional interactions occur. Robert Stolorow, Bernard Brandschaft and George Atwood spent fifteen years in collaborative effort in order to define a new construct: the concept of an intersubjective field, as the pivotal building block in the relationship between patient and therapist. Robert Stolorow, Bernard Brandschaft and George Atwood, *Psychoanalytic Treatment: An Intersubjective Approach* (Hillsdale, N.J.: Analytic Press, 1987), 4.

94. Bion, *Attention*, 7.

95. Christopher Bollas, *The Shadow of the Object* (New York: Columbia University Press, 1987), 4.

96. Michael Eigen, *The Psychoanalytic Mystic* (London: Free Association Books, 1998), 13. Eigen is a psychologist and psychoanalyst.

97. Trigant Burrow, *Preconscious Foundations of Human Experience* (New York: Basic Books, 1964), ix. Burrow (1875–1950) helped found the American Psychoanalytic

Association in 1911 and became its president in 1926. His work was 'ostracized' by the mainstream psychoanalysts of his time because of what they viewed as a radical departure from individual psychoanalysis to group dynamics.

98. Burrow, *Preconscious Foundations,* 47, 56.

99. Gustave Le Bon, *The Crowd* (1896; London: Ernest Benn, 1952), 72.

100. James Grotstein, *Who is the Dreamer Who Dreams the Dream? A Study of Psychic Presences* (Hillsdale, N.J.: Analytic Press, 2000), xvii.

101. Zen master Shunryu Suzuki, *Zen Mind, Beginner's Mind* (New York: Weatherhill, 1970), 111.

102. Chögyam Trungpa, *Glimpses of Abhidharma* (Boston: Shambhala, 2001), 75.

103. Ta'anit 25b. Compare *Zohar* 3:247b.

104. Freud, 1900, "Interpretation of Dreams," in *Standard Edition*, ed. James Strachey, vols. 4–5.

Chapter Ten

Opposites

Opposites are usually given to stress a word, idea or concept. The purpose of this intensification and magnification is to draw attention. As Shakespeare noted: "'Tis not enough our foes are this time fled, Being opposites of such repairing nature. . . ."[1] The metaphor of 'being opposites' exaggerates the importance of awareness of the enemy—the other—the 'foe.' For only when we realize through stressing or accentuating the importance of opposites, can we attend to the business at hand, or understand another state of mind.

We have previously pointed out that Jacques Lacan was fascinated by linguistic phenomena and stressed the importance of language in understanding clinical material. He was influenced clinically by Freud, linguistically by Ferdinand de Saussure, and philosophically by Hegel. There were also influences from the realm of mathematics. "Lacan criticises the way that other forms of psychoanalysis, such as Kleinian psychoanalysis and object-relations theory, tend to play down the importance of language and emphasize the 'non-verbal communication' of the analysand (his 'body language,' etc.) at the expense of the analysand's speech. . . . Lacan argues that language has both a symbolic and an imaginary dimension."[2] Language, therefore, allows us to understand the relationship between the signifier and signified.[3] In effect, there may be different or even opposite ways of understanding communication. But every linguistic expression has meaning.

A strong supporter of Freud during the difficult struggles with Jung, Adler and Rank, the physician and psychoanalyst Georg Groddeck made an astute comment regarding language and opposites or the negative: ". . . the word must have some other significance than the one usually accepted, and behind the word must lie hidden something which is powerful enough to allow us to think wrongly, without disturbing the course of events thereby."[4] Since

Groddeck was a very strong supporter of Freud and continually attempted to find organic medical or philosophical foundations for the 'master's' writings, this comment on the hidden meanings behind language must have had the blessing of Freud.

The work of Karl Abel,[5] the German philologist, on antithetical meanings of primary words, greatly influenced Freud. Freud had utilized some of Abel's ideas (as well as Talmudic primary sources, without attribution[6]) in his classic work on dreams.[7] Freud had commented that oftentimes dreams may take on a contrary or opposite expression. "There is yet another alternative way in which the dreamwork can deal with affects in the dream-thoughts. . . . It can *turn them into their opposite*."[8] Only through a thorough analysis can one know whether the meaning was actual, imagined, fantasized and/or opposite. "Dreams feel themselves at liberty . . . to represent any element by its wishful contrary; so that there is no way of deciding at first glance whether any element that admits of a contrary is present in the dream-thoughts as a positive or negative."[9] In our paper on the antithetical meaning of primary words, which we discussed in chapter four, on 'Good and Evil,' we looked at the primary word and concept 'breast.'[10] Utilizing Hebrew as a central representative of the Semitic language group, word opposites and reversals were shown as important ways to arrive at a closer, multidimensional appreciation and understanding of reality.

To demonstrate examples of the underlying meaning of opposites, we find in the Talmud the expression *sagi nahor*, which in Aramaic means 'an abundance of light.'[11] Another Talmudic description *me'or einayim,* in Hebrew, means 'full of light.'[12] Both of these idioms are used to describe a blind person! Rabbinic literature is replete with examples of utilizing opposites in order to define or clarify terms. These expressions are known as using a 'cleaner language,' a way of 'sweetening' a harsh term with a more poetic, metaphoric choice—generally an opposite in order to poignantly focus on the essence. In other words, we need to find the meaning behind the meaning.

Isaac the Blind, a twelfth-century French Kabbalist, was born blind. But the appellation referring to his lack of sight, even though a statement of fact, was given to accentuate the opposite. Although physically blind, he had the ability to search a person's soul and 'see' (i.e., read) his thoughts.

If we look at the first chapters in the Bible, in Genesis, we note that Creation is described as taking place in a void, a vacuum. There was darkness over the entire depth of the world. A decision is made to create 'light.' And, then there is a division created by God between the light that was just created and the previously existing darkness. Philosophers and Bible commentators pondered over this text in order to try to see if darkness was a separate creation by God or if it was *a priori* part of the existing constellation of materials and gases available for God's use in creating the world. Joseph Gikatilla, the Spanish Kabbalist, noted this philosophical problem and referred to it as "the power of opposites."[13] This fits in with the Midrashic idea of God having created and destroyed other worlds and using the 'leftovers' to create this world.[14]

Melanie Klein struggled with the same idea about the birth of the infant. When the fetus exits the mother's womb and cries, is that cry an expression of hunger and pain (meaning that there is already a primitive existing 'awareness' of these feelings) or is it an uncomfortable feeling that elicits crying as an instinctive response? And will it need further learning in order to define feelings, emotions and circumstances? This seemingly simple question has a great importance for Klein's conceptualization of early anxiety. At the moment the baby cries and is fed, he then experiences his proto object world as good—nurturing, warming and removing pain. This is 'the good breast.' However, if the hungry baby cries and is not fed, then he experiences his proto object world as bad—painful and persecuting. This opposite event is 'the bad breast.' Depending on whether the baby's mother is sensitive and available or not, we can see that the 'breast' can quickly change from good to bad, from *shad* to *shade*, from angel to devil, and back.

In an historical perspective, Klein's ideas follow Freud's 'break' with Otto Rank's concept that all anxiety stems from the birth trauma. "Freud[15] argued instead that the anxiety-situation changed at different stages in life. In doing so, he was in effect endorsing the importance of phantasy, and of reality, that is *content* which gives meaning to anxiety."[16] Klein's understanding of the causes of anxiety led her to formulate her double-thrusted theory of introjections and projections which, in effect, set the stage for flowing movement in two directions simultaneously: inwardly (introjections) and outwardly (projections). This is most clearly seen in her development of the concept of projective identification—which involves a complicated interplay of projections and identifications.[17]

Both the Creation story and Klein's investigation of the infant's birth are examples of the utilization of opposites, often in a metaphoric/theatrical manner, in order to accentuate, magnify and understand difference.

The psychoanalytical interest in contradictions, antithetical meanings,[18] slips of the tongue and pen, and other parapraxes can be matched by the Kabbalistic concern with opposites. Examples are receiving and giving/imparting, absence and presence of light, good and evil, light and dark, cause and effect. It is not by chance that opposites form a significant part of psychoanalytic interpretations during treatment and in mystical/Kabbalistic thinking and practice. We will now look at this further in light of Kabbalah.

The *Bahir* (*Book of Illumination*), the oldest of Kabbalistic texts,[20] in quoting a verse from Psalms, "Even darkness is not dark to You. Night shines like day—light and darkness are the same,"[21] is stating a fact regarding God's presence in the world. God is "both imminent and transcendental. . . . Light . . . refers to the Divine Essence, as perceived in the mystical state. Due to the constriction (*tzimzum*), we do not see this Light when we look toward God, and He therefore seems to be surrounded with darkness."[22] Again, we see the utilization of the technique of portraying opposites. By this exegetic method, polarity and differences help accentuate and highlight the importance of something by stressing the extremes.

This is also a technique that we find in the *Sefer Yetzirah* (*Book of Creation*), another early Kabbalistic text where the author lists opposites in terms of directions and depths.[23] Aryeh Kaplan notes in his commentary: "The Ten *Sefirot* are thus seen as consisting of five sets of opposites."[24] Nothing can be accepted at face value. There are always two (opposite) ways of looking at something. Since everything is affected by the *sefirotic* world, opposites are inherently built in, as polarized positions, in order to emphasize a thought, idea, direction or feeling. These oppositions are necessary in order to foster and engender "differentiation."[25] The clinical psychologist Sanford Drob summarizes this issue: "The Lurianic theosophy actually involves a dialectical play of opposites: Emanation and contraction, revelation and concealment, breaking of the vessels and restoration."[26]

Similarly, the famous Jewish ethicist Eliyahu Dessler was a master at weaving Hasidic, Kabbalistic and philosophical streams of thought.[27,28] His essays and letters were published in a multivolume set as *Michtav M'Eliyahu* (*A Letter from Eliyahu*). In a fascinating analysis of how soul and spirit can be harnessed for the striving for truth and understanding the self in the service of the Creator, Dessler notes the following:

> The world was created in (with) opposites. There is purpose that unites them and merges them. There is an electron (with a negative charge) and a proton (with a positive charge), and they both make up the atom. So too there is body and soul, this world and the next world (to come), upper and lower worlds, light and darkness, life and death, evil and good, spirituality and corporeality, revealed and hidden. . . . Opposites generate the purpose: misfortune brings salvation, darkness brings light, this world brings the next world (to come), death brings resurrection of the dead. The general rule is: from the hidden sprouts forth the revealed. . . .[29]

Dessler was influenced by the revered Tzadok HaCohen of Lublin, who himself was a genius at interlacing mystical and Hasidic philosophy and thought. We can see from the above quotation, one of the essential theses of

Tzadok HaCohen: the dialectic power of paradox.[30] In order to understand this further, we need to look at the concept of the dialectic.

Dialectic is a Greek term that refers to an exchange of propositions (known as theses) and counterpropositions (known as antitheses), which result in an argument or disagreement. The aim of the dialectical method is to resolve disagreement through rational discussion. The way to arrive at agreement is through knowing both sides of an argument. The opposite side needs to be taken in before a decision can be arrived at. The concept of the dialectic was advanced in Greece by Socrates and developed later by the eighteenth-century German philosopher Hegel. This is an interpretive method, whereby in order to arrive at an absolute concept of truth, an assertable proposition, known as a *thesis*, is opposed by an equally assertable and apparently contradictory proposition, known as an *antithesis*. The mutual contradiction can be reconciled on a higher level of truth by a third proposition, known as *synthesis*. These dichotomies between absolute and relative, finite and infinite, are found in other major philosophical systems as well as in psychoanalytic and psychological systems. This philosophy was adopted, albeit in a skewed manner, by Karl Marx. A frontal attack on the potential misuses of the Hegelian dialectic was advanced by philosopher Karl Popper. Popper accused the abuse of the dialectic as encouraging and even justifying fascism.[31]

We have seen how philosophy, as Kabbalah and psychoanalysis, makes use of the dialectic or 'exchange of opposites.'[32] In the Dessler quotation above, he writes that "the world was created in (with) opposites"! We see here an *a priori* decision to have opposites as part of the creation process. There is a built-in philosophical process that includes opposites as a necessary part of the universe. If we picture this in purely physical terms, we have Heisenberg's Uncertainty Principle, Einstein's Relativity Theorem, and the EPR (Einstein, Podolsky and Rosen) Paradox, for example. All three of these theories, which form the basis of quantum theory, take into account paradoxes and opposites.

By the same token, in Kabbalah, emanation and flow do not operate in a one-way system, but rather, there is a back-and-forth movement that oftentimes is oppositional and yet brings us back to the center so that we can move forward. This is the *Zohar*'s concept of utilizing the left and right poles in order to arrive at a centering.[33] Oppositional poles allow for mediation in order to arrive at a more balanced position. As Daniel Matt notes in his translation and notational comments on the *Zohar*, "The central pillar: *Tif'eret*, who mediates between the polar opposites of *Hesed* and *Gevurah*."[34] Strength needs to be modulated with mercy, stringency with compassion, in order for mankind to survive. If one is 'off' in any way, it emphasizes the need to tilt that person to a more 'right' or 'left' position. The modern term for this is 'off center.' Such directionality has a basic meaning as in describing an overly physical or emotional person, someone who is too warm or too cold or, for that matter, too active or too passive. Hence the significance of finding the 'just right' center of balance.[35]

Rachel Elior, a philosopher and professor of Jewish Studies, refers to the ". . . dialectical system founded upon the tension between the two tendencies in the relations between good and evil . . ."[36] and to "the dialectical law of the union of opposites,"[37] "which allows for contradictions."[38] Elior makes the interesting observation that opposites are not accidental but rather are part of a preconceived and ordered system of living and being that is a necessary part in the running of the world. By having opposites and polar extremes, we are forced to acknowledge the entire range of being and doing (feelings and behavior), and this allows us to arrive at the medium that is relevant for us at a certain moment in time. By having the entire spectrum open and available, we can then make an intelligent choice that accounts for the extremes and enables us to find our position on the continuum.

J. B. Soloveitchik furthered the thinking of Hegel and the nineteenth-century Danish philosopher Søren Kierkegaard, and pursued a study of the dialectic. The (seemingly) polar concepts of good and evil, of tension and suspension are subjects for his thinking and investigation. He notes: "Man is a dialectical being who is torn by conflict, and who is in a state of continual ontological tension and perplexity. It is this tension in man that ultimately results in Man's creative gesture, and is, therefore, responsible for Man's greatness and God's election of Man as a charismatic figure."[39] There is a constant and continuous dialectic that weighs like a balance scale. There is never a complete, one-sided decision, as there needs to be a weighing, an evaluation of the elements in order to arrive at a working formula. Soloveitchik sees God as having the final say: "Only God knows how to reconcile the inherent tension within Man. We do not."[40] In psychoanalysis and psychological processes, man has a major part to play. God, the 'mystical' element, the unconscious, cannot be overlooked, but man has 'input.' Soloveitchik doesn't rule out man's involvement. However, Man (capital 'M') is influenced by and in need of the God-input.

Freud, citing the famous German philologist Karl Abel, made reference to the "'antithetical meaning of primal words' . . . (and) not to suppose that communications made by one person to another with the help of such ambivalent words were on that account ambiguous. On the contrary, intonation and gesture must have made it quite certain in the context of the speech which of the two contraries the speaker intended to convey."[41] While the above quotation relates to how language develops, Freud later took this idea further in discussing deliberate and non-deliberate slips of the tongue or pen, "in which one says the precise opposite of what one intended to say . . . contraries have a strong conceptual kinship with each other and stand in a particularly close psychological association with each other."[42]

The Kabbalistic understanding of opposites is that there is an accentuation and deliberateness of purpose in utilizing opposites. Often the result is to arrive at a compromise, a middle road. We see this in Kabbalah's stress on the importance of seeing how both giving and receiving are not only related, but are the same! By giving to the other, one opens up paths and energy systems that can then be replenished and fortified by receiving. This follows the energy and/or light system that is the essence of the Kabbalah system. God needed to limit His presence (metaphorically and realistically), represented by light (i.e., energy), by the process of *tzimzum* (constriction), in order for man to have a hand in effectuating the creation process. In this system there is light in every person that is connected to the Godhead. If there is a lack of spiritual wellness, then there is an absence or lack of light. While it sounds like an either-or position, man's struggle in life is reflected by the need to arrive at a compromise position. Sometimes the compromise may tend toward one pole or the other—not necessarily a middle position.

Comparatively, Erik Erikson described different tasks for each stage in his developmental framework of the stages of man. These tasks were arranged as a polarity—i.e., extremes. A person would need to find his level—which, hopefully, would not be an extreme pole but rather a mixture of each pole.[43] Bion utilized the term 'valency' "to describe the type of relationship which accounts for the pull of the basic assumption group,"[44] which was defined as a polarity—two extremes. In order for a person to 'survive' in a group, he would have to gravitate toward a position which was given as an extreme, but the aim was to attenuate the extremist pull.

Freud explained: ". . . mental life is the arena and battle-ground for mutually opposing purposes or, to put it non-dynamically, that it consists of contradictions and pairs of contraries. Proof of the existence of a particular purpose is no argument against the existence of an opposite one; there is room for both."[45] We think that Freud 'borrowed' from the Kabbalistic tradition the idea that there can exist two opposing poles, and one does not have to negate the other. Rather we need to derive meaning from each pole in our quest to arrive at a position that is relevant to our understanding and 'being.'

In an earlier publication Freud wrote: "Reversal of an instinct into its opposite resolves on closer examination into two different processes: a change from activity to passivity, and a reversal of its content."[46] The reversal of content like "the transformation of *love into hate*"[47] is understandable in light of what we stated earlier regarding slips of the tongue and other stress-related parapraxes. These are not necessarily polar opposites, but emphasize the need to explore further the concept of the reversal of an instinct into its opposite, as this is a central feature of psychoanalytic theory.

Transpositions and reversals are distortions that enable us to change violent thoughts into sublimated expressions and feelings.[48] This parallels the idea of active-passive in patient and therapist thoughts, feelings and actions. It also allows us to become less (or more) paranoiac: being looked at instead of looking. In psychopathology this has been termed 'exhibitionism' rather than 'scopophilia.'[49] In Kabbalah this is represented by the world of *tohu* (confusion and disruption) and the world of *tikkun* (restoration). One cannot correct or restore something that is not broken or confused. The two poles work together in enabling us to recognize disruptions, unevenness and confusion and to work hard to fix and correct.

The Kabbalistic idea of balancing poles can be summarized in the following quotation from Dessler:

> . . . God's munificence is always giving. And us? If we just stand and receive His goodness, and continually ask for more—'give! give!'—then we are transfixed in the path of taking and loving (only) ourselves, (and) this leads to ingratitude, pitilessness and closing oneself off to spirituality.[50]

Parallel to this is the psychoanalytic concept of narcissism. A healthy balance of self-love is the ability to have enough emotional investment in the self and have enough left over to form relationships with the other. Pathological narcissism is the over-libidinal investment in the self to the exclusion of sharing with the other.

Jung's conceptualization of the psychical system followed Freud's fluid, physical, psychodynamic theoretical framework. However, Jung went further in viewing the energy system as consisting of internal polar opposites that complement one another. Frieda Fordham, who synthesizes 'what Jung really meant,' summarized Jung's ideas in the following manner:

> Jung usually refers to the opposing poles as 'the opposites.' The greater the tension between the pairs of opposites the greater the energy; without opposition there is no manifest energy. . . . The opposites have a regulating function . . . and when one extreme is reached libido passes over into its opposite. [51]

Since Jung admitted that he was 'influenced' and aware of the Kabbalistic theoretical system,[52] let us now look further at the Kabbalistic view of opposites. Gershom Scholem has written: "In addition to its positive aspect, the *tikkun*, the restoration of the right order, the true unity of things, has a corresponding negative aspect, which in the Lurianic Kabbalah is termed *berur*. *Berur* (literally 'selection') is the elimination of the negative factors that disturb the right order, that is the elimination of the powers of the demonic and Satanic, of the 'other side' (*sitrah achra*) as the Kabbalists call it."[53] Opposite poles are a part of the world order and we need both poles in order for the world to strive for perfection and correction.

Similarly, Ferenczi, a colleague and the *enfant terrible* of Freud's inner circle, exclaimed: ". . . Jung was right in his claim that psychoanalysis has its roots in Jewish mysticism."[54] In one of his brief notes[55] Ferenczi comments: ". . . some memories of childhood cannot be ever raised as such into the cs,[56] and even in physical symptoms and hallucinations are always mixed with dreamlike (wish-fulfilling) distortions of defence and of turning into the opposite. . . ."[57] Opposites become a way of transforming difficult material into another (opposite) form in order to reduce the anxiety associated with the original. The opposite form, in reality, places stress on both the original as well as the opposite. Ferenczi, as Freud, was aware that oppositional poles contribute greatly to the magnification and accentuation of ideas, thoughts and affects.

The issue of sexuality and bisexuality was a topic frequently discussed by Freud, Wilhelm Fleiss[58] and even Ferenczi. The idea of bisexuality is that "every human being is endowed constitutionally with both masculine and feminine sexual dispositions. . . ."[59] Freud wrote: "The dominant sex of the person, that which is the more strongly developed, has repressed the mental representation of the subordinated sex into the unconscious."[60]

There is nothing more 'opposite' than the two sexual gender roles: male and female. Earlier Freud had noted that while there were two gender roles, male and female, there was only one sexual organ that was important, the penis, and there were those who had it (males) and those who lacked it (females). On the other hand, Kabbalah recognizes the primacy and equal importance of both the male and the female. The tenth *sefira* (*Malkhut*—Kingship) is the feminine representative attribute of the Divine. This *sefira* is the power invested in man by God in order to be able to receive and, thereby, also to be able to give. This seems reminiscent of Erik Erikson's sixth stage which deals with intimacy. To paraphrase Erikson's idea, one becomes intimate when able to both give and receive. If this *sefira* represents both receiving and giving, then it functions as both a female and male representative of the Divine!

Kaplan tried to resolve the seemingly dichotomous way of seeing male and female, and notes that there isn't a weaker or inferior sex. Both are equal and both are important in one's development: ". . . when we look at ourselves in terms of our external relationships, we are looking at our masculine identity. When we look at our Self, our inner core, we are almost looking at a feminine entity."[61] This role sharing also helps us to understand the days of the week: ". . . all week long in our struggle to gain spirituality, we are on a male level.[62] On the Sabbath, we are on a female level because we can absorb the fruits of all we have done during the week."[63] This follows the Kabbalistic notion of the giver (symbolized by the male) and the receiver (symbolized by the female).

Since God is accessible only through the *Shekhinah* (Divine presence), which corresponds to the tenth *sefira* (*Malkhut*—kingship). This is the female characteristic of the Godhead, by which the upper sphere's God-element (Divine energies) pass into channels that can be understood in the lower worlds. Thus, the female (as opposite to male) is the funnel through which all of God's transcendence flows. This marriage between male and female, in the world of the *sefirot*, between *Tiferet* and *Shekhinah*, has its counterpart in the marriage couple on earth. Therefore, a healthy and productive marriage on earth will influence and unite the masculine and feminine elements in this world as well as in the worlds above. This is best symbolized by the Sabbath, the ultimate wedding that unites mankind with his Maker.

However, Elliot Wolfson, Professor of Hebrew and Judaic Studies, doesn't see the feminine and masculine aspects as truly equal.

> Even though the kabbalists consistently speak of the unity and perfection of God in terms of the union of masculine and feminine, the idea of ultimate wholeness or oneness is predicated on a reconstituted male androgyne. The kabbalistic representation of androgyny, therefore, is that of the one male force who represents the ideal anthropos that comprises both masculine and feminine traits.[64]

While "femaleness is, in fact, only an aspect of masculinity,"[65] the "mystical communion" and "mystical fellowship" is a heterosexual one—male and female.[66]

> . . . the Lurianic Kabbalists . . . upheld heterosexuality as the only legitimate and authorized form of sexual behavior. All forms of deviant sexuality outside the relationship of husband and wife are considered detrimental inasmuch as such actions create a division above between male and female.[67]

The concept of opposites, in this respect, does not refer to opposite in orientation but rather polar opposites in sexual role differentiation. Each form of sexual behavior has its own role, set of affects and self and object representations. Moreover, each form (male and female) has a major identity focus (maleness and femaleness, masculinity and femininity). It also has a minor sexual oppositional identifactory focus (male role with female influences, female role with male influences). This situation corresponds to biological science whereby every male has a minor infusion of female hormones and every female has a minor infusion of male hormones. Too much of the opposite hormone can cause an imbalance in the sexual role differentiation.

Both the male and female poles are important both as separate and in their coupling:

> Indeed, the negative valorization of the feminine in certain kabbalistic texts, especially the zoharic literature, is underscored by the fact that when the female potency is separated from the masculine, the potential exists that she will evolve into a punitive or even demonic force. Sexual coupling of male and female is indicative of an androgynous unity that has been fractured. In the ideal state gender differentiation is neutralized and the female is absorbed back into the male.[68]

Not surprisingly, there are many analogies between our study of opposites and contemporary thoughts on physics, quantum and string theory. According to the theoretical framework of the laws of dialectics, the universe is not an accidental conglomeration of isolated elements. Rather is an integral whole, with mutually interdependent relationships. All of nature is in a state of constant motion, a ceaseless state of movement and change. Everything contains contradictions and opposites. Seemingly insignificant changes can lead to major qualitative changes.

"In the quantum world, what you see is what you get, and nothing is real; the best you can hope for is a set of delusions that agree with one another."[69] The importance of quantum theory and (super)string theory is that influence can be exerted from different parts of space. The influence can be symmetrical or asymmetrical. It can be similarly positive or dissimilarly negative. "No drop comes down from above without having two drops come from below."[70] There is constant interplay and influence from one 'world' system to another. Physicists even posit ten or eleven dimensions to the universe.[71,72] There is always tension—as in the strings of a musical instrument. It is this tension that conducts and transmits energy impulses. The movement may be oppositional to the original intent or parallel and similar to it. What is clear is that the universe consists of similarities and opposites that work together in moving the universe forward.

Einstein, Podolsky and Rosen theorized in 1935 (the EPR Paradox): "There really is some underlying clockwork that keeps the universe running, and that only gives the appearance of uncertainty and unpredictability at the quantum level. . . ."[73] This 'timekeeper,' who is 'not throwing dice,' constructs the universe and world systems as many parts—often disparate—that need to work together in parallel and/or in opposition.

In 1957, the physicist Hugh Everett formulated his Many-Worlds interpretation of quantum mechanics, noting: ". . . the overlapping wave functions of the whole universe, the alternative realities that interact to produce measurable interference at the quantum level, do not collapse. All of them are equally real, and exist in their own parts of 'superspace' (and supertime)."[74] Everything is important and influential. Kabbalah teaches us that seemingly unrelated poles are in reality part and parcel of one unified superstring or quantum field. Our life's work is to strive for perfection of self as well as the universe.

Before concluding, it is essential to put all of this in the context of the psychoanalytic concept of ambivalence. Ambivalence "means the holding of contradictory feeling states in the relationship towards one object."[75] We see this in Freud's describing the importance of the duality of instincts (libidinal and aggressive), as well as the coexistence of love and hate. Melanie Klein "elevated this state of ambivalence to a central place in the key concept of the depressive position."[76] Freud mentions the issue of love and hate in his earlier writings as: "A battle between love and hate was raging in the lover's breast, and the object of both these feelings was one and the same person."[77] In addition to our noting the simultaneous occurrence of two contradictory feelings, attitudes or tendencies, one needs to take into account the clinical treatment of ambivalence. Freud relates to this when discussing the need to work through the negative as well as positive transference.[78]

What is important to emphasize is that we need to be aware of opposites, and to take them into account as a necessary part of our existence. Something on the surface may belie something else. Things aren't always what they seem!

NOTES

1. William Shakespeare, *King Henry VI*, act 5, scene 3 (1591–1592).
2. Dylan Evans, *An Introductory Dictionary of Lacanian Psychoanalysis* (London: Routledge, 1996), 97–98.
3. Lacan's 'objectified self' was inspired by Swiss linguist Ferdinand de Saussure's (1857–1913) insights and philosophy. De Saussure laid the foundation for the modern study of linguistics and signs, which came to be known as semiotics.
4. Groddeck, *The Unknown Self* (London: Vision Press, 1951), 37. This was originally given as a lecture in Berlin in 1926.
5. Karl Abel published his pamphlet in 1884.
6. For example, Talmud Berachot 54a–55b.
7. Sigmund Freud, "The Interpretation of Dreams," vols. 4–5 of *Standard Edition of the Complete Psychological Works of Sigmund Freud*, ed. James Strachey (1900; London: Hogarth Press, 1981).
8. Freud, "Interpretation of Dreams," vol. 5, 471.
9. Freud, "Interpretation of Dreams," vol. 4, 318.
10. Joseph Berke and Stanley Schneider, "Antithetical Meanings of 'the Breast,'" *International Journal of Psycho-Analysis* 75 (1994): 491–98.
11. Talmud Berachot 58b.

12. Talmud Haggigah 5b.

13. Joseph Gikatilla was a Spanish Kabbalist (1248–1305). See *Ginnat Egoz* (Garden of the Walnut) [in Hebrew] (1274; Jerusalem: Yeshivat Ha-Chaim v'Ha-Shalom, 1999), 47.

14. Midrashic literature consists of rabbinic commentaries on Biblical texts. They roughly span a period from the fifth to fourteenth centuries. This particular Midrash is from Bereshit Rabbah 3:7.

15. Sigmund Freud, 1926a, "Inhibitions, Symptoms and Anxiety," in *Standard Edition*, ed. James Strachey, vol. 20.

16. Robert Hinshelwood, *A Dictionary of Kleinian Thought* (London: Free Association Books, 1991), 113.

17. Melanie Klein, "Notes on Some Schizoid Mechanisms," *International Journal of Psycho-Analysis* 27 (1946): 99–110.

18. Berke and Schneider, "Antithetical Meanings"; Schneider and Berke, "Breast, Robbery and the Devil," *Jewish Bible Quarterly* 23 (1995): 86–90.

19. Freud, 1901, "The Psychopathology of Everyday Life," in *Standard Edition*, ed. James Strachey, vol. 6.

20. Attributed to Nehuniah ben HaKanna, a first-century Talmudic sage.

21. Psalms 139:12.

22. Aryeh Kaplan, *The Bahir* (Newburyport, Mass.: Samuel Weiser, 1979), part 2:1.

23. The dating of this work places it earlier than the sixth century. The section mentioned here is 1:5.

24. Aryeh Kaplan, *Sefer Yetzirah (The Book of Creation)* (Newburyport, Mass.: Samuel Weiser, 1990b), 45. This is a five-dimensional continuum that is enumerated as beginning/end, good/evil, above/below, east/west and north/south.

25. Gershom Scholem, *Origins of the Kabbalah* (1962; New York: Jewish Publication Society and Princeton University Press, 1987), 332.

26. Sanford Drob, *Symbols of the Kabbalah: Philosophical and Psychological Perspectives*, (Northvale, N.J.: Aronson, 2000a), 84–85, fn. 70.

27. An expounder of Mussar. Mussar is a path of contemplative practices and exercises that have evolved to help an individual soul to pinpoint and then to break through the barriers that surround and obstruct the flow of inner light. Mussar is a repository of techniques and understandings that offer guidance for one to improve one's life.

28. Eliyahu Dessler (1891–1954) was not only a profound thinker and prolific writer, but he was also a brilliant educator. He became actively involved in defining the educational direction of the Gateshead Educational network in England and the Ponovczh Yeshiva in Israel.

29. Eliyahu Dessler, *Michtav M'Eliyahu* [in Hebrew] (1943; Jerusalem: Sifriyati, 1997), vol. 5, 17–18.

30. Tzadok HaCohen (1823–1900), *Pri Zadik* [in Hebrew] (Lublin, Poland: no publisher listed, 1912), vol. 2, 38.

31. Karl Popper, *The Open Society and Its Enemies*, 5th ed. (1945; Princeton, N.J.: Princeton University Press, 1966).

32. From the Greek.

33. *Zohar*, 1:17b, 2:167a, 2:176a.

34. *The Zohar*, trans. D. Matt. Pritzker Edition (Stanford, Calif.: Stanford University Press, 2002), vol. 1, 125, fn. 131.

35. Stanley Schneider and Joseph Berke, "Discovering Oneself: Kabbalah and Psychoanalysis," *Midstream* 51 (November–December 2005): 6, 24–27.

36. Rachel Elior, "The Doctrine of Transmigration in Galya Raza," in *Essential Papers on Kabbalah*, ed. L. Fine (New York: New York University Press, 1995), 251.

37. Rachel Elior, "HaBaD: The Contemplative Ascent to God," in *Jewish Spirituality*, ed. A. Green (New York: Crossroad, 1997), 165.

38. Elior, "HaBaD," 164.

39. Joseph Soloveitchik, "The Dual Aspects of Jewish Morality," in *A Conspectus of the Public Lectures of Rabbi Joseph B. Soloveitchik*, ed J. Epstein (New York: Hamevaser/Yeshiva University, 1973/1974), 60.

40. Soleveitchik, "Dual Aspects."

41. Freud, 1915–16, "Introductory Lectures on Psycho-Analysis," in *Standard Edition*, ed. James Strachey, vol. 15, 229–30.

42. Freud, 1915–16, "Introductory Lectures," 33–34.

43. Erik H. Erikson, *Childhood and Society* (New York: Norton, 1950).

44. Gérard Bléandonu, *Wilfred Bion: His Life and Works 1897–1979* (London: Free Association Books, 1994), 90.

45. Freud, 1915–16, "Introductory Lectures," 76–77.

46. Freud, 1915, "Instincts and Their Vicissitudes," in *Standard Edition*, ed. James Strachey, vol. 14, 127.

47. Freud, 1915, "Instincts and Their Vicissitudes," 123.

48. Freud, 1918, "From the History of an Infantile Neurosis," in *Standard Edition*, ed. James Strachey, vol. 17.

49. Freud, 1915, "Instincts and Their Vicissitudes," 130. Scopophilia means pleasure in looking. In many of Freud's writings this is erroneously spelled as 'scoptophilia.'

50. Dessler, *Michtav M'Eliyahu*, vol. 1, 144.

51. Frieda Fordham, *An Introduction to Jung's Psychology* (1953; Harmondsworh, Middlesex, England: Penguin, 1991), 17–18.

52. Gerhard Adler, ed., *C. G. Jung Letters* (Princeton, N.J.: Princeton University Press, 1975), vol. 2, 356–60.

53. Gershom Scholem, *On the Kabbalah and Its Symbolism* (New York: Schocken Books, 1969), 128–29.

54. Tom Keve, *Triad: The Physicists, the Analysts, the Kabbalists* (London: Rosenberger & Krrausz, 2000), 85.

55. Sandor Ferenczi, "The Two Extremes: Credulity and Scepticism," in *Final Contributions to the Problems and Methods of Psycho-Analysis* (1932; New York: Brunner/Mazel, 1980).

56. Conscious.

57. Ferenczi, "Two Extremes," 264.

58. Wilhelm Fleiss (1858–1928) was a German otorhinolaryngologist who was very close with Freud and played a role in many of Freud's early ideas in psychoanalysis.

59. Jean Laplanche and Jean-Bertrand Pontalis, *The Language of Psycho-Analysis* (London: Hogarth Press, 1980), 52.

60. Freud, 1919a, "A Child Is Being Beaten," in *Standard Edition*, ed. J. Strachey, vol. 17, 200–201.

61. Aryeh Kaplan, *Innerspace* (Jerusalem: Vagshal/Moznaim, 1990a), 75.

62. We are in a 'giving' mode.

63. Kaplan, *Innerspace*, 75.

64. E. R. Wolfson, "Crossing Gender Boundaries in Kabbalistic Ritual and Myth," in *Ultimate Intimacy: The Psychodynamics of Jewish Mysticism*, ed. M. Ostow (London: Karnac, 1995b), 256. See also Moshe Idel, *Kabbalah and Eros* (New Haven, Conn.: Yale University Press, 2005).

65. Wolfson, "Crossing Gender Boundaries," 257.

66. E. R. Wolfson, *Circle in the Square: Studies in the Use of Gender in Kabbalistic Symbolism* (Albany: State University of New York Press, 1995a), 108.

67. Wolfson, *Circle in the Square*, 224, fn. 145.

68. Wolfson, "Crossing Gender Boundaries," 266.

69. John Gribbin, *In Search of Schrödinger's Cat: Quantum Physics and Reality* (London: Black Swan, 1991), 162.

70. Talmud Ta'anit 25b; *Zohar* 3:247b.

71. Michio Kaku, *Hyperspace* (New York: Anchor, 1995).

72. Brian Greene, *The Elegant Universe* (New York: Vintage, 1999).

73. Gribbin, *In Search of Schrödinger's Cat*, 182.

74. Gribbin, *In Search of Schrödinger's Cat*, 237.

75. Hinshelwood, *Dictionary*, 218.

76. Hinshelwood, *Dictionary*, 218.

77. Freud, 1909, "Notes upon a Case of Obsessional Neurosis," in *Standard Edition*, ed. James Strachey, vol. 10, 191.

78. Freud, 1912a, "The Dynamics of Transference," in *Standard Edition*, ed. James Strachey, vol. 12.

Chapter Eleven

Nothingness and Narcissism

The Bible reveals that God created man in his image. But, God is not a mirror, nor an Olympian ideal, nor can any words or concepts encompass 'His' 'awesome majesty.'

Although metaphorical allusions to 'His' brain, heart, torso, hands and feet abound, 'He' has no similitude or likeness to any creature, male or female, or any thing, anywhere. Indeed, the twelfth-century Jewish philosopher Moses Maimonides emphasized that God can only be approached in the negative—what he isn't, rather than what he is. For once God is defined, it limits His 'without end' (the *Ein Sof*).

According to the main body of Kabbalistic thought and contemplation, God is nothingness and everythingness, both the *Ayin* (nothing, the-no-thing, no-thing-ness) and the *Ein Sof* (the-without-end, all-things, infinity). Or, from another perspective, God is the Center, the Source, the Beginning and End, of Everything.

Then, what is man? A prayer, 'Master of all Worlds!' which Jews recite every morning, replies by comparing man to God, and also concludes, not what man is, but what he is not:

> Are not all the heroes like nothing before You, the famous as if they had never existed, the wise as if devoid of wisdom and the perceptive as if devoid of intelligence? For most of their deeds are desolate and the days of their lives are empty before You.[1]

In other words man, like his Creator, is nothing. This is a good starting point to consider how psychoanalysis and Kabbalah respond to what may be peoples' greatest fear, but also deepest truth.

From infancy to adulthood people long to see themselves as a 'universe unto themselves.' That is, they want to believe that they generate themselves and, in effect, are self-enclosed and self-sufficient. This is the natural condition of the newborn child, which Freud referred to as a state of 'primary narcissism' or 'auto eroticism,' meaning that the baby turns to his or her own body as in thumb sucking, to gain pleasure or avoid pain.[2] Here the 'self' or 'ego' (meaning the 'I') is fundamentally a physical experience. For months it is the focus of the baby's love as well as the center of the baby's life. And, as far as he is concerned, it is the center of everyone else's life too. Therefore at this time the world-view of the baby is 'egocentric.' His existence is dominated by libidinal or life-desiring pressures, that is, the needs of the animal self.

Later in his first year the baby begins to form relationships with members of his family, especially his parents, and others in his immediate social circle. This is the next developmental phase, when the child realizes that he needs people other than himself to satisfy his needs, and marks the point when the outside world, or one might say, 'actuality,' begins to impinge on his life. Freud termed the awareness and grudging acceptance of this point 'the reality principle.'[3]

Up until now the infants' relationships have been generally utilitarian, even slavish. People or things exist to serve him, mother to feed, take away pain, or stimulate; father likewise. As we have explained, this is what the neonate experiences as 'the breast,' and is what Kleinian psychoanalysts term 'a part object.'

Gradually, however, the baby perceives that his caretakers, or part objects, have lives of their own. They are not always available when he wants them. They have needs of their own and do things and relate to each other in ways that don't involve him. Both subjectively and objectively, they evolve into 'whole objects,' complete persons with their own interests and feelings, which sometimes conflict with those who depend on them.

This is the moment of psychological birth, when the infant experiences absence, separation and aloneness and is beset by unavoidable voids, externally and internally. As with physical birth, this is a very painful process. It coincides with Freud's 'reality principle,' and with what the Kleinians recognize as the onset of the 'depressive position.' Inevitably the infant becomes aware that the people he loves and the people he hates are one and the same. Few individuals manage an easy passage through the ensuing turmoil. Overcoming such 'depressive anxiety' is a lifelong project. Invariably mass culture and institutional religion serve to help people cope with ramifications of these intrapsychic and interpersonal processes. They include the refusal to be born, partial birth and later womb-wished regressions. These are negative conditions that generally encompass what psychoanalysts have described under the rubric of narcissistic states.

Kabbalists, on the other hand, are primarily concerned with the ways and means of achieving God consciousness. This includes an awareness of the unity of all things, from the lowest physical realms to the highest spiritual universes, and the connections between them.

Experientially there appears to be a remarkable coincidence between the states of mind from which the narcissist wants to escape (nothingness) and to which the Kabbalist wants to reach (nothingness). But their points of departure are different. The former finds it excruciating to engage the world—that is, people and relationships—and tries to avoid them by deceit, exaggeration and especially by the projection of parts of himself into others. In contrast, the Kabbalist celebrates existence, even though there are times when he tries to pass beyond it.[4]

If there is a point of convergence, it occurs when self-centered or mystically inclined individuals cannot contain their experiences, such as when their desires, emotions or 'energies' become too strong for a fragile ego or an incomplete spirituality. Then either the person may go 'off the tracks' and 'into space,'—that is, enter a manic or omnipotent state of being, with serious consequences for themselves, for actuality and for their divine aspirations.

We have been using, and will continue to use, descriptions like 'narcissist' or 'mystic' to denote two kinds of approaches to being or not being in the world. But either characterization hardly does justice to the complicated process of living or, for that matter, to the discordant structure of the self. Moreover, the few people who are true mystics are generally invisible to those who are not.

Certainly one can evince God consciousness without being a Kabbalist, just as ads in the New York subway used to declaim, "You don't have to be Jewish to eat Levy's rye bread." In truth, there are all too many times when religious figures fuel an exaggerated self-importance. The story is told of a synagogue crowded on Yom Kippur, the Day of Atonement, ostensibly the holiest day of the Jewish year. Having completed the prayer for the Confession of Sins, the rabbi added, "God, I am nothing." The chazan (cantor), having noticed the rabbi's fervor, exclaimed aloud to God: "Today I have led Your children in prayer. Together, we have offered words that crown you on High. But in truth, I know that I am nothing, absolutely nothing." Inspired by the rabbi and chazan, an unassuming congregant cried out from the back of the synagogue, "God, I am nothing, nothing." Whereupon the chazan leaned over toward the rabbi and whispered, "Look who thinks he is nothing!"[5]

But we also know that people are not necessarily solipsistic or absorbed in and with themselves every second. A lot depends on circumstances, who they are with, and what pressures they feel. That is why it is important to keep in mind that when we use the terms 'narcissist' or 'kabbalist' we are essentially discussing orientations between persons who are inclined to seek salvation by inflating themselves, or emanations of themselves, and those who tend toward self-effacement. To put it another way, the difference is between being prideful and being humble. The Kabbalist realizes that humbleness is a prerequisite to access God. The narcissist insists that pridefulness is the means to be God.

The paradox is that the less you are, the more you become. This, in turn, depends on the capacity and willingness to contract the self—which, of course, depends, in the first place, on having a self, or a sustained, consistent set of feelings and experiences, to contract.

Through humbleness an essential principle emerges: "as God recedes, creation unfolds." Hence, God generates existence by contracting His infinite essence. If this had not happened, life could not exist, because life is mobile, malleable, limiting and limited.

The question that the Kabbalah has long tried to answer is: how does a finite world emerge from an infinite being? Isaac Luria used the term *tzimzum* to denote each step in this process of Divine contraction. By so doing, "He concealed himself" and left a 'space' for something else to exist. This 'vacated space' is not a vacuum, and it is not completely vacated. Although devoid of substance, it retains possibility, that is, God's will. Therefore, it has also been termed a 'pregnant void,' full of creative potential.

The 'vacated space' can be compared to what physicists call a 'quantum vacuum.' This is a choppy sea of randomly fluctuating electromagnetic waves. Although the total energy of the vacuum averages zero over a long period of time, the waves, in the form of 'virtual photons' ('Divine sparks'), can pop in and out of existence for split seconds. In the presence of a powerful gravitational or accelerational field (that is, an energized input), the virtual photons can break free (from being virtual or ghostly) and become real and visible like ordinary photons.

According to Lurianic theory, the 'energized input' was a *kav*, equivalent to a line, or very fine beam of extremely intense energy. When this *kav* filled the vacated space or 'sea of potential,' existence came into being. At first existence was a unity, and was organized, as we have previously discussed, in keeping with the *sefirot*, or vessels of Divine emanation. But they couldn't hold the Divine input, for as Aryeh Kaplan has pointed out, they were not yet relational entities. They could only receive, but not yet give.[6]

This failure of containment led the lower seven *sefirot* to shatter. In Kabbalah this event is known as *Shvirat HaKelim*, the breaking or shattering of the vessels. It proved to be an indispensable next step because the shattering answered a second major question about the process of creation: how can a singularity (God's initial creation) give rise to multiplicity?

The *shvirah* or breaking was necessary for the differentiation of existence. Since oneness, which is also equal to infinity, could not be held or contained in a single vessel, it had to become many. The breaking vessels spilled out variety, and everything became what it was, and is. In consequence, the failure of containment by the primordial vessels was a positive event and an essential prerequisite for the creation of the world and everything in it.

An important aside is that the only vessel or entity that can contain itself, as well as everything else, is God. The mathematician Amir Aczel notes in his book *The Mystery of the Aleph* that Georg Cantor, who was descended from Marrano Jews, was the first to mathematically describe the concept of infinity (very much as delineated in the Kabbalah).[7] He also spent a lifetime trying to discover a certain vessel or set that could be or could contain the set of all things. He failed, a necessary failure proven by his younger colleague Kurt Gödel. Known as Gödel's law, it is one of the landmark discoveries of the twentieth century.[8] For if this were not the case, then God could be described by a mathematical formula. But then this entity would not be God, that is, 'the-no-thing' (*Ayin*) and 'the-without-end' (*Ein Sof*). Indeed this is exactly what Albert Einstein spent decades trying to describe, a 'unified field theory,' an equation that would unite all four major forces in the universe, and in his words, would allow him to "read the Mind of God."[9] Einstein failed, but the search continues for a 'Theory of Everything.' The latest candidate is 'super string theory,' as Michio Kaku relates in *Parallel Worlds*.[10]

The generative principle ("as God recedes, creation unfolds") not only helps to explain existence in itself, but also the existence of multiplicity, that is, an infinite universe of sets and subsets. As Lurianic Kabbalists contend, God, in 'His' unfathomable humbleness, contracts 'Himself' so that 'Mankind' (and everything else) can come into being, can be, and can continue to be.[11] The latter point is very important. Creation is not a singular, or one-off, event. It is a continuing process of Divine self-negation without which the universe would cease to exist.

In contrast, the narcissistic solution to existence is denial, projection, expansion and, ultimately, de-differentiation. Here individuals cannot tolerate variety or multiplicity. All they want is a world where every object, indeed, every aspect of reality, remains part of themselves and is in their total control. Like God they constrict reality, but not to create, rather to aggrandize and personify existence. For them oneness equals 'ME-ness.' It follows that those who embody the culture of narcissism are aptly called the 'ME' generation.

While the narcissist may abhor relationships, the Kabbalist perceives that the world, the universe and, indeed, everything everywhere, is an intricate array of interconnected events, energies and objects. Objects, whether people, rocks, *sefirot* or worlds, represent the agglomeration of physical and spiritual forces. That is why we can say that Kabbalah is nothing more, but also nothing less, than the systematic study of 'object relations,' that is, things and events in relation to each other, beginning with the *Ein Sof*, the source of all, the 'without end,' and extending to all mankind. In between, there exist a multitude of spiritual and physical entities from the highest, almost entirely spiritual realms, such as *Atzilut* (Emanation), down through the more embodied worlds of *Beriyah* (Creation) and *Yetzirah* (Formation), until finally reaching the world that we inhabit, *Asiyah* (Action). As we have previously discussed, the internal structure of each of these worlds consists of ten vessels or *sefirot*, which collectively and metaphorically comprise the *Etz Chaim* (Tree of Life). The vessels, in turn, contain ten Divine emanations and are connected in 22 different ways to each other.

A multiplicity of currents emanate from the highest realms, the Godhead, to the lowest creatures, and back up again. Moreover, the currents flow through an uncountable number of interrelated pathways. The result is a relational system that is akin to, but much greater than, the billions of possible neuro-synaptic transactions or interpersonal connections made by the brain or the Internet.

Abraham Abulafia touched on the point of all these relations when he noted that the aim of the game of life is to keep playing, seeking and discovering more about God. By this he was referring to the interconnectiveness of all things, whether on the highest level or the lowest.

How are such connections made and maintained? The answer: through love. We refer not to a self-obsessed preoccupation, but a reaching out to someone or something outside of oneself. From the earliest moments of the Jewish tradition, the Torah declaims: "Love your neighbor as yourself,"[12] and "You shall love the Lord your God with all your heart, with all your soul, and with all your might."[13] Significantly, the Midrash agrees: "Whatever you do, do it only out of love."[14] This is a view reiterated by the Baal Shem Tov, the founder of Hasidism, in the seventeenth century, and that continues to echo in popular culture today, through such songs as the Beatles' "All you need is love."[15]

Love may be the force that unifies our 'self' and connects us with the oneness of the cosmos, but in our day and age, it is a force decidedly difficult to access, activate and sustain. This problem demonstrates a further distinction between Kabbalah and psychoanalysis. The former focuses on the love of God, righteousness, while the latter focuses on perversity, the denial of God.

It is worth reiterating that Schneur Zalman, the 'spiritual grandson' of the Baal Shem Tov, differentiated in the *Tanya* between three types of individuals: the *Tzaddik*, the *Benoni* and the *Rashah*.[16] The *Tzaddik* is a person who is completely righteous; he does not possess, nor is possessed by, inherent evil or pride. Or to put it another way, he is someone who can see people as they are, in and of themselves, without feeling diminished or threatened by his perceptions. Therefore he can respond to their needs with loving guidance. The *Benoni* is a person who was born with evil and prideful impulses, but he was able to overcome them to the extent that he can also act in the world like a *Tzaddik*. His negative desires still exist, but remain in abeyance. Such a person has far surpassed any hint of envy, greed, jealousy or any form of self-aggrandizement. Both the *Tzaddik* and *Benoni* are rare individuals. Only a few exist in every generation. Both are forces for good.

In contrast, ordinary or even not-so-ordinary individuals come under the category of *Rashah*, or wicked one. Of course, the *Tanya* avers that there are many degrees and types of *Rashah*, but the basic feature of the *Rashah* is that he or she is more or less under the sway of negative impulses. With some effort, however it is possible to overcome negative states in order to become a *Benoni*, for a day, an hour, or even a minute. That is why the *Benoni* is known as the Intermediate Man, that is, intermediate between a *Tzaddik* and *Rashah*, between good and evil.

Schneur Zalman did not overlook negative states. His way to realign the world was to emphasize virtue and the oneness of all things, as well as a spirituality that delights in the unique individuality of every creature and every aspect of creation.

Sigmund Freud, on the other hand, trained in biological medicine as a neurologist and psychiatrist. So his basic outlook focused on pathology: what was wrong with people, not what was right about them. He developed psychoanalysis in order to gain a better understanding of abnormal states of mind. In so doing he found a dynamic method—'the talking cure,' 'free associations,' 'the couch,' 'the analytic hour'—that was able to effect a change in previously perverse experiences and relationships. It took a succeeding generation of psychoanalysts to expand and refine the depth of their inquires to encompass 'normal' mental processes.

Today the analytic emphasis remains on the psychopathological problems and symptomatology. Perhaps this is because of the medical legacy of psychoanalysis. Few people embark on a psychoanalysis for its own sake. On the contrary, what they want is to overcome emotional and social difficulties either in themselves or, in the case of trainees, their clients.

These difficulties inevitably involve a disturbance in interpersonal and intrapsychic relationships. This is an area in which Freud focused during the latter part of his working life, especially on the transference relationship. This occurs when a person perceives and acts toward another as if he or she were a significant figure in the other's mind, that is, an internal mental construct.

Freud recognized that the reason that many of his patients behaved so negatively toward him was that they perceived him as if he were actually their hated father, or mother, an example of transference phenomena.[17]

Later generations of analysts, in particular the early and later 'object relations' schools of Melanie Klein, Donald Winnicott, Ronald Fairbairn and others, have described the counter-transference, whereby a person induces feelings or actions in another. This happens in therapy, for example, when a patient can induce his or her therapist to unwittingly feel the patient's feelings or enact his behavior.[18] The therapist often experiences this event as if he were being taken possession of by an alien influence or force. Far more than in psychodynamic exchanges, transferential and counter-transferential events are the bread and butter of everyday life. They exemplify basic kinds of intrapsychic transactions and interpersonal transformations.

Projective processes continually affect the ebb and flow of internal relationships such as those that take place in a dream, and external relationships such as those which take place between people, groups or whole cultures. In fact, contemporary psychoanalysts have long recognized that the gist of projective as well as introjective processes do not just involve simple mental constructs, that is, emotionally charged images of parents or siblings. In particular, they include the relationships between internal images, between subject and external others as well as between the subject and his internal images. Therefore, it is essential to realize that complex representations of relationships are the psychic constructs that are projected or introjected together with all the attendant emotions and expectations.

Dependency or need is the most important of all such relationships. It begins before birth with the connection between mother and fetus and continues throughout one's life, whether between parent and child, husband and wife, group and group member, or at the end of one's life, between caretaker and cared for. Yet, in an age of narcissism, where the media bombards readers, listeners and viewers with the possibility of becoming the source of themselves, the dependency relationship seethes with ambivalence, frustration, resentment and envy.[19]

Certainly conflicts about dependency comprise the main reason why people are unhappy and enter therapy, or take drugs, or float from one unsatisfactory relationship to another. Therefore, it may not be so remarkable that one of the most frequently recited prayers in the Jewish liturgy, the 'Grace after Meals,' has to do with dependency and the conflicts it can arouse.

Such prayers are extremely sensitive to painful encounters, either with oneself or others. They emphasize that the way to avoid feeling ill at ease (embarrassment), at odds with how one wants to be (shame) or at odds with others (disgrace), and to get over feeling small and vengeful (humiliation), is not to be dependent on family or friends, but to realize that whatever one wants and needs comes from God, that is, from a source other than oneself and beyond one's control.

For the believer this realization is irrefutable. It is a further example of the importance of self-contraction or humility as a means of overcoming frustration and self-preoccupation. Or, from another angle, it connects with the struggle against narcissism and the need to achieve spiritual as well as psychological birth. This process is not easy or necessarily successful. In *Souls on Fire*, Elie Wiesel recounts the complaint of Reb Wolfe of Zhitomir, himself an anti-Hasid:

> I have troubles with my son-in-law. Since his Mezeritch adventure [visit to the Maggid of Mezeritch, the successor to the Baal Shem Tov], all he talks about is his fight against pride. I don't understand: what does he have to be proud of? He does nothing, has nothing, knows nothing. I, on the other hand, studied with the Gaon of Vilna, know half the Talmud by heart, am generous with the needy, attend services three times a day and lead a saintly life. And, yet look at me: do I look like I must fight pride?[20]

Freud struggled with this vein by developing a method for overcoming pride that might have been recognized by his Hasidic ancestors.[21] We refer to the psychoanalytic process, which involves talking freely and directing real as well as transferred dependency toward the analyst. These are steps whereby an individual is able to refocus early conflicts regarding need and caring and to learn humility. The person then becomes aware that outside figures, or even internal ones, are not preoccupied with his every whim, and that he is not the source of everything that happens.

For this lesson to be successful in psychoanalysis or psychotherapy, the patient has to actually experience the pain and pleasure of dependency, and to acknowledge, at least as far as his psychic development is concerned, that the analyst is a power greater than himself. Otherwise the treatment can continue indefinitely with no change occurring. Far from subduing narcissism, an analysis can feed it. After all, where else can one person pay another to pay attention, or pretend to pay attention, while he drones on about himself for years at a time? And without pridefulness being challenged, the individual soon believes, like an overindulged child, that he has become 'God,' a power unto himself.

An adult, an institution, a culture or an entire nation can act like a petulant child, unwilling to give and unable to receive, and frightened of the nothingness from which all things emerge. Then arrogance replaces humility, and the aggrandizement of power supersedes awe and love. In human terms we are describing the omnipotent solution to the loss of omnipotence. The latter is a fantasy that diverts a failure to comprehend true power: what Kabbalists call the Divine, which lies hidden within oneself and beyond, and what psychoanalysts like Donald Winnicott call 'the true self.'

Idolatry is the most common manifestation of this unwillingness to distinguish true from false power. And in our age the most common form of idolatry is narcissism, the worship of the self. We are not describing the natural and necessary developmental phase that infants must pass through. On the contrary, we refer to a stubborn preoccupation with one's own person and personality at the expense of everything and everyone else. The cause and effect of such intense self-centeredness are often the same: low self-esteem, an impoverishment of self, a retreat from relationships and an over-delicate sensitivity to life events.

The omnipotent solution is simple: Make sure that your mind and body appear bigger and bigger, so big that there is no room for others' needs or wishes or subjectivity. Use the mechanisms of projection and projective identification to invent reality and populate it with bits and pieces of your mind. Replace real people and whole object, I–Thou, genuine relationships with part object, I–it, contrived transactions where external people and things serve the sole purpose of feeding the ego and perpetuating pride.[22]

As Christopher Lasch pointed out in his bestseller, *The Culture of Narcissism*, the wish to be divine, and the equally strong wish to worship the results, are so pervasive in our society that most people cannot distinguish between who they are and who they want to be.[23] First and foremost, this leads to the worship of physicality where, as in ancient Greece, God becomes a process (body building, fashion, and sports, the Olympic games) and a product (the body beautiful, clothes, gold medals). Similarly 'God' can incarnate as food and sex. We refer to *haute cuisine* as the be-all and end-all of living, instead of the means to enjoy life; and to orgasms and sexual prowess, in place of giving love and making life.

In addition to physicality, some people with a particular talent or charisma, which we can define as the capacity to overwhelm others with parts of their personality, deify themselves and manage to convince others to also look upon them as 'Gods.' Typical examples are certain gurus, media personalities and cultural icons, all of whom may be famous for being famous, but tend to lack substantial accomplishment.

Not infrequently, charismatic politicians conceal their desire for power and self-glorification by directing and redirecting the attention of their fellow citizens to the state, as part of the process of transforming individual narcissism into suprapersonal nationalism. Then slogans take the place of thoughts, emotions beget patriotism, and men and women are able to conceal their longing for transcendence by identifying with their Motherland or Fatherland.

Nationalism is to the state what narcissism is to the individual, a form of national narcissism. It demands exclusive attention to concerns like size (bigness), shape (boundaries and borders), inner content (ethnic and religious purity) and outer appearances (pride and prestige). These preoccupations climax with the state taking the place of 'God' and its leaders taking the role as 'God's' chosen intermediaries.[24]

Eventually the omnipotence inherent in all of these illusions breaks down and the idols turn to clay and shatter. But as clay is earth, so we are describing a process of coming down to earth, grieving for a 'God that failed,' and relocating power. This is a non-narcissistic response. The narcissistic response is hatred and violence, a turning against all prior hopes and desires, and falling in love with death.

The British psychoanalyst Herbert Rosenfeld described this development as 'destructive narcissism.'[25] At a certain point of frustration and despair, a person stops longing for life-enhancing experiences and activities. Instead he reorients his omnipotence toward destructiveness, and takes pleasure in inflicting hatred and pain, as with religious or political cadres who lose sight of their initial aims and become obsessed with the mechanics of torture and killing. Indeed, many cultures celebrate death and destruction by idealizing murderous impulses and embodying them as omnipotent figures. These includes the Hindu Kali, the Zoroastrian Ahriman and, in contemporary terms, Muslim jihadists.

It seems that idolatry begins with the self and ends among the stars. But in addition to a devotion to projected impulses and disaffected forces, there exists one further example of the perversity of power that needs to be considered. We refer to the common attempt to overcome the agony of emptiness and nothingness, not by worshipping God but by becoming 'God.' This reaction includes the denial of pain, relationships, emotions and need. The denial can be so complete that many experiences or outside events are simply blocked out. But if not, they are feared, hated, treated as evil and become the focus of intense annihilative attacks. Melanie Klein, in particular, explored this reaction, which she called 'the manic response' or 'manic psychosis' or simply, 'mania.'[26]

The manic man or woman exists in a world beyond limits. This is the 'high' or manic phase of what psychiatrists refer to as a 'manic-depressive' or 'cyclothymic' cycle. The manic person feels totally powerful and beyond pain or food or sleep. He inhabits a state of transcendence until, like Icarus, he is brought back to earth by the myriad others he has bothered, who then impose restraints (hospitalization, medication or imprisonment). While the manic state is pathological, it is worth noting that some individuals can be creative as well as destructive during a manic phase, and can accomplish fantastic things. We knew a Cambridge don who would periodically get very excited and write continuously thirty to forty hours at a stretch. Later he liked to volunteer for a medical charity and could answer fifteen phones at once, always appropriately. He never took lithium and found therapy helpful only when he wasn't 'high.' After two or three weeks in this state, he invariably became exhausted and would sleep for a couple of days in a row before resuming his usual duties.

Manic omnipotence is also a very attractive state for Kabbalists who cannot control their thirst for power or who feel inflamed by their spiritual and emotional energies. Once arrogance displaces humility, and self-importance supplants self-abnegation, it is a short step before 'the thief comes out from hiding.'[27] This means that the *Rashah* or 'the bad one within' reveals himself by stealing credit for everything. Then, instead of serving as a channel for the Divine energy, he identifies with it, and can claim to be God's messenger, the Messiah, or God, 'Himself.'

One such individual was Shabbatai Zevi, who was born in Smyrna (now Izmir), Turkey, in 1626, allegedly on the ninth of Av, the anniversary of the destruction of the first and second Temples in Jerusalem. Also, according to Jewish tradition, the Messiah will be born on the ninth of Av. Zevi died a Moslem apostate in 1676. By the power of his personality and by his actions, he almost single-handedly brought about a disaster to world Jewry that is still being worked through to this day. Therefore, it is worth reviewing what took place.

The seventeenth century is a nadir in Jewish history. Hundreds of thousand of Jews had been massacred by the Cossack warlord Chmielnicki and his followers. Towns and villages throughout Russia, Poland and the Ukraine were ravaged to an extent not repeated until the twentieth century. It was a situation awaiting a savior, and Shabbatai Zevi was more than willing to take on that role. As a young man he was a gifted scholar, a Torah prodigy, well versed in Talmud and also Kabbalah. But by the age of 16 he began to demonstrate marked swings in mood from elation to severe depression, swings that continued throughout his life. During the periods of elation or, as he put it, 'illumination,' he would deliberately break all religious conventions and sensitivities. For example, he publicly pronounced the Tetragrammaton, the Ineffable Name of God, an act that under Jewish law could only be done by the High Priest in the Holy of Holies in Jerusalem on Yom Kippur, the Day of Atonement. He went so far as to declare the abolition of all commandments and to utter a blasphemous benediction to "Him, who allows the forbidden." He also began to refer to himself as the Messiah.

At first he was greeted with derision, called a madman, and banished from Smyrna. But because of his obvious charisma, Torah knowledge and, one might add, spiritual power, Shabbatai Zevi gradually accumulated more and more followers. The turning point occurred when he was acclaimed the true Messiah by Nathan of Gaza, an outstanding rabbi and Kabbalist, who became his disciple. And like the Pied Piper, he attracted Jews from all over the world. By 1666 Shabbatai proclaimed himself "the anointed of the God of Jacob," and prepared to march on Turkey to seize the crown "of the great Turk" and establish the Kingdom of the Jews.

At this point, the Sultan became thoroughly alarmed and ordered Shabbatai Zevi's arrest and possible execution. But the Sultan also offered him the opportunity to save himself by renouncing Judaism and becoming a Moslem. He agreed and was given a handsome pension and other honors. His followers, however, were totally demoralized. In consequence, leading European rabbis forbade the study of Kabbalah, and for years Judaism became the preserve of a narrow legalistic elite.

Paradoxically Shabbatai Zevi's apostasy did Judaism a great favor. If he had died a martyr, like Jesus of Nazareth, his followers might have created a new religion, and Judaism could have been marginalized. In fact a Shabbatean movement did remain in Turkey for hundreds of years. Outwardly his devotees, called *Doenmeh*, were practicing Moslems, but like the Marrano Jews in Spain after the Inquisition, they secretly continued to practice their old religion and only married among themselves. Indeed, in the year 2000 a group of Istanbul Shabbateans did reveal their roots and applied to return to Israel.[28]

On the other hand, there are 'tormented masters' like Rabbi Nachman of Bratslav, who was the direct descendent of the Baal Shem Tov and the founder of the Bratslav Hasidim. During his lifetime he achieved profound degrees of spiritual and temporal illumination, and his works continue to be fresh and insightful to this day. Yet, Nachman was a man who continually struggled with severe inner conflict and turmoil. He was a leader subject to tumultuous mood swings and a terrible sense of sin and self loathing.[29] Similarly we could cite the Kotsker Rebbe, who remained in his room for years at a time, yet remained a commanding presence and teacher.

Therefore we must ask, if mania denotes false power, and depression signifies great conflict, what is true power and where does it reside? A tale is told of a very old and venerable rabbi who lay on his deathbed surrounded by his disciples. They were gnashing their teeth and tearing their clothes at the thought of him passing away. One said, "No one is more pious than yourself. How can we survive when there is no one to lead us in piety?" Another cried, "You are the most learned man of our generation. Who can teach us the law as brilliantly as you have done?" A third exclaimed, "You are the most ethical man in the world. Who can show us the paths of righteousness as you have done?" Summoning up his last ounce of strength, the rabbi replied, "And about my humility you have nothing to say?"[30]

Clearly power does not reside with pride. On the contrary, as we have seen with this tale and the prior account of Reb Wolfe, pride, which expresses self-inflation and omnipotence, denotes a waning of power.

The answer lies in the paradox we have previously cited, "the less you are the more you become," for only by achieving nothingness can one be in touch with the infinite source of everything. Thus the prophet Moses came closest to God, and was allowed to view His back, because he had most closely reached a state of *bitul* or self- (ego-) annihilation. But even Moses wasn't perfect. When the Jews demanded water, God instructed him to touch a rock with his stick. Instead he hit it, thereby revealing sparks of self-indulgence and petulance. For this, the Torah says, he was punished. God refused to allow him to enter the Promised Land.[31]

The Maggid of Mezeritch put the issue succinctly when he discussed how to gain power, which, for him, was the same as attaining an awareness of God:

> Think of yourself as *ayin* (nothingness) and forget yourself totally. Then you can transcend time, rising to the world of thought, where all is equal: life and death, ocean and dry land.[32]

Narcissism is the perversion of power. It is the opponent of *ayin* and the opposite of *bitul* (self-abnegation). It gives the illusion of omnipotence, while draining the self of energy and influence. More specifically narcissism erects a barrier to spirituality. It presents the downchaining of *shefa* from flowing from our will to our mind to our heart and into our limbs. No wonder the age of narcissism yields the dearth of the spiritual.

So then, where is the power? It is everywhere because everything is a unity. Every person is both one with the universe and an individual incarnation of the universe. How does this happen? Because everything is interconnected. What is the power? It is the form and energy of the interconnections.

If pushed, psychoanalysis might come to a similar conclusion, although starting from a different perspective and using a distinctive vocabulary. We begin life as a slivered self. Gradually we develop an internal world (a subjective universe) replete with figures (objects) and part figures in relationship to each other. With luck and over time, these relationships expand and our subjectivity thrives in scope and complexity. Sanity is the strength to establish relationships, to contain and maintain them. Maturity is unity, the affirmation of divergent experiences, the power to see that we inhabit an interrelated universe. Where is this power? It is in ourselves. What is the power? It is our capacity to see beyond ourselves.

NOTES

1. *ArtScroll Siddur*, trans. Nosson Scherman (New York: Messorah, 1987), 27.
2. Sigmund Freud, 1914c, "On Narcissism," in *Standard Edition of the Complete Psychological Works of Sigmund Freud*, ed. James Strachey (1914c; London, Hogarth Press, 1981), vol. 12.
3. Sigmund Freud, 1911, "Formulations on the Two Principles of Mental Functioning," in *Standard Edition*, ed. James Strachey, vol. 12.
4. The two states of nothingness are also different in other ways. For the narcissist, nothingness is the annihilation of experience. For the Kabbalist, nothingness is the going beyond experience.
5. A traditional Mussar (moralistic) tale quoted by Daniel Matt, *God and the Big Bang: Discovering Harmony between Science and Spirituality* (Woodstock, Vt.: Jewish Lights, 1996), 76.
6. Aryeh Kaplan, *Innerspace* (Jerusalem: Vagshal/Moznaim, 1990a), 79.
7. Amir Aczel, *The Mystery of the Aleph: Mathematics, the Kabbalah, and the Search for Infinity* (New York: Four Walls Eight Windows, 2001), 109–10.
8. Aczel, *Mystery of the Aleph,* 194–95.
9. Michio Kaku, *Parallel Worlds* (London: Allen Lane/Penguin, 2005), 198.
10. Kaku, *Parallel Worlds,* 187–210.
11. Kaku points out that Man lives in what he calls the "Goldilocks zone," an improbable space where life is possible. Changing or deleting the parameters of this zone by the most minute amount would make life impossible. Kaku, *Parallel Worlds,* 241–46.
12. Leviticus 19:18; Aryeh Kaplan, trans., *The Living Torah: The Five Books of Moses*, (Jerusalem: Maznaim Publishing, 1981), 603.
13. Deuteronomy 6:5; Kaplan, *Living Torah*, 901.
14. The Midrash consists of commentaries on the Jewish Biblical Scriptures. This is discussed by Matt, *God and the Big Bang*, 97.
15. This is the refrain from a popular song of the Beatles, "The Yellow Submarine": "All you need is love" to vanquish the "blue meanies."
16. Schneur Zalman of Liadi, *Likutei Amarim: Tanya.* Bilingual ed., trans. N. Mindel (1797; Brooklyn, N. Y.: Kehot, 1984), chap. 1.
17. Sigmund Freud, 1912a, "The Dynamics of Transference," in *Standard Edition*, ed. James Strachey, vol. 12, 100–103.
18. Paula Heimann, "On Counter-Transference," *International Journal of Psycho-Analysis* 31 (1950): 81–84.
19. See Joseph Berke, *The Tyranny of Malice: Exploring the Dark Side of Character and Culture* (New York: Simon & Schuster, 1988), chap. 4, "On Attacking the Breast," 78–98.
20. Elie Wiesel, *Souls on Fire* (New York: Random House, 1972), 70.
21. Described in detail by Paul Roazen, *Meeting Freud's Family* (Amherst: University of Massachusetts Press, 1993) and by Marianne Krull, *Freud and His Father* (New York: Norton, 1986).

22. For a fuller discussion of I–Thou and I–It relationships, see Martin Buber, *I and Thou*, trans. R. G. Smith (New York: Scribner, 1958).

23. Christopher Lasch, *The Culture of Narcissism: American Life in an Age of Diminishing Expectations* (New York: Norton, 1978).

24. Berke, *Tyranny of Malice*, 257–59.

25. Herbert Rosenfeld, "A Clinical Approach to the Psychoanalytic Theory of the Life and Death Instincts: An Investigation in to the Aggressive Aspects of Narcissism," *International Journal of Psycho-Analysis* 52 (1971): 169–78.

26. Melanie Klein, "A Contribution to the Psychogenesis of Manic-Depressive States," *International Journal of Psycho-Analysis* 16 (1935): 145–74; and Melanie Klein, "Mourning and Its Relation to Manic-Depressive States," *International Journal of Psycho-Analysis* 21 (1940): 125–53.

27. Based on a saying by the Hasidic master Menachem Mendel of Kotsk (the Kotsker Rav): "The 'I' is a thief in hiding." In P. Z. Gliksman, *Der Kotsker Rebbe* (Warsaw: no publisher listed, 1938), quoted by Matt, *God and the Big Bang*, 78.

28. The background material about Shabbatai Zevi comes from (a) the section on Shabbatai Zevi, *Encyclopaedia Judaica*, 1221–54; (b) the monumental biography *Sabbatai Sevi: The Mystical Messiah* by Kabbalah scholar Gershom Scholem (London: Routledge & Kegan Paul, 1973). Scholem lays out a portrait of a very disturbed man whose episodic emotional eruptions are called 'manifestations.'

29. Arthur Green, *Tormented Master: The Life and Spiritual Quest of Rabbi Nahman of Bratslav* (Woodstock, Vt.: Jewish Lights, 1992). Rabbi Nachman was the great-grandson of the Baal Shem Tov.

30. Told by Norman Podhoretz in "Heard the One About the Rabbi?" *Daily Telegraph*, April 10, 2001.

31. Numbers 20:9–12; Kaplan, *Living Torah*, 763.

32. Rivka Schatz-Uffenheimer, ed., *Dov Baer: Maggid Devarav le-Ya'aqov* [in Hebrew] (Jerusalem: Magnes Press, 1976), 186, quoted by Matt, *God and the Big Bang*, 75.

Chapter Twelve

Repairing Worlds: Reparation and *Tikkun*

Tikkun has to do with correction, restoration and renewal. It is the core concept, the *raison d'être* of Kabbalah, and it coincides with the impetus for reparation, perhaps the most significant psychoanalytic formulation of Melanie Klein and her followers.

As in Kabbalah, Klein set out to describe how to overcome fragmentation and loss, evil and exile. But her terms of reference were different. Klein was concerned with the self in relation to 'internal objects,' internalized representations of significant persons, and to a lesser extent 'external objects,' actual life-important people. For her, exile meant separation from mother, while evil equaled death. For Kabbalists, however, evil means fragmentation of the soul and separation from God.

Reparation is the will, means and action of repairing an inner world shattered under the pressure of destructive impulses and an outer world of damaged relationships, peoples and things. Reparation, like *tikkun,* is both a goal and the movement toward this goal. According to Kleinian psychology, reparation is never complete; rather it is an active process of striving toward completeness, whether of the head or heart or entire being. It is intimately related to its Kabbalistic counterpart, which is also a constant ongoing process, but with a larger purpose: to unify the universe.

We all know a popular children's rhyme that expresses the fear and need to restore something that has been smashed to pieces:

> Humpty Dumpty sat on a wall.
> Humpty Dumpty had a great fall.
> All the King's horses and all the King's men
> Couldn't put Humpty together again.

The despair in this refrain expresses the difficulty, even impossibility, of effecting a repair. The sentiments are so moving because they are so elemental. How can one put back together a loved one, loved ones, after we have hurt them? And how strong are our reparative capacities when, as R. D. Laing has noted, "the dreadful has already happened?"[1] Surely this is the case with Humpty Dumpty. For he is not an ordinary creature. Rather he embodies the cosmic egg, the primal contents and container of all life.

It is fitting to conclude this extended study of psychoanalysis and Kabbalah with a discussion of *tikkun.* Essentially *tikkun* has to do with healing—physical, emotional and spiritual. For 'man' this has to do with healing the rifts within himself and between himself and others, in order to gain and regain *shlaimoot* (wholeness) and *shalom* (peace of mind).

Essentially, Kabbalah teaches that when a person restores his self-balance, that is, restores the proper weight of his thought, feelings and actions on a personal scale, he will simultaneously perform a *tikkun ha-olam,* a transformation of the cosmos. Therefore, what happens internally will happen externally, what happens on a micro scale will also happen on a macro scale. So we learn that there is a continual interplay between the ultimate goal of creation, which is to bring completeness to the world, *tikkin ha-olam*, and the action or personal praxis that has to be taken to bring this about.

There is a striking complementarity between the concept of *tikkun ha-olam* and psychoanalytic aims and actions. The analytic focus is the *olam ha-pnimi,* the internal object world of the patient. Initially Melanie Klein used the words *Weiderherstellung,* 'restoration,' and *Wiedergutmachung,* 'restitution,' to describe this process of correction. However, these translations were soon superseded by 'reparation,' which is a refinement of the previous versions and includes the idea of repairing as well as making reparation to someone.

According to Klein, the basic need, indeed the ongoing project of every person, is to overcome early infantile sadism. She insisted that such savagery usually took the form of intense phantasies of tearing, devouring and fragmenting the mother's body. Subsequently, these impulses extended to father and siblings, as well as all the relationships that went on among them, externally and internally. Even more terrifying, by 'the laws of revenge' this sadism soon rebounds on the child, and his or her own body, mind and relations. Hence the nightmares of early childhood are replete with the same monsters and demons, ghouls and goblins, that inhabit horror films.

In consequence Klein's concepts encompass not just the need and fact of repair—putting things back together again—but of 're-pair,' reestablishing torn and broken relationships, especially the one between the parental couple. By implication this leads to the idea of repairing social as well as personal and interpersonal reality, in other worlds, macro-social as well as micro-personal reality.

But both the Jewish and psychoanalytic traditions agree that an important first step has to occur before a correction or repair can take place. We refer to the recognition of a wrong, whether between man and God or between man and man. In Judaism this step is called *teshuvah* and is a formal process of taking responsibility for wrongdoing or sin. *Teshuvah* means repentance, but it also signifies 'return,' a turning back toward one's primary source, or God.

Neither the fact nor process of repentance is formalized in psychoanalysis. Rather this step appears to be noted as regret, remorse, sorrow, or, in general, a concern for a lost or damaged other or 'object.' In Kleinian terms this concern arises during the 'depressive position' when a person, the subject, sees another as 'a whole object'—that is, as he or she exists in 'his' own right, with his own needs, problems and desires. But we think that a basic aspect of the Kleinian view, and indeed, the whole idea of repentance, can also be accommodated under Sigmund Freud's formulation of the 'reality principle' and related 'reality-testing' and 'reality adaptation.' Here 'reality' denotes the point where a person is no longer under the sway of instinctual, narcissistic and purely personal desires or perceptions.

It is a major accomplishment when a child or adult is able and willing to see people or things as they are, as well as the connections between them. This denotes a state of mind that can acknowledge loss, injury or absence. Moreover, it can embrace mental or physical capacities or the foci of these feelings such as beauty, nature and cognition. We refer to the maturational moment when a person perceives a misfortune and accepts responsibility for his or her contribution to a damaged world.

Teshuvah is the conscious, and, more important, heartfelt acceptance of the dark side of oneself. Or, as Adin Steinsaltz observes, it is the reaching into "the nadir of the abyss."[2] Only then, when one has dug down to the very bottom of one's soul, can the descent into badness and madness stop and the ascent toward redemption begin.

The RaMBaM (Maimonides) outlined several stages of *teshuvah* in his seminal work *Mishnah Torah*.[3] The first step is recognition. A person has to see that he has done something wrong. Next is confession, when he openly acknowledges what he has done. Third is regret. This allows the person to learn from his mistakes. And finally there is resolve, the decision not to repeat the wrongdoing in the future. Collectively these four stages comprise repentance, which is only complete when the impetus to act wrongly or wickedly has ended. In fact, for sins against one's fellowman, the RaMBaM adds a fifth step, which includes apology, asking forgiveness and restitution.

This process has been institutionalized during the Jewish festival of Yom Kippur. Also known as the 'Day of Atonement,' it demands three essential elements for redemption: *tefillah* or prayer (change of consciousness), *teshuvah* or repentance (change of heart), and *tzeddakah* or charity (change of action).

Hence the further meaning of 'atonement' is 'attunement,' the attuning or realigning of one's material as well as spiritual vessel, in order to become 'at-one' with one's source. For these reasons 'The Day of Atonement' has also been seen as 'The Day of At-One-Ment' as well as 'The Day of Attunement.'

The psychotherapist Estelle Frankel has discussed these issues at length in her paper "Yom Kippur, Teshuvah and Psychotherapy."[4] In particular she uses the analogy of the *ketoret*, incense used in the temple service in Jerusalem, to point out that sin is not only an evil aspect of life, but also a necessary contributor toward the course of emotional realignment and growth. The incense was made up from 11 basic ingredients. One of the most important of these was *chelbanah* or galbanum, a bitter, foul-smelling gum resin.[5] In itself galbanum is disgusting. But as part of the incense mixture, it adds passion and pungency. Sin is also repugnant. But like galbanum, when integrated into the totality of our personality, it can add strength and vigor. In this regard Frankel quotes from Avraham Kook, a noted Kabbalist and the first Chief Rabbi of Israel:

> When a person sins he has entered the world of fragmentation, and then every particular being stands by itself, and evil is evil in and of itself, and it is evil and destructive. When he repents out of love there at once shines on him the light from the world of unity, where everything is integrated into one whole, and in the context of the whole, there is no evil at all. The evil is joined with the good to invest it with more attractiveness and to enhance its significance. Thus the willful wrongs become transformed into real virtues.[6]

Kook's further point is that repentance occasioned by love gives people a second chance, another opportunity to rectify their existence. This follows the dictum described in the *Zohar* that it is possible to re-approach the shadow side of the soul in order to unblock and reclaim the light hidden within it.[7] Similarly one of the functions of psychoanalysis is to dis-cover, un-cover and ultimately re-cover a love of life that lies hidden amid a morass of suffering and symptoms. We would not suggest, however, that the overt expression of *teshuvah* was part of Freud's therapeutic agenda, all the more so because we know that he despised (or feared) formalized religious practices. Indeed, soon after marrying Martha Bernays, who grew up in an observant family, he forbade her to light Sabbath candles on Friday night. Martha complied until after Freud died, after which she resumed this custom. Indeed, she exclaimed after his passing, ". . . on Friday night evenings good Jewish women light candles for the approach of the Sabbath. But this monster—*Unmensch*—will not allow this because he says that religion is superstition."[8]

It is important to consider the underlying influences that contributed to Freud's 'mind formulations.' Psychoanalysis itself, and, in particular, the whole process of acknowledging reality, can be seen and understand as a form of repentance or *teshuvah.* This is not as outlandish a statement as it may seem. Freud was born in Galicia, a central area of Jewish mysticism, and was the son, grandson and great-grandson of Hasidim—pious, mystically inclined Jews.[9] In our paper, "Sigmund Freud and the Lubavitcher Rebbe," we show that there was an overt Freud, who denigrated his background, and a covert Freud, who was knowledgeable of and fascinated by Jewish ideas and practices.[10] Thus, in 1891 on the occasion of Sigmund's 35th birthday, his father, Jakob, presented him with a copy of the Philippsohn Bible, which Sigmund had studied as a child. Jakob wrote in it an elaborate Hebrew inscription replete with fragments and phrases from the Torah and rabbinic literature. We must assume that Sigmund was familiar with the Jewish sources.[11]

Phyllis Grosskurth, in her biography of Melanie Klein, notes that Klein had a formidable Jewish pedigree. Her father came from an orthodox family and her mother was the daughter of a rabbi. Although Klein was not observant or formally religious in adult life, Grosskurth relates that she retained a special fondness for Yom Kippur, the Day of Atonement.[12] Similarly, Freida Fromm-Reichmann was strongly influenced by an orthodox Jewish upbringing and a Lurianic world view, such as expressed by the title of her biography, *To Redeem One Person Is to Redeem the World.*[13]

Perhaps most tellingly, the physicist Tom Keve documents in his study *Triad: The Physicists, the Analysts, the Kabbalists* the extent to which many of the founding fathers of psychoanalysis, including Joseph Breuer, Robert Breuer, Abraham Brill, Sandor Ferenczi (originally Fraenkel), Heinz Hartmann and Lajos Levy, were direct descendants of rabbis, Kabbalists or purveyors of mystical texts.[14]

While psychoanalytic practice may explore penitence, contrition, remorse or sorrow—different ways of recognizing and responding to wrongdoing—it seems to do so without a specific set of procedures or steps for finalizing repentance, such as described by Maimonides or as elaborated by later scholars. Analysis is more concerned with the mental anguish, the self-reproach, the self-blame and especially the sense of guilt that arise from internal conflict. According to Freud's structural model of the mind, the central conflict occurs between the id, the ego and the superego. This has to do with sexuality and socialization: the internalization of parental injunctions, infringement of moral imperatives and doubts about the worth or value of the self. This aspect of Freudian psychology fits in well with the theories of ChaBaD (Lubavitch)

Hasidism, where the goal of replacing one's base instincts with intellectual, aesthetic and spiritual pursuits is a constant reminder of Freud's dictum, "where id was, there ego should be."[15] The failure to accomplish such socialization may manifest itself as a vague inner dread often synonymous with 'neurotic anxiety,' or a life dominated by endless rounds of 'cops and robbers,' pursuit and punishment.

In comparison to the structural theory, the psychological model of Melanie Klein emphasized the conflict between *Thanatos* and *Eros*, the forces of death and disintegration versus love and life. This parallels the Jewish mystical tradition, which emphasizes a psychology of conflict featuring *tohu* (chaos, the without-form, void) versus *bohu* (emptiness, but literally the 'it is in it,' reconciliation, integration).[16] In conjunction with the origin of the *sefirot* (the divine characteristics), *tohu* has to do with the world of points (*nikudim*), which is roughly comparable to a state of part object relations. On the other hand, *bohu* pertains to a developmentally later world of interrelated streaks (*berudim*) and is roughly comparable to a state of whole object relations. The inability of the divine containers, or *sefirot,* to give and take, to interrelate, leads directly to *Shvirat HaKelim,* the 'Breaking of the Vessels,' and the disintegration of the universe. But when the *sefirot* are reconstituted and they are able to engage with each other, then the universe can be re-created and life can be reestablished.

Psychologist and writer Sanford Drob points out that Kabbalah constantly describes the dialectical clash between opposing thoughts, emotions, states and values (*midot*) as well as the process of integrating and re-integrating them on higher, that is, more complex levels of being.[17] From this perspective, that is, continuous de-constructive, if not destructive, conflict, the capacity to feel guilt is a major accomplishment. It demonstrates an active concern for friends and relatives, internal as well as external objects, and encompasses the excruciating torment when one cannot protect them from oneself or from others.

In contemporary psychoanalysis or psychoanalytic psychotherapy, the transference relationship provides the means for working through the carnage of an ambivalently lived life. The cut and thrust of projection and introjection, transference and counter-transference between the patient and analyst enable both parties to transcend all boundaries of time, space and person. In such a relationship, the patient does not *represent* an angry child, but he *is* that angry child. The analyst doesn't appear to be an injured parent, he is that parent. Similarly, the present is the past, while the consultation room becomes the place, the space where everything happened, but where every 'thing' can also be overcome.

The beauty of an analytic relationship is that it provides a second chance to put things right. Klein captured this possibility by her original choice of the term *Wiedergutmachung*, which signifies restitution or reparation. In German the word can be subdivided into *wieder + gut + machung.* Literally this means *second chance (again?) + good + making* or 'the making good for a second time.' From a Kleinian perspective we might say that such second, third and more chances are back-up mechanisms for getting through the depressive position, and becoming 'human.'

Interestingly, Hasidic masters like the late Lubavitcher Rebbe, Menachem Mendel Schneerson and the nineteenth-century sage, Tzadok HaCohen of Lublin, came to kindred conclusions when they illustrated the transformative benefits of *teshuvah* ('transformation,' 'repentance'). The Lubavitcher Rebbe taught that every person is allowed a second chance to reinvigorate and rehabilitate himself by achieving a greater degree of understanding and by returning to his source, or as he put it, to godliness.

Nothing is irretrievable. One must never give up hope. Given application and motivation, even the greatest sinner or regressed institutionalized patient can leap over limitations, whether self-imposed or not, and achieve a higher degree of functioning. In fact, we have both been privileged to observe and contribute to such changes at first hand both at the Arbours Crisis Centre in London, and the Summit Institute in Jerusalem.[18] Individuals who were willing to spend a lot of time and effort to rehabilitate themselves have been able to transcend their diagnostic categorizations and resume their family and community activities.

Tzadok HaCohen of Lublin emphasized the temporal aspects of the extra chance. When *teshuvah* is done *me'ahavah*—out of love (for family, for God)—an individual can travel in time in order to reverse a wrongdoing, so that it appears that the event, and its effects, never happened. This view coincides with what the Lubavitcher Rebbe and Rav Kook meant when they declared that a heartfelt repentance can reverse time and overturn a bad decree.[19]

These reversals are also consistent with positive developments during the course of therapy or analysis. When the positive transference is activated, we can observe that love in the present can obliterate the pain of the past. This love is transferential in that it emanates from the deepest recesses of the patient toward 'internal objects' projectively identified with the analyst, an 'other' who is willing and able to receive the feeling and be affected by it. The love is also transactional and tangible, because it involves a mutually satisfying interplay by both the patient and analyst. Such transformations allow people to transcend pain or illness by reframing their experiences and shifting them into a higher or different state of consciousness. The ensuing time flows are transferential and non-transferential, backward and forward. Like the intricate counterpoint of a Bach partita, the process of repentance is only complete when past turmoil and hardships are mitigated by present warmth and affection.

Although we have been discussing the changes that *teshuvah* can bring about in and of itself, *teshuvah* is a necessary, but not a sufficient, condition for effecting a *tikkun* or correction, in a person or in the world as a whole. For a man and woman, the first steps are a willingness to perceive reality and a mellowing of the heart. But the third step involves specific actions designed to redress and elevate a fragmented self and chaotic world. We now wish to address this third element, both from the perspective of what needs to be corrected and the actions that have to be taken to bring forth and complete the realms of reparation and *tikkun.*

When we began this study, we quoted the conundrum that Heinz Kohut repeatedly posed: how can man "cure his crumbling self"? So the *first focus* of our discussion of *reparation / tikkun* will be the individual in relation to himself. We can call this the world of self. *Second*, we shall explore the individual in relation to others. We can call this the world of relationships. *Third*, we shall consider everything else, animate and inanimate, the totality of existence that comprises 'the world.' In truth all of these areas, as well as their creation, destruction and re-creation, are interconnected.

The world of self begins even inside the womb when the child-to-be exists as an undifferentiated being complete with potential for thoughts to be thought, feelings to be felt and relationships to be lived. For a brief moment he or she is akin to a cosmic egg waiting to be shattered under the impact of existence. It is even said that the newly incarnated soul emerges with a full knowledge of the Torah, the oral and written codes of law.[20]

But beset by bits and pieces of rudimentary experiences, hunger and frustration, tension and rage, the nascent self and infantile ego soon succumb to dissolution and chaos. The newborn baby 'forgets' whatever it may have known and reverts to a crumbled state where its mind and bodily sensations become broken and fragmented. Moreover, replete with indigestible internal events, the infant evacuates these bits and pieces, which Bion has called 'beta elements,' into his environment through cries, vomit, wind, feces, urine and kindred products and activities.[21] The remnants lodge in everyone and everything around him which, in turn, appear dangerous and life-threatening.

We are obviously describing the developmentally early or regressive situation that in Kleinian psychology is known as the paranoid-schizoid position. Here the infant, or adult as may be the case, suffers ominous fears that his being is constantly under attack, and relies on mechanisms of projection and division to defend himself from death and destruction. Significantly, Kabbalah describes a similar intermediate stage during the creation of reality. This is the 'Universe of *Tohu*,' when the vessels that reflect and contain the divine condition emerge as separate entities. But, as we have previously described, these *sefirot* cannot interact with each other nor hold the intense light or energies that flow into them. So the lower seven vessels (lower in a spiritual sense) shatter and explode outward, imbuing everything around them with shards or fragments of themselves. This shattering event is the harbinger of evil in existence, because both the *sefirot* and their contents then become separated from their source.

From any standpoint, non-containment is intolerable. The infant does have an external container, its mother or caretaker, who holds or should be able to hold its disparate experiences together. He is overwhelmingly dependent on these containing capacities, just like a patient in therapy or analysis is very dependent on the containing capacities of his therapist or analyst to keep the various threads of his mind together and to keep him from falling apart.

Even at this maturational moment, however, there do exist certain proto-reparative capacities. These are physical and cognitive skills that help to overcome fragmentation and promote psychic and emotional integration. One of the most important of these has to do with language. As we saw in the chapter on language, a baby creates reality through sounds, gestures and words. And if the baby can create reality, then he can change it and make it better.

The story of Helen Keller illuminates this process. By grasping words and by realizing the meaning of words, Keller was able to emerge from a primitive state of chaotic darkness. Moreover, her life clarifies the Kabbalistic maxim "Redemption comes with the birth of the word." Why? Because words delineate time and define space. Moreover, they reveal what has been concealed, and in so doing, they release an idea of the inner essence of persons and things. Or, they permit a preconception to become a conception. These conceptions become containers that nourish 'meaning' and generate subjective or internal reality. They reduce projective outbursts and allow fragments of self that have been embedded in others 'to come home.'

A strong container allows a child or adult to enter the world of relationships. This means that he can become a giver as well as taker. So the containing/contained function becomes more flexible and much stronger. Feelings don't have to well up until the bursting point, nor be explosively discharged. They can be held, processed, digested, modulated and otherwise transformed from bad to good, from noxious to useful.

There is a striking resemblance between the Lurianic account of creation, *tikkun ha-olam,* which can be roughly translated as 'repairs to the tears in the universe,' and the Kleinian concept of reparation, which can also be seen as 'making good the tears of separation.'[22] This is one of Klein's greatest contribution, for it conveys the possibility of overcoming the shock of the depressive position with all its painful discoveries: separateness, aloneness, loss, jealousy, but especially guilt for the damage one has inflicted on beloved relatives and friends.

What can one do in the face of such shattering experiences? How is it possible to constitute 'the self,' with all its thoughts, feelings, images and intentionality? The Israeli poet Pinchas Sadeh has described what the process *tikkun ha-lev*, or Restoration of the Heart, has meant for him:

> This evening, while I was still engrossed in thought on a certain topic, a thought entered my mind regarding 'repair of the heart.' A few years ago, when I edited a book of the writings of Rabbi Nachman of Breslov, I chose to call it *Tikkun Ha-Lev*, repair of the heart. I thought that the meaning of the name, simple in itself, was absolutely clear to me. But I am thinking that perhaps only now its meaning is becoming clear to me. . . . Time, fate, life and death—all these powerful forces prevent the possibility of repairing that which is broken. If so, what is possible? What remains for man to do, after all? What can save and rescue the things that are smashed? Maybe only—and even this only through tremendous effort, through difficult struggle, through great pain—this; repairing the heart. In other words, repairing the heart, which was broken when all those things were broken.[23]

A broken heart, of course, denotes a damaged self—not just a part of the body, but a whole range of ruptured thoughts and feelings. It describes an inner world that lies bleeding, shattered and in ruins. Hasidim, in particular, has tried to address this problem through prayer, meditation and introspection.

In his book on traditional Jewish healing, *The Wings of the Sun*, the Bratslav lecturer and writer Avraham Greenbaum goes into great detail about how to overcome a broken body and mind. Ultimately he quotes Rabbi Nachman of Bratslav: "The basic cause of illness is unhappiness, and the great healer is joy."[24]

Similarly, the late Lubavitcher Rebbe, Menachem Mendel Schneerson, emphasized the power of faith and reflection to overcome inner confusion and chaos. "Everything has its limits, even darkness. As the *Zohar* says, 'When the world was made, a limit was set how long it will function in confusion.'"[25]

All of these activities can bring about *tikkun* by joining divisions and mitigating inner turmoil. But the question arises, how can they be effective in predominantly secular Western societies, when, long after Nietzsche declared that 'God is dead,' a post-modern skepticism invites disbelief in the existence of the soul or the self?

There is a subjective state that everyone experiences, although few people realize how effective it can be in solving problems or reorganizing inner reality. We refer to the capacity to dream, remember dreams and learn from dreams. Of course, Freud brought dreams and dreaming to the forefront of our collective consciousness with his seminal work *The Interpretation of Dreams*.[26] But long before Freud's exposition, there was an extensive literature on the power of dreams to affect and effect the present as well as predict the future in the Torah, the Talmud and other writings. Perhaps the most notable example of this process was the Biblical figure of Joseph.[27]

The authors have experienced the healing balm of dreams at first hand. Both of us come from Newark, New Jersey, although we did not meet until many years later in Jerusalem. Stanley Schneider moved to Brooklyn as an adolescent, but Joseph Berke only left the city in the early 1960s to attend Columbia University in New York. He often thought of the area in which he had lived and felt devastated when it was destroyed in the Newark riots of 1967. It seemed as if something in him had been destroyed, too. Years later after moving to London to continue his career, he kept yearning to go back and explore his old neighborhood. Rationally he knew it no longer existed. But the wish to return remained strong.

Then in the late 1970s Berke had a remarkable dream that fulfilled this hope. He found himself walking down a road leading to the street, Farley Avenue, where he had grown up. He recognized the bushes where he used to play and the trees he used to climb. As a child he was intimidated by them, as well as by the sewer openings in the road. But in the dream they were friendly and non-threatening. He continued to walk down Farley Avenue. The houses had all been renewed and painted a brilliant white. They were very beautiful. And around their sides, gardens and spacious fields had replaced asphalt driveways and dilapidated garages. Then he awoke and felt suffused with happiness. 'Home' had reestablished itself inside him, and he felt 'at home' with himself. The dream had renewed his urban landscape. From that day on he was no longer bothered by thoughts and fantasies about Newark.

Dreams like this are closely related to the process of symbol formation, which is an essential means to create inner reality and to repeatedly re-create it. Symbols literally have to do with a bringing together of thoughts, images, ideas, emotions and sensations so that both child and adult can transform and transcend concrete things. Symbols are plastic and infinitely malleable; they represent, but are not the equivalent of, people and part people—or in the language of psychoanalysis, 'objects' and 'part objects.'

As Hanna Segal has pointed out, symbols are the means to overcome both a mind and relationships that have been devastated by primary aggression, or, as Kabbalists conclude, by the non-containment of primary energies. In chapter 8, "The Language of Creation," we showed how the initial symbols are letters and words. In the Nazi concentration camps, 'mules' were people who were so traumatized that they could not speak. Only by regaining their power of speech were they able to become human again. The implication was that they could now reestablish symbolic connections and meaning in their lives.

The Master of Slonim cites a passage in the *Zohar* that describes the exile of the Jews from Egyptian slavery as 'the exile of speech.'[28] Why? Because for Jewish mystics every biblical nation represents a different organ of the body. Egypt symbolized the throat, a place of narrowness and constriction. In

Egypt the Jews were dumb and mute, their words got 'stuck in the throat,' they couldn't cry out and were condemned to a state of despair. Again, it was through the power of speech as mediated by the festival of Passover (*Pesach*, in Hebrew, which according to Isaac Luria, equals *Peh* + *Sach,* literally the 'mouth' that 'talks') and the Haggadah that they were and are able to retrieve their 'Hi-Story,' and undergo a redemptive transformation or *tikkun ha-nefesh,* repair of the soul, every spring.[29]

In fact, all artistic endeavor serves the same purpose: to effect a *tikkun ha-nefesh.* Contemporary psychoanalysts conclude that this action has to do with restoring a lost, damaged or dead internal object, while Kabbalists insist such activity has to do with restoring a connection with the Divine. About this Avraham Yitzchak HaCohen Kook stated:

> Usually the mind conceals the divine extremely by imagining that there is a separate mental power that constructs the mental images. But by training yourself to hear the voice of God in everything, the voice reveals itself to your mind as well. Then right in the mind, you discover revelation.[30]

These two perspectives may not be radically different, for it is often said that the highest level of achievement is akin to the artist being touched by the Divine. The artist is able to 'speak' with his hands, legs, eyes and indeed with all his sensorium in order to construct externally, in actuality, what he or she wants to reconstruct internally.[31] In discussing this issue, British psychoanalyst Robert Hinshelwood adds that 'beauty' represents the quality of the struggle to revive a lost and broken person or thing, or, as we shall soon consider, relationship.[32] He also refers to Bion's view that the oscillation between the part and the whole, or between the *shard* and the *sefira,* is a symbolic expression of the movement between Klein's paranoid-schizoid and depressive positions. In fact, Bion thinks such swings underlie all scientific as well as artistic creativity.[33]

In a brief report entitled "Magical Regeneration by Dancing," Joan Rivière gives a charming example of this very process. Rivière describes a visit she had with the mother of a four-year-old girl. The woman had recently given birth to a baby boy and was concerned about her daughter's jealousy. The mother explained:

> Jane shows a striking tendency to ritualistic performances and ceremonies. It makes me think of savage rites. For instance, this is the sort of game she plays now. She and I are at the table pretending to eat: we have little toy plates and dishes with sham food stuck on them, like bacon, a loaf, a fish, etc. When we have pretended to eat them, Jane gets down from her chair and says, 'Now I must

make them grow on the plates again.' She then performs an elaborate dance . . . round and round the table. She then says, 'Now they are all grown again.'[34]

For Jane, we can surmise that the bacon, the loaf, the bread and the other foods spread out on the plate were all symbolic of parts of her mother's body and the new baby that she had savaged and then brought back to life again. Thus, she wasn't stuck with a dead and dying mishmash in her mind. She had successfully 'elevated' her inner world by dancing. In a similar vein we have described the process by which a guest at the Arbours Centre in London 'elevated' or overcame badness by doodling.[35] He acted like the Hasidic figure of the *Benoni,* or intermediate man (halfway, that is, between all bad and truly righteous) who becomes a righteous person by 'elevating' his bad or immoral impulses (this is related to the *Nefesh B'haimit,* the animal soul). Here the term 'elevation' includes reframing perception, sublimating desires and 'sweetening' existence.[36]

Perhaps the ultimate 'sweetener,' and therefore, the main means to achieve *tikkun ha-nefesh,* is to discover and recover meaning or significance in all the elements of one's life. This project is closely related to the psychotherapy that Victor Frankl, who was a veteran of the concentration camps, termed 'Logotherapy.' The Greek word *Logos* represents the word, the will of God, the controlling principle of the universe or meaning. Frankl preferred the latter translation and strove to help his patients get better through gaining spiritual meaning in their lives.[37] But what does this mean? And how can people find meaning when their minds are in chaos? For many individuals the very delusions that they believe and the symptoms that they produce are an attempt to overcome an inner world-catastrophe, whereby nothing makes any sense. Then their 'illness' gives their life meaning, although neither they, nor the doctors brought in to treat them, may understand this. No wonder patients often refuse to 'get better.'

In contrast, Bion postulated an 'epistemophillic instinct,' the innate ability to find meaning in things, which was represented by what he called the 'K' symbol. 'K' stands for *gnosis* or knowledge. For Bion the search for knowledge, 'K,' had equal importance with Love and Hate, or Eros and Thanatos. It is related to 'alpha-function,' the mental activity by which a person processes raw sense data (psychic mush) and transforms this mush into meaningful elements that can be used to promote thinking. There is no doubt such an activity is in itself a form of psychic restitution or *tikkun*. Bion pointed out that without a strong 'epistemophillic instinct,' people faced a demoralization and dread leading to psychic collapse. Essentially Bion anticipated the contemporary 'dis-ease' which tends to be rationalized as 'post-modern' amorality.[38] This occurs when specific actions to bring about *tikkun* are blocked.

Tikkun actions initially focus on the self, hence *tikkun ha-nefesh*. They include a variety of internal and external events: prayer, meditation, introspection, dream-processing, symbol formation, speech, artistic endeavor, reframing perception, sublimation, gnosis and the search for meaning. Collectively all of these activities allow the individual to contain previously uncontainable experiences and to heal wounds to the psychic fabric and personal identity.

These wounds or divisions must reach beyond self-structure to the next stage of *tikkun,* to healing or reunifying human relationships as well as to the physical environment and spiritual universe. In Kleinian psychology this is the action-time for overcoming the depressive position. For Kabbalists the comparable time is *bohu,* the World of *Tikkun*. It is the occasion for reconciliation and rectification, when the *sefirot* come together (both in themselves and in combination as the *partzufim*) and when the male and female expressions of God's presence on earth establish and re-establish relations with each other.

Hanna Segal has narrated a dream by a woman that went a long way toward rectifying relationships in her inner and outer realities.[39] She dreamt she was driving her car to work, but began to experience intense anxiety that the electric current in the car could be cut off. Then the woman realized she had a torch battery of her own and that the battery was in working order. When she arrived for work, she waited for a doctor to help her, but when he turned up his arm was in a sling and he was useless. She slowly realized that the work she had to do was the opening-up of an enormous mass grave. She started digging alone by the light of what she considered was a 'little torch.' Gradually, however, she realized that not all the people who were buried in the grave were dead. To her great joy and encouragement, those who were still alive promptly started to dig with her. At the end of the dream she had a strong sense that two things had been accomplished: (1) Anyone who was still alive had been rescued from the mass grave, and (2) those individuals who were dead could be extracted from the anonymous tomb, recognized and given a proper burial.

The woman had various associations to the dream. She thought that all the people in the grave were themselves women. The burial place had to do with the Warsaw ghetto. Her own mother was partly Jewish. Anxiety about the continued flow of electric current had to do with the continuation of her analysis. Finally, the torch and battery equaled the insight that she had acquired through her analysis.

According to Segal, the dream represented the work the woman had undertaken to solve her depressive anxieties, that is, her fears about the effects of her hostility and her ability or inability to redress the damage she had caused. This included facing the reality of her vicious attacks on her mother and everything Jewish that her mother represented.

Much of this effort was directed toward rescuing and restoring the internal figures who were still alive in her. These restored 'internal objects' became helpers and co-workers in her project of reparation, and they were available to become part of a renewed self and strengthened. But not everyone could be restored to life. The woman had to face the fact that many of her actual and 'inner' relatives were really dead, and that some of the baleful effects of her sadistic anti-Semitism could not be undone. Only then could the process of mourning be completed. In turn, when these people were properly named and buried (laid to rest in herself), then her emotional attachments to them could be freed and her libido could become available for creative purposes.

Segal makes a further very important point. The woman's reparative efforts did not just bring certain internal figures back to life, especially images of her mother and father. Rather the restoration served to repair the parental couple, and, by implication, the sexual relationship between them. In other words the person was able to overcome her oedipal jealousies (such as arise during the depressive position when the child recognizes that parents have a life of their own). We would add that the restored relationship was not exclusively, nor necessarily, sexual. It meant that they could have fun and do all sorts of productive things together.

This account describes a redemptive transformation on many levels. In the transference the dream has given the woman a second chance to revitalize a dead and deadening relationship with her mother. Therefore she doesn't have to continuously evacuate dread and hatred into Segal. Segal can and did become a 'good object.' Her patient became more able to listen and take in (introject) what Segal had to say. In actuality, the relationship became more real, tangible and satisfying, both for Segal and her patient. This carries tremendous implications. An effective therapeutic relationship (and this applies to all relationships) has to be a two-way street. Each side has to participate in the give and take. Thus, for Segal's dreamer to be truly healed, she has to know that her therapist had recognized and been affected by her reparative actions. In effect, these were gifts to her analyst, not unlike the gifts that children give to their parents. That is why the loving exchange of presents between parent and child, husband and wife, lover and loved, or just plain friends, are such basic human activities. The principle is reciprocity, which carries on to many levels of give and take, recognition and receptivity, not unlike a Jacob's ladder of ascending and descending angels.

Bohu, the world of *tikkun,* also denotes an interplay of reciprocal relationships that leads to the creation of the spiritual and physical universe. It is the point where the devastation caused by the *Shvirat HaKelim,* breaking of the vessels, begins to be rectified. As we recently reviewed, the original difficulty occurred because of the lack of reciprocity. The lower *sefirot* were only able to take in Divine energies, but not give them out. So the vessels shattered. Once a system of relationships is established, then, according to Lurianic Kabbalah, the *sefirot* and their cosmic structure, the *Etz Chaim* (The Tree of Life, the *sefirotic* tree) and the *partzufim* (archetypal personas or spiritual analogues of the human body) can be constituted and reconstituted.

The *Etz Chaim* itself is a structure of 22 relationships that correspond to the 22 letters of the Hebrew alphabet. Hence Hebrew is a language of creation that closely follows the relationship between godly qualities and their syntheses. These syntheses, in turn, depend on the union of the masculine and feminine aspects of the Godhead, symbolized by the *partzufim,* wisdom and understanding, *abba* and *ima*, father and mother, as well as the conjunction of *zer anpin*, the short face, the masculine, giving qualities of the Godhead, and *nukva,* the *Shekhinah,* the feminine, receptive qualities.

Chaim Vital elaborated the Lurianic view that when this intercourse (*zivug*) takes place between the male principle (the *zachar,* the *zer anpin*) as God, and the female principle (*the Shekhinah*) as humankind, then humanity is impregnated by God's qualities or characteristics, so that they permeate *'her'* existence and allow humankind to perceive things through *'his'* eyes, that is, to see and respond to the world as God does.[40] Therefore, the whole process of the rectification of the cosmos is dependent on a cosmic drama (or should we say dream) of the erotic coupling of the divine personas. Sanford Drob explains:

> These unifications (*zivug*) symbolize the dialectical union of such 'opposites' as male and female, good and evil, being and nothingness, creation and destruction, self and other, past and present, mind and world, material and spiritual, etc.[41]

On the other hand, *bitul* is the precondition for reestablishing the link between man and his maker, the third and highest level of *tikkun.* Even now, traditional Jews may spend hours scouring the fridge or vacuuming carpets in Passover cleaning. Everyone involved in this process explains that the work is time-consuming and very exhausting. But that is the point, one must become so engaged in these tasks that pride and self-importance along with dirt and grime rub away. Then the purification of pots can lead to an inner cleansing whereby self-inflation yields nothingness.

The primary feature of Passover (*Pesach*) is the eating of *matzot* (flat unleavened bread) and the absolute prohibition of utilizing leavening or leavened products (loaves, rolls, cakes, etc.). Moreover, the very possession of leaven is forbidden. Any residue must be destroyed. The *Torah* instructs:

> Be careful regarding the matzot, for on this day I have brought your masses out of Egypt. You must carefully keep this day for all generations. It is a law for all

> times . . . you must eat only matzah. During seven days, no leaven may be found in your homes. If someone eats anything leavened his soul shall be cut off from the community of Israel.[42]

This injunction is the physical analogue of the imperative to eliminate the evil of Egypt from our souls. Why? Because it is said that the Egyptians were a puffed-up people, swollen with pride and self-aggrandizement, which justified all manner of perversions and perversities. By carrying out the commandment to root out leaven, every Jew achieves a personal Exodus by overcoming the 'Egypt' in himself or herself.

Observant Jews aim to uproot 'Egypt' by meticulously cleaning their house, car or office before *Pesach*. Many begin weeks before the festival to personally dust every book and scrub every nook and cranny of their abode. As Seder night approaches the pace of activity increases, with rugs taken up, shelves polished and ovens cleaned with a blow torch. Separate sets of milk and meat dishes, pots and cutlery all will be carefully cleaned and sealed away before being replaced in entirety for the week. This flurry of energy culminates in the evening before *Pesach* when the final bits of leaven are ceremoniously removed with a feather. The resultant crumbs and scraps will be set aside and burned the following morning.

But why carry out these exhausting practices? Why spend a week eating restricted food and less-than-appetizing flat breads? Because the Kabbalah asserts that God is a source of infinite energy like the sun. Nothing can get near it without being burned away. Only the lowly neutrino, a particle which carries no mass or charge, can reach the sun and pass right through it. Similarly, only a person who has rid himself of the leaven of self-inflation and nullified his ego can get close to the Godhead.

The practices (*avodah*) of Jewish festivities like *Pesach* are all vehicles for the formalized renunciation of narcissism. In so doing they serve as *tikkunim,* the means for rectifying relationships, whether between man and man or man and the universe, which have become damaged by envy, jealousy and, generally, the wish for power and domination.

The renewal of relationships leads to this third and most important level of reparation, which is no less than *tikkun ha-olam,* rectification of the whole world. The *Zohar* hints at what this means when it describes four paths to wisdom. The highest, that is, the most advanced, is ". . . to know and contemplate the world one is in. What is its purpose? And then to seek to know the supernal mysteries of the higher worlds. . . ."[43]

Essentially the *Zohar* is calling for self-perfection or self-completion through the process of self-discovery, not unlike a long and deep psychoanalysis. But this is a path that avoids personal enhancement or narcissistic satisfaction. Rather it has to do with raising the sparks or elements of one's existence by the realization of one's 'Godly self' or *Nefesh Elokit,* an event that is simultaneously psychological, spiritual, ethical and political. Each of these goals and actions is dependent on and identical with the other, and leads not only to the redemption of the individual, but to the whole of existence.

In other words, in everyone there is something of his fellow man. This expresses the view of the great sixteenth-century Kabbalist Moshe Cordovero, that every person contains worlds within worlds within worlds, or an infinite array of Divine sparks. "Everything is in Him, and He is in everything and beyond everything, and there is nothing besides Him."[44]

Tikkun ha-olam is a collective task. We depend on every prayer, every act of kindness, every bit of self-sacrifice to bring it about. And like the figures in the dream that Hanna Segal described, every time a therapist helps to restore a person to sanity, he or she becomes a helper to restore another person to sanity, and so on. Thus, to reconstitute one person, is to redeem the world.

This view is consistent with what Freud said, or is said to have said, when asked what should a normal person be able to do: "To love and to work" (*"Lieben und arbeiten"*).[45] The formulation is deceptively simple, but is quite profound. To love is to treat another with respect, mutuality and kindness. It is the most healing of balms.

Concomitantly, to work is to give added value back to the world, to repay it for the blessings that one has received. Love, work, prayer, charity, self-sacrifice and kindred deeds all comprise the active component of *tikkun ha-olam.* But as we explained at the beginning of this chapter, and have been trying to demonstrate through subsequent examples, *tikkun ha-olam* is both a means to an end, and the end itself. The ultimate purpose of the rectification of realms spiritual and physical is *shalom* and *shlaimoot,* peace and wholeness, which Kabbalists consider to be the harbinger of, if not the tangible realization of, the messianic age. In human terms the equivalent achievement is a state of self-actualization. Then a person would be able to heal, through an act of will, whatever wounds he or she has suffered, whether intrapersonally, interpersonally or transpersonally. Indeed recent research shows that adults carry within themselves stem or precursor cells that can differentiate and repair damaged tissues when activated.[46] Essentially, people are plastic and restorable. Therefore they can recognize that they are part of a multidimensional hologram like the *Etz Chaim,* or *sefirotic* tree, instead of clinging to the narcissistic idea that they are the center of a whole.

All this is very well. However, the question remains, what about individuals who abuse this process? What about those who use love, work and countless deeds of activity for purposes of self-aggrandizement? Many observers, including Freud, have asserted that ritual practices are obsessive-compulsive, neurotic mannerisms—or worse, offensive stratagems designed to insulate the self and project superiority over others.

We could hardly disagree with the perfectly obvious, that actions which appear to be expressions of *tikkun* are often perversions of it. Far from repairing broken hearts and helping others, work and worship, self-sacrifice and charity may simply serve as vehicles of control, contempt and ways of triumphing over relatives and friends. This very common situation arises when arrogance replaces repentance. Then one refuses to face reality, acknowledge damage, feel regret, make amends or ask for forgiveness. In Kleinian terms this state of affairs is known as manic reparation, which is a psychological and interpersonal maneuver that aims to avoid the awareness of loss and hate and guilt.

Certain charities where the beneficiaries are of different racial, religious or class origins are primary foci of manic reparation. This is not to say that such organizations do not do good work or receive generous and selfless donations. But it is a basic feature of manic reparation that it is directed toward persons or things that are seen as inferior, dependent and far removed from the primary figures one may have actually damaged. Sadly, when under the sway of manic states of mind, one doesn't really fix up anything. The whole point is to avoid depression.

Even when true reparation does take place, such as in the dream of Segal's patient, there can be manic elements. Segal described several disturbing and unresolved aspects of the dream, particularly in relation to the woman's father. Still the overall trend was reparative. This indicates that repairs to one's inner world, if not outer figures, is not a one-off event. Rather it is a lifelong process of putting 'Humpty Dumpty' back together again in the face of tremendous inner resistance and struggle.

Interestingly, there does not seem to be a related concept of 'anti-*tikkun*' in Kabbalah. However, Shmuel Lew, the Lubavitch emissary in London, has recounted a story about the second Lubavitcher Rebbe, Dov Ber Shneuri, also known as the Mittler Rebbe, which may illustrate the equivalent of manic reparation.[47]

The office of the Rebbe was like a 'court' where his followers and strangers would gather to tell him their problems and ask for advice. One day a rather agitated Hasid came to meet him. After ushering him in and listening to what he had to say, the Rebbe suddenly turned white, dismissed the man from his presence, and afterward his whole court. Then he went into seclusion and insisted that no one interrupt him. This was highly unusual behavior and elicited great surprise and anxiety among his followers and family. The Rebbe remained in his room for over a week. Finally he came out and requested that the man be brought before him. After meeting for some while the man left and the Rebbe resumed his daily activities.

His Hasidim were very curious about what had happened. Eventually the Rebbe explained that when someone came to him with a problem, in order to help him, he had to discover a similar problem in himself. In this instance the man's problem was necrophilia. He used to have sexual relations with dead bodies. As you can imagine, the Rebbe himself was shocked by what he had heard and was hard put to relate this to his own experiences. Eventually he did. For him the commensurate problem was praying without proper intention. But proper intention means more than intentionality. It implies the right focus and intensity. In other words the praying has to be vital, alive, a true reaching out to God. Only after the Rebbe came to this realization was he able to help the man overcome his difficulties. From the Rebbe's perspective praying without true intention is the equivalent of manic reparation, because it denies the source of all reality and leads to a disjunction rather than conjunction with the Godhead.

The Rebbe especially needed time to find and face such a horrific reality in himself. But by doing so he was able to help the man make amends for what he had done as well as utilize prayer in order to mend the fabric of his existence. Thus the person gained a second chance through repentance (*teshuvah*) to accomplish a *tikkun ha-nefesh* (repair of the self) and concurrent *tikkun ha-ola*—(repair of the universe). As the Kabbalah asserts, the one leads to the other. Similarly, the analytic patient who truly feels intense remorse when discovering the extent of his own depravities has the opportunity to heal his inner world as well as bring *shalom* and *shlaimoot* to family and friends.

The Piacezna Rebbe, Kalonymous Kalman, who died in the Warsaw ghetto, wrote that the special characteristic of the time of *tikkun* (or as he saw it, Messianic times) is that every person will be his own spiritual master (or as we would say, his own psychoanalyst).

The meaning is that every person will find his 'real voice,' a voice whose words will serve as a transcendent guide. At that moment people will realize that they carry the sacred texts within themselves and that they and the texts are one. Or, from another angle, everyone will see that 'phylogony recapitulates ontogeny' and that they carry the entire story of creation in their genes and in their hearts.

Significantly, the Hasidic maestro Nachum of Chernobyl asserted that the Hebrew word for Messiah can be subdivided as *Mah—Siach,* which roughly translates as 'from—dialogue' or 'of—conversation.' The implication is that the corrector of the universe is potentially present in all human conversation. However, such exchanges do not refer to ordinary chit-chat or the passing of information, but rather to acts of mutual voice-giving, one to another. Then the words can rise to the level of authentic (non-alienated) conversation, which is a special speech, at once both whole and holy. Even a single letter or vowel has the power to transform evil into amity.[48]

The same holds true with a certain breath or intense silence. Indeed, the Book of Ezekiel employs the word *chashmal* to covey the prophet's meeting with God. Usually this is translated as 'luminescence' (from which emerged four angels). But Isaac Luria asserted that *chashmal* can also be interpreted as the 'color of the speaking silence,' or the silence from which divine speech emerges.

Maybe this explains why mystics, in general, conclude that transformative speech is connected to the higher sound of silence and why Kabbalists, in particular, insist that the greatest light comes from the darkness. Such views are certainly not inconsistent with a successful therapy or analysis. The effort may be long and difficult and painfully silent. But from bitter experience, we have seen that many of the most brilliant truths radiate from the deepest depths, and the loudest truths tend to be unspoken.

NOTES

1. Personal communication. R. D. Laing (1927–1989) was a Scottish psychiatrist and a major advocate of the anti-psychiatry movement.
2. Adin Steinsaltz, *Teshuva* (London: British Friends of Rabbi Steinsaltz, 2002), 2.
3. Maimonides (Moses ben Maimon), 1135–1204, was a physician, rabbinic sage and philosopher.
4. Estelle Frankel, "Yom Kippur, Teshuvah and Psychotherapy" *Tikkun* 9 (1994): 5, 23–24, 104–5.
5. Galbanum was obtained from various Asiatic plants (genus Ferula) of the umbel family.
6. Avraham Yitzchak HaCohen Kook, *Orot Teshuvah* [in Hebrew] (Jerusalem: Mossad HaRav Kook, 1975), chap. 12, no. 5.
7. Parts of the *Zohar* date back to discussions of a group of scholars in Israel of the second century, led by Simeon bar Yochai. Most of the book deals with the inner, esoteric meaning of Scripture. Modern scholarship has concluded that the main part of the *Zohar* was written down toward the end of the thirteenth century by Moses de Leon, a Castillian Kabbalist who died in 1305.
8. Peter Gay, *A Godless Jew* (New Haven, Conn.: Yale University Press, 1987), 153.
9. Freud's father, Jakob, was a Hasid until his early adolescence. Then he became secularized. Still he retained his appreciation for many Jewish traditions, especially the Passover Seder and the guidebook for the Seder, the Haggadah, which he knew by heart. See J. B. Heller, "Freud's Mother and Father," *Commentary* 21 (1956): 419. Also see M. Krull, *Freud and His Father* (New York: Norton, 1986), 78, 95, 98.

10. Stanley Schneider and Joseph Berke, "Sigmund Freud and the Lubavitcher Rebbe," *Psychoanalytic Review* 87 (2000): 1, 39–59.

11. Yosef Hayim Yerushalmi, *Freud's Moses: Judaism Terminable and Interminable* (New Haven, Conn.: Yale University Press, 1991), 70–74, 76–79, 104–5.

12. Phyllis Grosskurth, *Melanie Klein* (London: Hodder & Stoughton, 1985), 13.

13. Gail Hornstein, *To Redeem One Person Is to Redeem the World: The Life of Frieda Fromm-Reichman* (New York: Free Press, 2000).

14. Tom Keve, *Triad: The Physicists, the Analysts, the Kabbalists* (London: Rosenberger & Krausz, 2000), i–ix.

15. Sigmund Freud, 1933, "New Introductory Lectures on Psycho-Analysis—Lecture 30: Dreams and Occultism," in *Standard Edition of the Complete Psychological Works of Sigmund Freud*, ed. James Strachey (1933; London: Hogarth Press, 1981), 80.

16. Aryeh Kaplan, *Innerspace* (Jerusalem: Vagshal/Moznaim, 1990a), 78–83.

17. Sanford Drob, *Symbols of the Kabbalah: Philosophical and Psychological Perspectives* (Northwale, N.J.: Aronson, 2000a), 376–77.

18. Joseph Berke is the founder and director of the Arbours Centre (est. 1973). See: www.arbourscentre.org.uk. Stanley Schneider was one of the founders and executive director of the Summit Institute (est. 1973; Schneider left the executive directorship in 1995).

19. We can find parallels for this in quantum theory. "Black holes do not destroy information but merely transmit it elsewhere." M. Tegmark, "Parallel Universes," *Scientific American* 288 (2003): 38.

20. The Talmud Niddah 30b teaches us that the fetus is taught all of the Torah and, as it is born, an angel slaps his mouth and causes it to forget the Torah completely.

21. The process of generating meaning out of sensations. W. R. Bion, "A Theory of Thinking," *International Journal of Psycho-Analysis* 43 (1962b): 306–10.

22. The Kleinian and Lurianic systems are discussed at length by Harriet Lutsky, "Reparation and Tikkun: A Comparison of the Kleinian and Kabbalistic Concepts," *International Journal of Psycho-Analysis* 16 (1989): 449–58.

23. Translated by Shmuel Lew and Naphtali Loewenthal. Quoted in Joseph Berke, "Psychoanalysis and Kabbalah," *Psychoanalytic Review* 83 (1996): 857.

24. Avraham Greenbaum, *The Wings of the Sun: Traditional Jewish Healing in Theory and Practice* (Jerusalem: Breslov Research Institute, 1995), 5.

25. Menachem Mendel Schneerson, *Bringing Heaven Down to Earth: 365 Meditations*, comp. Tzvi Freeman (New York: Class One Press, 2002), 286.

26. Sigmund Freud, 1900, "The Interpretation of Dreams," vols 4–5 of *Standard Edition*, ed. James Strachey.

27. In truth, many cultures and peoples demonstrate an intense fascination with dreams and dreaming. For example, Freud himself was not only influenced by the Jewish literature, but by dream scholars such as Hervey de Saint-Denys (1822–1892), a French orientalist, who detailed the problem-solving powers of dreams. Discussed in Morton Schatzman, ed., *Dreams and How to Guide Them* (London: Duckworth, 1982). See also Stephen Frosh, "Freud and Jewish Dreaming," *Psychoanalysis and History* 3 (2002): 18–27.

28. Discussed by Mordechai Gafni, *Soul Prints* (New York: Pocket Books, 2001a).

29. The Haggadah is the written account of the liberation from Egypt. It is read at the Seder, the special meal celebrated during the first night(s) of the Festival.

30. This quotation from Avraham Yitzchak HaCohen Kook is brought down by Daniel Matt, *God and the Big Bang: Discovering Harmony between Science and Spirituality* (Woodstock, Vt.: Jewish Lights, 1996), 74.

31. "Bion was able to show us that what we think we know is the emanations of the sense organs, that is, we 'know' the object by the impressions that our sense organs emanate from the object's impressions on them." J. S. Grotstein, "Bion's Transformation in 'O,' the 'Thing-in-Itself' and the 'Real': Toward the Concept of the 'Transcendent Position,'" *Journal of Melanie Klein and Object Relations* 14 (1996): 111.

32. Robert Hinshelwood, *A Dictionary of Kleinian Thought* (London: Free Association Books, 1991), 450–51.

33. W. R. Bion, *Learning from Experience*, in *Seven Servants* (New York: Aronson, 1977), referred to in Hinshelwood, *Dictionary*, 451.

34. Joan Rivière, "Magical Regeneration by Dancing," *International Journal of Psycho-Analysis* 11 (1930): 340.

35. J. Berke, *The Tyranny of Malice: Exploring the Dark Side of Character and Culture* (New York: Simon & Schuster, 1988), 283–84.

36. Discussed by Schneur Zalman of Liadi, the first Lubavitcher Rebbe, in *Likkutei Amarim—Tanya*. Bilingual ed., trans. N. Mindel (1797; Brooklyn, N.Y.: Kehot, 1984).

37. Victor Frankl, *Man's Search for Meaning* (New York: Washington Square Press/Pocket Books, 1984).

38. Hinshelwood, *Dictionary*, 296–301, 448–49.

39. Hanna Segal, *Introduction to the Work of Melanie Klein* (London: Hogarth Press, 1975a), 92–95.

40. Chaim Vital, *Etz Chaim* [in Hebrew] (1587; Jerusalem/B'nai Brak: Videvsky, 1988), Hechal 6, Gate 1 (Shaar Tikkun Nukvah—Gate of the Restoration of the Feminine), 1146–56.

41. Sanford Drob, *Symbols of Kabbalah*, 365.

42. Exodus 12:17–19; A. Kaplan, trans., *The Living Torah: The Five Books of Moses* (Jerusalem: Maznaim Publishing, 1981), 311.

43. *Zohar*, Song of Songs: 18. Quoted by S. Drob, *Symbols of Kabbalah*, 273.

44. Moshe Cordovero, 'Elima Rabbai,' fol. 25a, quoted by Rachel Elior, *The Paradoxical Ascent to God* (Albany: State University of New York, 1993), 50.

45. These words, which are very familiar to all psychoanalysts, may not have been written down, but seem to be part of an oral tradition. They have been quoted in several places including by Erik Erikson in *Childhood and Society* (New York: Norton, 1950), 264–65.

46. "From bone marrow, the raw material of cures," *International Herald Tribune*, June 22–23, 2002. This is an example of *tikkun* from within. It is also possible, as in the case of certain neurological impairments, to accomplish *tikkun* from without: "Firing up artificial memory: Scientists develop circuits to mimic neural activity." *International Herald Tribune*, June 22–23, 2002.

47. Dov Ber Schneuri (1773–1827) was the son of the founder of ChaBaD, Schneur Zalman of Liadi. He adopted the family name of Schneuri after his father's name. Succeeding generations changed it to Schneersohn or Schneerson.

48. Thus the Hebrew word for evil and for friend have the same two consonants, *resh* and *ayin.* Their only difference is a vowel. This is why the mystics say that *Golah*, 'exile,' is only an aleph away from *Geulah*, 'redemption.'

References

Abulafia, A. 1280. *Chayei HaOlam HaBah* (Life in the World to Come) [in Hebrew]. Edited by Amnon Gross. Jerusalem: Barazani, 2001.

———. 1286. *Otzer Eden Ganooz* (Hidden Eden) [in Hebrew]. Edited by Amnon Gross. Jerusalem: Barazani, 2000.

———. 1291. *Imrei Shefer* (Beautiful Words) [in Hebrew]. Edited by Amnon Gross. Jerusalem: Barazani, 1999.

Aczel, A. D. 2001. *The Mystery of the Aleph: Mathematics, the Kabbalah, and the Search for Infinity.* New York: Four Walls Eight Windows.

Adler, G., ed. 1975. *C. G. Jung Letters*. Vol. 2. Princeton, N.J.: Princeton University Press.

Alexander, F., and S. T. Selesnick. 1966. *The History of Psychiatry*. New York: Harper & Row.

Andrews, R., M. Biggs, and M. Seidel, eds. 1996. *Columbia World of Quotations*. New York: Columbia University Press.

Arica, Y. 1998. *Practical Kabbalah* [in Hebrew]. Kefar Sava: Aryeh Nir/Modan.

Ariel, D. S. 1988. *The Mystic Quest*. New York: Schocken.

ArtScroll Siddur. 1987. Translated by Nosson Scherman. New York: Messorah.

Atwood, G., and R. Stolorow. 1984. *Structures of Subjectivity: Explorations in Scientific Phenomenology*. Hillsdale, N.J.: Analytic Press.

Bakan, D. 1965. *Sigmund Freud and the Jewish Mystical Tradition*. New York: Schocken.

Bar-Lev, Y. 1994. *Song of the Soul*. Petach Tikvah, Israel: Sefer ve Sefel.

Barnes, M., and J. H. Berke. 2002. *Mary Barnes: Two Accounts of a Journey through Madness*. 3rd ed. New York: The Other Press.

Bentall, R. 2003. *Madness Explained: Psychosis and Human Nature*. London: Allen Lane.

Berke, J. H. 1988. *The Tyranny of Malice: Exploring the Dark Side of Character and Culture*. New York: Simon & Schuster.

———. 1996. "Psychoanalysis and Kabbalah." *Psychoanalytic Review* 83:849–63.

——. 2006. *Malice through the Looking Glass*. London: Teva Publications.
Berke, J. H., et al., eds. 2002. *Beyond Madness: Psychosocial Interventions in Psychosis*. London: Jessica Kingsley.
Berke, J. H., and S. Schneider. 1994. "Antithetical Meanings of 'the Breast.'" *International Journal of Psycho-Analysis* 75:491–98.
——. 2001. "A Tale of Two Orphans: The Limits of Categorization." *Mental Health, Religion and Culture* 4:81–93.
——. 2003. "Repairing Worlds: An Exploration of the Psychoanalytical and Kabbalistic Concepts of Reparation and Tikkun." *Psychoanalytic Review* 90:723–49.
——. 2006. "The Self and the Soul." *Mental Health, Religion and Culture* 9: 333–54.
Bettelheim, B. 1983. *Freud and Man's Soul*. London: Chatto & Windus/Hogarth Press.
Bick, E. 1964. "Notes on Infant Observation in Psycho-Analytic Training." *International Journal of Psycho-Analysis* 45:558–66.
——. 1968. "The Experience of the Skin in Early Object Relations." *International Journal of Psycho-Analysis* 49:484–86.
Bion, W. R. 1959. "Attacks on Linking." *International Journal of Psycho-Analysis* 40:308–315.
——. 1962a. *Learning from Experience*. In *Seven Servants*. New York: Aronson, 1977.
——. 1962b. "A Theory of Thinking." *International Journal of Psycho-Analysis*. 43:306–10.
——. 1965. *Transformations*. In *Seven Servants*. New York: Aronson, 1977.
——. 1970. *Attention and Interpretation*. In *Seven Servants*. New York: Aronson, 1977.
Birnbaum, D. 1989. *God and Evil: A Unified Theodicy / Theology / Philosophy* Hoboken, N.J.: Ktav.
Bléandonu, G. 1994. *Wilfred Bion: His Life and Works 1897–1979*. London: Free Association Books.
Bloom, H. 1993. *Kabbalah and Criticism*. New York: Continuum.
Bollas, C. 1987. *The Shadow of the Object*. New York: Columbia University Press.
Boyman, S. 1936. *Miftachei Chochmat HaEmet* (Entrance to the Wisdom of Truth) [in Hebrew]. Warsaw (republished in Jerusalem): 1987.
Breuer, J., and S. Freud. 1895. *Studies on Hysteria*. In Strachey, *Standard Edition*, Vol. 2.
Brian, D. 1996. *Einstein: A Life*. New York: Wiley.
Buber, M. 1958. *I and Thou*. Translated by R. G. Smith. New York: Scribner.
Budge, E. A. W. 1930. *Amulets and Talismans*. New York: Collier-Macmillan, 1970.
Burrow, T. 1964. *Preconscious Foundations of Human Experience*. New York: Basic Books.
Buzaglo, S. 1750. *Mikdash Melech* (The Temple of the King) [in Hebrew]. Jerusalem: Machon Bnai Yissachar, 1995.
Cassirer, E. 1954. *An Essay on Man: An Introduction to a Philosophy of Human Culture*. Garden City, N.Y.: Doubleday Anchor Books.

Castaneda, C. 1968. *The Teachings of Don Juan: A Yaqui Way of Knowledge*. New York: Pocket Books.

The Chumash: Stone Edition. 1998. New York: Mesorah Publications.

Cole, K. C. 1998. *The Universe in a Teacup*. New York: Harcourt Brace.

Cordovero, M. 1548. *Pardes Rimonim* (Orchard of Pomegranates) [in Hebrew]. Jerusalem: Yerid Hasefarim, 2000.

———. n.d. *Shiur Koma* [in Hebrew]. Jerusalem: Yeshiva Kol Yehudah.

Crick, F. 1994. *The Astonishing Hypothesis: The Scientific Search for the Soul*. New York: Simon & Schuster.

Dalai Lama. 1989. *Ocean of Wisdom: Guidelines for Living*. Santa Fe, N.M.: Clear Light Publishers.

———. 1997. *The Four Noble Truths*. London: Thornsons.

Damasio, A. 1999. *The Feeling of What Happens*. New York: Harcourt Brace.

Davis, A. 1996. "Sefer Haredim" (sixteenth century). In *The Way of the Flame: A Guide to the Forgotten Mystical Tradition of Jewish Meditation*. San Francisco: Harper.

Dennett, D. C. 1991. *Consciousness Explained*. Boston: Little Brown.

Derrida, Jacques. 1995. *The Gift of Death*. Translated by David Wills. Chicago: University of Chicago Press.

Dessler, E. L. 1943. *Michtav M'Eliyahu* [in Hebrew]. Jerusalem: Sifriyati, 1997.

Donahue, H. 2004. "My 5-Year Addiction to the Knife." *London Times*, September 1.

Dov Ber of Lubavitch. 1963. *On Ecstasy*. Edited and translated by L. Jacobs. Chappaqua, N.Y.: Rossel Books.

Drob, S. 2000a. *Symbols of the Kabbalah: Philosophical and Psychological Perspectives*. Northvale, N.J.: Aronson.

———. 2000b. *Kabbalistic Metaphors*. Northvale, N.J.: Aronson.

Drosnin, M. 1997. *The Bible Code*. New York: Simon & Schuster.

Eigen, M. 1998. *The Psychoanalytic Mystic*. London: Free Association Books.

Eliade, M. 1964. *Shamanism*. Princeton, N.J.: Princeton University Press.

Elior, R. 1993. *The Paradoxical Ascent to God*. Albany: State University of New York Press.

———. 1995. "The Doctrine of Transmigration in Galya Raza." In *Essential Papers on Kabbalah*, edited by L. Fine. New York: New York University Press.

———. 1997. "HaBaD: The Contemplative Ascent to God." In *Jewish Spirituality*, edited by A. Green. New York: Crossroad.

Ellenberger, H. 1970. *Discovery of the Unconscious: The History and Evolution of Dynamic Psychiatry*. New York: Basic Books.

Elyashiv, Shlomo. 1909. *Leshem Shvo v'Achlamah* [in Hebrew]. Pietrekov: Zederboim Press.

Encyclopaedia Judaica. 1972. Vol. 14. Jerusalem: Keter Publishing.

Erikson, E. 1950. *Childhood and Society*. New York: Norton.

Evans, D. 1996. *An Introductory Dictionary of Lacanian Psychoanalysis*. London: Routledge.

Fairbairn, W. R. D. 1946. "Object-Relations and Dynamic Structure." In *Psychoanalytic Studies of the Personality*. London: Routledge & Kegan Paul, 1986.

———. 1952. *Psychoanalytic Studies of the Personality*. London: Routledge & Kegan Paul, 1986.

Ferenczi, S. 1919. "Technical Difficulties in the Analysis of a Case of Hysteria." In *Further Contributions to the Theory and Technique of Psycho-Analysis*. New York: Brunner/Mazel, 1980.

———. 1920. "The Further Development of an Active Therapy in Psycho-Analysis." In *Further Contributions to the Theory and Technique of Psycho-Analysis*. New York: Brunner/Mazel, 1980.

———. 1932. "The Two Extremes: Credulity and Scepticism." In *Final Contributions to the Problems and Methods of Psycho-Analysis*. New York: Brunner/Mazel, 1980.

Fleer, G. 1988. "On Containment." Personal communication, Jerusalem.

Flusser, D. 1980. *Jewish Sources in Early Christianity* [in Hebrew]. Tel Aviv: Ministry of Defense.

Fordham, F. 1953. *An Introduction to Jung's Psychology*. Harmondsworth, Middlesex, England: Penguin, 1991.

Frankel, E. 1994. "Yom Kippur, Teshuvah and Psychotherapy." *Tikkun* 9:5, 23–24, 104–5.

Frankl, V. 1984. *Man's Search for Meaning*. New York: Washington Square Press/ Pocket Books.

Freud, A. 1937. *The Ego and the Mechanisms of Defense*. New York: International Universities Press, 1971.

Freud, S. 1886. "Report on My Studies in Paris and Berlin." In Strachey, *Standard Edition*, Vol. 1.

———. 1889. "Review of August Forel's Hypnotism." In Strachey, *Standard Edition*, Vol. 1.

———. 1894. "The Neuro-Psychoses of Defence." In Strachey, *Standard Edition*, Vol. 3.

———. 1895/1950. "Project for a Scientific Psychology." In Strachey, *Standard Edition*, Vol. 1.

———. 1900. "The Interpretation of Dreams." In Strachey, *Standard Edition*, Vols. 4–5.

———. 1901. "The Psychopathology of Everyday Life." In Strachey, *Standard Edition*, Vol. 6.

———. 1904. "Contributions to the Neue Freie Presse: Obituary of Professor S. Hammerschlag." In Strachey, *Standard Edition*, Vol. 9.

———. 1905a. "Three Essays on Sexuality." In Strachey, *Standard Edition*, Vol. 7.

———. 1905b. "Psychical (or Mental) Treatment." In Strachey, *Standard Edition*, Vol. 7.

———. 1909. "Notes upon a Case of Obsessional Neurosis." In Strachey, *Standard Edition*, Vol. 10.

———. 1910a. "The Antithetical Meaning of Primary Words." In Strachey, *Standard Edition*, Vol. 11.

———. 1910b. "Five Lectures on Psycho-Analysis." In Strachey, *Standard Edition*, Vol. 11.

——. 1911. "Formulations on the Two Principles of Mental Functioning." In Strachey, *Standard Edition*, Vol. 12.
——. 1912a. "The Dynamics of Transference." In Strachey, *Standard Edition*, Vol. 12.
——. 1912b. "Recommendations to Physicians Practising Psycho-Analysis." In Strachey, *Standard Edition*, Vol. 12.
——. 1912–1913. "Totem and Taboo." In Strachey, *Standard Edition*, Vol. 13.
——. 1913. "On Beginning the Treatment." In Strachey, *Standard Edition*, Vol. 12.
——. 1914a. "Remembering, Repeating and Working-Through." In Strachey, *Standard Edition*, Vol. 12.
——. 1914b. "On the History of the Psycho-Analytic Movement." In Strachey, *Standard Edition*, Vol. 14.
——. 1914c. "On Narcissism." In Strachey, *Standard Edition*, Vol. 12.
——. 1915. "Instincts and their Vicissitudes." In Strachey, *Standard Edition*, Vol. 14.
——. 1915–1916. "Introductory Lectures on Psycho-Analysis." In Strachey, *Standard Edition*, Vol. 15.
——. 1917. "Introductory Lectures on Psycho-Analysis—Lecture 19: Resistance and Repression." In Strachey, *Standard Edition*, Vol. 16.
——. 1918. "From the History of an Infantile Neurosis." In Strachey, *Standard Edition*, Vol. 17.
——. 1919a. "A Child Is Being Beaten." In Strachey, *Standard Edition*, Vol. 17.
——. 1919b. "The Uncanny." In Strachey, *Standard Edition*, Vol. 17.
——. 1919c. "Lines of Advance in Psycho-Analytic Therapy." In Strachey, *Standard Edition*, Vol. 17.
——. 1920. "Beyond the Pleasure Principle." In Strachey, *Standard Edition*, Vol. 18.
——. 1923. "The Ego and the Id." In Strachey, *Standard Edition*, Vol. 19.
——. 1924. "The Economic Problem of Masochism." In Strachey, *Standard Edition*, Vol. 19.
——. 1926a. "Inhibitions, Symptoms and Anxiety." In Strachey, *Standard Edition*, Vol. 20.
——. 1926b. "The Question of Lay Analysis." In Strachey, *Standard Edition*, Vol. 20.
——. 1927. "The Future of an Illusion." In Strachey, *Standard Edition*, Vol. 21.
——. 1930. "Civilization and Its Discontents." In Strachey, *Standard Edition*, Vol. 21.
——. 1933. "New Introductory Lectures on Psycho-Analysis—Lecture 30: Dreams and Occultism." In Strachey, *Standard Edition*, Vol. 22.
——. 1936. "A Disturbance of Memory on the Acropolis." In Strachey, *Standard Edition*, Vol. 22.
——. 1937a. "Analysis Terminable and Interminable." In Strachey, *Standard Edition*, Vol. 23.
——. 1937b. "Constructions in Analysis." In Strachey, *Standard Edition*, Vol. 23.
——. 1938/1941. "Findings, Ideas, Problems." In Strachey, *Standard Edition*, Vol. 23.
——. 1939. "Moses and Monotheism." In Strachey, *Standard Edition*, Vol. 23.
Friedman, L. J. 2000. *Identity's Architect: A Biography of Erik H. Erikson*. Cambridge, Mass.: Harvard University Press.
Frosh, S. 2002. "Freud and Jewish Dreaming." *Psychoanalysis and History* 3:18–27.

Gafni, M. 2001a. *Soul Prints*. New York: Pocket Books.
———. 2001b. "Shattered Vessels, Stained Hands." *Wellsprings*, no. 48.
Gay, P. 1987. *A Godless Jew*. New Haven, Conn.: Yale University Press.
———. 1998. *Freud: A Life for Our Time*. New York: Norton.
Gikatilla, J. 1274. *Ginnat Egoz* (Garden of the Walnut) [in Hebrew]. Jerusalem: Yeshivat Ha-Chaim v'Ha-Shalom, 1999.
———. 1561. *Sha'are Orah* (Gates of Light) [in Hebrew]. Edited by J. Bakar. Jerusalem: privately printed, 1995.
Gilligan, C. 1982. *In a Different Voice*. Cambridge, Mass.: Harvard University Press.
Ginsburgh, E. K. 1989. *The Sabbath in the Classical Kabbalah*. Albany: State University of New York Press.
Ginsburgh, Y. 1990. *The Hebrew Letters: Channels of Creative Consciousness*. Jerusalem: Gal Einai Publications.
Gliksman, P. Z. 1938. *Der Kotsker Rebbe* [in Yiddish]. Warsaw: no publisher listed.
Green, A. 1992. *Tormented Master: The Life and Spiritual Quest of Rabbi Nahman of Bratslav*. Woodstock, Vt.: Jewish Lights.
Greenbaum, A. 1995. *The Wings of the Sun: Traditional Jewish Healing in Theory and Practice*. Jerusalem: Breslov Research Institute.
Greene, B. 1999. *The Elegant Universe*. New York: Vintage.
———. 2004. *The Fabric of the Cosmos*. New York: Vintage.
Gribbin, J. 1991. *In Search of Schrödinger's Cat: Quantum Physics and Reality*. London: Black Swan.
Groddeck, G. 1951. *The Unknown Self*. London: Vision Press.
Grosskurth, P. 1985. *Melanie Klein*. London: Hodder & Stoughton.
Grotstein, J. S. 1996. "Bion's Transformation in 'O,' the 'Thing-in-Itself' and the 'Real': Toward the Concept of the Transcendent Position." *Journal of Melanie Klein and Object Relations* 14:109–41.
———. 2000. *Who Is the Dreamer Who Dreams the Dream? A Study of Psychic Presences*. Hillsdale, N.J.: Analytic Press.
Guttmann, J. n.d. *Philosophies of Judaism*. London: Routledge & Kegan Paul.
HaCohen, Tzadok. 1912. *Pri Zadik* [in Hebrew]. Lublin, Poland: no publisher listed.
Ha-Levi, Y. 1905. *The Kuzari*. New York: Schocken, 1964.
Hartmann, H. 1958. *Ego Psychology and the Problem of Adaptation*. New York: Imago.
Heimann, P. 1950. "On Counter-Transference." *International Journal of Psycho-Analysis* 31:81–84.
Heller, J. B. 1956. "Freud's Mother and Father." *Commentary* 21:418–21.
Herrigel, E. 1974. *Zen and the Art of Archery*. New York: Vintage.
Hinshelwood, R. 1991. *A Dictionary of Kleinian Thought*. London: Free Association Books.
Hornstein, G. 2000. *To Redeem One Person Is to Redeem the World: The Life of Frieda Fromm-Reichman*. New York: Free Press.
Hugo, V. 1977. *Les Miserables*. New York: Washington Square Press.
Idel, M. 1985. "Prophetic Kabbalah and the Land of Israel." In *Vision and Conflict in the Holy Land*, edited by R. I. Cohen. New York: St. Martin's Press.

——. 1988. *Kabbalah: New Perspectives*. New Haven, Conn.: Yale University Press.
——. 1998. *Messianic Mystics*. New Haven, Conn.: Yale University Press.
——. 2005. *Kabbalah and Eros*. New Haven, Conn.: Yale University Press.
Isaacs, S. 1948. "On the Nature and Function of Phantasy." *International Journal of Psycho-Analysis* 29:73–97.
Jacobson, E. 1964. *The Self and the Object World*. New York: International Universities Press.
Jacobson, S. 1995. *Toward a Meaningful Life: The Wisdom of the Rebbe*. London: Piatkus.
——. 2001. "A Cup of Vinegar." *Meaningful Life* 12(49).
James, D. C. 1984. "Bion's 'Containing' and Winnicott's 'Holding' in the Context of the Group Matrix." *International Journal of Group Psychotherapy* 34:201–13.
James, W. 1890. *The Principles of Psychology*. New York: Holt.
——. 1901. *The Varieties of Religious Experience*. New York: Mentor Books, 1958.
Jones, E. 1916. *Papers on Psycho-Analysis*. London: Balliere, Tindall & Cox, 1948.
Jung, C. G. 1928. "The Spiritual Problem of Modern Man." In *The Portable Jung*, edited by J. Campbell. New York: Penguin, 1976.
——. 1951. *Aion*. In *The Collected Works of Carl G. Jung*, Vol. 9. Bollingen Series XX. Princeton, N.J.: Princeton University Press.
——. 1963. *Memories, Dreams, Reflections*. New York: Pantheon.
——. 1964. *Man and His Symbols*. London: Aldus.
Kaku, M. 1995. *Hyperspace*. New York: Anchor.
——. 2000. "It's All So Clear in 10-Dimensional Hyperspace." *London Independent*, January 19.
——. 2005. *Parallel Worlds*. London: Allen Lane/Penguin.
Kant, I. 1922. "Metaphysik der Sitten" [in German]. In *Samtliche Werke*, edited by K. Vorlander, Vol. 3. 4th ed. Leipzig: Felix Meiner.
Kaplan, A. 1978. *Meditation and the Bible*. Newburyport, Mass.: Samuel Weiser.
——. 1979. *The Bahir*. Newburyport, Mass.: Samuel Weiser.
——, trans. 1981. *The Living Torah: The Five Books of Moses*. Jerusalem: Maznaim Publishing.
——. 1982. *Meditation and Kabbalah*. Newburyport, Mass.: Samuel Weiser.
——. 1984. *Chassidic Masters and Their Teachings*. New York: Moznaim.
——. 1990a. *Innerspace*. Jerusalem: Vagshal/Moznaim.
——. 1990b. *Sefer Yetzirah (The Book of Creation)*. Newburyport, Mass.: Samuel Weiser.
Karo, J. 1875/1990. *Magid Meisharim* [in Hebrew]. Edited and translated by Y. Bar-Lev. Petach Tikvah: privately printed.
Keller, H. 1903. *The Story of My Life*. New York: Bantam, 1990.
Keve, T. 2000. *Triad: The Physicists, the Analysts, the Kabbalists*. London: Rosenberger & Krausz.
Kierkegaard, S. 1843. *Fear and Trembling*. Harmondsworth, Middlesex, England: Penguin, 1985.
Klein, M. 1935. "A Contribution to the Psychogenesis of Manic-Depressive States." *International Journal of Psycho-Analysis* 16:145–74.

———. 1940. "Mourning and Its Relation to Manic-Depressive States." *International Journal of Psycho-Analysis* 21: 125–53.

———. 1946. "Notes on Some Schizoid Mechanisms." *International Journal of Psycho-Analysis* 27:99–110.

———. 1957. *Envy and Gratitude*. New York: Delta.

———. 1975. *The Psycho-Analysis of Children*. New York: Delta.

Kohut, H. 1971. *The Analysis of the Self*. New York: International Universities Press.

———. 1977. *The Restoration of the Self*. New York: International Universities Press.

Kook, A. I. H. 1975. *Orot Teshuvah* [in Hebrew]. Jerusalem: Mossad HaRav Kook.

Krull, M. 1986. *Freud and His Father*. New York: Norton.

Lacan, J. 1954–1955. *The Seminar, Book II: The Ego in Freud's Theory and in the Technique of Psychoanalysis*. Edited by J. A. Miller, translated by S. Tomaselli. Cambridge: Cambridge University Press, 1988.

———. 1964. *The Seminar, Book XI: The Four Fundamental Concepts of Psycho-analysis*. Translated by Alan Sheridan. London: Hogarth Press and the Institute of Psycho-Analysis, 1977.

Laplanche, J., and J-B Pontalis. 1980. *The Language of Psycho-Analysis*. London: Hogarth Press.

Lasch, C. 1978. *The Culture of Narcissism: American Life in an Age of Diminishing Expectations*. New York: Norton.

Le Bon, G. 1896. *The Crowd*. London: Ernest Benn, 1952.

Leet, L. 2003. *The Kabbalah of the Soul: The Transformative Psychology and Practices of Jewish Mysticism*. Rochester, Vt.: Inner Traditions.

Locks, G. 1985. *The Spice of Torah: Gematria*. New York: Judaica Press.

Loewenthal, N. 1990. *Communicating the Infinite: The Emergence of the Habad School*. Chicago: University of Chicago Press.

———. 2004. Personal communication, December.

López-Corvo, R. E. 2003. *The Dictionary of the Work of W. R. Bion*. London: Karnac.

Lutzky, H. 1989. "Reparation and Tikkun: A Comparison of the Kleinian and Kabbalistic Concepts." *International Journal of Psycho-Analysis* 16:449–58.

Luzzatto, M. H. 1989. *Sefer Ha-Kllalim* [in Hebrew]. Edited by C. Friedlander. B'nai Brak: Gittler. ("Kllalei Maamar Ha-Chochmah").

———. n.d. *Kalach Pitchei Chochmah* (138 Windows to Wisdom) [in Hebrew]. Edited by C. Friedlander. Bnai Brak: Gittler.

Machzor for Rosh Hashanah. 1993. New York: Merkos L'inyonei Chinuch.

Mahler, M. 1968. *On Human Symbiosis and the Vicissitudes of Individuation*. New York: International Universities Press.

Maslow, A. H. 1968. *Toward a Psychology of Being*. New York: Van Nostrand Reinhold.

———. 1970. *Religions, Values, and Peak-Experiences*. New York: Viking Press/ Penguin.

Matt, D. C. 1990. "*Ayin*: The Concept of Nothingness in Jewish Mysticism." In *Essential Papers on Kabbalah*, edited by L. Fine. New York: New York University Press, 1995.

——. 1996. *God and the Big Bang: Discovering Harmony between Science and Spirituality*. Woodstock, Vt.: Jewish Lights.
Matte-Blanco, I. 1988. *Thinking, Feeling and Being*. London: Routledge.
May, R., E. Angel, and H. Ellenberger, eds. 1958. *Existence: A New Dimension in Psychiatry and Psychology*. New York: Basic Books.
McEvoy, J. P., and O. Zarate. 1999. *Introducing Quantum Theory*. Cambridge: Icon Books.
Menaker, E. 1982. *Otto Rank: A Rediscovered Legacy*. New York: Columbia University Press.
Micklem, N. 1990. "I Am Not Myself: A Paradox." In *Jung's Concept of the Self: Its Relevance Today.* Papers from the Public Conference, Jungian Postgraduate Committee, British Association of Psychotherapists, no. 3.
Mitchell, S. A. 1988. "The Intrapsychic and the Interpersonal: Different Theories, Different Domains, or Historical Artifacts?" *Psychoanalytic Inquiry* 8:472–96.
Mozeson, I. 1989. *The Word: The Dictionary That Reveals the Hebrew Source of English*. New York: Shapolsky.
Nachmanides (RaMBaN). 1971. *Commentary on the Torah: Genesis*. Translated by C. Shavel. New York: Shilo Publishing House.
Ogden, T. H. 1994. "The Analytic Third: Working with Intersubjective Clinical Facts." *International Journal of Psycho-Analysis* 75:3–19.
Otto, R. 1958. *The Idea of the Holy*. London: Oxford University Press.
Pagels, E. 1995. *The Origin of Satan*. New York: Random House.
Panek, R. 2004. *The Invisible Century: Einstein, Freud, and the Search for the Hidden Universes*. New York: Viking.
Pine, F. 1990. *Drive, Ego, Object, and Self*. New York: Basic Books.
Podhoretz, N. 2001. "Heard the One about the Rabbi?" *Daily Telegraph*, April 10, p. 18.
Polatin, P. 1966. *A Guide to Treatment in Psychiatry*. Philadelphia: Lippincott.
Popper, K. 1945. *The Open Society and Its Enemies*. 5th ed. Princeton, N.J.: Princeton University Press, 1966.
Rank, O. 1945. *Will Therapy & Truth and Reality.* New York: Knopf, 1950.
——. 1950. *Psychology and the Soul*. New York: Perpetua, 1961.
Reich, W. 1980. *Character Analysis*. 3rd ed. New York: Farrar, Straus & Giroux.
Reik, T. 1948. *Listening with the Third Ear: The Inner Experience of a Psychoanalyst*. New York: Grove Press.
Rivière, J. 1930. "Magical Regeneration by Dancing." *International Journal of Psycho-Analysis* 11:340.
Roazen, P. 1993. *Meeting Freud's Family*. Amherst: University of Massachusetts Press.
Robinson, I. 1994. *Moses Cordovero's Introduction to Kabbalah: An Annotated Translation of His 'Or Ne'erav.'* New York: Yeshiva University Press.
Rosen, J. N. 1953. *Direct Analysis*. New York: Grunne & Stratton.
Rosenfeld, H. 1971."A Clinical Approach to the Psychoanalytic Theory of the Life and Death Instincts: An Investigation into the Aggressive Aspects of Narcissism." *International Journal of Psycho-Analysis* 52:169–78.

——. 1987. "Destructive Narcissism and the Death Instinct." In *Impasse and Interpretation*. London: Tavistock.
Rosman, M. 1996. *Founder of Hassidism: A Quest for the Historical Ba'al Shem Tov*. Berkeley and Los Angeles: University of California Press.
Rycroft, C. 1972. *A Critical Dictionary of Psychoanalysis*. Harmondsworth, Middlesex, England: Penguin.
Saadia Gaon. 1948. *The Book of Beliefs and Opinions*. Edited by Samuel Rosenblatt. New Haven, Conn.: Yale University Press.
Sagan, C. 1996. *The Demon-Haunted World*. New York: Ballantine.
Samuels, A. 1986. *A Critical Dictionary of Jungian Analysis*. London: Routledge & Kegan Paul.
Sandler, J., and A.-M. Sandler. 1999. *Internal Objects Re-Visited*. New York: International Universities Press.
Schatzman, M., ed. 1982. *Dreams and How to Guide Them*. London: Duckworth.
Schatz-Uffenheimer, R., ed. 1976. *Dov Baer: Maggid Devarav le-Ya'aqov* [in Hebrew]. Jerusalem: Magnes Press.
Schneersohn, S. D. B. 1905. *Kuntres Etz HaChayim: The Tree of Life* [in English]. New York: Sichos, 1998.
Schneerson, M. M. 1944. *Igrot Kodesh* [in Hebrew]. Vol. 1. New York: Kehot.
——. 1998. *On the Essence of Chassidus*. Trans. Y. Greenberg and S. S. Handelman. New York: Kehot.
——. 1998. *Week in Review* 9(18).
——. 1999. *Week in Review* 10(39).
——. 2002. *Bringing Heaven Down to Earth: 365 Meditations*. Compiled by Tzvi Freeman. New York: Class One Press.
——. 2003. *Forces in Creation*. New York: Kehot.
Schneider, S. 2003. "The Mystical and the Spiritual in the Large Group." In *The Large Group Re-Visited*, edited by S. Schneider and H. Weinberg. London: Jessica Kingsley.
Schneider, S., and J. H. Berke. 1995. "Breast, Robbery and the Devil." *Jewish Bible Quarterly* 23:86–90.
——. 2000. "Sigmund Freud and the Lubavitcher Rebbe." *Psychoanalytic Review* 87:1, 39–59.
——. 2005. "Discovering Oneself: Kabbalah and Psychoanalysis." *Midstream* 51 (November–December): 6, 24–27.
——. In press. "The Oceanic Feeling, Mysticism and Kabbalah: Freud's Historical Roots." *Psychoanalytic Review*.
Schneur Zalman of Liadi. 1797. *Likutei Amarim: Tanya*. Bilingual ed. Translated by N. Mindel. Brooklyn, N.Y.: Kehot, 1984.
Schochet, J. I. 1985. "Gematriya: The Principles of Numerical Interpretation." In *The Spice of Torah: Gematria*, edited by G. Locks. New York: Judaica Press.
——. 1988. *Mystical Concepts in Chassidism*. New York: Kehot.
Schoeck, H. 1970. *Envy: A Theory of Social Behavior*. Translated by M. Glenny and B. Ross. New York: Harcourt Brace.

Scholem, G. 1941. *Major Trends in Jewish Mysticism*. New York: Schocken Books, 1995.
———. 1962. *Origins of the Kabbalah*. New York: Jewish Publication Society and Princeton University Press, 1987.
———. 1969. *On the Kabbalah and Its Symbolism*. New York: Schocken Books.
———. 1973. *Sabbatai Sevi: The Mystical Messiah*. London: Routledge & Kegan Paul.
———. 1974. *Kabbalah*. Jerusalem: Keter.
———. 1991. *On the Mystical Shape of the Godhead*. New York: Schocken.
Segal, H. 1957. "Notes on Symbol Formation." *International Journal of Psycho-Analysis* 38: 391–97.
———. 1975a. *Introduction to the Work of Melanie Klein*. London: Hogarth Press.
———. 1975b. "A Psycho-Analytic Approach to the Treatment of Schizophrenia." In *Studies of Schizophrenia*, edited by M. Lader. Ashford, Kent, England: Headley Bros.
Shearer, A. 2004. Personal communication, December.
Shulman, Y. D. 1996. *The Sefirot: Ten Emanations of Divine Power*. Northvale, N.J.: Aronson.
Siddur Tehillat HaShem. 1978. Translated by N. Mangel. New York: Merkos L'inyonei Chinuch.
Solms, M., and O. Turnbull. 2002. *The Brain and the Inner World*. London: Karnac.
Soloveitchik, J. B. 1973/1974. "The Dual Aspects of Jewish Morality." In *A Conspectus of the Public Lectures of Rabbi Joseph B. Soloveitchik*, edited by J. Epstein. New York: Hamevaser/Yeshiva University.
———. 2000. *Family Redeemed: Essays on Family Relationships*. New York: Toras HoRav Foundation.
Spitz, R. 1946. *The First Year of Life*. New York: International Universities Press, 1965.
Steiner, J. 1996. "The Aim of Psychoanalysis in Theory and in Practice." *International Journal of Psycho-Analysis* 77:1073–83.
Steinsaltz, A. 1980. *The Thirteen Petalled Rose*. New York: Basic Books.
———. 1988a. *The Strife of the Spirit*. Northvale, N.J.: Aronson.
———. 1988b. *The Long Shorter Way*. Northvale, N.J.: Aronson.
———. 1995. *In the Beginning: Discourses on Hassidic Thought*. Edited and translated by Y. Hanegbi. Northvale, N.J.: Aronson.
———. 2002. *Teshuva*. London: British Friends of Rabbi Steinsaltz.
———. 2003. *Opening the Tanya*. New York: Jossey-Bass.
Stolorow, R. D., B. Brandschaft, and G. E. Atwood. 1987. *Psychoanalytic Treatment: An Intersubjective Approach*. Hillsdale, N.J.: Analytic Press.
Strachey, James, ed. *Standard Edition of the Complete Psychological Works of Sigmund Freud*. 24 vols. London: Hogarth Press, 1981.
Sullivan, H. S. 1953. *The Interpersonal Theory of Psychiatry*. New York: Norton.
Sutherland, J. D. 1980. "The British Object Relations Theorists: Balint, Winnicott, Fairbairn, Guntrip." *Journal of the American Psychoanalytic Association* 28: 829–60.

Suzuki, S. 1970. *Zen Mind, Beginner's Mind*. New York: Weatherhill.
Tegmark, M. 2003. "Parallel Universes." *Scientific American* 288:31–41.
Tenen, S. 2006. *The Alphabet in Genesis*. Sharon, Mass.: Meru Foundation.
Trachtenberg, J. 1939. *Jewish Magic and Superstition: A Study in Folk Religion*. New York: Atheneum, 1970.
Trungpa, C. 2001. *Glimpses of Abhidharma*. Boston: Shambhala.
Tyson, P., and R. Tyson. 1990. *Psychoanalytic Theories of Development*. New Haven, Conn.: Yale University Press.
Ulman, S. 1996. *Maftaychot HaChochmah* (The Keys to Wisdom) [in Hebrew]. Jerusalem: HaMesorah.
Underhill, E. 1912. *Mysticism*. London: Methuen.
Vital, C. 1587. *Etz Chaim* [in Hebrew]. Jerusalem/B'nai Brak: Videvsky, 1988.
Whybrow, P. 2005. *American Mania: When More Is Not Enough*. New York: Norton.
Wiesel, E. 1972. *Souls on Fire*. New York: Random House.
Wineberg, L. 1987. *Lessons in 'Tanya.'* New York: Kehot.
Winnicott, D. W. 1952. "Psychoses and Child Care." In *Through Paediatrics to Psycho-Analysis*. London: Hogarth Press, 1975.
——. 1953. "Transitional Objects and Transitional Phenomena." In *Through Paediatrics to Psycho-Analysis*. London: Hogarth Press, 1975.
——. 1958. "The Capacity to Be Alone." In *The Maturational Processes and the Facilitating Environment*. London: Hogarth Press, 1985.
——. 1960a. "The Theory of the Parent-Infant Relationship." In *The Maturational Process and the Facilitating Environment*. London: Hogarth Press, 1972.
——. 1960b. "Ego Distortion in Terms of True and False Self." In *The Maturational Processes and the Facilitating Environment*. London: Hogarth Press, 1972.
——. 1963. "The Mentally Ill in Your Caseload." In *The Maturational Process and the Facilitating Environment*. London: Hogarth Press, 1972.
Wolf, L. 1999. *Practical Kabbalah*. New York: Three Rivers Press.
Wolfson, E. R. 1995a. *Circle in the Square: Studies in the Use of Gender in Kabbalistic Symbolism*. Albany: State University of New York Press.
——. 1995b. "Crossing Gender Boundaries in Kabbalistic Ritual and Myth." In *Ultimate Intimacy: The Psychodynamics of Jewish Mysticism*, edited by M. Ostow. London: Karnac.
Yadin, Y. 1990. *The Temple Scroll* [in Hebrew]. Tel Aviv: Maariv.
Yerushalmi, Y. H. 1991. *Freud's Moses: Judaism Terminable and Interminable*. New Haven, Conn.: Yale University Press.
Young, R. 1994. *Mental Space*. London: Process Press.
The Zohar. 1931–1934. Translated by H. Sperling, M. Simon, and Paul Levertoff. London: Soncino Press.
The Zohar. 2002–2006. Translated by D. Matt. Pritzker Edition. 3 vols. Stanford, Calif.: Stanford University Press.

Index

About the Authors

Joseph H. Berke is a psychoanalytic psychotherapist working with individuals and families. He graduated from the Albert Einstein College of Medicine in New York and completed his analytic training in London where he now lives and works. In 1973 he founded and is now the director of the Arbours Crisis Centre, a pioneering psychosocial facility for supporting severely disturbed people. He is a lecturer and teacher and a prolific author of many articles and books including *Mary Barnes: Two Accounts of a Journey Through Madness* (with Mary Barnes) and *Malice Through the Looking Glass.* Web: www.jhberke.com. E-mail: jhberke@aol.com

Stanley Schneider is a supervising and training psychoanalyst and full member of the Israel Psychoanalytic Society. He is professor and chairman of the Program for Advanced Studies in Integrative Psychotherapy, Hebrew University. Jerusalem. He was a founder and director of the Summit Institute for emotionally disturbed adolescents and young adults in Jerusalem. He is also a group analyst and has written many books, chapters and articles, including several with Joseph Berke. E-mail: stanley@actcom.co.il.

www.ingramcontent.com/pod-product-compliance
Ingram Content Group UK Ltd.
Pitfield, Milton Keynes, MK11 3LW, UK
UKHW012036150926
475560UK00001B/45

9 780765 705006